EU Regional Trade Agreements

This book unveils the potential of utilizing European Union Regional Trade Agreements (EU RTAs) as an instrument of promoting the rule of law to third states.

In doing so, the book combines development economics, foreign policy and legal perspectives at three levels of analysis of four sectors to introduce the concept of "EU value-promoting RTAs". The book demonstrates that the EU RTAs bear considerable potential to be strategized as instruments of promoting the rule of law in third states, requiring, however, overcoming strict divides between EU political and economic cooperation, and values and *acquis* conditionality in its relations with third countries.

This book will be of key interest to scholars and students of European studies, European Union law, EU external action/foreign policy, EU trade agreements and development studies, as well as to NGOs and think tanks that work on European affairs.

Maryna Rabinovych is Assistant Professor at the Department of Public Policy and Governance at the Kyiv School of Economics, Ukraine.

Routledge Studies in European Foreign Policy
Series Editors: Richard Whitman
University of Kent, UK

Richard Youngs
University of Warwick, UK

This series addresses the standard range of conceptual and theoretical questions related to European foreign policy. At the same time, in response to the intensity of new policy developments, it endeavours to ensure that it also has a topical flavour, addressing the most important and evolving challenges to European foreign policy, in a way that will be relevant to the policy-making and think-tank communities.

The European Union's Approach to Conflict Resolution
Transformation or Regulation in the Western Balkans?
Laurence Cooley

The Proliferation of Privileged Partnerships between the European Union and its Neighbours
Edited by Sieglinde Gstöhl and David Phinnemore

EU – Turkey Relations
Civil Society and Depoliticization
Özge Zihnioğlu

The Politics of the European Neighbourhood Policy
Agnieszka K. Cianciara

European Identities and Foreign Policy Discourses on Russia
From the Ukraine to the Syrian Crisis
Marco Siddi

The EU in Southeast Asian Security
The Role of External Perceptions
Ronja Scheler

EU Regional Trade Agreements
An Instrument of Promoting the Rule of Law to Third States
Maryna Rabinovych

For a full list of titles in this series, please visit www.routledge.com

EU Regional Trade Agreements
An Instrument of Promoting the Rule of
Law to Third States

Maryna Rabinovych

LONDON AND NEW YORK

First published 2021
by Routledge
2 Park Square, Milton Park, Abingdon, Oxon OX14 4RN

and by Routledge
52 Vanderbilt Avenue, New York, NY 10017

Routledge is an imprint of the Taylor & Francis Group, an informa business

© 2021 Maryna Rabinovych

The right of Maryna Rabinovych to be identified as author of this work
has been asserted by her in accordance with sections 77 and 78 of the
Copyright, Designs and Patents Act 1988.

All rights reserved. No part of this book may be reprinted or reproduced or utilised
in any form or by any electronic, mechanical, or other means, now known or
hereafter invented, including photocopying and recording, or in any information
storage or retrieval system, without permission in writing from the publishers.

Trademark notice: Product or corporate names may be trademarks or
registered trademarks, and are used only for identification and explanation
without intent to infringe.

British Library Cataloguing-in-Publication Data
A catalogue record for this book is available from the British Library

Library of Congress Cataloging-in-Publication Data
Names: Rabinovych, Maryna, author.
Title: EU regional trade agreements : an instrument of promoting the rule
    of law to third states / Maryna Rabinovych.
Description: 1 Edition. | New York : Routledge, 2021. | Series: Routledge
    studies in european foreign policy | Includes bibliographical references
    and index.
Identifiers: LCCN 2020048449 (print) | LCCN 2020048450 (ebook) |
    ISBN 9780367468460 (hardback) | ISBN 9781003031505 (ebook)
Subjects: LCSH: Free trade—European Union countries. | Trade
    regulation—European Union countries. | European Union countries—
    Commercial policy. | Rule of law—European Union countries. |
    European Union countries—Foreign economic relations—European
    Free Trade Association countries. | European Free Trade Association. |
    European Free Trade Association countries—Foreign economic
    relations—European Union countries.
Classification: LCC KJE5177 .R33 2021 (print) | LCC KJE5177 (ebook) |
    DDC 343.2408/7—dc23
LC record available at https://lccn.loc.gov/2020048449
LC ebook record available at https://lccn.loc.gov/2020048450

ISBN: 978-0-367-46846-0 (hbk)
ISBN: 978-0-367-75858-5 (pbk)
ISBN: 978-1-003-03150-5 (ebk)

Typeset in Times New Roman
by Apex CoVantage, LLC

Contents

Acknowledgements		vii
Preface		viii
List of abbreviations		ix
	Introduction	1
1	The concept of the rule of law in the EU external action	11
2	EU external economic policy: history and the legal basis	28
3	The interplay between trade liberalization and the rule of law in the development context: towards the concept of EU value-promoting Regional Trade Agreements (RTAs)	44
4	EU rule of law promotion through RTAs in third states: the "regulation" dimension	68
5	EU rule of law promotion through RTAs in third states: the "action" dimension	106
6	Coherence between the "regulation" and "action" dimensions of rule of law promotion through RTAs (internal coherence)	144
7	Coherence between the rule of law promotion through RTAs and EU broader rule of law promotion activities (external coherence): the case of justice sector reforms	168

vi *Contents*

8   The EU-Ukraine DCFTA as an instrument of promoting
    the rule of law: conflict, unique approaches to assistance
    and unexpected spillovers   190

    Outlook and recommendations   216
    Index   222

Acknowledgements

I would like to use the chance to express my gratitude to people and institutions without whom completing this book would be hardly possible.

First, I am profoundly grateful to Prof. Dr. Karsten Nowrot, who patiently supported me and listened to tonnes of ideas, looking for hidden gems. I am also grateful to Prof. Dr. Markus Kotzur, Prof. Dr. Thomas Bruha and Martin Lieberich for discussions and ideas at the University of Hamburg and Europa-Kolleg Hamburg. Parts of my research were completed during my research stays in Thessaloniki and Vienna, and I would like to thank my academic hosts, Prof. Dr. Panayotis Glavinis and Prof. Dr. Irmgard Marboe, for their feedback and our insightful debates. Having presented parts of my research at a number of academic conferences and workshops in Europe, the USA and Canada, I have benefited from the support of many colleagues including Dr. Anne Pintsch, Dr. Cindy Wittke, Prof. Dr. Jan Orbie, Prof. Dr. Nicolas Levrat, Dr. Vsevolod Samokhvalov, Dr. Andreas Umland, Dr. Andriy Tiushka, Prof. Dr. Joan DeBardeleben and many others. For me, the participation in academic events also means making new close friends – and I would like to thank Zuzana Novakova, Diana Potjomkina, Mihai Chihaia, Kostiantyn Fedorenko, Yuliya Kaspiarovich and Paolo Pizzolo for inspiration, nice informal discussions and constant support. I would also like to thank the DAAD (German Academic Exchange Service), the OeAD (Austrian Academic Exchange Service), the European Commission, the International Studies Association, the European International Studies Association and UACES (the academic association for contemporary European studies) for generous financial and ideational support, and Europa-Kolleg Hamburg for being my home during several years, while I was doing the research that underlies the book.

There are no words that can express my gratitude to my family and friends, back to my hometown, Odesa (Ukraine), without whom this work would never be completed. To my Mom and Dad–for all the support, care and encouragement. I am especially thankful to Milena Golovina, my English teacher back to high school, for teaching me English, helping with my very first academic works and being a person, I can always call. My life would be grey without my soulmates – Stanislav, Anastasiia and Kateryna – and thank you for our offline and online time together, and for reading my works.

Preface

The book contributes to the growing body of knowledge about the pursuit of non-trade policy objectives through the European Union (EU) trade policy. In particular, it explores the actual and potential suitability of the EU Regional Trade Agreements (RTAs) as an instrument of promoting the rule of law in partner countries.

The book introduces the concept of EU value-promoting RTAs, based on the combination of the foreign policy, legal and development economics perspectives. It offers a detailed account of the legal pathways through which the RTAs advance the rule of law standards and their interplay with the EU's application of unilateral assistance instruments in the Balkans, the "associated" Eastern Neighbourhood and the CARIFORUM countries. The final part of the book applies the concept of EU value-promoting RTAs to the case of the EU-Ukraine Deep and Comprehensive Free Trade Agreement (DCFTA). It suggests a number of recommendations for relevant EU institutions as to strategizing the use of RTAs as a value-promotion instrument.

The text will be of key interest to scholars, students and practitioners in the field of EU external relations and their legal regulation, especially those focusing on the EU trade and development policies.

Abbreviations

AA	Association Agreement
AASM	Associated African States and Madagascar
ACAA	Agreement on Conformity Assessment and Acceptance of Industrial Products
ACP	African, Caribbean and Pacific States
AETS	Institutional Strengthening Risk Managing Sustainable Development
AfCFTA	African Continental Free Trade Agreement
AG	Attorney General
AMCU	Anti-Monopoly Committee of Ukraine
ASEAN	Association of Southeast Asian Nations
BRICS	Brazil, Russia, India, China and South Africa
CA	Cotonou Agreement
CARDS	Community Assistance for Reconstruction, Development and Stabilization
CARICOM	Caribbean Community
CARIFORUM	Caribbean Forum
CBC	Cross-Border Cooperation
CCP	Common Commercial Policy
CEFTA	Central European Free Trade Agreement
CEPS	Centre for European Policy Studies (Brussels)
CETA	Comprehensive Economic and Trade Agreement
CFR	Charter of Fundamental Rights of the European Union
CFSP	Common Foreign and Security Policy
CJEU	Court of Justice of the European Union
CoE	Council of Europe
COMECON	Council for Mutual Economic Assistance
CRIP	Caribbean Regional Indicative Programme
CSDP	Common Security and Defense Policy
CSME	Caribbean Single Market and Economy
CSO	Civil Society Organization
CSP	Country Strategy Paper
DCFTA	Deep and Comprehensive Free Trade Agreement

x *Abbreviations*

DCI	Development Cooperation Instrument
DG	Directorate-General
DSM	Dispute Settlement Mechanism
EACU	Eurasian Customs Union
EaP	Eastern Partnership
EAS	European Administrative Space
EEAS	European External Action Service
EBA	Everything But Arms (initiative that is part to the EU Generalized Scheme of Preferences)
EBRD	European Bank for Reconstruction and Development
EC	European Community
ECHO	European Community Humanitarian Aid Office
ECHR	European Convention on Human Rights
ECJ	European Court of Justice
ECtHR	European Court of Human Rights
ECOWAS	Economic Community of West African States
ECtHR	European Court of Human Rights
EDF	European Union Development Fund
EEC	European Economic Community
EEU	Eurasian Economic Union
e.g.	for example
EIB	European Investment Bank
EIDHR	European Instrument for Democracy and Human Rights
EIF	Enhanced Integrated Framework
EIPA	European Institute of Public Administration (Luxembourg)
EMA	Euro-Mediterranean Agreements
ENI	European Neighbourhood Instrument
ENP	European Neighbourhood Policy
ENPI	European Neighbourhood and Partnership Instrument
EP	European Parliament
EPA	Economic Partnership Agreements
EPC	European Political Cooperation
EPRS	European Parliament Research Service
ESA	Eastern and Southern Africa
ESDP	European Union Security and Defence Policy
ETUI	European Trade Union Institute
EU	European Union
EUAM	European Union Advisory Mission (to Ukraine)
EUBAM	EU Border Assistance Mission to Moldova and Ukraine
EUI	European University Institute (Florence)
EUJUST THEMIS	EU Rule of Law Mission to Georgia
EU-LAC	EU, Latin America and the Caribbean
EULEX	European Union Rule of Law Mission
EUR	Euro
FDI	Foreign District Investment

Abbreviations xi

FTA	Free Trade Agreement
FYROM	Former Yugoslav Republic of Macedonia
GATS	The General Agreement on Trade in Services
GATT	The General Agreement on Tariffs and Trade
GCC	Gulf Cooperation Council
GDP	Gross Domestic Product
GPA	Agreement on Government Procurement
GSF	General Support Facility
GSP	Generalized System of Preferences
HIV/AIDS	Human Immunodeficiency Virus Infection and Acquired Immune Deficiency Syndrome
Ibid.	An abbreviation from the Latin word "ibidem", meaning "the same place", often used in footnotes and endnotes
IBSA	India, Brazil and South Africa
ICCPR	International Covenant on Civil and Political Rights.
ICESCR	International Covenant on Economic, Social and Cultural Rights
IcSP	Instrument contributing to Stability and Peace
ICTY	International Criminal Tribunal for the former Yugoslavia
IP	Intellectual Property
IPA	Instrument of Pre-Accession Assistance
JHA	Justice and Home Affairs
KFG	Kolleg-Forschergruppe (Research Group)
LAC	Latin America and the Caribbean
LDC	Least Developed Countries
LDM	Law and Development Movement
MDA	Multi-Donor Account
MDG	Millennium Development Goals
MEDT	Ministry of Economic Development and Trade
MENA	Middle East and North Africa
MERCOSUR	Southern Common Market
MFA	Macro-Financial Assistance
MFF	Multiannual Financial Framework
MFN	Most Favoured Nation
MIP	Multiannual Indicative Programme
MIPD	Multiannual Indicative Planning Document
MISEREOR	Latin: misereor, I have mercy
MoU	Memorandum/Memoranda of Understanding
MPE	Market Power Europe
n.d.	no date
NCTS	New Computerized Transit System
NGO	Non-Government Organization
NIP	National Indicative Programme
NPE	Normative Power Europe
ODA	Official Development Assistance
OJ	Official Journal

xii *Abbreviations*

OECD	Organization for Economic Co-operation and Development
OSCE	Organization for Security and Co-operation in Europe
p.	page
para	paragraph
PCA	Partnership and Cooperation Agreement
PCD	Policy Coherence for Development
PCSD	Policy Coherence for Sustainable Development
PEM	Pan-Euro-Mediterranean
PHARE	Poland and Hungary: Assistance for Restructuring their Economies
RSCAS	Robert Schuman Centre for Advanced Studies (at the European University Institute in Florence, Italy)
RST	Reform Support Team
RTA	Regional Trade Agreement
SAA	Stabilisation and Association Agreement
SAFE	Framework of Standards to Secure and Facilitate Global Trade
SAP	Stabilization and Association Process
SDGs	Sustainable Development Goals
SEA	Single European Act
SGUA	Support Group for Ukraine
SME	Small and Medium-sized Enterprise
SPS	Sanitary and Phytosanitary Measures
SSF	Single Support Framework
STABEX	European Commission Compensatory Finance Scheme to Stabilise Export Earnings of the ACP countries
TAIEX	Technical Assistance and Information Exchange Instrument
TBT	Technical Barriers to Trade
TCA	Trade and Cooperation Agreement
TEC	Treaty establishing the European Community
TEU	Treaty on European Union
TEU(A)	Treaty on European Union (Amsterdam)
TEU(M)	Treaty on European Union (Maastricht)
TEU(L)	Treaty on European Union (Lisbon)
TFA	Trade Facilitation Agreement
TFEU	Treaty on the Functioning of the European Union
THEMIS	European Union Rule of Law Mission in Georgia
TiSA	Trade in Services Agreement
TRIPS	Trade-Related Aspects of Intellectual Property Rights
TTIP	Transatlantic Trade and Investment Partnership
UEMOA	West African Economic and Monetary Union
UN	United Nations
UNCITRAL	The United Nations Commission on International Trade Law
UNCTAD	United Nations Conference on Trade and Development
VPA	Voluntary Partnership Agreements
WCO	World Customs Organization
WTO	World Trade Organization

Introduction

The European Union (EU) is one of the major players on the international arena that both holds a significant power *in* trade and exercises power *through* trade (Poletti and Sicurelli, 2018, pp. 1–2). Over the history of its trade policy, the EU has continuously used its power *through* trade to achieve development and normative objectives abroad. Hence, since 1971, the European Union (formerly the European Community [EC]) has been running the Generalized Scheme of Preferences (GSP) that uses preferential access to the Union's market as a means to assist developing countries in their effort to counter corruption and develop good governance. Non-reciprocal trade benefits also constituted the foundation of the Community's early trade and aid agreements with African, Caribbean and Pacific (ACP) countries, starting with the Lomé I Convention (1976–1981). In the 1990s and early 2000s, the EU further strengthened the development dimension of its trade policy through concluding a number of novel regional trade agreements (RTAs), such as the comprehensive Cotonou Agreement with ACP countries and Association Agreements (AAs) with Southern Neighbours, and launching the Everything But Arms (EBA) initiative. Moreover, the EU has been an active promoter of the Doha Development Agenda under the World Trade Organization (WTO) in the early 2000s, advocating for the improvement of developing countries' trading prospects and a stronger nexus between trade and aid (Dee, 2015, p. 63).

Ironically, particularly the deadlock of the WTO Doha Round served as a crucial impetus for the EU to boost the development, regulatory and normative aspects of its trade policy. Following trade negotiators' inability to reach agreement at the meetings in Cancún (2003), Paris (2005) and Hong Kong (2005), signifying the stalemate of the Doha Round, in 2006 the Commission substituted its "multilateralism first" strategy by an ambitious bilateral and plurilateral trade liberalization agenda.[1] In geographic terms, the post-2006 EU trade liberalization agenda encompasses Canada, Mexico and Central American states, MERCOSUR countries, the Andean Community, South Korea, Singapore, Vietnam, Australia and

---

1 European Commission, Communication to the Council, the European Parliament, the European Economic and Social Committee and the Committee of the Regions: Global Europe, Competing in the World, A Contribution to the EU's Growth and Job Strategy, COM(2006) 567 final of 4 October 2006.

2 Introduction

New Zealand, as well as Eastern and Southern Neighbourhoods. Substantively, the EU "new generation" regional trade agreements (RTAs)[2] remove beyond-the-borders barriers to trade through regulating the so-called "deep" disciplines, such as public procurement, competition, financial services and IP rights protection. Noteworthy, alongside and largely in synergy with "deep" disciplines, post-2006 EU RTAs are characterized by the proliferation of non-trade policy objectives (NTPOs), including human rights protection, sustainable development and countering corruption (Fiorini, 2019). Foremost, a surge in NTPOs, not immediately connected to trade, can be explained by the fact that, according to Art. 21(1) and 21(2)(a)(b) of the Treaty on European Union (TEU), EU fundamental values (human rights, democracy, the rule of law, equality and solidarity, and respect for the principles of the UN Charter and international law) acquired the legal status of the principles and objectives of the EU external action.[3] In line with Art. 21(2)(f), sustainable development was also recognized as a general objective of the whole spectrum of EU external policies, including its trade policy. Subsequently, the image of the EU as a normative trade power was consolidated in the 2015 European Commission's Communication "Trade for All. Towards a More Responsible Trade and Investment Policy".[4] In particular, the Communication stipulates that the EU trade strategy "is not just about interests but about values" and addresses EU trade agreements and preferential trade schemes as "levers" to promote values beyond the EU borders. At the same time, the 2015 Communication states that an effective trade policy shall "dovetail with the EU's development and broader foreign policies, as well as the external objectives of EU internal policies, so that they mutually reinforce each other".[5] Subsequently, an emphasis on NTPOs is important in light of the EU's ambition to ensure coherence of its external policies, in general, and the Policy Coherence for Development (PCD), aimed at "minimizing contradictions and building synergies between different EU policies to benefit developing countries" (Council of the EU, 2019). Moreover, synergies between development objectives lie at the heart of the Agenda 2030 – a global consensual "action plan for people, planet and prosperity" the EU is committed to.[6]

In this vein, a recent surge of academic interest towards the EU power through trade and NTPOs with third countries does not come as a surprise. A systematic analysis of studies on NTPOs demonstrates allows conditionally distinguishing them into three research strands. The first strand uses the proliferation of NTPOs

---

2 For the purposes of this study, the notion "regional trade agreement" (RTA) refers to any bilateral or plurilateral free trade agreement or customs union between the EU, on the one side, and one (or more) third state(s), on the other side.

3 Consolidated version of the Treaty on European Union, OJC 326, 26.10.2012, p 13–47 (hereinafter referred to as "TEU" or "TEU"[L]) in the context of treaty reforms).

4 European Commission, Communication to the Council, the European Economic and Social Committee and the Committee of the Regions "Trade for All: Towards a More Responsible Trade and Investment Policy", COM (2015)0497final of 14 October 2015.

5 Ibid.

6 United Nations General Assembly, Resolution "Transforming Our World: the 2030 Agenda for Sustainable Development", A/RES/70/1 of 25 September 2015.

Introduction 3

as a case to research the peculiarities and dynamics of the EU international actor-ness and power in foreign relations. A starting point for this discussion deals with a two-fold role the EU plays via its trade policy: (i) fostering Europe's growth and (ii) promoting sustainable development abroad (Poletti and Sicurelli, 2018, pp. 5–7). Thus, the EU seeks to increase its international competitiveness (acting as a market power Europe [MPE]) while protecting human rights and promoting good governance and sustainable development (acting as a normative power Europe [NPE]) (Orbie, 2016). Hence, a number of contributions juxtaposes the NPE to the MPE, based on the perceptions of norm-takers. While this research strand attributes the NTPOs' promotion to the NPE "side of the coin", an important limitation to the exercise of the EU's normative power through trade is constituted by the divergence of perspectives between the EU and a norm-taker (Orbie and Khorana, 2015; Hoang and Sicurelli, 2017). Moreover, the normative dimension of the EU trade policy is hindered by the conflicts between market and normative objectives (Gstöhl and Hanf, 2014), as well as insufficient capacities of the Union, stemming from the "hybrid state of European integration" (Orbie, 2016, p. 80). The second research strand brings together single-case and comparative studies of the legal design of RTAs' clauses, containing NTPOs (Douma, 2017; Morin and Jonnah, 2018). Notably, these studies tend to consider the legal design of either the trade and sustainable development chapters (TSDs) (Douma, 2017; Stoll, Gött and Abel, 2018; Marx, Ebert and Hachez, 2017) of EU RTAs or human rights conditionality (Velutti, 2016; Araujo, 2017). A single project that takes stock of all the NTPOs is the Horizon 2020 project "Realizing Europe's Soft Power in External Cooperation and Trade" (RESPECT), aimed at studying the effects of trade on NTPOs.[7] While this project refers to "trade agreements" as a unified mechanism of pursuing NTPOs and does not consider specific legal mechanisms they include, the legal framing of some NTPOs – such as the promotion of the rule of law, good governance and countering corruption – remains under-researched. In turn, the literature strand, dedicated to NTPOs' implementation, tends to focus on the impact, effectiveness and partner countries' compliance with their obligations under the TSDs, paying significantly lesser attention to values' conditionality (e.g. Orbie and Van Den Putte, 2016).

Hence, the point of departure for this book stems from an observation that, despite its foundational nature for EU external policies, the rule of law has never been researched either as an NTPO or, more specifically, in the context of the EU RTAs with third countries. Studying the rule of law in the context of the EU trade policy is, however, relevant for at least three reasons. First, while the rule of law is broadly recognized as an "essentially contested" concept (Waldron, 2002), the ongoing rule of law crises in Poland and Hungary led to the "consensualiza-tion" of the EU concept of the rule of law (European Parliament, 2020). Inquiries into the roots of the crises demonstrated that an important reason behind them

---

7 For more information about the "RESPECT" project, please visit: http://respect.eui.eu/ [accessed 5 October 2020]. Note that all electronic sources and pdfs were last accessed and checked on 5 October 2020.

4 *Introduction*

has been the lack of the autonomous EU concept of the rule of law and, subsequently, clear benchmarks and criteria to assess Candidate countries' compliance with political criteria prior to the 2004 "Big Bang" enlargement (Kochenov and Bárd, 2018, p. 17). As a part of the EU response, the 2014 Commission's Communication "A new EU Framework to Strengthen the Rule of Law" introduced the consensual concept of the rule of law – a move that can potentially spillover to EU external policies, including trade.[8] Second, such a move creates an impetus for studying the substance of the rule of law as stipulated by EU trade agreements, while: (i) neither of EU trade agreements explicitly defines the substance of the rule of law and (ii) as opposed to TSD chapters, the rule of requirements pierce different disciplines under RTAs.

Moreover, it can be hardly debated that the rule of law is conducive to trade liberalization and FDI (e.g. Anderson, 2013; Ngatat, 2016). However, no contributions addressed the impact trade liberalization exerts on the rule of law, as well as the legal mechanisms that make such impact possible, especially in view of the rise of the "deep" trade agenda. The promotion of the rule of law and sustainable development, as well as the implementation of "deep" trade arrangements, represent critical vectors of the EU external action in different policy contexts. However, the EU lacks a pronounced and coherent approach to the trade-sustainable development–rule of law nexus. This statement can be supported by the recourse to Policy Coherence for Development reports that never referred to the rule of law prior to 2017, despite aiming to synergize EU policies that influence development.[9] As it will be demonstrated later, the incoherencies between the EU support of trade liberalization and the rule of law promotion in the Enlargement and EU Neighbourhood Policy (ENP) contexts are to a great extent determined by the structure of the Copenhagen criteria (that strictly delimit between the political and economic criteria and cooperation domains).

Statement of aims and research strategy

Against this background, the book seeks to provide answers to five mutually intertwined questions, appearing in bold italic type in what follows.

• ***What are the peculiarities of EU value-promoting RTAs?***

Based on the study of the evolution of the EU external economic policy, and the interplay between the normative and market objectives of the Union, the book

---

8 European Commission, Communication to the European Parliament and the Council: A New EU Framework to Strengthen the Rule of Law, COM(2014) 158 final/2 of 11 March 2014.

9 See, for instance: European Commission, Commission Staff Working Document accompanying the Commission Working Paper "EU Report on Policy Coherence for Development" (COM(2007)545final), SEC (2007) 1202 of 20 September 2007; European Commission, Commission Staff Working Document accompanying the Report from the Commission to the Council "EU 2009 Report on Policy Coherence for Development" (COM(2009)461final), SEC(2009) 1137final of 17 September 2009.

introduces the concept of the EU "value-promoting RTAs". In this respect, particular attention is paid to analyzing the political prerequisites of the EU value-promotion through RTAs, as well as distinguishing the peculiarities of the EU value-promoting RTAs *vis-à-vis* other EU trade agreements. The analysis distinguishes EU Stabilization and Association Agreements (SAAs) with Western Balkans countries, EU Association Agreements (AAs) with Eastern and Southern Neighbours, and Economic Partnership Agreements (EPAs) with ACP countries as the examples of EU value-promoting RTAs that can be illustrative of a variety of legal mechanisms the EU RTAs utilize to promote values. Transferring to the rule of law-specific inquiry, we ask:

- *How do the EU bilateral and plurilateral RTAs promote the rule of law?*

To answer this question, the book uses the concepts of "regulation" and "action". "Regulation" can be defined as a process of "controlling, governing or directing", immediately exercised by the EU with respect to selected areas of the rule of law in partner countries through rules contained in RTAs (Black, 2002, p. 4). Stemming from development cooperation field, "action" refers to the application of any policy and legal instruments that aim to promote the rule of law and/or support the implementation of trade liberalization arrangements, but cannot immediately regulate legal relations within a target country. Hence, "action" may embrace the use of "soft" (diplomatic) instruments, financial and technical assistance instruments, non-reciprocal market access and the creation of monitoring and coordination institutions and missions (Pech, 2012/2013). Given the framework nature of the EU's unilateral arrangements for sustainable development and good governance (i.e. the GSP, the GSP+ and the EBA initiatives) and the fact that they were not recently applied to the countries under study (European Commission, High Representative of the Union for Foreign Affairs and Security Policy, 2020), the analysis only tangentially engages with these mechanisms.

Based on this, the book zooms in on the rule of law in four categories of RTAs' norms and related "action":

- "Essential element" clauses – a foundational instrument of values' conditionality across virtually all EU trade agreements.
- "Transparency" chapters in trade-related parts of the Association Agreements with Eastern Neighbours, illustrative of far-reaching rule of law clauses in the "new generation" EU RTAs.
- Administrative and technical cooperation chapters, offering an insight into the rule of law dimension of treaty obligations pertaining to exchange of information and cooperation and related unilateral instruments.
- Public procurement, competition and state aid chapters, belonging to the category of "deep" disciplines and related unilateral instruments.

The action-regulation dichotomy represents the core of analyzing the mechanism of the value-promoting RTAs' impact on the state of the rule of law in areas,

6 *Introduction*

highlighted previously. The introduction of such dichotomy also helps to answer the subsequent research question:

- *Are the "regulation" and "action" dimensions of the EU value-promoting RTAs coherent between each other?*

Apart from exploring the coherence of the rule of law promotion through trade liberalization, the book also intends to answer the following question:

- *How can the EU value-promoting RTAs be integrated into the existing system of the EU instruments of promoting the rule of law to generate synergies?*

The book uses the case of justice sector reform in the Western Balkans, Eastern Neighbourhood and the Caribbean Forum (CARIFORUM) to illustrate the nexuses between the EU rule of law promotion through trade liberalization and the EU promotion of the rule of law, broadly defined. The choice of the justice sector reform is determined by the fact that independent and impartial judiciary is both an essential component of the rule of law and one of the key points on the EU "rule of law promotion menu", offered to third countries worldwide. Insights, acquired in terms of answering the previous and this research question, are used as a foundation for developing recommendations on how to strategize the EU rule of law promotion through trade liberalization.

Ultimately, the inquiry aims to apply the concept of EU value-promoting RTAs and the findings regarding the legal mechanisms of the EU rule of law promotion through trade liberalization to the single case study of the EU-Ukraine Deep and Comprehensive Free Trade Agreement (DCFTA, i.e. a trade-related part of the EU-Ukraine AA). An emphasis will be made on the key rule of law-relevant changes within Ukraine's domestic legal system, stemming from the application of the DCFTA and legal instruments, directed at its implementation, and the problématique of coherence. Hence, the fifth research question can be formulated as:

- *In which ways has the EU-Ukraine DCFTA and related implementation instruments impacted the rule of law in Ukraine, and to which extent such support is coherent with the Union's other efforts to promote the rule of law in Ukraine?*

The choice of the EU-Ukraine DCFTA as a case study is determined by three reasons. First, the EU-Ukraine AA (that comprises the DCFTA) represents one of the most ambitious agreements the EU has ever concluded with a third country in terms of Single Market integration. Second, since 2014 (the change of power in Ukraine following the Euromaidan Revolution[10] and the annexation of Crimea),

---

10 The Euromaidan Revolution (the Revolution of Dignity) signifies the revolutionary movement in Ukraine, provoked by then President Viktor Yanukovych's refusal to sign the EU-Ukraine Association Agreement. The revolution took place over the period from 21 November 2013 through 23 February 2014, resulting in the appointment of the interim government and the subsequent elections of the President and Verkhovna Rada (the Parliament).

Introduction 7

the EU has been implementing an unprecedented multiannual state-building programme in Ukraine, worth €11.2 billion that includes multiple rule of law components (Wolczuk and Žeruolis, 2018, pp. 3–4). Third, Ukraine represents an interesting case study due to the uniquely high popular support for EU integration, manifested by the Euromaidan Revolution, and the tensions in the EU-Russia relationships due to the latter's annexation of Crimea and aggression in Eastern Ukraine. Thus, the single case of the EU-Ukraine DCFTA is utilized to downscale from the general idea of value-promoting RTAs to the operation of such an RTA in a specific country context, and produce recommendations for EU institutions regarding the promotion of the rule of law in countries, experiencing "unfinished transition".

In sum, the book contributes to understanding the actual and potential suitability of "deep" trade agreements as a means of promoting fundamental values, as well as the substance and prospects of the rule of law as an NTPO.

A note on theoretical framework and methodology

The theoretical framework of the study comprises five elements.

First of all, the book is based on the concept of the rule of law. It introduces the rule of law as a fundamental value of the EU and uses a number of the EU and Council of Europe primary sources, as well as secondary sources to distinguish the consensual components of the rule of law. It also explains the conceptual problématique of the rule of law in the context of the EU trade policy and trade liberalization with third countries. The second crucial pillar of the research is represented by the understanding of the political and legal foundations of the EU external economic policy. Third, based on this and insights into the literature on law and development, and the interplay of market and normative power Europe, the book introduces the concept of the EU value-promoting RTAs.

Fourth, as mentioned previously, the book applies the concepts of "regulation" and "action". These concepts form the core of understanding the logic of the RTAs' impact on the rule of law and help to present the ways of integrating RTAs into the broad spectrum of the EU rule of law promotion instruments in a structured manner. Fifth, the study applies the concept of coherence, understood beyond the simple avoidance of overlaps, to encompass the opportunities for creating synergies. In particular, the book focuses on the horizontal dimension of coherence to explore the interplay between the "regulation" and "action" dimensions of the EU rule of law promotion through RTAs and locate value-promoting RTAs in the context of the EU broader rule of law promotion efforts.

In methodological terms, the book combines the "black letter law" analysis with the analysis of official documents, such as those relating to EU human rights dialogues with third countries, multiannual and annual programming of the EU financial and technical assistance, technical assistance project documentation and EU mission mandates. The "black letter law" methodology provides for concentrating solely on the "letter of the law", contained in primary sources, such as official texts of the EU trade agreements with third countries and case law of the European Court of Justice (ECJ), and is, first of all, used to analyze

8 *Introduction*

the "regulation" dimension of the EU rule of law promotion through RTAs. In turn, document analysis serves to explore related "action". The combination of the "black letter law" approach and document analysis is applied to explore the problématique of coherence.

Structure of the book

This book is divided into eight chapters.

Chapters 1–3 introduce the conceptual and theoretical foundations of the book. Chapter 1 discusses the conceptual problématique of the rule of law and introduces the consensual components of the rule of law to serve as benchmarks for the analysis. In turn, Chapter 2 traces the history and the peculiarities of the legal basis of the EU external economic policy. Chapter 3 constructs the concept of the EU value-promoting RTAs and explains the added value of distinguishing between the value-promoting RTAs and the RTAs without the value-promoting component.

The book continues with the analysis of the mechanisms of the EU rule of law promotion through trade liberalization in Chapters 4 and 5. Chapter 4 looks at the "regulation" dimension of the EU rule of law promotion through RTAs, focusing on the "essential element" clauses, the "Transparency" chapters of the EU DCFTAs with Eastern Neighbours, and administrative and technical cooperation clauses across the whole spectrum of the RTAs in question, as well as the public procurement, competition and state aid chapters. Chapter 5 covers the EU "action" in the aforementioned domains.

Based on Chapter 4 and Chapter 5, Chapter 6 and Chapter 7 explore the coherence of the EU rule of law promotion through RTAs from two standpoints. Chapter 6 looks at the interplay between the "regulation" and "action" dimensions of the EU rule of law through RTAs ("internal coherence"). Chapter 7 discusses the EU value-promoting RTAs in the broader context of the Union's rule of law promotion policy and the PCD ("external coherence"). Using the case of the EU support of justice sector reforms in the enlargement, the ENP and development policy contexts, Chapter 7 offers a remarkable insight into the RTAs' potential to supplement the EU traditional rule of law promotion efforts.

Chapter 8 applies the concept of "EU value-promoting RTAs" and the findings of Chapters 4–7 to the single case study of the EU-Ukraine DCFTA.

Finally, the book concludes with a discussion of the prospects of "strategizing" EU RTAs for the purposes of promoting the rule of law.

References

Anderson, R. (2013). Linking rule of law and trade liberalization in Jamaica. *Berkeley Journal of African-America Law and Policy*, 7(1), pp. 51–91.

Araujo, B. M. (2017). *Labour standards and mega-regionals: Innovative rule-making or sticking to the boilerplate?* Institute of European Law Working Paper 03/2017. [online] Available at: http://epapers.bham.ac.uk/2991/1/IEL_Working_Paper_03-2017_-_melo-araujo.pdf.

Black, J. (2002). Critical reflections on regulation. *Australian Journal of Legal Philosophy*, 27, pp. 1–36.

Council of the EU. (2019). *Policy coherence for development: Council adopts conclusions.* [online] Available at: www.consilium.europa.eu/en/press/press-releases/2019/05/16/policy-coherence-for-development-council-adopts-conclusions/.

Dee, M. (2015). *The European Union in a multipolar world.* Basingstoke: Palgrave Macmillan.

Douma, W. (2017). The promotion of sustainable development through EU trade instruments. *European Business Law Review*, 28(2), pp. 193–212.

European Commission, High Representative of the Union for Foreign Affairs and Security Policy. (2020). *Report on the generalized scheme of preferences covering the period 2018–2019.* [online]. Available at: https://trade.ec.europa.eu/doclib/docs/2018/january/tradoc_156536.pdf.

European Parliament. (2020). *Rule of law in Poland and Hungary has worsened.* [online] Available at: www.europarl.europa.eu/news/en/press-room/20200109IPR69907/rule-of-law-in-poland-and-hungary-has-worsened.

Fiorini, M. (2019). *Future of EU's trade policy and non-trade objectives. German development institute.* [online] Available at: https://blogs.die-gdi.de/2019/05/08/future-of-eus-trade-policy-and-non-trade-objectives/.

Gstöhl, S.M. and Hanf, D. (2014). The EU's post-Lisbon free trade agreements: Commercial interests in a changing constitutional context. *European Law Journal*, 20(6), pp. 733–748.

Hoang, H. and Sicurelli, D. (2017). The EU's preferential trade agreements with Singapore and Vietnam. Market vs normative imperatives. *Contemporary Politics*, 23(4), pp. 369–387.

Kochenov, D. and Bárd, P. (2018). *Rule of law crisis in the new member states of the EU. The pitfalls of overemphasizing enforcement.* RECONNECT Working Paper No. 1. [online] Available at: https://reconnect-europe.eu/wp-content/uploads/2018/07/RECONNECT-KochenovBard-WP_27072018b.pdf.

Marx, A., Ebert, F. and Hachez, N. (2017). Dispute settlement for labour provisions in EU free trade agreements: Rethinking current approaches. *Politics and Governance*, 5(4), pp. 49–59.

Morin, J.F. and Jonnah, S. (2018). The untapped potential of preferential trade agreements for climate governance. *Environmental Politics*, 27(3), pp. 541–565.

Ngatat, E. T. (2016). Trade liberalization within intra-BRICS and the rule of law. *Asian Journal of Law and Economics*, 8(2), pp. 33–48.

Orbie, J. (2016). The European Union's role in world trade: Harnessing globalization? In: J. Orbie, ed., *Europe's global role. External policies of the European Union*. London: Routledge, pp. 51–82.

Orbie, J. and Khorana, S. (2015). Normative versus market power Europe? The EU-India trade agreement. *Asia Europe Journal*, 13(3), pp. 253–264.

Orbie, J. and Van Den Putte, L. (2016). *Labour rights and the EU trade agreement: Compliance with the commitments under the sustainable development chapter.* OFSE Working Paper 58. [online] Available at: https://biblio.ugent.be/publication/8055501/file/8055504.pdf.

Pech, L. (2012/2013). *Rule of law as a guiding principle of the European Union's external action.* CLEER Working Papers. [online] Available at: www.asser.nl/media/1632/cleer2012-3web.pdf.

Poletti, A. and Sicurelli, D. (2018). *The political economy of normative trade power Europe.* Basingstoke: Palgrave Macmillan.

10   *Introduction*

Stoll, P.T., Gött, H. and Abel, P. (2018). A model labour chapter for future EU trade agreements. In: H. Gött, ed., *Labour standards in international economic law*. Berlin: Springer, pp. 381–430.

Velutti, S. (2016). The promotion and integration of human rights in EU external trade relations. *Utrecht Journal of International and European Law*, 32(83), pp. 41–68.

Waldron, J. (2002). Is the rule of law an essentially contested concept (In Florida?) *Law and Philosophy*, 21(2), pp. 137–164.

Wolczuk, K. and Žeruolis, D. (2018). *Rebuilding Ukraine. An assessment of EU assistance: Chatham house Ukraine forum research paper*. [online] Available at: www.chatham house.org/sites/default/files/publications/research/2018-08-16-rebuilding-ukraine-eu-assistance-wolczuk-zeruolis.pdf.

1 The concept of the rule of law in the EU external action

Part 1. Conceptual problématique of the rule of law

The rule of law represents an "expansive" and "essentially contested" concept, characterized by multi-aspect problématique, including unclear relations to other concepts, and varying interpretations in scholarship (Fallon, 1997; Waldron, 2002). These understandings vary from associating the rule of law with the formal presence of transparent and predictable rules to complex conceptualizations, entailing formal, substantive and institutional aspects. While these understandings are not mutually exclusive, the difficulties emerge on the rule of law's path from a theory to the "solution of the world's troubles" (Ringer, 2007, p. 178) and the objective of reforms, funded by international donor institutions. The global "conceptual anarchy" (*Ibid.*) surrounding the rule of law, divergent constitutional traditions of EU Member States and the peculiarities of supranational EU law turn the solidification of the EU's rule of law concept into a uniquely challenging task. Hence, this chapter will discuss the status of the rule of law in the EU legal system, as well as the relevant theoretical approaches to conceptualizing the rule of law.

1. Rule of law in the EU legal order

Marked by both structural and aspirational nature, "the rule of law already manifests itself in the very existence of the Union and its predecessors" (Larik, 2016, p. 220). Addressing the European Economic Community (EEC) as a "phenomenon of law" (Hallstein, 1979, p. 51), the first EEC President Walter Hallstein coined the notion of *Rechtsgemeinschaft* (addressed in English-language scholarship as a "European supranational legal community") and, subsequently, gave rise to the theory of European integration though law" (Müller, 2012, p. 10). Importantly, Hallstein conceptualized the Community as *Rechtsgemeinschaft* in four senses: as a creation of law (*Rechtsschöpfung*), a source of law (*Rechtsquelle*), the legal order (*Rechtsordnung*) and a legal policy (*Rechtspolitik*) (Hallstein, 1979, p. 53). In terms of the first connotation, Hallstein emphasized the fact that the Community was not just an economic but a legal project, wherein the relations between the Member States and their relations to the Community had to be governed by law, rather than economic power or force (Tuori, 2015, p. 213). In turn, ensuring

12 *The rule of law in the EU external action*

such a functioning of the *Rechtsgemeinschaft* requires strong *Rechtsstaat* or the rule of law.

Since the concepts of the *Rechtsgemeinschaft*, *Rechtstaat* and the rule of law significantly differ in their substance (Tuori, 2015, p. 213), the European Court's of Justice (ECJ's) referral to the former European Community (EC) as a "Community based on the rule of law" in its *Les Verts* judgement brought about crucial conceptual disarray.[1] The Court underlined that the rule of law plays a founding role for the Community "inasmuch as neither its Member States nor its institutions can avoid a review of the question whether the measures adopted by them are in conformity with the basic constitutional Charter, the Treaty", thus, evoking the components of both *Rechtsgemeinschaft and Rechtstaat*.[2] The analysis of the described formula leads us to three takeaways important for understanding the rule of law concept within the legal system of the EU as a successor of the European Community.

First, the Court implicitly addressed the rule of law as a "positive good in itself" (Pech, 2009, p. 13) or, put it differently, as a value. Second, since this formulation defines the Treaty as a Constitutional Charter, the rule of law can be regarded as a constitutional principle of the EC to be upheld not only by the ECJ, but national courts that become "decentralized" Union courts (Reding, 2013). Third, the Court approached the rule of law in the EC from the formal standpoint, primarily associating it with the EC institutions and Member States being subject to the rules, contained in Treaties, rather than the substance of Treaty rules.

The rule of law was the first time formalized in the Preamble of the TEU(M), which reflected the Member States' "attachment to the principles of liberty, democracy and respect for human rights and fundamental freedoms and of the rule of law".[3] This reference did not, however, either define the status of the rule of law or refer to its substance. Art. 6(1) of the Treaty of Amsterdam (TEU [A]) mentioned the rule of law among the principles the Union is founded upon.[4] Moreover, the TEU(A) pioneered in introducing sanctions for the Member States' "serious and persistent breach . . . of principles, mentioned in Art. 6(1) TEU (A) and Art. 49 TEU (A)" (respect for the rule of law as a criterion for the EU accession). Art. 11 (1) TEU(A) also mentioned the rule of law among the objectives of the Union's Common Foreign and Security Policy (CFSP). Thus, particularly the TEU(A) reaffirmed the constitutional nature of the rule of law for the EU legal system, giving rise to its conceptualization as a "meta-norm" pertaining to both the EU and its institutions, and the Member States (Palombella, 2009).

---

1 European Court of Justice, Parti écologiste "Les Verts"/European Parliament, Case294/83, Judgment of 23 April 1986.
2 *Ibid.*, para 23.
3 Treaty on European Union, OJ C 191 of 29 July 1992, Preamble; hereinafter referred to as "TEU(M)".
4 Treaty of Amsterdam amending the Treaty on European Union, the Treaties establishing the European Communities and certain related acts, OJ C 340 of 10 November 1997; hereinafter referred to as "TEU(A)".

The rule of law in the EU external action 13

As opposed to Art. 6(1) TEU(A) that viewed the rule of law as a founding *principle* of the Union, Art. 2 TEU as modified by the Lisbon Treaty mentions the rule of law among the EU's common *values*. Such a vocabulary change was repeatedly assessed by scholars as "regrettable", since the concept of founding principles "expresses the overarching normative frame of reference for all primary law, indeed, for the whole of the EU's legal order" (von Bogdandy, 2010, p. 22). Nevertheless, the analysis of the further referrals to the founding values in EU primary law reveals that the change of wording (though, hard to explain) is most likely unrelated to any ideas to change the nature or substance of the founding principles as formulated by Art. 6(1) TEU(A). On the contrary, the Treaty of Lisbon (TEU[L]) consolidated the functions the rule of law plays in the EU legal order. Alongside Art. 2 that refers to the rule of law as a fundamental value, Art. 3(1) and 13(1) TEU position the rule of law as an objective of both the EU and its institutions. Next, the TEU(L) mentions the rule of law among the criteria for EU membership. Furthermore, following the trend to the constitutionalization of foreign policy objectives (Larik, 2016), the TEU(L) distinguishes the promotion of EU values, including the rule of law, as a general objective of the whole spectrum of EU external policies.

Despite the detailed regulation of various functions of the rule of law in the TEU(L), it did not shed light on the substance of the rule of law. However, important developments of the EU rule of law agenda took place due to the ongoing rule of law crises in Poland and Hungary. First of all, the "Great Rule of Law Debate" led to the acknowledgement of the lack of genuinely common understanding of the rule of law as a crucial reason behind Member States' non-compliance with the foundational rule of law requirements, such as judicial independence and impartiality (Kochenov, Magen and Pech, 2016). It was also stressed that, alongside Art. 7 TEU, offering a straightforward way to address a breach via sanctions, the EU has lacked instruments to react to Member States' non-compliance with fundamental values. Having recognized the rule of law problem but being reluctant to immediately proceed with sanctions, the European Commission started with introducing a new EU Framework to Strengthen the Rule of Law ("2014 Rule of Law Framework").[5]

Conceived as an early warning tool to address the rule of law threats through the dialogue with a concerned Member State, the 2014 Rule of Law Framework applies the consensual approach to the rule of law, introduced by the Venice Commission. Even though the Framework allows for a particular degree of vagueness to accommodate differences in Member States' constitutional traditions, the Commission's first attempt to map the substance of the rule of law testifies to the ongoing consolidation of the concept at the Union level. Importantly, the formulation of Art. 21(2)(a) TEU ("The Union shall define and pursue common policies and actions, and shall work for a high degree of cooperation in all fields

---

5 European Commission, Communication to the European Parliament and the Council: A New EU Framework to Strengthen the Rule of Law, COM (2014)158 final/2 of 19 March 2014.

14   *The rule of law in the EU external action*

of international relations, in order to (a) safeguard *its* values", emphasis added) points to an immediate notional link between the Union's understanding of the rule of law as a fundamental value of the Union and an objective of the EU external action. Subsequently, the adoption of the Rule of Law Framework is crucial not only for streamlining the protection of the rule of law as a fundamental value but defining the substance of this concept that can be, *inter alia*, extrapolated to the EU enlargement and external action.

The second significant trend that emerged as a result of the intra-EU rule of law crises has been the elaboration of new instruments to promote the rule of law. In this vein, the Commission's 2019 Communication "Strengthening the rule of law within the Union. A blueprint for action" introduced the Rule of Law Review Cycle and Annual Rule of Law Report to both monitor significant developments in EU Member States and engage into dynamic dialogue with them.[6] Thus, although the rule of law crises in the EU were not yet resolved, and the infringement procedures are ongoing, the Great Rule of Law Debate in the EU promoted the search for a consensual concept of the rule of law.

2. Scholarly approaches to the substance of the rule of law

The easiest-to-capture controversy in the rule of law debate relates to its substance. Such a controversy manifests itself in the co-existence and complex interplay of formal (including institutional) and substantive approaches to the rule of law in the doctrinal interpretation of the concept and the rule of law promotion practice. The core of the formal approaches to the rule of law directly stems from the opposition between the "rule of law" and the "rule of men", i.e. "the condition of government absent of law, where men rule, according to their fancies, not according to general rules" (Cheeseman, 2015, p. 20). In turn, alongside the prevention of the "rule of men" through effective and binding rules, substantive approaches to the rule of law zoom in on the contents of legal regulations. Both approaches are considered in more detail in what follows.

Formal perspectives on the rule of law

Focusing on the ways to effectively bind the governments, the main representatives of the formal approach, such as the Israeli philosopher Joseph Raz (1979) and the British constitutionalist Albert Venn Dicey (1985), emphasized clear, prospective and predictable rules as the foundation of the rule of law. In this vein, Raz (1979) argued in favour of a clear distinction between the rule of law and other features of the political and legal systems, such as democracy, justice and the protection of human rights. The impressive formality of Raz's approach to the rule of law is manifested by the fact that he "readily admits that the rule of law

---

6 European Commission, Communication to the European Parliament and the Council: Strengthening the rule of law within the Union. A blueprint for action, COM/2019/343final of 17 July 2019.

could be met by regimes, whose laws are morally objectionable, provided that they comply with the formal precepts that comprise the rule of law" (Craig, 1997, p. 468). According to Raz (1979), these formal precepts of the rule of law include prospective nature, openness and clarity of laws; relative stability of laws; open, stable and clear rules of law-making; guaranteed independence of the judiciary; observance of the principles of "natural justice" (p. 217) (open and fair hearing, the absence of bias etc.); review powers of the courts; and accessibility of courts and limited discretion of the crime-preventing agencies.

Although Raz (1979) tries to distinguish the rule of law from other features of government, the analysis of formal approaches to the rule of law, introduced by him and other scholars, reveals tight links between the formal rule of law, on the one hand, and equality, fairness and the protection of individual rights, on the other hand. First, he himself goes beyond the solely formal approach to the rule of law, when mentioning the concept of "natural justice", characterized by profound substance. Second, the fact that Raz (1979, p. 217) mentions that "the courts should be easily accessible" among the formal precepts of the rule of law, can be interpreted as individuals' right to equal access to courts. Third, the non-arbitrariness of the state's actions, mentioned by Locke (2015), Dicey (1985) and Hume (1994), is widely recognized as a prerequisite of equality and fairness. In particular, the prohibition of arbitrary punishments and individuals' equality before the law represent two out of three components of the Dicey's famous three-element formula of the rule of law. Relevant for the British legal system, characterized by the absence of the written Constitution, the third element of the Dicey's formula stipulates that "the Constitution (the law) is the result of previous judicial decisions, determining the rights of private persons" (Dicey, 1985, p. 349). Despite these links to substantive issues, the key problem with the formal conceptualizations of the rule of law is that it can be, nevertheless, observed by undemocratic regimes that deny human rights and practice racial segregation or religious persecution.

Substantive approaches to the rule of law

Adherents to the substantive perspective of the rule of law argue that the formalist view of the concept contributes to the government's "rule by law", rather than bounds the state to treat individuals acceptably (Tamanaha, 2005, p. 92). An emphasis on the contents of the law dates back to Aristotle, who argued that "laws, when good, should be supreme" (Frank, 2007, p. 37). While recognizing that the rule of law serves an important purpose of countering the rule of men, John Locke (2015) linked the rule of law to "peace, safety and the public good of the people" (p. 68). A similar position was expressed by Dworkin (1986), who views formal rules as a crucial means of enforcing moral rights and substantive justice (pp. 11–12).

In Germany, the opposite to the formal rule of law (*formaler Rechtsstaat*) is represented by the concept of the material rule of law (*materieller Rechtsstaat*). According to Kelsen (2009), the notion of the "formal rule of law" applies to a

16 *The rule of law in the EU external action*

situation, where a state bases its action on its legal order – independent on the specific substance of such order (p. 121). On the contrary, *materieller Rechtsstaat* requires particular institutions, such as the democratic law-making, responsibility of the executive, observance of the individual freedoms, independent judiciary and the presence of administrative courts system (*Verwaltungsgerichtsbarkeit*) (*Ibid.*, p. 45). Having been first applied in the legal tradition of the Weimar Republic (1919–1933), *materieller Rechtsstaat* gained the new momentum in the value-based order, created by the German Basic Law (*Grundgesetz für die Bundesrepublik Deutschland*) (Enzmann, 2012, pp. 51–57). The modern concept of *materieller Rechtsstaat* emphasizes material justice (*materielle Gerechtigkeit*) and the need for ensuring the order, directed to the public good (*am Gemeinwohl orientierte Ordnung*) (*Ibid.*, p. 51). Thus, beyond the formal characteristics of laws, the substance of the respective concept encompasses human rights (including socially ensured rights to education and healthcare), and justice. Interestingly, while Kelsen (2009) tended to underline the importance of democratic institutions and processes for the material rule of law, nowadays *materieller Rechtsstaat* is viewed not only as means to promote human rights observance and justice but limit the discretion of the parliamentary majority (Möllers, 2008).

In English legal scholarship, the three-level substantive conceptualization of the rule of law was developed by Lord Tom Bingham (2011). As opposed to the German concept of the material rule of law, Bingham's model is strongly rights oriented, rather than focusing on justice and social security dimensions. The basic level of Bingham's understanding of the rule of law is founded on the principle that "all persons and authorities within the state, whether public or private, shall be bound by and entitled to the benefit of laws, publicly made, taking effect (generally) in the future and publicly administered in courts" (Bingham, 2011, p. 13). The second level encompasses several normative principles, such as the clarity of laws, everybody's equality before the law, limits to authorities' discretion and fair adjudicative procedures (*Ibid.*). Finally, underlining that the genuine rule of law goes beyond institutional and procedural benchmarks, Lord Bingham (2011) distinguished adequate protection of human rights, and a state's compliance with its international obligations as the necessary substantive elements of the rule of law.

Substantive elements of the rule of law are present across a broad array of the conceptualizations of the rule of law, applied by international organizations. For instance, the United Nations (UN) views "accountability to laws, consistent with the international human rights norms and standards", "strengthening states' compliance with international law" and "fostering an enabling environment for sustainable human development".[7] Similarly, the OSCE vision of the Rule of law is strongly linked to the "fulfillment in good faith of obligations under international law", "justice, based on the recognition and full acceptance of the supreme value

---

7 United Nations Secretary-General, Report "Delivering Justice: Programme of Action to Strengthen the Rule of Law at the National and International Levels", A/66/749 of 16 March 2012.

The rule of law in the EU external action 17

of human personality" and democracy and human rights.[8] Finally, the Council of Europe's concept of the rule of law also includes respect for human rights and compliance with international law.[9] Thus, in the post-World War era, marked by a uniquely strong common ambition to sustain the hard won peace, substantive components of the rule of law have become an essential for the international rule of law effort. In view of all of this, this book will adhere to the substantive approach to the rule of law, considering human rights to constitute a part of the concept. At the same time, given the fuzzy boundaries between democracy and the rule of law in the EU external action, further analysis is needed to draw the boundaries between democracy and substantive rule of law, and between the rule of law and democracy promotion.

3. Relationship between the rule of law and democracy in the EU political and legal orders

Similar to the rule of law, the concept of democracy lacks a unified understanding in the EU constitutional law, with multiple variations of democratic models, suggested in scholarship, and a long-lasting debate as to countering the EU "democratic deficit" (e.g. Moravcsik, 2004; Follesdap and Hix, 2006; Innerarti, 2018) In conceptual terms, the EU's understanding of democracy is claimed to be founded on the classical "liberal" or "Lockean" view (Merkel, 2004, pp. 34–35). According to this understanding, "the democratic process accomplishes the task of programming the government in the interest of society, where the government is represented as an apparatus of public administration, and society as a market-structured network of interactions among private persons" (Habermas, 1996, p. 21). In practice, such a programming takes the form of "collective decision-making, characterized by the kind of equality among the participants of the decision-making process" (Christiano, 2004, p. 266).

Despite the rigorous academic discourse on the applicability of the notion of *Demos* to conceptualizing EU democracy, "the institutional model of the nation-state theory of democracy" (Nettesheim, 2005, p. 371) is used to discuss democracy and its peculiarities in the Union. According to Art. 10(1) TEU, "the functioning of the Union shall be founded on the principle of representative democracy". Institutionally, the EU model of democracy is marked by the presence of two pivotal channels of democratic representation: Member States' representation in the European Council and in the Council by their democratically accountable

---

8 Conference on Security and Cooperation in Europe, Helsinki Final Act, 1975. [online] Available at: www.osce.org/helsinki-final-act?download=true; Conference on the Human Dimension of the CSCE, Concluding Document of the Copenhagen Meeting, 1990. [online] Available at: www.osce.org/odihr/elections/14304?download=true.

9 European Commission for Democracy through Law, "Rule of Law Checklist", Study No 711/2013 of 18 March 2016. [online] Available at: www.venice.coe.int/webforms/documents/default.aspx?pdffile=CDL-AD(2016)007-e (hereinafter referred to as "Venice Commission Rule of Law Checklist" or "The Rule of Law Checklist").

18   *The rule of law in the EU external action*

governments and citizens' direct representation in the European Parliament. Additionally, the Lisbon Treaty reinforced the intra-EU democracy by strengthening the role of national parliaments in the EU decision-making processes (Art. 12 TEU) and introducing the European Citizens' Initiative (Art. 11 [4] TEU). In turn, citizens' rights to representation, openness of decision-making procedures and the application of the principle of subsidiarity, provided for in Title II TEU, can be distinguished as functional prerequisites of the EU democracy.

While the substance of the EU model of democracy is shaped by the peculiarities of the EU as a *sui generis* legal entity, the democratic model the Union seeks to promote abroad has long been a contested issue in scholarship (e.g. Merkel, 2004; Wetzel, 2015). Simultaneously, a number of authors stress the technocratic nature of the EU's rule transfer under the auspices of democracy promotion (e.g. Radaelli, 1999; Korosteleva, 2016). Mapping the substance of the Union's external democracy promotion, Wetzel (2015) applies the complex "embedded democracy" model (Merkel, 2004, p. 33), developed by the German political scientist Wolfgang Merkel. In his model, he distinguished five internal characteristics of democracy (or "partial regimes" (Merkel, 2004, p. 33)), such as electoral regime, political rights, civil rights, horizontal separation of powers and elected officials' effective power to rule. In turn, external conditions of democracy, emphasized by Merkel (2004), are the degree of socio-economic development, functioning civil society, as well as international and regional integration.

The analysis of the EU internal and external perspectives on democracy, and substantive conceptualization of the rule of law, allows distinguishing a range of shared components. The key component, shared by the concepts, is represented by the focus on civil rights that Merkel (2004) explicitly links to the protection of an individual from violations of own rights by the state or private parties. Moreover, virtually all models of democracy, including "embedded democracy", encompass political or citizens' rights, such as the right to vote and stand as a candidate at elections, right to good administration, right of access to documents and right to petition, contained in Chapter V of the EU Charter of Fundamental Rights (CFR).[10] Second, the conceptualizations of both democracy and the rule of law tend to refer to the delineation of powers between authorities, the checks and balances system, and accountable and transparent law- and decision-making procedures. In the rule of law-related understanding, the delineation of powers between authorities and the functioning "checks and balances" system represent the essential prerequisites for the observance of the legality standard that requires *inter alia* authorities' compliance with laws. Simultaneously, the separation of powers and, especially, the limitedness of the executives' powers are necessary for ensuring the proper role for a parliament within the representative democracy system. The system of powers' delineation becomes even more complex in the case of the EU, where the Member States' and citizens' representation co-exist. With regard

10 Charter of Fundamental Rights of the European Union, OJ C 364/101 of 18 December 2000, pp. 1–17 (hereinafter referred to as "CFR").

The rule of law in the EU external action   19

to both democracy and the rule of law, the institutionalized practices of public accountability serve as crucial means to ensure officials' adherence thereto. In turn, exercising public accountability requires openness and transparency of law- and decision-making processes. Scholars' confidence in the inextricable nature of the relationship between the rule of law and democracy (e.g. O'Donnell, 2004), and important components they share, raise a question regarding the concepts' interdependence and functions they fulfil with respect to each other. Can the rule of law exist in a non-democratic state or can democracy function under no rule of law? What is the relationship between democracy and the rule of law, on the one hand, and human rights, on the other hand? Answers to these questions significantly depend on one's understanding of the very idea behind the rule of law and democracy and the choice of conceptual premises for the analysis.

Understood in formal terms, the rule of law can exist in an authoritarian state, where human rights are poorly observed. The case is more controversial with the substantive rule of law. Theoretically, one can argue that substantive rule of law requirements can be fulfilled within the authoritarian state, provided that such state observes individual human rights. In the same vein, Möllers (2008) states that democracy shall be associated with the particularities of the decision-making, while the outcomes of such processes (e.g. a majority's decision to violate minority rights) do not anymore belong to the concept of democracy. However, the essential nature of political rights for both the rule of law and democracy, and the fact that political rights' violations are typical for states, testify to the tight nexus between the rule of law and democracy.

Despite the scholarly criticism regarding the formal approach to the rule of law, particularly formal characteristics of the rule of law serve as crucial prerequisites for both democracy and the observance of human rights. Sufficiently general, publicly promulgated prospective rules public institutions comply with serve as the fundamental basis for creating transparent, accountable and inclusive processes that lie at the heart of democracy. Next, the formal rule of law principle is essential for ensuring the functionality of a classic liberal government, wherein the state takes "its traditional minimalist, night watchman form" (Stewart, 2004, p. 136), the powers are separated and the exceptions to democracy and fundamental rights are stipulated in laws. As it can be exemplified by Art. 51–52 CFR, the rule of law principle presupposes multiple limitations to an individual's discretion, such as an individual's and institutions' obligation to comply with laws, the separation of powers and, finally, the requirement of lawful exceptions to fundamental rights and democratic processes. Different from the formal rule of law, both the British substantive rule of law concept and the German material rule of law (*materieller Rechtsstaat*) are broadly understood as a means to limit the discretion of the ruling majority. In scholarship, a similar role is attributed to individual rights that are included in the core of the substantive rule of law. Importantly, the rule of law–democracy nexus shall not be viewed as a one-way road, where the rule of law contributes to creating an "enabling environment" for democracy and limits the discretion of democratically elected officials. Various components of democracy also facilitate the rule of law. For instance, as argued by Merkel (2004),

20 *The rule of law in the EU external action*

compliance with laws and their social acceptance depend on the properties of processes through which laws are enacted, such as transparency, accountability, deliberative nature and exclusiveness.

The preceding analysis reveals that, despite the "inextricable linkage" between the concepts of democracy, the rule of law and human rights, they require delimitation in both the theory and practice of international value-promotion. In practical terms, such delimitation is of particular importance in view of the far-reaching critique of the EU and others international actors' technocratic or "institutions-only" approach to value-promotion that focuses on institutional capacities, rather than carefully applying the rule of law and democracy concepts to particular political and socio-economic contexts.

Part 2. Consensual components of the rule of law

An insight into the conceptual problématique of the rule of law demonstrates that despite (and by virtue of) the "essentially contested" nature of the rule of law, the debate on its uncontested components gains momentum both due to the ongoing intra-EU rule of law crises and the EU's ambition to increase the coherence of its external action. In this vein, the analysis proceeds with the development of the working conceptualization of the rule of law, embracing its consensual (or at least most widely spread) components, as distinguished in: (i) EU primary and secondary legislation; (ii) ECJ case law; (iii) the Commission's and Council's non-binding documents; (iv) Council of Europe documents (referred to by the 2014 Rule of Law Framework) and (v) secondary sources.

Implied in the ECJ's judgement in *Les Verts*[11] in the context of Member States' compliance with EU law, the principle of **legality** has been affirmed as an essential component of the rule of law in both early and most recent ECJ jurisprudence.[12] Since neither EU primary and secondary law nor ECJ judgements offer a conceptualization of legality, this analysis is primarily based on the 2019 Commission's Communication "Strengthening the rule of law within the Union. A blueprint for action" and the 2016 Venice Commission's Rule of Law Checklist the former document refers to.[13] The Checklist suggests considering legality as an umbrella concept, bringing together substantive, institutional, procedural and law enforcement aspects. In substantive terms, the core of the legality requirement is represented by the principle of supremacy of law that emphasizes the presence of legal obstacles to an abuse of power or, in other words, seeks to prevent the "rule of men". Such understanding of the supremacy of law is traceable in the scholarly approaches to both the rule of law and *Rechtstaat*. For instance, in his major work

---

11 European Court of Justice, Parti écologiste "Les Verts"/European Parliament, Case294/83, Judgment of 23 April 1986.

12 See, for instance: ECJ, Joined Cases C-7/56 and C-3/57 to C-7/57 Algera/Common Assembly of European Coal and Steel Community, Judgment of 12 July 1957; ECJ, Case C-90/95 P Henri de Compte/European Parliament of 17 April 1997.

13 See Venice Commission Rule of Law Checklist.

Introduction to the Study of the Law of the Constitution, Dicey (1985) pointed to the need for the "absolute supremacy or predominance of regular law as opposed to arbitrary power" (p. 202). The need for the binding laws limiting the authority of those in power also lies at the heart of the German concept of the supremacy of Constitution and laws (*Vorrang von Verfassung und Gesetzes*) (Unger, 2008, p. 17). Alongside the supremacy of law, substantive dimension of legality requirement encompasses general nature of laws, clear and understandable nature of legal norms, and the appropriate formulations of exceptions in emergency situations. Institutionally, legality is, foremost, linked to institutions' compliance with laws (including the delineation of powers between authorities; law-based nature of procedures, governing institutions' activities and authorities' compliance with their positive obligations). In turn, the Checklist refers to two critical types of procedures: transparent, accountable and inclusive law-making procedures, as well as transparent and accountable procedures of applying exceptions in emergency situations. Finally, the enforcement aspect of legality deals with officials' duty to implement the law, including the availability of effective remedies against the non-implementation of legislation and consistent application of sanctions for the non-implementation of the legislation.

Similar to the principle of legality, the principle of **legal certainty** is deeply rooted in constitutional traditions of EU Member States (Fenwick, Siems and Wrbka, 2017; Raitio, 2003, pp. 10–14). Despite the fact that it was never explicitly provided for in EU Treaties, the ECJ jurisprudence recognizes legal certainty as an essential condition for the rule of law in its jurisprudence.[14] According to the Rule of Law Checklist, legal certainty foremost means the accessibility of legislation and court decisions, with the exceptions duly justified. Accessibility of legislation and court decisions serves as a foundation for adhering to the transparency principle, as well as creating stable and foreseeable legal environment. In turn, the major function of the sub-principle of foreseeability of laws under the umbrella of legal certainty is to "enable legal subjects to regulate their conduct in conformity with it".[15] Foreseeability of laws is also ensured through their stability. In terms of the Checklist, stability does not mean that laws remain unchangeable. On the contrary, the design of the legal system needs to provide for laws' "capability to adapt to changing circumstances" and "fair warning" in the case of changes to legislation and consistency of introducing changes or amendments to the legal system. A further component of legal certainty is the principle of legitimate expectations. The primary idea behind this principle is that public authorities shall not only adhere to laws but take into account their promises and arising

---

14 The concept of legal certainty found its reflection in numerous European Court of Justice cases, such as: Kühne & Heitz NV/Produktschap voor Pluimvee en Eieren, Case C-453/00, Judgment of 13 January 2004, Stergios Delimitis/Henninger Bräu AG, Case C-234/89, Judgment of 28 February 1991; Syndicat français de l'Express international (SFEI) and others/La Poste and others, C-39/94, Judgment of 11 July 1996.

15 European Court of Human Rights (ECtHR), *The Sunday Times v the United Kingdom*, Case 6538/74, Judgment of 26 April 1979, para 49.

22   *The rule of law in the EU external action*

expectations (stemming not only from laws but individual decisions). As formulated by the Checklist, "according to the legitimate expectations doctrine, those, who act in a good faith on the basis of the law as it is, should not be frustrated in their legitimate expectations" (p. 26). Next, legal certainty requires laws to be prospective to ensure their general nature, predictability and coherence. Building upon the principles of foreseeability and non-retroactivity of law, the Checklist refers to the foundational principles of international criminal law and domestic criminal law of many countries: "*nullum crimen sine lege*" ("no crime without the law") and "*nulla poena sine lege*" ("no penalty without the law"). Finally, the umbrella legal certainty principle will not be complete without the mentioning the concept of *res judicata*, providing for the "respect of final judgments, unless there are cogent reasons for revising them" (p. 28).

Ensuring institutions' compliance with the law and preventing their abuse (misuse) of powers requires promoting accountability of institutions and transparency of decision-making processes. While the 2016 Rule of Law Checklist directly provides for **accountability** of the law-making process, it does not explicitly refer to this concept, when addressing the activities of the executive branch of the government. However, given the concept's broad application in EU law (e.g. with respect to the functioning of EU administrative agencies), it is suggested to include it into the scope of this working conceptualization of the rule of law. Having compared definitions of accountability across domestic laws of EU Member States, Busuioc (2013) defined it as "a relationship between an actor and a forum, characterized by three main stages or elements" (p. 32). At the first stage, an actor provides a forum with information regarding its decisions and actions retrospectively ("information phase"). The central debating stage of accountability provides for a forum's engaging an actor into a discussion or debate, based on the above information. Finally, the notion of accountability would hardly be complete without the element of the so-called "redistributive justice" – i.e. the forum's right to impose sanctions on an actor. Tightly linked to public accountability and integrity as "essential prerequisites of a democracy based on the rule of law", the principle of **transparency** contributes to all the previously mentioned dimensions of the rule of law. According to the European Commission, transparency provides for, *inter alia*, the disclosure of information on policy-making and spending, while ensuring citizens' access to such information.[16] Notably, as stipulated in the ECJ judgement in *Commission v Spain*, the transparency requirement applies to all the EU institutions, bodies and agencies.[17] Alongside this, the principle of transparency applies to the Directives' transposition into domestic legislation of EU Member States.[18] Further crucial components of the transparency principle include citizens' right to access EU institutions' documents (provided for in the Regulation 1049/2001/

---

16 European Commission, Communication to the European Parliament, the Council, the European Economic and Social Committee and the Committee of the Regions "A European strategy for data", COM(2020) 66 final of 19.2.2020.
17 European Court of Justice, Commission/Spain, Case C-417/99, Judgment of 13 September 2001.
18 *Ibid.*, para 21.

The rule of law in the EU external action 23

EC)[19] and the institutions' "duty to give reasons" for legislative and administrative acts, provided for in Art. 41CFR. In terms of the EU external rule of law promotion, transparency is frequently seen as both a component of the rule of law and a means to advance it, in particular, for the purposes of effective judicial review.[20]

Along with the principle of legality, already the ECJ judgement in *Les Verts* affirmed the availability of **judicial review** as a condition for Member States' observance of EU law. Subsequently, according to the ECJ reasoning in Rosneft' case, "the very existence of effective judicial review designed to ensure compliance with provisions of EU law is of the essence of the rule of law".[21] In this vein according to the 2014 Rule of Law Framework, "the Union based on the rule of law" means that "the EU institutions are subject to judicial review of the compatibility of their acts not only with the Treaty but with 'the general principles of law which include fundamental rights".[22] This both affirms the substantive nature of the EU understanding of the rule of law and underlines the inextricability of the link between the rule of law and fundamental rights in the EU legal system. Importantly, in its recent case law pertaining to the intra-EU rule of law crises, the ECJ repeatedly referred to Art. 19 TEU, obliging EU Member States to provide remedies sufficient to ensure "effective legal protection" in the domains covered by EU law.[23] In line with the ECJ judgement in the case *Commission v Poland*, the observance of Art. 19 TEU requires *inter alia* ensuring independence of the judiciary.[24] According to the ECJ earlier judgement in *Wilson*, **judicial independence** represents an autonomous concept in EU law, providing that judges need to be protected against any external interventions or pressures that can potentially jeopardize independent judgements.[25] Furthermore, the principle of judicial independence is tightly interconnected with the principle of **separation of powers**, distinguished by the European Commission as a consensual component of the

19 Regulation (EC) No 1049/2001 of the European Parliament and of the Council of 30 May 2001 regarding public access to European Parliament, Council and the Commission documents, OJL 145 of 31 May 2001.

20 European Commission, Communication to the European Parliament, the European Council and Council "Strengthening the rule of law within the Union. A blueprint for action", COM/2013/ 343final of 17 July 2019, p. 6; European Commission, Communication to the European Parliament, the Council, the European Economic and Social Committee and the Committee of the Regions "EU Enlargement Strategy", COM(2015)611final of 10 November 2015, p. 2; European Commission, Communication to the European Parliament, the Council, the European Economic and Social Committee and the Committee of the Regions "2019 Communication on EU Enlargement Strategy", COM(2019)260final of 29 May 2019, p. 4.

21 ECJ, *PJSC Rosneft Oil Company v Her Majesty's Treasury and Others*, Case C 72/15, Judgment of 28 March 2017.

22 European Commission, Communication to the European Parliament and the Council: A New EU Framework to Strengthen the Rule of Law', COM (2014)158 final/2 of 19 March 2014.

23 See, for instance, ECJ, Associação Sindical dos Juízes Portugueses, Case C-64/16, Judgment of 27 February 2018, para 32–34; ECJ, *Commission v Poland*, Case C-619/18, Judgment of 24 June 2019, para 71.

24 ECJ, *Commission v Poland*, Case C-619/18, Judgment of 24 June 2019, para 77.

25 ECJ, *Wilson v Ordre des avocats du barreau de Luxembourg*, Case C/506–4, Judgment of 19 September 2006, para 52–53.

24   *The rule of law in the EU external action*

rule of law in its 2014 Rule of Law Framework. In its 2014 judgement in *Celmer*, the ECJ highlighted the need for **impartiality** of national courts to ensure "equal distance" from the parties and their respective interests in the proceedings.[26] The principles of judicial independence and impartiality are also enshrined in the 2019 Communication "Further strengthening the Rule of Law within the Union. State of play and possible next steps".[27]

Next, the principles of **equality** and **non-discrimination** play a significant role in the EU legal order, founded upon the values of democracy and the rule of law. According to Rossi and Casolari (2017), the principle of equality in EU law embraces numerous dimensions, ranging from equality among the Member States to equality among EU citizens. However, both the 2014 Rule of Law Framework and the subsequent 2019 Commission's Communication "Strengthening the rule of law within the Union. A blueprint for action" stress solely equality before the law as the component of the rule of law.[28] Simultaneously, the Venice Commission's Rule of Law Checklist underlines an inextricable link between equality before the law and non-discrimination, with the latter principle encompassing the constitutional prohibition of discrimination, and individuals being guaranteed equal and effective protection against discrimination. Lying at the crossroads of fundamental rights and the rule of law, the principles of equality and non-discrimination are enshrined in Art. 20 and 21 CFR, respectively, ECJ case law,[29] as well as the 2015 and 2019 Enlargement Strategies.[30]

Finally, it is suggested to accentuate **the relationship between domestic and international law** as a part of the working conceptualization of the rule of law. The rationale behind this suggestion stems from the EU ambition to contribute to "contribute to the strict observance and development of international law" (Art. 3(5) TEU), as well as the importance of regulatory convergence for the EU external trade policy. Although the Venice Commission's Rule of Law Checklist limits its consideration of the relationship between domestic and international law

---

26 ECJ, Celmer, Case C-216/18 PPU, Judgment of 25 July 2018.

27 European Commission, Communication to the European Parliament and the Council: Further strengthening the Rule of Law within the Union. State of play and possible next steps, COM (2019)163final of 3 April 2019.

28 European Commission, Communication to the European Parliament and the Council: A New EU Framework to Strengthen the Rule of Law', COM (2014)158 final/2 of 19 March 2014, p. 4; European Commission, Communication to the European Parliament and the Council: Strengthening the rule of law within the Union. A blueprint for action, COM/2019/343final of 17 July 2019, p. 3.

29 See, for instance, ECJ, Criminal proceedings against Etablissements Fr. Colruyt NV. Request for a preliminary ruling from the Hof van beroep te Brussel, C 221/15, Judgment of 21 September 2016; ECJ, Wolfgang Glatzel/Freistaat Bayern, Case C 356/12, Judgment of 22 May 2014; ECJ, Blanka Soukupová/Ministerstvo zemědělství, Case C 401/11, Judgment of 12 April 2011.

30 European Commission, Communication to the European Parliament, the Council, the European Economic and Social Committee and the Committee of the Regions "EU Enlargement Strategy", COM(2015)611final of 10 November 2015; European Commission, Communication to the European Parliament, the Council, the European Economic and Social Committee and the Committee of the Regions "2019 Communication on EU Enlargement Strategy", COM(2019)260final of 29 May 2019.

to international human rights law, it is suggested to expand the scope of analysis to include other relevant branches of international law, such as the international trade, environmental and health law. In this vein, it shall be mentioned that, apart from undertaking particular obligations under international public law, facilitating the rule of law at the national level requires clear rules on the fulfillment of these obligations to be entailed into the national legislation, the fulfillment of obligations under international treaty law and respect for customary international law.

Conclusion

The analysis presented in this chapter confirmed the "essentially contested" nature of the EU rule of law concept. Nonetheless, the ongoing rule of law crises in Poland and Hungary urged EU policy-makers, civil society leaders and scholars to engage into the "Great Rule of Law Debate" that pursues a two-fold task. Foremost, the Debate seeks to introduce new ways to ensure EU Member States' compliance with the rule of law. However, accomplishing this task requires, at a first stage, determining what the rule of law actually is. In this vein, the 2014 Commission's Rule of Law Framework, produced in terms of the Great Rule of Law Debate, offered the Member States a lowest common denominator in the rule of law debate. Guided by the Framework and relevant EU secondary law, case law of the ECJ and the Council of Europe documents, we introduced the working conceptualization of the rule of law, comprised of seven components. They include the principles of legality, legal certainty, accountability and transparency, judicial review (including the requirements of judicial independence and impartiality, as well as the protection of fundamental rights), equality and non-discrimination and the relationship between domestic and international law. While sticking to such conceptualization, subsequent analysis will continue regarding the rule of law as an "essentially contested" concept and accentuate nuances in the understandings of the rule of law, embedded in the EU RTAs in question and related unilateral documents.

References

Bingham, T. (2011). *The rule of law*. London: Penguin.
Bogdandy, A. von. (2010). Founding principles of EU law: A theoretical and doctrinal sketch. *European Law Journal*, 16(2), pp. 95–111.
Busuioc, E.M. (2013). *European agencies: Law and practices of accountability*. Oxford: Oxford University Press.
Cheesman, N. (2015). *Opposing the rule of law*. Cambridge: Cambridge University Press.
Christiano, T. (2004). The authority of democracy. *Journal of Political Philosophy*, 12, pp. 266–290.
Craig, P. (1997). Formal and substantive approaches to the rule of law: An analytical framework. *Public Law*, 1, pp. 467–487.
Dicey, A. V. (1985). *Introduction to the study of the law of the constitution*, 1st ed. Berlin: Springer.
Dworkin, R. (1986). *A matter of principle*. Oxford: Clarendon Press.

26 The rule of law in the EU external action

Enzmann, B. (2012). *Der demokratische verfassungsstaat: Entstehung, elemente, herausforderungen*. Berlin: Springer.

Fallon, R.H. (1997). The rule of law as a concept in constitutional discourse. *Columbia Law Review*, 97, pp. 1–56.

Fenwick, M., Siems, M. and Wrbka, S., eds. (2017). *The shifting meaning of legal certainty in comparative and transnational law*. Oxford: Hart Publishing.

Follesdap, A. and Hix, S. (2006). Why there is a democratic deficit in the EU: A response to Majone and Moravcsik. *Journal of Common Market Studies*, 44(3), pp. 533–562.

Frank, J. (2007). Aristotle on constitutionalism and the rule of law. *Theoretical Inquiries in Law*, 8, pp. 37–50.

Habermas, J. (1996). Three normative models of democracy. In: S. Benhabib and E. Meyer, eds., *Democracy and difference: Contesting the boundaries of the political*. Princeton: Princeton University Press, pp. 21–31.

Hallstein, W. (1979). *Die Europäische Gemeinschaft*. Berlin: Bundeszentrale für politische Bildung.

Hume, D. (1994). *Political essays*. Cambridge: Cambridge University Press.

Innerarti, D. (2018). *Democracy in Europe. A political philosophy of the EU*. Basingstoke: Palgrave Macmillan.

Kelsen, H. (2009). *General theory of state and law*. Translated by A. Wedberg. Clark, NJ: The Lawbook Exchange.

Kochenov, D., Magen, A. and Pech, L. (2016). The great rule of law debate in the EU. *Journal of Common Market Studies*, 54(4), pp. 1045–1049.

Korosteleva, E. (2016). The European Union and Belarus: Democracy promotion by Technocratic Means? *Democratization*, 23, pp. 678–698.

Larik, J. (2016). *Foreign policy objectives in European constitutional law*. Oxford: Oxford University Press.

Locke, J. (2015). *The second treatise of civil government*. Peterborough: Broadway Press.

Merkel, W. (2004). Embedded and defective democracies. *Democratization*, 11(5), pp. 33–58.

Möllers, C. (2008). *Demokratie – Zumutungen und Versprechen*. Frankfurt am Main: Politik bei Wagenbach.

Moravcsik, A. (2004). Is there a 'democratic deficit' in world politics? A framework for analysis. *Government and Opposition*, 39(2), pp. 336–363.

Müller, H. (2012). *The point of no return. Walter Hallstein and the EEC commission between institutional ambitions and political constraints*. Les Cahiers Europeans de Sciences Po 03. [pdf] Sciences Po. Available at: www.sciencespo.fr/centre-etudes-europeennes/sites/sciencespo.fr.centre-etudesEuropeanness/files/n_3_2012%20Muller_dec_2012_final.pdf.

Nettesheim, M. (2005). Developing a theory of democracy for the European Union. *Berkeley Journal of International Law*, 23, pp. 358–400.

O'Donnell, G. (2004). The quality of democracy: Why the rule of law matters. *Journal of Democracy*, 15(4), pp. 32–46.

Palombella, G. (2009). The rule of law beyond the state: Failures, promises and theory. *International Journal of Constitutional Law*, 7(3), pp. 442–467.

Pech, L. (2009). *The rule of law as a constitutional principle of the European Union*. Jean Monnet Working Paper 2009/04. [online] Available at: https://papers.ssrn.com/sol3/papers.cfm?abstract_id=1463242.

Radaelli, C.M. (1999). The public policy of the European Union: Whither politics of expertise? *Journal of European Public Policy*, 6, pp. 757–774.

Raitio, J. (2003). *The principle of legal certainty in EC law*. Netherlands: Springer.

Raz, J. (1979). *The authority of law: Essays on law and morality*. Oxford: Clarendon Press.

Reding, V. (2013). *Speech: The EU and the rule of law – What next?* [online] Available at: https://ec.europa.eu/commission/presscorner/detail/en/SPEECH_13_677.

Ringer, T. (2007). Development, reform, and the rule of law: Some prescriptions for a common understanding of the "rule of law" and its place in development theory and practice. *Yale Human Rights and Development Journal*, 10(1), pp. 178–208.

Rossi, L.C. and Casolari, F. (2017). *The principle of equality among member states of the European Union*. [online] Available at: www.springer.com/gp/book/9783319661360.

Stewart, C. (2004). The rule of law and the Tinkerbell effect: Theoretical considerations, criticisms and justifications for the rule of law. *Macquarie Law Journal*, 4, pp. 135–164.

Tamanaha, B.Z. (2005). The tension between legal instrumentalism and the rule of law. *Syracuse Journal of International Law and Commerce*, 33(1), pp. 1–24.

Tuori, K. (2015). *European constitutionalism*. Cambridge: Cambridge University Press.

Unger, S. (2008). *Das Verfassungsprinzip der Demokratie: Normstruktur und Norminhalt des grundgesetzlichen Demokratieprinzips*. Tübingen: Mohr Siebeck.

Waldron, J. (2002). Is the rule of law an essentially contested concept (In Florida?) *Law and Philosophy*, 21(2), pp. 137–164.

Wetzel, A. (2015). The substance of the EU democracy promotion: Introduction and conceptual framework. In: A. Wetzel and J. Orbie, eds., *The Substance of EU democracy promotion: Concepts and cases*. Berlin: Springer, pp. 1–23.

2 EU external economic policy

History and the legal basis

Chapter 2 offers an overview of the Communities' and, later on, the EU's external economic policy, essential for developing the conceptual framework for researching the interplay between the rule of law promotion and trade liberalization in the EU external action. Additionally, it provides the analysis of the legal basis behind the EU's external economic policy with a focus on reforms introduced by the Lisbon Treaty.

Part 1. History of the EU external economic policy

For the purposes of clarity and structure, the book divides the history of the EU external economic policy into three stages:

- **The first stage (1957–beginning of the 1990s)** embraces the timeframe from the establishment of the European Economic Community (EEC) to the preparation to the conclusion of the Maastricht Treaty, the EU's participation in the Uruguay Round of the multilateral trade negotiations.
- **The second stage (beginning of the 1990s–2006)** is marked by the finalization of the EU Internal Market, the Union's joining the WTO, re-launch of the relationships with ACP countries, the conclusion of the Partnership and Cooperation Agreements (PCAs) with former Soviet states and the Association Agreements with Southern Neighbours.
- **The third stage (2006–present)** has started with the Commission's Communication "Global Europe – Competing in the World – A Contribution to the EU's Growth and Job Strategy" that marked the EU's turn to an ambitious "deep" bilateral and plurilateral free trade agenda.[1]

1. First stage (1957–beginning of the 1990s)

Due to the failure of the European Defense Community project in 1954, the Rome Treaties did not contain independent foreign policy-related provisions

---

1 European Commission, Communication to the Council, the European Parliament, the European Economic and Social Committee and the Committee of the Regions: Global Europe, Competing in the World, A Contribution to the EU's Growth and Job Strategy, COM(2006) 567 final of 4 October 2006.

EU external economic policy 29

(Wyatt-Walter, 1979, p. 15). However, the introduction of the common external tariff under the customs union, provided for by the 1957 Treaty establishing the EEC, could not have been completed without granting the Community competences in the external trade domain. Subsequently, the very fact of the launch of the internal customs Union between the EEC states conditioned the start of the Common Commercial Policy (CCP) that "constitutes the 'centrepiece' of EU external relations" (Eeckhout, 2012, p. 239). Moreover, in Art.110 of the Treaty, the EEC Member States expressed their commitment to contribute "to the harmonious development of world trade, the progressive abolition of restrictions on international trade and the lowering of customs barriers".[2] Although before the conclusion of the Maastricht Treaty, the Community lacked competence in the field of development cooperation, the EEC Treaty provided for the creation of associations with overseas countries and territories, having special relations with the EEC Member States (Art.131–136) and establishing the European Fund for Development (Art.131).

An insight into the preceding clauses reveals that since the beginning of its history, the EU's external trade policy has been tightly linked to development. This statement can be also illustrated by the 1963 Yaoundé Convention between the EEC and the Associated African States and Madagascar (AASM). Under the Convention, the EEC and the AASM countries agreed to continue their cooperation, based on the conditions, aiming to contribute to the "economic and social wellbeing of the latter" (European Community Information Service, n.d., p. 6) The EEC linked trade and development in the Yaoundé Convention by unilaterally granting the products, originating in the associated states, free access to the domestic markets of the six EEC countries. Moreover, the Convention provided for the development aid in the form of grants and special loans, financed by the European Development Fund and loans, granted by the European Investment Bank (European Community Information Service, n.d., pp. 10–11). In 1969, the Yaoundé Convention was renewed. Compared to the Yaoundé I Convention, the Yaoundé II included a strengthened emphasis on financial and technical aid and diversified the purposes of aid provision to include the stabilization of agricultural prices, production aid, technical assistance and emergency aid (Bartels, 2007, pp. 722–725).

Alongside the birth of the EEC development policy, the evolution of the Union's external economic policy in the late 1960s and early 1970s was marked by three other noteworthy trends. First, in accordance with the EEC's competence to represent the Member States in external trade relations,[3] the EEC acted in this position during the Kennedy Round of negotiations under the GATT. Apart from signing trade agreements with Greece, Turkey, Lebanon and others, the EEC agreed to make significant trade concessions (especially in favour of developing countries), under the GATT, currently known as an "enabling clause" (Nsour, 2010, pp. 110–115). The EEC's representation of the Member States during the

---

2 Treaty establishing the European Economic Community [Not published in the OJ]. [online] Available at: http://aei.pitt.edu/37139/1/EEC_Treaty_1957.pdf, p. 92 (hereinafter referred to as "EEC Treaty").

3 EEC Treaty, Art. 3(b).

30 *EU external economic policy*

Kennedy Round led to the consolidation of the Member States' common position in the global multilateral trade process and strengthening of the development dimension of the EEC external trade policy, *inter alia*, via the launch of the Generalized Scheme of Preferences in 1971. Second, the EEC strengthened its foreign policy dimension by launching the European Political Cooperation. The 1970 Davignon Report, adopted by the foreign ministers of the EEC states in 1970 in Luxembourg, provided for the informal institutionalization of consultations on foreign policy matters (Salmon and Nicoll, 1997, pp. 107–110). The institutional framework of such consultations was further strengthened by the 1973 Copenhagen Report and the founding of the European Council in 1973–1974. Third, in 1973 the EEC experienced the first enlargement, with the UK, Denmark and Ireland joining the EEC, leading to the need to include the British Commonwealth's Least Developed Countries into the EEC trade and development partnership with African countries (Yard, 1985, pp. 634–635).

Coupled with the need for launching trade relations with the Commonwealth states, the evolution of the Community's development policy led to the negotiations for the new partnership-based agreement between the EEC and 71 ACP countries. As a result of long-lasting negotiations, the parties signed the Lomé I Convention, appearing to be far more profitable for the associated states than the Yaoundé conventions, primarily due to the broadened scope of the trade preferences, and the creation of the STABEX system and the Centre for Industrial Development (Rhodes, 1998, pp. 129–135). Although these benefits were development friendly by design, critics argue that the strict rules of origin and a safeguard clause limited exports from African countries to the EEC and discouraged private investments, respectively (e.g. Yard, 1985). Notably, despite the formal absence of conditionality clauses in the Convention, the EEC used its spirit as the basis for its first-time application of conditionality policy, when unilaterally suspending aid allocation to Uganda following the 1977 massacre of Acholi and Langi people (Koch, 2015, pp. 97–108). Signed in 1979, the Lomé II Convention did not introduce significant changes to the Lomé I framework, except for launching the System for Mineral Products (SYSMIN) to provide targeted support of the mining industry of the ACP states (*Ibid.*). In turn, an emphasis on the ACP states' self-reliance in development matters and strengthening of the decentralized cooperation between the Community and the ACP states can be distinguished as a major feature of the Lomé III Convention, signed in 1984.

In view of a renewed emphasis on fulfilling the EEC's original goal of launching the Internal Market, the 1980s laid down the foundations for the respective broadening the scope of the CCP and, subsequently, the EEC commercial agreements. The development of the policy was also nurtured by the 1986 Single European Act (SEA) that re-launched the European Political Cooperation, clearly providing for the European Council's, European Parliament's and the Commission's roles in the Community's foreign policy[4] The consolidation of the EEC's

---

4 European Communities, Single European Act, OJ L 169/1 of 26 September 1987.

EU external economic policy 31

position in external trade negotiations and the so-called "Lomé fatigue" resulted in significant changes, introduced by the 1990 Lomé IV Convention, as compared to the previous ones. Most importantly, the Lomé IV was the first EU trade and association agreement that explicitly provided for economic and political conditionality. Building upon the Lomé III logic of self-reliant development, the Lomé IV Convention linked access to aid to the partners' implementation of Structural Adjustment Programs (Commission of the European Communities, 1990). Art. 5 of the Lomé IV Convention referred to the adherence to democratic principles, the consolidation of the rule of law and good governance as the principles, representing an "essential element" of cooperation under the Convention (Hachez, 2015).[5] The departure from political neutrality of the previous Lomé opened up a new era in the Community's trade and development policies, marked by the tightening links between trade, aid and fundamental values. Subsequently, the observance of democratic principles, human rights and the rule of law found their reflection in the EEC's agreements, for instance, with Argentina (1990) and Albania (1992).[6]

Ultimately, over the period from 1957–1990, the external economic policy of the EEC underwent a profound transformation, shaped by the consolidation of the Community's foreign policy and the evolution of the multilateral trade liberalization. A significant trend, overseen in this period in the EEC-ACP relations, was the tightening nexus between trade and investment promotion, on the one hand, and the monitoring of partner countries' observance of fundamental values, such as democracy, human rights and the rule of law, on the other hand.

2. Second stage (beginning of the 1990s–2006)

The second stage of the EU external economic policy's evolution was marked by the Union's active participation in the multilateral trade liberalization process, further evolution of its relationships with the ACP countries and the conclusion of ten PCAs with Russia, countries of Eastern Europe, the Southern Caucasus and Central Asia, as well as the Association Agreements with Southern Neighbours (Israel, Jordan, Lebanon, Algeria, Morocco and Egypt).

Pursuant to Art. XI of the 1994 Marrakesh Agreement Establishing the World Trade Organization, both the European Community and its Member States became Members of the WTO.[7] The choice of such a "double membership" strategy was determined by the fact that not all the issues addressed by the WTO were covered by the exclusive competence of the Community, stemming from

---

5 ACP-EEC Council of Ministers, Fourth ACP-EEC Convention, signed at Lomé on 15 December 1989. [online] Available at: www.epg.acp.int/fileadmin/user_upload/LomeIV1989.pdf.

6 Framework Agreement for trade and economic cooperation between the European Economic Community and the Argentine Republic – Exchange of Letters, OJL 295 of 26 October 1990, pp. 67–73; Agreement between the European Economic Community and the Republic of Albania, on trade and commercial and economic cooperation, OJL343 of 25 November 1992, p. 2.

7 Marrakesh Agreement Establishing the World Trade Organization, 1994. [online] Available at: www.wto.org/english/docs_e/legal_e/04-wto_e.htm.

32 *EU external economic policy*

Art.113 of the EEC Treaty and, hence, required the active involvement of the EU Member States. In particular, according to the 1994 Opinion 1/94 of the ECJ, the Community has "sole competence, pursuant to Art.113 of the EC Treaty, to conclude the multilateral agreements on trade in goods"[8], while the Community and its Member States are jointly competent to conclude the General Agreement on Trade in Services (GATS) and the Agreement on Trade-Related Aspects of Intellectual Property Rights (TRIPS). Even before the Court issued Opinion 1/94, the EC Commission, the Council and the Member States managed to develop the "code of conduct", providing for the basis of the cooperation between the EC and its Member States in the field of trade in services negotiations (Elsig, 2017, p. 33). However, no general conduct of cooperation between the EC (EU) and its Member States was so far concluded.

Since the 2001 Doha Ministerial Conference, the EC has been active in the new round of the WTO negotiations, including three major focus areas, such as markets' opening (industrial goods, agricultural goods and services), regulatory cooperation (subsidies and countervailing measures, trade facilitation) and development (Jacobsson and Stocchetti, 2013, pp. 3–4). It is noteworthy that during the early Doha Round negotiations, the EU demonstrated a strong stance on protecting developing countries' interests through Aid for Trade, Special Measures for Least Developed Countries (LDCs) and Special and Differential Treatment provisions (Van den Hoven, 2006, pp. 188–189). Notwithstanding the Members' multiple commitments to finalize the Round, already after several years after the launch of negotiations, scholars and practitioners started to talk about the "*deadlock*" of the Doha Round following the Members' decision not to include crucial "Singapore issues" (namely, investment and competition) into the Doha Development Agenda (Woolcock, 2003, p. 249). In this period, the deadlock of negotiations has become even more evident after subsequent failures to reach agreement on agricultural exports subsidies during the 2005 Paris talks, the 2005 Sixth Ministerial Conference in Hong Kong and the 2006 meeting in Geneva (*Ibid.*). From this point onward, the increased resort to bilateral and regional free trade agreements can be witnessed in the external trade policies of major powers, such as the USA and the EU.

Prior to this shift to a bilateral trade agenda, the EU marked the beginning of the new millennium by signing the ambitious Cotonou Agreement (CA) that became the comprehensive framework for the partnership between the EU, the EU Member States and 79 ACP countries. According to Art. 1 CA, "the partnership shall be centred on the objective of reducing and eventually eradicating poverty consistent with the objectives of sustainable development and the gradual integration of the ACP countries into the world economy".[9] Notably, as compared to Lomé

---

8 ECJ, Opinion 1/94 "Competence of the Community to conclude international agreements concerning services and the protection of intellectual property – Article 228 (6) of the EC Treaty" of 15 November 1994, para VII.

9 Partnership Agreement between the members of the African, Caribbean and Pacific Group of States of the one part, and the European Community and its Member States, of the other part, signed in Cotonou on 23 July 2000, OJ L 317/3 of 15 December 2000, Art.1 (hereinafter referred to as "CA").

EU external economic policy 33

I Convention, the CA is marked by ambitious political cooperation clauses, as well as the first fully-fledged "essential element" clause in the history of the EU external economic policy. Art. 9 of the Agreement distinguishes the respect for human rights, democratic principles and the rule of law as the essential elements of the Agreement; in turn, Art. 96(2)(c) provides for the application of "appropriate measures", such as the refusal to renew developmental support or redirecting aid from government to civil society in case a breach of an "essential element" cannot be dealt with through consultations. Furthermore, following the its commitment to create more differentiated relations with the ACP countries in compliance with the WTO rules, the EU launched the preparation of Economic Partnership Agreements (EPAs) with groups of ACP countries such as, for instance, the East African Community (Burundi, Kenya, Rwanda, South Sudan, Tanzania and Uganda) and the Caribbean Forum (CARIFORUM), including 15 Caribbean Community states and the Dominican Republic (Meyn, 2008).

As mentioned earlier, the third critical trend shaping the history of the EU external economic policy in the end of the 20th and beginning of the 21st century has been the conclusion of the PCAs with the former Soviet countries (the Republic of Armenia, the Republic of Azerbaijan, Georgia, the Republic of Kazakhstan, the Kyrgyz Republic, the Republic of Moldova, the Russian Federation, Ukraine, the Republic of Uzbekistan and Tajikistan).[10] While not liberalizing trade, the PCAs established the framework for political dialogue, provided for the application of the Most favoured nation (MFN) principle in trade in goods, free transit of goods via parties' territories and the elimination of quantitative restrictions on imports. Further provisions of the PCAs concerned the focus on social and economic development of the partner states, cross-border supply of services and protection of intellectual, industrial and commercial property, as well as employment and social standards.

Fourth, the 1995 Euro-Mediterranean Conference of Foreign Affairs Ministers, held in Barcelona, marked the start of the Euro-Mediterranean Partnership, also referred to as the "Barcelona Process" (Joffe and Vasconcelos, 2000, pp. 3–9). The Barcelona Declaration, adopted as a resulted of the Conference, provided, *inter alia*, for "creating the area of shared prosperity" and, subsequently, "the progressive establishment of a free trade area".[11] Pursuant to the Declaration, the EU concluded Euro-Mediterranean free trade agreements with Algeria (2005), Egypt (2004), Jordan (2002), Lebanon (2006), Tunisia (1998), Israel (2000) and Morocco (2000). The Interim Association Agreement on Trade and Cooperation

---

10 Council and Commission Decisions 99/602/EC, 99/514/EC, 99/515/EC, 99/490/EC, 99/401/EC, 98/401/EC, 99/5937EC and 2009/989/EC on the conclusion of the Partnership and Cooperation Agreement between the European Communities and their Member States, of the one part, and the Republic of Armenia, the Republic of Azerbaijan, Georgia, the Republic of Kazakhstan, the Kyrgyz Republic, the Republic of Moldova, the Russian Federation, Ukraine, and the Republic of Uzbekistan, Tajikistan of the other part, respectively.

11 Barcelona Declaration adopted at the Euro-Mediterranean Conference on 27–28 November 1995 [Not published in the OJ. [online] Available at: https://ec.europa.eu/research/iscp/pdf/policy/bar celona_declaration.pdf.

34   *EU external economic policy*

between the EU and Palestine was concluded in 1997. In line with the Barcelona Declaration's ambition to promote regional cooperation in the Mediterranean, in 2004 Egypt, Jordan, Morocco and Tunisia signed the Adagir Agreement, oriented on the intra-regional trade liberalization.[12] For the time being, the Euro-Mediterranean Agreements and the Adagir Agreement constitute the foundation for the development of more comprehensive RTAs between the EU and Southern Neighbours (Tunisia, Morocco and Egypt) (Van der Loo, 2015).

In a nutshell, over the second stage of the history of the EU external trade policy, the EU experienced a surge and a deadlock in multilateral trade negotiations, strengthened the political dimension of its association relations with the ACP countries and set the framework for trade and development cooperation with the former Soviet states and Southern Neighbours.

3. Third stage (2006–ongoing)

As noted earlier, in the Annex to its 2006 Global Strategy, the EU stressed the need to facilitate its bilateral and plurilateral trade liberalization agenda, while acknowledging that the "multilateral rules-based system under the WTO is the most effective means of expanding and managing trade".[13] That is why it would be a mistake to argue that the EU's re-concentration on bilateral trade liberalization would mean virtually refraining from the previous focus on multilateral trade. Thus, the ongoing stage of the evolution of the EU's external economic policy is marked by the combination of the EU's efforts to finalize the WTO Doha Round, and to broaden and deepen its bilateral and plurilateral trade relations with third countries.

Regarding the Doha Round, it shall be mentioned that in 2011 the WTO Members managed to reach agreement on a package of debated issues regarding agriculture and non-agricultural market access (European Parliament, 2017). Following the subsequent slowdown in all the areas of negotiations, in April 2011 the Chairman of the Council on Trade and Services presented a report on the state of play of the Doha Round negotiations, distinguishing market access for services, GATS reform and preferential treatment for LDCs as major issues to be further negotiated (WTO, 2011). Largely in view of the EU's lobbying efforts, the 2011 Eighth Ministerial Conference resulted in adopting a waiver to let preferential treatment for services and service suppliers, stemming from the LDCs (WTO, 2017).

Subsequently, an important achievement of the WTO Doha Round, actively promoted by the EU, has been the 2013 agreement on the Bali package, including the Trade Facilitation Agreement, food security-related issues and the establishment

---

12 Agreement, setting up a free trade area between the Arab Mediterranean countries of 8 May 2001. [online] Available at: https://wits.worldbank.org/GPTAD/PDF/archive/agadir.pdf.

13 European Commission, Commission Staff Working Document – Annex to the Communication to the Council, the European Parliament, the European Economic and Social Committee and the Committee of the Regions: Global Europe, Competing in the World. A Contribution to the EU's Growth and Job Strategy (COM (2006) 567 final of 4 October 2006), SEC(2006)1228 SEC(2006)1229, p. 7.

of the WTO monitoring mechanism to review the provisions on special and differential treatment for developing countries.[14] In 2015, the WTO Members came up with the Nairobi Package, containing six Ministerial Decisions on agriculture, cotton and issues related to LDCs (preferential treatment in the area of services and the criteria for determining whether exports from LDCs may qualify for trade preferences) (WTO, 2015). During the Conference, the EU presented the phase two of the multi-donor Enhanced Integrated Framework[15], directed to supporting developing countries' integration of trade issues into their national development plans, and a range of commitments regarding technical assistance for developing countries to implement the Trade Facilitation Agreement. Although the Nairobi Package is presented in literature as the culmination of the Doha Round, the Nairobi Conference produced major ambiguities as regards the future of the WTO as a multilateral trade system, in general, and the Doha Development Agenda, in particular (Schmieg and Rudloff, 2016). In this vein, the EU, however, reaffirmed the need "to keep working on outstanding Doha Development Agenda issues but with new approaches" and work together on emerging issues, such as investment, e-commerce and digital trade, regulatory issues related to the cross-border trade in goods and service and subsidies (European Commission, 2015, p. 1).

The contemporary stage of the evolution of the EU bilateral and plurilateral trade agenda is marked by four major directions: (i) broadening the geography of the EU RTAs' negotiations; (ii) deepening the scope of trade liberalization; (iii) continuing emphasis on the links between trade and development and (iv) strengthening the normative dimension of trade. As mentioned in the introductory part of this book, the geography of the EU post-2006 RTAs spreads to all the continents except Antarctica, encompassing Canada, Central American states, the Andean Community, Mercosur countries, the Andean Community, Singapore, Vietnam, South Korea, Japan and the EU's Eastern and Southern Neighbours. The negotiations with Mexico, Myanmar, Philippines, Australia and New Zealand, and with the ACP countries as to the "continent-to-continent" RTA, are ongoing. The negotiations of RTAs with Gulf Cooperation Council countries (e.g. Bahrain, Oman, Qatar, Kuwait), Thailand, India, the USA, Central African countries (e.g. Chad, Congo, Gabon) and Eastern and Southern Africa (e.g. Comoros, Djibouti, Eritrea) were put on hold until further notice.[16]

Second, given the ever-growing importance of the global value chains in international trade, the Accompanying document to the 2006 Global Europe Strategy suggested the new trade policy of the EU, addressing "the whole operating

---

14 9th WTO Ministerial Conference, Bali Package and November 2014 Decisions, 2014. [online] Available at: www.wto.org/english/thewto_e/minist_e/mc9_e/balipackage_e.htm; WTO, Agreement on Trade Facilitation of 27 November 2014. [online] Available at: www.wto.org/english/docs_e/legal_e/tfa-nov14_e.htm (hereinafter referred to as "WTO TFA").

15 For more information on the concept and activities of the Enhanced Integrated Framework, please visit: www.enhancedif.org/.

16 For the up-to-date information about the state-of-play of the EU trade agreements and negotiations, please visit: https://ec.europa.eu/trade/policy/countries-and-regions/negotiations-and-agreements/.

36 *EU external economic policy*

environment in third countries and . . . the barriers and transactional costs, derived from fragmentation for productive processes".[17] The Strategy also emphasized the "leading role" the Union shall play in "sharing best practice and developing global rules and standards"[18], thus inspiring the Commission to intensify its regulatory cooperation with third states. Going beyond traditional tariff discussions and strengthening regulatory cooperation were also underlined as the crucial external trade policy objectives under the Commission's 2015 Strategy "Trade for All: Towards a More Responsible Trade and Investment Policy".[19] Subsequently, the RTAs recently concluded and currently negotiated by the EU contain numerous provisions going beyond the liberalization of trade in goods, such as public procurement, competition, trade facilitation and sustainable development.

Third, the EU commitment to promoting development through trade liberalization is manifested not only through its support for the respective components of the Doha Round, but the Union's 2014 GSP Preferential Trade and Everything But Arms Schemes, flexible EPAs with African countries,[20] and the support for foreign direct investment in developing countries and LDCs. Moreover, based on the 2007 EU Strategy on Aid for Trade,[21] the Union and its Member States aspire to include Aid for Trade into the scope of the official development assistance (ODA), continually increase collective volumes of respective aid and the donors' capacity, and support the monitoring and reporting in the field of Aid for Trade. Furthermore, since its 2006 FTA with South Korea, the EU has included trade and sustainable development chapters (TSDs) in its trade agreements to legalize the parties' commitment to upholding environmental and social standards, contained in relevant international treaties, such as the Paris Agreement on climate change and the International Labour Organization's (ILO) conventions (Bartels, 2014). It is, however, noteworthy that the TSDs do not include enforceable dispute settlement mechanisms or envisage financial penalties for non-compliance, thus attracting much criticism of the EU and international civil society groups and scholars (e.g. Füller, 2018; Orbie et al., 2016). Due to such criticism, enforcement mechanisms of the EU TSD chapters expect review.

---

17 European Commission, Accompanying document to the Communication from the Commission to the Council, the European Parliament, the European Economic and Social Committee and the Committee of the Regions – Global Europe: a stronger partnership to deliver market access for European exporters – Impact Assessment (COM(2007) 183 final) (SEC(2007) 453), p. 7.

18 European Commission, Communication to the Council, the European Economic and Social Committee and the Committee of the Regions "Global Europe: Competing in the World", COM (2006)567final of 4 October 2006, p. 7.

19 European Commission, Communication to the Council, the European Economic and Social Committee and the Committee of the Regions "Trade for All: Towards a More Responsible Trade and Investment Policy", COM (2015)0497final of 14 October 2015.

20 Regulation (EU) No 978/2012 of the European Parliament and of the Council of 25 October 2012 applying a scheme of generalised tariff preferences and repealing Council Regulation (EC) No 732/2008, OJ L 303 of 31 October 2012.

21 European Council (2008). Note to the WTO General Secretariat "EU Strategy on Aid for Trade: Enhancing EU Support for Trade-related Needs in Developing Countries". [online] Available at: http://trade.ec.europa.eu/doclib/docs/2008/november/tradoc_141470.pdf.

EU external economic policy 37

Fourth, the 2015 Commission's Communication "Trade for All. Towards a More Responsible Trade and Investment Policy" consolidated the image of the EU as a normative power through trade (Poletti and Sicurelli, 2018, pp. 1–2). Arguing that trade "is not an end in itself" but a "tool to benefit people", the Communication calls for using EU trade and investment policy to support inclusive growth in developing countries, promote sustainable development, fair and ethical trade standards, as well as promote and defend human rights, fight against corruption and promote good governance. In this vein, the Communication suggests anchoring normative and development objectives in EU trade policy in a united and coherent manner that requires the EU to speak with one voice and ensure equal treatment of all EU Member States, people and companies.[22]

Concluding, the present stage of the EU's external economic policy's evolution involves the interplay of its efforts to further develop the Doha Round (that is not yet formally over) and promote its ambitious bilateral and plurilateral trade liberalization, marked by an emphasis on development and normative aspects.

Part 2. Legal basis

Trade is oldest and one of the most important exclusive competences of the European Economic Community and, later on, the EU. The Treaty on the Functioning of the European Union addresses the Common Commercial Policy (CCP) in Art.206–207 that are designed to amend and modernize Art. 131(1) and 133 of the EEC Treaty.[23] One of the key innovations, introduced by the Lisbon Treaty and concerning, *inter alia*, the EU trade policy has been the introduction of general objectives to be pursued through the whole spectrum of the EU external policies. Among the objectives of the Union's "relations with the wider world", Art. 3(5) TEU mentions upholding and promoting its values and interests, peace, security, sustainable development, solidarity and mutual respect among people, as well as the protection of human rights and the rights of the child. A slightly more expanded list of objectives is presented in Art. 21(2) TEU. Notably, both Art. 3(5) TEU and 21(2) TEU contain trade-specific objectives. Art.3(5) TEU mentions promoting and upholding "free and fair trade" as an objective of the EU external action. In turn, Art.21(2) TEU suggests a more elaborate formulation, stipulating that the EU shall "encourage the integration of all countries into the world economy, including through the progressive abolition of restrictions on international trade". The rule of law and adherence to the international law are reflected as both the principles of the Union's external action (Art.21[1] TEU) and its objectives, Art. 3[5] and Art.21[2] TEU). In terms of Art.21(1) TEU, the rule of law and adherence to international law refer to the principles the Union shall stick to in its

---

22 European Commission, Communication to the Council, the European Economic and Social Committee and the Committee of the Regions "Trade for All: Towards a More Responsible Trade and Investment Policy", COM (2015)0497final of 14 October 2015.

23 Consolidated version of the Treaty on the Functioning of the European Union, OJC 326, 9.05.2008, pp. 47–390 (hereinafter referred to as "TFEU").

38 *EU external economic policy*

external action, while Art.3(5) and Art.21(2) TEU touch upon the external uphold-ing and promotion of fundamental values, including the rule of law. Thus, along with other external action domains (e.g. development cooperation and humanitar-ian aid), the CCP shall *inter alia* aim to uphold and promote the rule of law.

The understanding of the importance of extending the general objectives of the EU's external action to the domain of the CCP would not be complete without referring to the legal value of Art. 21(2) TEU. According to Kube (2016), the textual analysis of the EU's human rights-related foreign policy objectives, stipu-lated in Art. 21(2)(b) TEU, testifies to the EU's adoption and constitutionalization of the extraterritorial human rights responsibility. This approach was authorita-tively reaffirmed by the ECJ in its landmark Opinion 2/15, stipulating that the EU is under the obligation to integrate the respective general objectives and princi-ples into the CCP.[24] In this vein, the concept of responsibility can be understood both with regard to the EU responsibility under international human rights law, such as the International Covenant on Civil and Political Rights (ICCPR) and the International Covenant on Economic, Social and Cultural Rights (ICESCR), and the extraterritorial application of the CFR. The latter is of special interest for the EU law scholarship in view of the emerging body of case law on the application of the CFR beyond the EU's border[25] and, subsequently, the growing topicality of defining the interplay between the CFR (as a primary law act) and the EU's trade liberalization agreements with third states. Despite the relative novelty of this problématique, it is already possible to distinguish several legal effects of the EU's undertaking the extraterritorial human rights responsibility. First, the introduction of the overarching objectives of the EU's external action enabled the EU to depart from the fragmentary external human rights policy, lacking a con-stitutional foundation, to a more consistent responsibility-based model (Ryngaert, 2018). Second, human rights commitments shall serve as a foundation for cov-ering particular human rights issues during the trade liberalization negotiations or addressing human rights concerns in terms of the agreements' implementa-tion. Last, but not least, since the extraterritorial human rights responsibility falls within the scope of the EU's primary law, the institutions' failure to observe the objectives, set by the Art.21(2) TEU, may potentially lead to the EU's and/or its institutions' liability.

According to Art. 206 TFEU, specific policy objectives of the CCP encompass "the harmonious development of world trade, the progressive abolition of restric-tions on world trade and lowering of customs and other barriers". As compared to the previous version of the Treaty, Art. 206 TFEU underlines the binding nature of the EU's commitment to the harmonious development of world trade. Moreo-ver, reflecting the change in the scope of the CCP, Art.206 TFEU introduced the

---

24 ECJ, Opinion C-2/15. Opinion pursuant to Article 218(11) TFEU, 16 May 2017, para 141–142.

25 See, for instance, ECJ, *Muhamad Mugraby v Council of the European Union and European Com-mission*, Case C-581/11P, Judgment of 12 July 2012; General Court, Case T-512/12 *Frente Polisa-rio v Council*, Judgment of 10 December 2015.

abolition of restrictions on foreign direct investment as a further specific objective of the policy.

Building upon the previously existing body of the ECJ case law, Art. 3(1)(e) TFEU explicitly refers to the CCP as the exclusive competence of the EU (Krajewski, 2010). According to Art.2(1) TFEU,

> when the Treaties confer on the Union exclusive competence in a specific area, only the Union may legislate and adopt legally binding acts, the Member States being able to do so themselves only if so empowered by the Union or for the implementation of Union acts.

Importantly, the Treaties do not directly link the EU's right to conclude international agreements with the exclusive nature of the Union's competences in a respective area. Thus, Art.3(2) TFEU provides for the EU's exclusive competence to conclude an international agreement, when "its conclusion is provided for in a legislative act of the Union or is necessary to enable the Union to exercise its internal competence, or in so far as its conclusion may affect common rules or alter their scope". Art.216 TFEU distinguishes four set of circumstances under which the Union possesses the respective competence ("when the Treaties so provide", "where the conclusion of an agreement is necessary in order to achieve, within the framework of the Union's policies, one of the objectives referred to in the Treaties" or where the conclusion of the agreement is "provided for in a legally binding act" or "is likely to affect common rules or alter their scope"). Referring to the rules and procedures, contained in Art.218 TFEU, Art.207 TFEU provides the Union with the explicit competence to conclude international agreements, thus, representing the first circumstance, mentioned by Art.3(2) and 216 TFEU. However, since vast majority of EU RTAs encompass numerous cooperation areas and, hence, appeal to several domains of the EU activities, many of the RTAs are founded on several legal bases. Moreover, virtually all EU RTAs have to be concluded as "mixed agreements", since they include cooperation areas, falling within the scope of both the EU's and Member States' competences.

An important novelty, introduced by the Lisbon Treaty into the field of the CCP, is the extension of the policy's scope. First, Art. 207(1) TFEU spreads exclusive competence of the Union to all kinds of services, eliminating previously existing shared competences in the fields of educational, cultural and audiovisual services. Furthermore, Art. 207(1) TFEU mentions "commercial aspects of intellectual property" as the component of the CCP's scope. Importantly, the Treaties do not apply the conventional TRIPS terminology ("trade-related aspects of intellectual property rights"), conditioning an intense scholarly discussion regarding the scope of the notion, applied by the EU (e.g. Krajewski, 2010). Finally, following the trend to the establishment of the EU comprehensive investment policy, the Lisbon Treaty extended the scope of the CCP to include foreign direct investment (FDI). Art. 207(1) TFEU does not, however, cover portfolio investment and other forms of foreign investment, as well as investment protection rules. The major practical consequence, stemming thereof, is the "mixed" nature of international agreements

40 *EU external economic policy*

that cover different forms of foreign investment and investment protection (Wu, 2011). In more general terms, the integration of the EU's international trade and investment policies reflects the trends towards the deeper Europeanization of the EU external economic policies and "rendering" of the policy's subject to its principles, such as the sustainable management of global resources and progressive improvement of the environment and good global governance.

The consolidation of the goals, competences and scope of the CCP can be hardly imagined without the reform of the institutional aspects of the policy. In the pre-Lisbon era, the institutional design of the CCP was primarily determined by the relationship between the Commission and the Council (Kleimann, 2011, p. 3). The European Parliament's lacking role in the realm of the CCP, combined with the activities of trade experts-led committee under Art. 133 of the EEC Treaty conditioned the CCP's being characterized in scholarship as the "black-box nature" policy, requiring greater openness and legitimacy (Kleimann, 2011; Ginsberg, 2010, pp. 243–244). Aiming to open up the "black box" of the CCP, the Treaty of Lisbon significantly enhanced the role of the European Parliament in the CCP in two major ways. First, pursuant to Art. 207(2) TFEU, the Parliament acts as a fully-fledged co-legislator on the Union's own trade legislation (e.g. trade defence instruments) and the legislation directed to the implementation of the Union's international agreements. With regard to international agreements, the European Parliament (along with the Council's *ad hoc* Trade Policy Committee) acquired the right to be informed on the progress of the international agreements' negotiations. Moreover, Art. 218(6) TFEU provided for the need for the Parliament's consent for concluding international agreements, whose subject matter falls within the scope of the ordinary legislative procedure. Noteworthy, the European Parliament has been increasingly active in using its powers to impact the Union's international agreements (e.g. the requirement to include the so-called "Singapore issues" in the EU-South Korea FTA; emphasis on the removal of non-tariff trade barriers in the EU-Japan FTA) (European Parliament Directorate-General for External Policies, 2014, pp. 8–10)

Ultimately, the Lisbon Treaty introduced a number of innovations pertaining to the CCP, including the consolidation of the CCP's goals and their enhanced coherence with the general objectives of the EU external action, the extension of the CCP's scope, and the European Parliament's strengthened role in decision-making pertaining to the CCP.

Conclusion

The overview of history and the legal basis of the EU external economic policy testifies to the long-lasting nature of the relationship between trade liberalization and fundamental values in the EU external economic policy. The nexus between the EU trade policy, EU development policy and the Union's promotion of fundamental values has significantly strengthened during the most recent phase of the EU trade policy's evolution due to the EU's turn to an ambitious bilateral and

EU external economic policy 41

plurilateral trade liberalization agenda. Recently, an important trend, also reinforcing the strengthening of such a nexus has been the contestation of the universal and EU values both within the EU and by illiberal actors abroad, as mentioned
in the introduction to the book. In legal terms, an increasingly active interplay
between the different aspects of the EU external action has found its reflection in
the notion of the "general objectives" of the EU external action. The institutions'
obligation to pursue the consolidation and promotion of the rule of law across the
whole spectrum of the EU external policies creates a legally binding inextricable
nexus between the Union's trade agreements with third countries and its value-
promoting policies.

References

Bartels, L. (2007). The trade and development policy of the European Union. *The European Journal of International Law*, 18(4), pp. 715–756.
Bartels, L. (2014). Human rights and sustainable development obligations in EU free trade
agreements. In: J. Wouters, A. Marx, D. Geraets, and B. Natens, eds., *Global governance
through trade. EU policies and approaches.* London: Edward Elgar, pp. 73–91.
Commission of the European Communities, DG for Information, Communication and Culture. (1990). *LOME IV 1990–2000. Background, innovation, improvements*, March 1990.
Available at: http://aei.pitt.edu/7561/1/31735055261238-1.pdf.
Eeckhout, P. (2012). *EU external economic relations law.* Oxford: Oxford University Press.
Elsig, Manfred. (2017). *The EU's common commercial policy: Institutions, interests and
ideas.* Abingdon: Routledge.
European Commission. (2015). *Joint statement by Commissioners Malström and Hogan
ahead of the 10th ministerial conference in Nairobi.* [online] Available at: http://trade.
ec.europa.eu/doclib/press/index.cfm?id=1416.
European Community Information Service. (n.d.). *Community topics 26. Partnership
in Africa: the Yaoundé association.* [pdf] Available at: http://aei.pitt.edu/34505/1/
A674.pdf.
European Parliament. (2017). *The Doha round and agriculture.* [online] Available at:
www.europarl.europa.eu/factsheets/en/sheet/112/the-doha-round-and-agriculture.
European Parliament Directorate-General for External Policies. (2014). *The role of the EP
in shaping the EU's trade policy after the entry into force of the treaty of Lisbon.* [pdf]
Available at: www.europarl.europa.eu/RegData/etudes/briefing_note/join/2014/522336/
EXPO-JOIN_SP(2014)522336_EN.pdf.
Füller, V. (2018). *How to make TSD chapters more effective?* TEPSA Brief. [pdf] Available
at: www.tepsa.eu/download/Briefing-Verena-Fuller.pdf.
Ginsberg, R.H. (2010). *Demystifying the European Union: The enduring logic of regional
integration.* Plymouth: Rowman and Littlefield.
Hachez, N. (2015). *'Essential elements' clauses in EU trade agreements making trade
work in a way that helps human rights?* Leuven Centre for Global Governance Studies
Working Paper, 2015/158. [online] Available at: https://ghum.kuleuven.be/ggs/publica
tions/wp158hachez.pdf.
Jacobsson, J. and Stocchetti, M. (2013). *The WTO under pressure. Tackling the deadlock
in multilateral trade.* FIIA Briefing Paper, 2013/142. [pdf] Available at: www.fiia.fi/wp-
content/uploads/2017/01/bp142.pdf.

42 EU external economic policy

Joffe, G. and Vasconcelos, A. (2000). Towards Euro-Mediterranean regional integration. In: G. Joffe and A. Vasconcelos, eds., *The Barcelona process: Building a Euro-Mediterranean regional community*. Abingdon: Routledge, pp. 3–9.

Kleimann, D. (2011). *Taking stock: EU common commercial policy in the Lisbon era*. CEPS Working Document, 2011/345. [pdf] Available at: ceps.eu/system/files/book/2011/04/WD%20345%20Kleimann%20on%20EU%20CCP.pdf.

Koch, S. (2015). A typology of political conditionality beyond aid: Conceptual horizons, based on lessons from the European Union. *World Development*, 75, pp. 97–108.

Krajewski, M. (2010). The reform of the common commercial policy. In: A. Biondi, P. Eekhout, and S. Ripley, eds., *EU law after Lisbon*. Oxford: Oxford University Press, pp. 292–312.

Kube, V. (2016). *The European Union's external human rights commitment: What is the legal value of the art.21 TEU?* EUI Working Papers 2016/10. [online] Available at: http://cadmus.eui.eu/handle/1814/40426.

Meyn, M. (2008). Economic partnership agreements: A 'historic step' towards a 'partnership of equals'? *Development Policy Review*, 26, pp. 515–528.

Nsour, M.F. (2010). *Rethinking the world trade order: Towards a better legal understanding of the role of regionalism in the multilateral trade regime*. Leiden: Sidetone Press.

Orbie, J., Martens, D., Oehri, M. and Van den Putte, L. (2016). Promoting sustainable development or legitimising free trade? Civil society mechanisms in EU trade agreements. *Third World Thematics (A TWQ Journal)*, 4, pp. 526–546.

Poletti, A. and Sicurelli, D. (2018). *The political economy of normative trade power Europe*. Basingstoke: Palgrave Macmillan.

Rhodes, C. (1998). *The European Union in the world community*. Boulder: Lynne Reiner Publishers.

Ryngaert, C. (2018). EU trade agreements and human rights: From extraterritorial to territorial obligations. *International Community Law Review*, 3–4, pp. 374–393.

Salmon, T. and Nicoll, W. (1997). *Building European Union: A documentary history and analysis*. Manchester: Manchester University Press.

Schmieg, E. and Rudloff, B. (2016). *The future of the WTO after the Nairobi Ministerial council*. SWP Comments, 2016/12. [online] Available at: www.ssoar.info/ssoar/bitstream/handle/document/46429/2016C12_scm_rff.pdf?sequence=1.

Van den Hoven, A. (2006). European Union regulatory capitalism and multilateral trade negotiations. In: S. Lucarelli and I. Manners, eds., *Values and principles in European Union foreign policy*. London: Routledge, pp. 185–200.

Van der Loo, G. (2015). *Enhancing the prospects of the EU's deep and comprehensive free trade areas in the Mediterranean: Lessons from the eastern partnership*. CEPS Commentary, 2015/06. [online] Available at: www.ceps.eu/publications/enhancing-prospects-eu%E2%80%99s-deep-and-comprehensive-free-trade-areas-mediterranean-lessons.

Woolcock, S. (2003). The Singapore issues in Cancun: A failed negotiation ploy or a litmus test for global governance. *Treeconomics*, 38, pp. 249–255.

WTO. (2011). *Lamy sees support for advancing negotiations in more promising areas of the round*. [online] Available at: www.wto.org/english/news_e/news11_e/gc_rpt_30nov11_e.htm.

WTO. (2015). *Nairobi package*. [online] Available at: www.wto.org/english/thewto_e/minist_e/mc10_e/nairobipackage_e.htm.

WTO. (2017). *Trade in services and LDCs*. [online] Available at: www.wto.org/english/tratop_e/serv_e/ldc_mods_negs_e.htm.

Wu, Ch. (2011). Foreign direct investment as common commercial policy: EU external economic competence after Lisbon. In: P.J. Cardwell, ed., *EU external relations law and policy in the post-Lisbon era*. Berlin: Springer, pp. 375–401.

Wyatt-Walter, H. (1979). *The European community and the security dilemma, 1979–92*. Basingstoke: Palgrave Macmillan.

Yard, T.I. (1985). Critical analysis of Lomé III's private investment provisions. *Fordham International Law Journal*, 9, pp. 634–679.

3 The interplay between trade liberalization and the rule of law in the development context

Towards the concept of EU value-promoting Regional Trade Agreements (RTAs)

In the present era, the relationship between the rule of law and economic development is characterized by a paradox. On the one hand, the rule of law is discussed as "a panacea for the ills of the countries in transition" (Carothers, 1998). On the other hand, despite the Western donors' almost missionary zeal to promote the rule of law as a means to induce economic development in third countries, the economies of BRICS countries and the Middle East exemplify economic growth under the lacking rule of law (Ramanujam et al., 2012). Moreover, while the second half of the 20th century was marked by an intense economic integration movement, the positive correlation between trade liberalization and domestic economic growth was hardly challenged by many states. Nowadays, however, protectionism and further anti-establishment movements represent a major threat to economic growth (Rodrik, 2017). Against this background, an insight into the theoretical perspectives regarding the rule of law-economic development nexus is required to understand the conceptual foundations behind the EU value-promoting RTAs.

Part 1. Theoretical perspectives on the linkage between economic development/economic integration and the rule of law

1. Modernization theory and the Law and Development Movement, dependency and world-systems theories and the Washington Consensus (1950s–1980s)

According to law and development theorists[1], law has been embedded into the economic development agenda since the post-war attempts to define the relationship between the theories of economic development and major policy objectives of that time (e.g. promotion of savings, investment and industrialization; expansion of the local supply and demand) (e.g. Kennedy, 2013, pp. 23–24). Thus, law

---

1 As an academic field of study, Law and Development emerged in the USA in the middle of the 1940s (as argued earlier, due to the demands of the post-war time), became highly prominent in the 1960s and, following the disillusionment of the 1970s and 1980s, re-emerged following the emphasis on the governance agenda by the World Bank.

was mainly viewed as a tool to "translate leading postwar economic theories into policy", rather than an independent development driver (*Ibid.*).

The dominant perceptions about role of law in the development economics context changed with the rise of the modernization theory that fuelled the USA-driven "Law and Development Movement" (1960s and early 1970s). Pursuant to key modernization theorists (e.g. Rostow [1959], Organski [1965], and Parsons [1964]), the root cause of societies' underdevelopment lies in its traditional economic, political, legal and cultural structures that require undergoing the evolutionary modernization process, already experienced by more developed societies. Hence, the key ambition of the LDM had been to promote the political, social and economic development of the "Third World" through legal reforms (Kroncke, 2012, p. 505). Importantly, the LDM understood law not only as a means of economic development, but developing states' multifaceted convergence with the West (*Ibid.*). Such an orientation without a due account to local contexts, class cleavages and customary rules, however, led to the failure of both the movement itself and the modernization theory:

> The decline of the modernization ethos [was] a complex story that played out differently in different locations and in various academic fields, but one key area of dissatisfaction with the approach had to do with its tendency to trust in the Third World state as representing the public interest.
>
> (Ohnesorge, 2014, p. 239)

Wide-spread criticism of the modernization theory resulted in the growing popularity of substantively new development economic theories: dependency (Singer, 1949; Prebisch, 1949) and the world-systems theory (Wallerstein, 1974). Both theories explain the differences in countries' economic development by analyzing their roles in the international system. Notably, the shift towards considering economies' dependencies and inequalities under the auspices of the present international markets systems changed the previously existing state-centric focus of development economics (Ohnesorge, 2014, p. 240). Such a change brought about controversial consequences. Its major negative effect deals with the sense of disillusionment, presupposing that developing countries are "victims" of the international system (*Ibid.*). On a positive side, the dependency and world-systems theories proved the impossibility of promoting development by simply transplanting new substantive rules to a state's legal system without changing a country's role in global value chains (Trubeck and Galanter, 1974). Consequently, trade liberalization and economic integration started to be widely viewed as crucial factors of economic development.

The trend of linking development to market policies was also reflected in the Washington Consensus, a set of specific policy reforms employed by the development agencies to support economic growth in developing countries during the 1980s (Williamson, 1990). The basis for the Consensus had been represented by the World Bank's study "Accelerated Development in Sub-Saharan Africa". The author of this study, Elliott Berg, mentioned three key areas vital for a country's economic success, namely trade and exchange rate policies, efficient use of resources in the public sector and suitable agricultural policies (The World Bank, 1982). Alongside this, the original Washington Consensus has included the policy of small budgetary deficits, the broadening of the tax base, strict state aid and social policies financial liberalization, and the liberalization of trade and investment policies as a means to promote economic development. Hence, the Consensus led to a radical change in the perceptions of a state's role in development, limiting it to private sector support.

While neither the dependency and the world-systems theories nor the Washington Consensus contained any particular legal ideas, the mainstream post-LDM assumptions about law turned back to post-war pragmatism. Flourishing legal instrumentalism of the late 1970s and 1980s can be, on the one hand, addressed as a positive phenomenon that underlined the potential of using law for the purposes of promoting multifaceted vectors of economic development, including economic integration and trade liberalization. This positive effect was, nevertheless, levelled on the other hand by the theorists' pre-eminence with public law and ignorance towards private law rules, vital for implementing the Washington-backed market-oriented agenda (e.g. guaranteeing the security of property rights) (Kennedy, 2013, p. 45).

Thus, over the period from the 1950s to the 1980s, the evolution of the development economics' view on law and its role in economic progress and economic integration underwent a circular development. Following the post-war understanding of law as a functional tool of policy realization, substantive laws played the central role in the LDM paradigm and were again devalued to the solely instrumental status under the predominance of the dependency and world-systems theory. All the considered theories do not mention the idea of the rule of law *per se*, rather referring to substantive law and legal culture (the LDM), the instrumental value of law or addressing the rule of law problématique implicitly ("abolishing impediments to foreign direct investment" and "guaranteeing secure property rights" under the Washington Consensus) (The World Bank, 1982).

2. New institutionalism and governance

In the late 1980s and the beginning of 1990s, "two separate currents seem to have converged to bring law and legal institutions back into the development picture" (Ohnesorge, 2014, p. 244). According to Ohnesorge (2014), these currents were, first, an increase in the influence of the new institutional economics and, second, the challenge to support the economies of Eastern Europe and Central Asia following the collapse of the Soviet Union. Moreover, the neoliberal idea of a state's minimalist market role was leveled by the macroeconomic successes of East and Southeast Asian countries, backed by strong state interventionism.

Sometimes considered to date back to the article "The Nature of the Firm" by Coase (1937), the "new institutional economics" (NIE) represents a reconsideration of the neoclassical model of economy with an emphasis on the quality of institutions' functioning. Renowned institutional theorist Douglass North (1991)

Trade liberalization and the rule of law 47

defines institutions as "humanly devised constraints that structure political, economic and social interaction" (p. 97). In informal terms, institutions encompass sanctions, taboos, traditions and codes of conduct. In turn, the formal institutions are "constitutions, laws and property rights". According to North (1991), the key context, where the society needs institutions as a constraint in human interactions, deals with "capturing the gains from trade" that otherwise can be prevented by "personal ties, voluntaristic constraints and ostracism" (*Ibid.*, p. 100). In turn, the centrepiece of preventing such voluntarism and high transaction costs is represented by the system of precisely defined and coherently enforced private property rights. The popularity of the NIE and previous implicit referrals to the rule of law components in the Washington Consensus were among the factors, conditioning the Washington institutions' recognition of the significance of laws and institutions for the purpose of development economics.

As argued by Krever (2011) in relation to the World Bank, "the turn to the new institutional economics was incorporated into a broader discursive shift in Bank policy in the early 1990s", i.e. a turn to the broader governance framework (p. 304). In 1992, the Bank defined governance as "the manner in which power is exercised in the management of a country's economic and social resources for development" (The World Bank, 1992, p. 1). In turn, "good governance" encompasses "predictable, open and enlightened policymaking", professional bureaucracy, an accountable executive branch of power and strong civil society, and the application of the rule of law principle (*Ibid.*, p. vii). As a result, the Washington Consensus was supplemented with several new dimensions, such as corporate governance, labour standards, WTO agreements, financial and accounting rules and standards, and independent central banks. Moreover, the new focus on governance attracted international and national development agencies' attention to two major aspects of states' legal system: (i) constitutional law, allowing for the observance of fundamental values (democracy, human rights and the rule of law) and (ii) private law.

The "pro-judiciary" "new constitutionalism" doctrine and an emphasis on the fundamental values in development cooperation receive ambiguous judgements in scholarship. For instance, Farber (2002) views constitutional reforms mostly as "costly commitments that political elites undertake in order to signal the investors the strength of their commitment to the rule of law and economic liberalization" (p. 83). George and Sabelli (1994) argue that the governance provides "the opportunity both to instil Western political values in borrowing countries and blame them if things go wrong" (p. 194). On the other hand, modern scholarship tends to recognize the link between development and fundamental constitutional values and principles. There are studies illustrating that democratic regimes are overall more conducive to economic growth than the undemocratic ones, *inter alia*, due to the fact that democracies tend not to engage in conflicts among each other. Rodrik (2017) points to the fact that democratic deliberative processes help to aggregate local knowledge necessary for creating development-friendly laws and regulations, as well as to facilitate compromises. The separation of powers, emphasized under the auspices of both democracy and the rule of law, is also

48   *Trade liberalization and the rule of law*

essential for ensuring high-quality laws, conducive to development. The reasons for that deal with creating obstacles to interest groups' capturing power, dropping commitments and the inter-institutional competition.

Viewed both in general terms and specifically from the governance angle, the rule of law is considered to favour economic growth. The Worldwide Governance Indicators (WGI), introduced by the World Bank, link the rule of law to

> capturing perceptions of the extent to which agents have confidence in and abide by the rules of society, and in particular the quality of contract enforcement, property rights, the police, and the courts, as well as the likelihood of crime and violence.
>
> (The World Bank Group, n.d.)

Such a stance towards the rule of law is also reflected in modern theorists' perspectives on the role of the rule of law in the external trade and investment domains. For instance, De Cara (2006/2007) discusses three functions of the rule of law in international trade. First, it regulates the behaviour of economic actors in order to protect property rights, maintain fair competitive environment and enforce contracts. Second, the rule of law tends to regulate and limit states' interventionism into economic and commercial activities. Third, in line with the 1994 Marrakesh Declaration, it also serves as a foundation for the multilateral trading system.[2] Subsequently, according to Shihata (1996), the key substantive law aspects that impact international trade liberalization include:

- Developed contract law and ensuring respect for contractual obligations.
- Effective regulation and protection of property rights.
- Functioning competition legislation.
- Functioning banking system and the prevention of criminal offences in economic sphere.

They are, in turn, close to the rule of law properties, distinguished by the World Bank Doing Business Index, such as regulatory conditions for starting the business; ease of obtaining necessary permits and licences; enforcement of contracts, and the environment for cross-border trade and investor protection (The World Bank Group, 2020).

In a nutshell, the World Bank's shift from the neoliberal Washington Consensus to the NIE and governance agenda significantly changed the development economics' perceptions of the role law and the rule of law standard play with regard to economic development. While the post-war period was marked by the instrumental approach to law (except for the LDM), the emergence of the NIE and the governance paradigm led to the diversification of such understandings. First, law

---

2 WTO, 1994. Marrakesh Declaration of 15 April 1994. [pdf] WTO. Available at: www.wto.org/english/docs_e/legal_e/marrakesh_decl_e.pdf.

Trade liberalization and the rule of law   49

continued to be understood as an instrument of macroeconomic policy implementation. Second, due to the strengthened focus on laws and institutions in NIE and governance paradigms, law started to be regarded as essential of the environment, conducive to economic activities. Third, given donors' increased interest to developing countries' constitutional law, law and the rule of law regained independent value in the development economics context. Hence, the rule of law regained *momentum* as a crucial prerequisite for a state's success in the world trade and attracting investors.

3. Promoting the rule of law through free trade and functional cooperation

The historical analysis of the role of law in development economics shows that law (and the rule of law) can be conceptualized as both an instrument and an objective of the development policy. It is, however, questionable, whether the reverse effect exists, and trade liberalization represents a pathway to promoting fundamental values, and the rule of law in particular. So far, there have been highly limited theoretical insights and empirical evidence regarding both the *mechanisms* through which trade liberalization can affect the state of the rule of law and the rule of law *effects* of RTAs (e.g. Ewing-Chow, Losari and Slade, 2014; Frensch, Horváth and Huber, 2018). This statement applies not only to European studies, but the studies of the multilateral trade liberalization and regional trade relations (e.g. the ASEAN Free Trade Area, MERCOSUR). In this vein, the conceptualization of the EU value-promoting RTAs requires insights into several blocks of literature.

First, the problématique of the EU externalization of its policies and its external trade are linked in the context of the power Europe debate. The foundational concept for understanding the essence and avenues of the EU rule transfer is the normative power Europe (NPE), coined by Manners (2002). The NPE emphasizes a value-driven nature of the EU identity and behaviour, determined by the peculiarities of the EU's history, and the interplay of the supranational and intergovernmental components in the EU as a polity and the legal system. In Manners' view, such an identity distinguishes the EU from other international actors and determines its ability "to shape the conceptions of 'normal' internationally" (Manners, 2002, p. 239). Manners (2002) describes six major ways of the diffusion of the EU's norms, namely: contagion (unintentional diffusion of norms), informational, procedural (through institutionalizing relations with non-Member States and international organizations), transference (through trade, aid and technical assistance, including conditionality), overt diffusion (EU's presence in third states) and cultural filter. Importantly, the NPE was repeatedly criticized in view of the concept being too close to the Union's own descriptions of its identity, multiple manifestations of self-interest in the EU development cooperation policies and emphases on economic power and incentives (e.g. Sjursen, 2006; Hyde-Price, 2006). Nonetheless, the NPE is widely applicable in scholarship, including rather recent contributions on EU normative power through trade (Poletti and Sicurelli, 2018) and, hence, offers a useful lens to understand EU external value-promotion.

50 *Trade liberalization and the rule of law*

Second, also based on the nexus between the EU identity and power, Damro (2012) emphasized the material existence of the EU's Single Market for the purposes of the debate relating to EU power. Subsequently, Damro's market power Europe (MPE) concept takes recourse to Majone's (1994) idea of the EU as a "regulatory state" that promotes others' convergence with its standards through regulatory expertise, regulatory coherence and sanctioning powers. Another foundational component of understanding the MPE deals with viewing the EU as an "arena of interest contestation", wherein the important role belongs to the non-institutionalized interest groups (Damro, 2012, p. 687). Hence, the EU exercises its market power through "the externalization of its market-related policies and regulations", employing both persuasive and coercive means (*Ibid.*, p. 692). As opposed to the NPE, the MPE is, thus, to a significant extent based on coercive power and material incentives. Nonetheless, as argued by Parker and Rosamond (2013), the NPE shall not be completely delimited from the economic liberalism ideas due to the latter's constitutive importance to the Union's post-Westphalian aspirations and the rich normative basis of market cosmopolitanism.

Another relevant concept is the EU trade power, presupposing that "the EU could become an important foreign policy actor through the back door, by using trade instead of more traditional diplomatic or military means" (Meunier and Nicolaïdis, 2017, p. 231). Noteworthy, the concept distinguishes between the EU power in trade (export of goods, services and capital) and the EU power through trade (exporting standards and norms). The size of the EU market and elaborateness of the respective *acquis communautaire* allow the EU to bear *power in trade* within the bilateral, inter-regional and global settings. EU *power through trade* signifies its ability to use trade to achieve NTPOs. Thus, not elaborating on the mechanisms of policies' externalization and rule transfer, Meunier and Nicolaïdis (2017) illustrate that trade represents a crucial pathway for the EU's influence on the domestic developments in third states.

Moving from the power Europe debate to the scholarship on the mechanisms and institutional set-up of the EU's external rule transfer, it is worth emphasizing the theory of democracy promotion through functional cooperation. This theory is of particular value for conceptualizing EU value-promoting RTAs, since it is the only EU-centred theory that zooms in on the interplay of functional cooperation (e.g. competition, state aid, environmental standards) and the EU value-promotion. Based on empirical analysis on the EU's rule transfer in the Eastern and Southern Neighbourhoods, Freyburg et al. (2011) proved that the adoption of the transparency, accountability and participation principles in sectoral terms may be "one step in the mobilization of a more vivid civil society and a stronger societal control of state power, both of which would constitute important preconditions for democracy promotion" (p. 1017). Since EU RTAs encompass numerous functional cooperation domains, the findings of research on democracy promotion through functional cooperation can be extrapolated to the rule of law domain to an extent that the democracy and the rule of law principles intersect.

Ultimately, we found the NPE, MPE, trade power Europe concepts and the theory of democracy promotion through functional cooperation useful for exploring the rule of law dimension of the EU RTAs. Since neither of these approaches immediately addressed the externalization of the rule of law, it is especially relevant to discuss the political and legal aspects of the EU value-promotion through RTAs.

Part 2. The political and legal aspects of EU value-promotion through RTAs

This part of the analysis addresses the following aspects of the politics and law behind the EU value-promoting RTAs: (i) the interplay between the economic, normative and security objectives in the EU's foreign policy; (ii) conceptual foundations of the EU's power; (iii) bargaining power of the Union in trade negotiations; (iv) policy contexts of the EU's value-promotion through RTAs; (v) the legal basis behind the value-promoting RTAs and, finally, (vi) major value-related standards, encompassed by the value-promoting RTAs.

1. EU foreign policy objectives in external economic policies

Art. 21(2) TEU points to a broad range of objectives of the EU foreign policy objectives that play a crucial role in the application of the EU law in light of the ECJ's "hallmark teleological approach, and the ongoing discussion about "the finalité of European integration" (Larik, 2016, p. 5). According to Art. 21(2)(b), the EU external action shall be directed to the consolidation and support of democracy, the rule of law, human rights and the principles of international law. The normative character of the EU external action is also manifested in Art.21(2)(d) and Art. 21(2)(g) TEU that underline its commitment to fostering economic, social and environmental development of developing countries with the primary objective of poverty eradication and providing humanitarian assistance to the societies in need respectively. In economic terms, the Union seeks to "encourage the integration of all countries into the world economy, including through the progressive abolition of restrictions on international trade" (Art. 21[2][e]). Reaching such an objective can be hardly imagined without the EU ambition to promote multilateral cooperation and global good governance (Art.21[2][h] TEU).

An analysis of the extensive list of the EU foreign policy objectives in the context of the EU value-promotion through RTAs surfaces the following two questions. How shall the EU balance self-interest and values in its external economic policy? How is the set of objectives behind the value-promoting RTAs different from the one behind other agreements? With regard to the first question, scholars increasingly often opine that the EU needs to be tightly instrumental and ends-oriented when pursuing its interests. Moreover, the EU's orientation on self-interest is embedded into the 2016 EU Global Strategy[3] that uses the concept of

---

3 EU External Action Service, Shared Vision, Common Action: A Stronger Europe. A Global Strategy for the European Union's Foreign and Security Policy. [online] Available at: https://europa.eu/globalstrategy/en (hereinafter referred to as "EU Global Strategy").

52 *Trade liberalization and the rule of law*

"principled pragmatism" to balance the EU interests and its normative aspirations. As argued by Juncos (2017), the notion of "principled pragmatism" contains an internal contradiction, implying that the EU shall act according to universal values but then utilize a pragmatic approach that may contradict moral imperatives of respective values. In certain cases, such as the EU promotion of environmental and labour standards through RTAs, both the internal support for values and external value-promotion can be combined with self-interest and even be beneficial for the realization of such interest (Poletti and Sicurelli, 2018, pp. 1–5).

Distinguishing the factors that enable the EU to pursue its interests and values simultaneously requires an insight into the EU bargaining power in the negotiations with different groups of countries. However, the preceding analysis already allows us to distinguish objectives behind the conclusion of the EU value-promoting RTAs. As opposed to the RTAs that do not contain the value-promotion components, value-promoting RTAs shall combine the objectives of using trade liberalization as a means to support countries' integration into the world economy (Art. 21[2][e] TEU), safeguarding EU values (Art.21[2][a] TEU), consolidating democracy, human rights and the rule of law (Art. 21[2][b] TEU) and promoting development (Art.21[2][d]TEU). Furthermore, given the proliferation of TSD chapters in EU RTAs with third countries, EU value-promoting RTAs would most likely contribute to realizing the EU's commitment to improving the environment and management of natural resources internationally (Art. 21[2][f] TEU).

Ultimately, the EU foreign policy is characterized by the complex relationship between the pursuit of self-interest and fundamental values. In some cases, balancing fundamental values and self-interest (or different values) requires a trade-off. However, the EU value-promoting RTAs exemplify the situation when the EU tends to combine numerous intertwined foreign policy objectives.

2. EU Power behind value-promoting RTAs and diffusion of norms

As explained earlier, EU value-promotion through RTAs is marked by the combination of different types of EU power. In theory, value-promotion is primarily associated with the NPE (Manners, 2002). Based on its normative power, the EU applies a range of norms diffusion avenues, such as norm contagion, informational diffusion, overt diffusion, procedural diffusion, transference and cultural filter (*Ibid.*). Thus, an important peculiarity of the NPE (and a frequent and important critique of Manners' concept), deals with the fact that the NPE is not "primarily exercised through persuasion and normative justification, but through a skilful application of political and economic conditionality" (Aggestam, 2013, p. 464). As noted by Haukkala (2011) in relation to the EU enlargement process, "it is only through the unique and rich combination of stick and carrots that are present in the accession process that the EU can exert the strongest normative influence on its partners" (p. 47). Similarly, economic conditionality is actively applied by the EU in its Neighbourhood and development policies.

Thus, alongside the NPE, market and trade power Europe play an essential role in diffusing EU values and norms. In MPE terms, the key driver behind the EU's

Trade liberalization and the rule of law   53

power is that it represents the world's largest economy with over half a billion potential consumers and €37,104 GDP per capita[4] (e.g. Damro, 2012). Drezner (2007) argues that the EU market size supports the externalization of its internal rules in two major ways: (i) creating material incentives for governments to coordinate their regulatory standards with the ones of a larger market and (ii) influencing their perceptions regarding the outcomes of adopting the respective standards. Furthermore, the EU market is attractive due to its scope that encompasses not only goods and services but also public procurement and Digital Single Market. On top of that, the EU demonstrates a coherent commitment to lowering trade and investment barriers and openness to trade with developing countries. Hence, the attractiveness of its market, including the availability of trade-related aid, is an important factor, enabling the Union to use RTAs as a means to diffuse its values and norms.

To sum up, the EU's value-promotion through RTAs is founded upon the unique fusion of normative and market powers of the Union. Since diffusion of the EU norms would not be possible without the benefits of liberalized access to the EU Single Market and other economic incentives, it is suggested that the *transference* dimension of the NPE shall be primarily associated with the MPE, rather than NPE.

3. Who is the counterpart? The EU bargaining power in trade negotiations

While in theory the NPE-MPE combination enables the EU to incorporate its values into the RTAs, an extent of such incorporation will significantly depend on an EU counterpart. What will make a counterpart agree? The most evident idea would be that a counterpart seeks democratic transformation and gladly accepts the challenge of adopting respective rules and standards. In reality, however, it is also possible that the government agrees to the conditions set by the EU, driven by economic motives or just lacking bargaining power to negotiate the non-inclusion of respective standards into an RTA. In both cases, however, the bargaining powers of the parties would be unequal or asymmetric to the benefit of the EU. It is, however, worth noting that the EU bargaining power is not endless, and the contemporary modern world system knows multiple examples of undemocratic, yet economically successful, regimes the EU has to establish trade relations with. As noted by Del Sarto (2016), in some cases (e.g. the MENA region), the EU may also consciously refrain from the genuine value-promotion, emphasizing security and stability. According to the literature on bargaining power in trade negotiations, the key properties of an EU negotiations partner, influencing the ratio of bargaining powers, include: (i) its economic characteristics and the role in global and regional markets; (ii) dependence on development assistance; (iii) political regime and openness to fundamental values and (iv) a state's vision of the future

---

4 Eurostat, Real GDP per capita. [online] Available at: https://ec.europa.eu/eurostat/web/products-datasets/-/sdg_08_10.

54 *Trade liberalization and the rule of law*

relations (e.g. Tussie and Saguier, 2011). On the other side of the negotiating table, a counterpart's importance for the EU shall be considered from the realist and liberal perspectives.

From the realist perspective, a state's bargaining power in trade negotiations primarily depends on its economic resources and capabilities that are, in turn, attributed to market size. As a general rule, a large and economically powerful market will have more leverage in bilateral trade negotiations with the EU than will a small and economically weak market. In their study of asymmetries in trade negotiations, Tussie and Saguier (2011) point to the relational nature of the "market power" concept and argue that market size does not matter as much in trade negotiations as the economy's dependence on imports and exports does. In the same vein, Hirschman (1945) argued that a small country's vulnerability in its relations with a larger country or a trading bloc is determined by the orientation of its imports and/or exports on the respective larger country. Furthermore, a crucial factor increasing a country's bargaining power in trade negotiations deals with its participation in negotiating coalitions – or, to put it differently, a degree of its integration into global and regional markets (Lamprecht, 2014). Based on this, it can be argued that a counterpart's imports and/or exports orientation on the EU and the lack of/insignificance of its involvement in trade blocs is conducive to the EU promotion of NTPOs through RTAs.

Second, while EU power in international relations is largely about "sticks" and "carrots", a counterpart's dependence on irrevocable aid and/or unilateral market access is likely to increase the Union's leverage as to the negotiations of the value-related components of an agreement. This statement can be exemplified by the evolution of the references to human rights and other fundamental values in the EU-ACP relations. As summarized by Clapham (1996, p. 101), "the renegotiations of the Convention, from Lomé II onwards essentially consisted in the EC telling the ACP states how much aid they were going to get, and the ACP complaining that it was not enough". Amid such a tough foreign aid dependence of a counterpart, the EU became able to continuously raise the importance of fundamental values in its relations with the ACP, until the emergence of the "essential element" clauses. On the one hand, the example of the ACP countries testifies to the effectiveness of the EU economic conditionality. At the same time, economic conditionality borders with foreign aid dependence that hinders development via fostering corruption and a "rentier state" effect (Abuzeid, 2009). These effects are to be considered by EU institutions, when preparing for the negotiations of value-promoting components in the EU RTAs.

Third, an important factor impacting a counterpart's bargaining power in trade negotiations deals with a counterpart's existing political regime. Evidently, the costs of accepting genuine external democratization efforts would be too high for authoritarian regimes (Del Sarto, 2016; Risse and Babayan, 2015). In such cases, the peculiarities of the EU trade liberalization with it and the design of the value-promoting component (if any) would depend on a regime's economic strength and the degree of its reliance on the EU's market and aid, as well as the EU's strategy *vis-à-vis* a region and a particular country (Wetzel, 2015). For instance,

Trade liberalization and the rule of law 55

while the MENA countries tend to rely on the EU in exports and imports terms, receive foreign aid and are strategically important for the EU, the Union is likely to pursue a limited value-promotion agenda in the region, in general, and through the RTAs, in particular.

The situation would, however, look different, in case of economically powerful authoritarian counterparts. (e.g. China, Russia, the GCC countries). Geopolitical discontents, the inability to reach agreement as to tariff concessions within specific sectors and – not least – the contestation of fundamental values by the above regimes underlie the lack of trade liberalization between them and the EU. Sometimes, cooperating with these regimes, the EU may still put the rule of law on the agenda, conceptualizing it as an essential for doing business rather than a value.[5]

The third combination encompasses the EU trade with economically powerful actors, such as Canada, Japan or South Korea, committed to the shared values of democracy, human rights and the rule of law. Subsequently, the CETA, the EU-Japan FTA and the EU-South Korea FTA provide for regulatory convergence, rather than unilateral norm transfer by the EU. In turn, a unilateral norm transfer is peculiar to the EU relations with young democracies and countries in transition that depend on the Union in terms of exports, imports and development aid. This statement is especially relevant for the relations with "flawed democracies", namely, the ones that comply with the basic requirements of democracy (e.g. free and fair elections) but still experience major democracy-related issues (e.g. restraints on the media freedom or the NGOs' activities). In such cases, the EU rule transfer is ensured both via the MPE (due to economic and aid dependence) and its normative appeal (regimes' official democratic aspirations).

Fourth, the ratio of bargaining power in the negotiations of value-promoting RTAs is influenced by both a counterpart's and the EU's visions of future relations, such as a membership perspective. However, as it can be exemplified by the evidence from the official aspirations of the "associated" Eastern Neighbourhood countries (Ukraine, Moldova, Georgia) to join the EU, not substantiated by the membership perspective, also add value to the Union's bargaining power. On the other side of the coin, the bargaining powers' ratio is also influenced by an extent and nature of the EU strategic interests in a region or in a specific country. Given an emphasis on EU interests in the 2016 Global Strategy and the Commission's ambition to reshape the EU into a "geopolitical force", one can predict the rising importance of the EU strategic interests in the negotiations of the value-promoting component in EU RTAs.

Based on the described factors, it becomes possible to distinguish four "ideal types" of the relationship between the EU and its counterpart in trade negotiations:

Type 1. If the EU negotiates a trade deal with an undemocratic state (or group of states), yet economically oriented on trade with the EU and dependent

---

5 For an example of such approach, see: European Commission/High Representative of the Union for Foreign Affairs and Security Policy, Joint Communication to the European Parliament and the Council: Elements for a New EU Strategy on China, JOIN (2016) 30 final of 22 June 2016.

56 *Trade liberalization and the rule of law*

on the EU aid, the Union can pursue a limited value-promotion agenda in a state (or region), promoting the rule of law primarily as an instrument of developing environment, conducive to business, rather than the value in itself. The most vocal example of such situation is the MENA region (Southern Neighbourhood). Importantly, in the case of the MENA region, the Union's interest in sustaining stability and preventing conflicts therein to a significant extent determines its value-promotion strategy.

Type 2. The most unfortunate situation for the EU value-promotion through trade emerges in relations with economically powerful yet undemocratic countries that also play a prominent role in regional economic integration projects other than the EU (e.g. Russia, China, the GCC countries).

Type 3. The third "ideal type" concerns the EU trade liberalization with high-income democracies, such as Canada, Japan or South Korea, and is marked by the convergence of the parties' regulatory rules, rather than the unilateral transfer of the EU rules.

Type 4. The most fruitful basis for the EU value-promotion through trade emerges under the combination of a counterpart's democratic aspirations and its ambitions pertaining to the EU membership or close association relations, coupled with its dependence on the exports/imports to the EU and development aid. Such an "ideal type" is exemplified by the cases of the EU candidate and Potential Candidate countries such as Albania, Montenegro, Macedonia, Serbia, Turkey, the "associated" Eastern Neighbourhood (Ukraine, Moldova and Georgia) and the ACP countries.

Based on these "ideal types", the following analysis will concentrate on the RTAs, concluded within the framework of the EU enlargement policy, the European Neighbourhood Policy (ENP) and the EU development policy.

4. EU value-promoting RTAs contextualized

Enlargement

Since the foundation of the EEC in 1957, the original Community, comprised of six Members, underwent seven enlargement rounds; the last time with Croatia joining the Union in 2013. The treaty basis for the EU's enlargement is represented by Art.49 TEU, stipulating that "any European state which respects the values referred to in Article 2 and is committed to promoting them may apply to become a member of the Union". The enlargement process aims at reinforcing peace, democracy and stability in Europe, enabling the EU "to be better positioned to address the global challenges" and boosting the EU transformative power.[6] Moreover, both the 2015 and 2018 Enlargement Strategies emphasize that the

---

6 Regulation (EU) No 231/2014 of the European Parliament and of the Council of 11 March 2014 establishing the Instrument of Pre-Accession Assistance (IPA II), OJ L 77/1 of 15 March 2014.

enlargement process offers a "win-win" strategy for both the EU and the partner countries.[7]

Although Art. 49 TEU tends to concentrate on the procedural dimension of enlargement, its in-depth analysis enables us to distinguish major substantive issues, shaping the enlargement process. Foremost, to be eligible for submitting the membership application, a state has to be "European". Although many states geographically comply with the "*Europeanness*" requirement, the EU has created two differentiated layers of the relations with its neighbours, treating some states as "*prospective Members*" and others as "Neighbours" or "wider Europe" (Kochenov, 2005). Alongside the broadly discussed case of Turkey's prospective membership, this testifies to the politicized nature of the EU enlargement policy, being extensively influenced by the "enlargement capacity" considerations and the security-focused "post-Sovereign logic of enlargement" (Jakovlevski, 2010). Although the 2019 Enlargement Strategy provides for the objectivity of the accession criteria and equal treatment of all the applicants[8], substantive accession criteria, identified in the EU primary law, remain subject to broad interpretations.

This criticism is of special relevance for a Candidate state's respect for the EU fundamental values, distinguished as an accession criterion in Art. 49(1) TEU and the Copenhagen criteria.[9] Along with human rights, economic development and competitiveness, and the functioning of democratic institutions, the rule of law represents one of the fundamentals of the enlargement process that "reflects the core values and general policy priorities of the EU" (Doyle, Enache and Merja, 2016, p. 6). However, the "essentially contested" nature of the EU rule of law concept results in the lack of any clarity as to what is actually expected from the Candidate countries (Zhelyazkova et al., 2018). In turn, the absence of specific benchmarks Candidate states shall achieve, and the publicly available standards the Commission shall adhere to while conducting the quality assessments of situation on the ground, leaves much room open for both the selective application of the EU conditionality tools and the politicization of enlargement negotiations.

According to Art.1 and Annex 1 of the Regulation establishing the Instrument for Pre-Accession Assistance (IPA II), the present geographical scope of the EU's Enlargement policy encompasses Albania, Bosnia and Herzegovina, Iceland (negotiations on hold since 2013), Kosovo, Montenegro, Serbia, Turkey

---

7 European Commission, Communication to the European Parliament, the Council, the European Economic and Social Committee and the Committee of the Regions: EU Enlargement Strategy, COM (2015) 611 final of 10 November 2015; European Commission, Communication to the European Parliament, the Council, the European Economic and Social Committee and the Committee of the Regions: A Credible Enlargement Perspective for and Enhanced Engagement with the Western Balkans, COM (2018) 65 final of 6 February 2018.

8 European Commission (2019). European Commission, Communication to the European Parliament, the Council, the European Economic and Social Committee and the Committee of the Regions: EU Enlargement Policy, COM(2019) 260 final of 25 May.

9 Copenhagen European Council (1993). Conclusions of the Presidency, of 21–22 June 1993, SN 180/1/93 REV1.

58 *Trade liberalization and the rule of law*

and the Republic of North Macedonia.[10] Free trade between the EU and Western Balkans is realized in terms of the Stabilization and Association Process.[11] The legal framework for the EU Customs Union with Turkey is constituted by the 1977 Agreement establishing the Association between the EEC and Turkey.[12] The EU unilateral assistance to partner countries is channelled via the IPA II, *inter alia* directed to "strengthening of democracy and its institutions, including an independent and efficient judiciary, and of the rule of law, including its implementation".[13] In line with the 2019 EU Enlargement Strategy, the reforms in the area of rule of law, fundamental rights and good governance remain "the most pressing issue" for the Western Balkans, and "the key benchmark., against which the prospects of these countries will be judged by the EU".[14] Amid the controversy surrounding the substance of values as a part of the political criterion, the EU enlargement policy offers an interesting case for exploring the nexus between trade liberalization and the EU promotion of the rule of law.

European Neighbourhood Policy

Frequently conceptualized as a "substitute for EU membership" (Cadier, 2013) or an "alternative regional integration scheme" (Gstöhl, 2015, p. 254), the European Neighbourhood Policy (ENP) was launched by the EU in 2004 and substantially revised in 2015.[15] The ENP's legal framework is constituted by Art. 8 TEU that obliges the EU to develop "a special relationship with neighbouring countries, aiming to establish an area of prosperity and good neighbourliness, founded on the values of the Union". In line with Art. 8(1) TEU, the 2014 Regulation establishing the European Neighbourhood Instrument (ENI) also refers to the ENP as a framework for privileged relationship between the EU and its Neighbours, "building upon a mutual commitment to, and promotion of, the values of democracy and human rights, the rule of law, good governance, and the principles of a market economy and sustainable and inclusive development".[16] As compared to Enlarge-

---

10 Regulation (EU) No 231/2014 of the European Parliament and of the Council of 11 March 2014 establishing the Instrument of Pre-Accession Assistance (IPA II), OJ L 77/1 of 15 March 2014.

11 See, for instance, Stabilization and Association Agreement between the European Union and the European Atomic Energy Community, of the one part, and Kosovo, of the other part, OJ L 71 of 16 March 2016, pp. 3–321 (hereinafter referred to as "EU-Kosovo SAA").

12 Agreement establishing the Association between the European Economic Community and Turkey, OJ L 361/1 of 31 December 1977, Art.2(2).

13 Regulation (EU) No 231/2014 of the European Parliament and of the Council of 11 March 2014 establishing the Instrument of Pre-Accession Assistance (IPA II), OJ L 77/1 of 15 March 2014.

14 European Commission (2019). European Commission, Communication to the European Parliament, the Council, the European Economic and Social Committee and the Committee of the Regions: EU Enlargement Policy, COM(2019) 260 final of 25 May.

15 For the ENP Revision, see European Commission, Joint Communication to the European Parliament, the Council, the European Economic and Social Committee and the Committee of the Region: Review of the European Neighbourhood Policy, JOIN 2015 (50) final of 18 November 2015.

16 Regulation (EU) No 232/2014 of the European Parliament and the European Council of 11 March 2014, establishing a European Neighbourhood Instrument, OJ L 77/27 of 15 March 2014.

Trade liberalization and the rule of law 59

ment, the post-2015 ENP is marked by a tight nexus between economic prosperity and the advancement of fundamental values, on the one hand, and stability, on the other hand, with conflict prevention, counter-terrorism and anti-radicalization policies at the core of the reviewed policy.

Geographically, the ENP encompasses two groups of countries, the Eastern Neighbourhood (Armenia, Azerbaijan, Belarus, Georgia, the Republic of Moldova and Ukraine) and the Southern Neighbourhood (Algeria, Egypt, Israel, Jordan, Lebanon, Libya, Morocco, occupied Palestinian territories and Tunisia).[17] Due to the variation in Neighbours' geopolitical orientations and foreign policies, the ENP is featured by a significant degree of differentiation that is, *inter alia*, manifested in the different scope of the EU RTAs with Neighbours. Thus, the EU Association Agreements (AAs) with Southern Neighbours, concluded over the period from 1995–2002, offer a limited room for political dialogue, despite referring to democracy and the rule of law as "essential elements".[18] In economic terms, the scope of the EMAs is limited to trade in goods. To deepen its trade relations with Morocco and Tunisia, the EU currently intends to supplement existing AAs with Deep and Comprehensive Free Trade Areas (DCFTAs) (Van der Loo, 2015). As opposed to the Southern Neighbourhood, the AAs /DCFTAs with Eastern Neighbours provide for an intense political dialogue between the EU and partner countries, as well as "deep" trade liberalization, encompassing trade in services, public procurement and non-tariff barriers to trade.[19] Since Armenia and Belarus joined the Eurasian Customs Union (EACU) and adopted the common tariff *vis-à-vis* third states, these countries are prevented from liberalizing their trade with the EU and, subsequently, their relations with the EU are governed by cooperation, rather than Association Agreements. Similar refers to the Azerbaijan that chose not to join the EACU, but also not to proceed with trade liberalization negotiations with the EU.

Nowadays, the ENP faces a range of external and, subsequently, conceptual challenges. Key external pressures stem from violent conflicts in Syria and Eastern Ukraine, and the geopolitical tensions with the Russian Federation, involved in both conflicts. Moreover, considerable variations in political regimes, foreign policy goals and the stages of political and economic development across the Neighbourhood make it difficult for the EU to keep all the Neighbours under the single policy umbrella. A particular conceptual difficulty arises with regard to Ukraine, Moldova and Georgia that require new incentives for deepening their relations with the EU following the AAs' entry into force. Furthermore, it remains important to continue advancing the Mediterranean dimension of the Union's external action, *inter alia*, through deepening trade and intensifying

---

17 *Ibid.*, Art. 1, Annex I.

18 See, for instance: Euro-Mediterranean Agreement establishing an association between the European Communities and their Member States, of the one part, and the Republic of Tunisia, of the other part, OJ L097 of 30 March 2008, pp. 2–183 (hereinafter referred to as "EU-Tunisia AA").

19 See, for instance: Association Agreement between the EU and its Member States, of the one part, and Ukraine, of the other part, OJ L 161/3 of 29 May 2014 (hereinafter referred to as "EU-Ukraine AA").

60 *Trade liberalization and the rule of law*

value-promotion. Besides, it is crucial for the EU not to lose leverage in Armenia, Belarus and Azerbaijan. In this vein, the differentiation and flexibility of the ENP and the demand for the new value-promotion avenues represent a promising framework for strengthening the interplay between the EU external trade and the rule of law promotion.

EU development policy

The "restructuring of the Europe's relations with its colonies and former colonies" has represented a substantial aspect of the European Communities' evolution (Mold, 2007, p. 29). Since the first game-changing provisions of the 1957 Rome Treaty regarding the EC's association with third states, the Communities and, later on, the EU, managed to shape a multifaceted development policy, encompassing Africa; Latin America; Northern, Southern and Eastern Asia; and the Middle East.[20] The policy framework of the post-Lisbon EU development policy is predominantly inspired by the 2030 Agenda, conceptualized by the UN as a "plan of action for people, planet and prosperity" and identifying 17 Sustainable Development Goals (SDGs).[21] In 2017, the EU adopted a new European Consensus on Development, aimed to consolidate its role as an international development actor, committed to "be a frontrunner in implementing the 2030 Agenda for Sustainable Development".[22] In terms of this commitment, the EU dedicates particular attention to coordinating its action with other donors in terms of the Global Partnership for Sustainable Development and ensuring the coherence of EU policies that may impact third countries through Policy Coherence for Development.

Art. 208(1) TFEU emphasizes poverty eradication as the major long-term objective of the EU development cooperation. Alongside this, the EU development policy shall pursue the whole spectrum of the general objectives of the EU external action. According to Art. 4(4) TEU, the EU shall have competence to "carry out activities and conduct a common policy" in the domains of development cooperation and humanitarian aid, yet the exercise of its competence shall not prevent the Member States from exercising their competences in these domains.

The geographical scope of EU development cooperation is defined in Art. 1(a) of the DCI. It includes the countries that are signatories to the 2000 CA (excluding South Africa); countries eligible for the European Development Fund; countries,

---

20 EEC Treaty, Part IV.

21 United Nations General Assembly Resolution: Transforming our World: the 2030 Agenda for Sustainable Development, A/RES/70/01 of 21 October 2015.

22 The Council, the representatives of the governments of Member States meeting within the Council and the European Commission, New European Consensus on Development: Our World, Our Dignity, Our Future, Joint Statement of 8 June 2017. [pdf] Available at: https://ec.europa.eu/euro peaid/sites/devco/files/european-consensus-on-development-final-20170626_en.pdf (hereinafter referred to as "New European Consensus on Development"); Joint declaration by the Council and the representatives of the governments of the Member States meeting within the Council, the European Parliament and the Commission on the development policy of the European Union entitled "The European Consensus", OJ C 46 of 24 February 2006.

Trade liberalization and the rule of law   61

eligible for the European Neighbourhood Instrument funding, as well as the acceding countries (those, eligible for the IPA II funding).[23] In October 2018, the EU launched the negotiations of the new framework of relations with the ACP states, represented by the Central Negotiating Group (CNG) to replace the Cotonou Agreement with the new one. Notably, the ACP negotiating mandate pertaining to the Post-Cotonou Agreement encompasses the alignment to the Agenda 2030 and the SDGs as a fundamental framework and the parties' commitment to peace, democracy, security and the rule of law as values, "pre-eminent to sustainable development".[24] Besides, the EU-ACP relations are founded on the WTO-compatible Economic Partnership Agreements (EPAs), "tailor-made to suit specific regional circumstances" and promote regional integration (Leonard and Taylor, 2016, p. 262).

The implementation and advancement of the EU development policy is concerned with numerous conceptual and coordination-related difficulties. The key challenge doubtlessly deals with the "growing skepticism about the effectiveness of aid as an instrument and the need to get value for money with the risk of focusing on 'quick fixes' producing immediate measurable results without deeper 'social change'" (Concord Cotonou Working Group, 2013) or, put it differently, the rise of post-development concerns as to the effectiveness of development assistance (Delputte and Orbie, 2020). Moreover, given the long-lasting lack of equal partnership between the EU as a donor and aid-receiving countries, it is challenging for the EU to ensure the joint ownership of its development cooperation projects. Third, certain EU Member States tend to question the present allocation of the 0.7% of the EU budget for development aid, willing to put greater emphasis on security and climate change–related issues (*Ibid.*). Nonetheless, the continuous expansion of aid industry makes it increasingly difficult to ensure the coordination of donors, policy coherence and the well-justified prioritization among the cooperation areas.

5. *Value-promoting disciplines under the EU RTAs*

The RTAs' ability to promote values immediately depends on their scope. The key RTAs' value-promoting disciplines are as follows.

First, while the "augmented" Washington Consensus links the law and development through financial liberalization and developed markets of financial services (Rodrik, 2006), the RTAs in question include provisions regarding the circulation of capital and the rapprochement of financial standards. Importantly, recent RTAs concluded by the EU, such as the EU DCFTAs with Eastern Neighbours,

---

23 Regulation (EU) No 233/2014 of the European Parliament and the European Council of 11 March 2014, establishing a financing instrument for development cooperation for the period of 2014–2020, OJ L 77/44 of 15 March 2014.
24 Decision No. 2/CVII/18 of the 107th Session of the ACP Council of Ministers on the ACP Negotiating Mandate for the post-Cotonou Partnership Agreement with the EU, held in Lomé, Togo, from 29th to 30th May 2018.

62 *Trade liberalization and the rule of law*

also contain provisions on establishment, trade in services and electronic commerce.[25] Aiming to integrate Eastern Neighbours to the EU's market of services and create mutual investment opportunities, the previously mentioned chapters introduce multiple standards, directed to improving **legal certainty** and **transparency**. These standards primarily concern the domestic regulations of business and the legislation on financial services and electronic commerce, as well as postal and courier services.[26] Notably, deregulation and the resulting openness to FDI represent the crucial law-related requirements for development, as understood in terms of the original Washington Consensus (Rodrik, 2006).

Next, virtually all the RTAs under study contain the rules pertaining to fair competition and state aid. Substantively, such rules touch upon the standards of **legality**, **transparency** and **accountability**, **equality** and **non-discrimination** through obliging the parties to ensure functional antitrust legislation.[27] The RTAs' competition-related chapters require the parties to maintain the institutions that would guarantee companies' access to the markets of each other, not restricted by the discriminatory practices.[28] Modern "deep" trade liberalization provides not only for eliminating barriers to trade in goods and services but ensuring parties' mutual access to public procurement markets. As it can be exemplified by the relevant chapters of the EU-Kosovo SAA or the EU-Ukraine DCFTA, granting such an access requires, *inter alia*, the adherence to a range of the rule of law standards, such as **transparency** of information regarding the tender procedures, **equality**, **non-discrimination guarantees** and the **availability of remedies**.[29] Another RTA discipline that contributes to the promotion of fundamental values, including the rule of law, is the recognition and protection of IP rights.[30] IP rights–related chapters of the RTAs complement the obligations of the EU and its counterparts under the WTO TRIPS Agreement and concern, among other things, the rules on trademarks, copyrights and geographical indications.[31] The recognition and protection of intellectual, industrial and commercial property serve as the necessary prerequisite for attracting FDI and exercising cross-border trade in services.

Furthermore, the RTAs may include provisions on trade-related **transparency**, consonant with the ones under the WTO TBT and SPS Agreements.[32] More general

---

25 See, for instance, EU-Ukraine AA, Part IV, Chapter 6.

26 *Ibid.*

27 See, for instance, EU-Kosovo SAA, Title VI; EU-Ukraine AA, Part IV, Chapter 10; Economic Partnership Agreement between the CARIFORUM States, of the one part, and the European Community and its Member States, of the other part, OJ L 289/1/4 of 30 October 2008, Title IV, Chapter 1 (hereinafter referred as "EU-CARIFORUM EPA").

28 See, for instance, EU-Ukraine AA, Art.255.

29 EU-Kosovo SAA, Art. 79; EU-Ukraine AA, Art.151.

30 See, for instance, EU-Kosovo SAA, Art.77; EU-Ukraine AA, Part IV, Chapter 9; EU-CARIFORUM EPA, Title IV, Chapter 5.

31 WTO, Agreement on Trade-Related Aspects of Intellectual Property Rights, 1869 UNTS 299, 33 ILM 1197 of 1994.

32 WTO, Agreement on Technical Barriers to Trade, 1186 U.N.T.S 276 (entered into force 1 January 1980) (hereinafter referred to as "WTO TBT Agreement"); WTO, Agreement on the Application of Sanitary and Phytosanitary Measures, 1867 U.N.T.S 493 (entered into force 1 January 1995).

Table 3.1 The Politics and Law of the EU Value-Promoting RTAs

	Value-promoting RTAs	Other RTAs
EU foreign policy goals	The interplay of normative and market foreign policy goals (can be also coupled with security and stability concerns)	Primarily market goals (in many cases, coupled with the Union's strategic vision of the relationships with a particular country or region)
EU power	Complex combination of normative and market power. While norms' diffusion is primarily associated with the NPE, economic/market access conditionality serves as an essential for incentivizing change in partner countries.	Complex combination of normative and market power. Normative power is primarily used with regard to the EU's negotiating sustainable development, product safety and other standards.
Balance of power between the EU and its counterpart	Asymmetric bargaining powers of the EU and a partner country in the negotiations; two basic types of relations, determining the differences in the normative agenda: 1) Negotiating with a democracy/"flawed democracy" that is dependent on the EU in terms of imports/exports and development aid, and may have European aspirations 2) Negotiating with an authoritarian state that is dependent on the EU in terms of imports/exports and development aid	Symmetric bargaining powers of the EU and a partner country in the negotiations; a partner does not depict a high level of economic or strategic dependency on the EU.
Mechanisms of rule transfer	NPE-specific ways of norms' diffusion (e.g. contagion, procedural diffusion, overt diffusion), coupled with strong economic/ market access conditionality	Regulatory convergence, rather than the unilateral transfer of the EU norms
Policy framework/ legal basis	CCP, coupled with enlargement, Neighbourhood and development agendas	CCP
Legal nature	Most commonly, any RTA represents "mixed agreements"	
Scope	While the value-promoting and other RTAs may include similar "deep" disciplines (e.g. competition, liberalization of public procurement), the source of standards would differ. In case of value-promoting RTAs, standards are predominantly set by the EU, and conditionality mechanisms are used to promote them. On the contrary, symmetrical bargaining powers in the negotiations would mean parties' voluntary commitments to values and standards, developed as a result of regulatory convergence, rather than the EU's unilateral norms' diffusion.	
Examples	SAAs with Western Balkans, DCFTAs with Eastern Neighbours, AAs with Southern Neighbours, the Cotonou Agreement and EPAs with African countries	CETA, EU-Korea FTA, EU-Singapore FTA

64 *Trade liberalization and the rule of law*

provisions on **transparency** and **accountability** are frequently included in the RTAs' chapters, dedicated to administrative, industrial and technical cooperation between the parties. Particular RTAs (e.g. the EU-Moldova DCFTA) even contain separate "Transparency" chapters that encompass different dimensions of **transparency, accountability** and **due process**.[33] Last but not least, in line with the "augmented" Washington Consensus, a crucial dimension of the law-development nexus is a country's compliance with the WTO standards and other widely spread international trade and sustainable development rules (Rodrik, 2006).

These elements demonstrate that, given their "depth", contemporary RTAs offer significant room for the promotion of fundamental values.

Conclusion

In Chapter 3, we demonstrated that the history of development economics is marked by divergent visions of the role of law in economic development, ranging from considering law solely from instrumental standpoint to assigning it the key role in the development process. Both of these extremes, however, recognize that law is essential for creating the atmosphere conducive to economic development and international trade. On the other hand, as substantiated by the referrals to the NPE and MPE concepts, and the evidence from the research on democracy promotion by functional cooperation, trade liberalization and market integration are likely to facilitate the promotion of fundamental values. Based on the presented evidence, the study proceeded with elaborating on the concept of value-promoting RTAs that will be applied as a foundation for the investigation of the mechanisms of the EU promotion of the rule of law through RTAs to be presented in Chapter 4 and Chapter 5. The key peculiarities of the EU value-promoting RTAs can be summarized in Table 3.1.

References

Abuzeid, F. (2009). Foreign aid and "big push" theory: Lessons from Sub-Saharan Africa. *Stanford Journal of International Relations*, 1, pp. 16–23.

Aggestam, L. (2013). Global norms and European power. In: K.E. Jorgensen and K.V. Laatikainen, eds., *Handbook on the European Union and international institutions*. Basingstoke: Palgrave Macmillan, pp. 457–472.

Cadier, D. (2013). Is the European neighbourhood policy a substitute for enlargement? In: Luc-Andre Brunet, ed., *LSEIDEAS special report "the crisis of EU enlargement"*. London: LSE, pp. 53–58.

Carothers, T. (1998). The rule of law revival. *Foreign Affairs*, 95, pp. 95–106.

Clapham, C. (1996). *Africa and the international system: The politics of state survival*. Cambridge: Cambridge University Press.

Coase, R.H. (1937). The nature of the firm. *Economics,* 4, pp. 386–405.

---

33 Association Agreement between the EU and its Member States, of the one part, and the Republic of Moldova, of the other part, OJ L 260/4 of 30 August 2014, Chapter 11 (hereinafter referred to as "EU-Moldova AA"), Chapter 12.

Concord Cotonou Working Group. (2013). *Trends and challenges in the EU development policy*. [pdf] Available at: http://concordeurope.org/wp-content/uploads/2016/07/Brussels_Briefing_Papers__Agenda_for_Change_En.pdf?1855fc.

Damro, Ch. (2012). Market power Europe. *Journal of European Public Policy*, 19, pp. 685–686.

De Cara, J-Y. (2006/2007). International trade and the rule of law. *Mercer Law Review*, 58, pp. 1357–1380.

Delputte, S. and Orbie, J. (2020). Bridging EU-&post-development studies: Four avenues. *EADI Blog*. [blog] 30 January. Available at: www.developmentresearch.eu/?p=618.

Del Sarto, R.A. (2016). Normative empire Europe: The European Union, its borderlands, and the 'Arab Spring'. *Journal of Common Market Studies*, 54(2), pp. 215–232.

Doyle, N., Enache, A.M. and Merja, A. (2016). *Rule of law conditionality in the stabilization and association agreement between Kosovo and the EU*. Group of Political and Legal Studies. [pdf] Available at: www.legalpoliticalstudies.org/wp-content/uploads/2016/11/Rule-of-Law-Conditionality-in-the-Stabilization-and-Association-Agreement-between-Kosovo-and-the-EU-F.pdf.

Drezner, D.W. (2007). *All politics is global: Explaining international regulatory regimes*. Princeton: Princeton University Press.

Ewing-Chow, M., Losari, J. and Slade, M. (2014). The facilitation of trade by the rule of law: The cases of Singapore and ASEAN. In: M. Jansen, J. Mustafa, and M. Smeets, eds., *Connecting to global markets*. Geneva: WTO, pp. 129–146.

Farber, D.A. (2002). Rights as signals. *Journal of Legal Studies*, 31(1), pp. 83–98.

Frensch, R., Horváth, R. and Huber, S. (2018). *World trade and endogenous rule of law: Size and pattern effects*. Working Paper of the University of Regensburg. [pdf] Available at: www.uni-regensburg.de/wirtschaftswissenschaften/vwl-moeller/medien/huber/frensch_horvath_huber.pdf.

Freyburg, T., Lavenex, S., Schimmelfennig, F., Skripka, T. and Wetzel, A. (2011). Democracy promotion through functional cooperation? The case of European neighbourhood policy. *Democratization*, 18, pp. 1026–1054.

George, S. and Sabelli, F. (1994). *Faith and credit. The world bank's secular empire*. London: Westview Press.

Gstöhl, S. (2015). Models of external differentiation in the EU's neighbourhood: An expanding economic community? *Journal of European Public Policy*, 22, pp. 854–870.

Haukkala, H. (2011). The European Union as regional normative hegemon: The case of European neighbourhood policy. In: Richard G Whitman, ed., *Normative power Europe: Empirical and theoretical perspectives*. Berlin: Springer, pp. 45–64.

Hirschman, A. (1945). *National power and the structure of foreign trade*. Reprint 1980. Berkeley: University of California Press.

Hyde-Price, A. (2006). 'Normative' power Europe: A realist critique. *Journal of European Public Policy*, 13, pp. 217–234.

Jakovlevski, V. (2010). The logic of EU enlargement: Exporting stability or inheriting an empire? *Journal of Public and International Affairs*, 21, pp. 23–48.

Juncos, A. (2017). Resilience as the new EU foreign policy paradigm: A pragmatist turn? *European Security*, 26(1), pp. 1–18.

Kennedy, D. (2013). Law and development economics: Toward a new alliance? In: D. Kennedy and J. Stiglitz, eds., *Law and economics with Chinese characteristics. Institutions for promoting development in the twenty-first century*. Oxford: Oxford University Press, Chapter 1.

66 *Trade liberalization and the rule of law*

Kochenov, D. (2005). *EU enlargement law: History and recent developments: Treaty-custom-concubinage?* European Integration Online Papers 2005/10–11. [pdf] Available at: http://eiop.or.at/eiop/pdf/2005-006.pdf.

Krever, T. (2011). The legal turn in late development theory: The rule of law and the world bank's development model. *Harvard International Law Journal*, 52(1), pp. 288–319.

Kroncke, J. (2012). Law and development as anti-comparative law. *Vanderbilt Journal of Transnational Law*, 45, pp. 477–555.

Lamprecht, J. (2014). *Bargaining power in multilateral trade negotiations: Canada and Japan in the Uruguay round and Doha development agenda.* PhD. London School of Economics. Available at: http://etheses.lse.ac.uk/903/1/Lamprecht_Bargaining_power_multilateral_trade_negotiations.pdf.

Larik, J. (2016). *Foreign policy objectives in European constitutional law.* Oxford: Oxford University Press.

Leonard, D. and Taylor, R. (2016). *The Routledge guide to the European Union.* London: Routledge.

Majone, G. (1994). The rise of the regulatory state in Europe. *West European Politics*, 17, pp. 77–101.

Manners, I. (2002). Normative power Europe: A contradiction in terms. *Journal of Common Market Studies*, 40(2), pp. 235–258.

Meunier, S. and Nicolaïdis, K. (2017). The European Union as a trade power. In: C. Hill, M. Smith, and S. Vanhoonacker, eds., *International relations and the European Union.* Oxford: Oxford University Press, pp. 210–234.

Mold, A. (2007). *EU development policy in a changing world: Challenges for the 21st century.* Amsterdam: Amsterdam University Press.

North, D.C. (1991). Institutions. *The Journal of Economic Perspectives*, 5, pp. 97–112.

Ohnesorge, J.K. (2014). Developing development theory: Law and development orthodoxies and the northeast Asian experience. *University of Pennsylvania Journal of International Law*, 28, pp. 220–308.

Organski, A. (1965). *The stages of political development.* New York: Alfred A. Knopf.

Parker, O. and Rosamond, B. (2013). 'Normative power Europe' meets economic liberalism: Complicating cosmopolitanism inside/outside the EU. *Cooperation and Conflict*, 48(2), pp. 229–246.

Parsons, T. (1964). Evolutionary universals in society. *American Sociological Review*, 29, pp. 339–357.

Poletti, A. and Sicurelli, D. (2018). *The political economy of normative trade power Europe.* Basingstoke: Palgrave Macmillan.

Prebisch, P. (1949). Growth, disequilibrium and disparities: Interpretation of the process of economic development. *Economic Survey of Latin America*, 9, pp. 3–85.

Ramanujam, N., Verna, M., Betts, J., Charamba, K. and Moore, M. (2012). *Rule of law and economic development: A comparative analysis of approaches to economic development across the BRICS countries.* Montreal: McGill University.

Risse, T. and Babayan, N. (2015). Democracy promotion and the challenges of illiberal regional powers: Introduction to the special issue. *Democratization*, 22, pp. 381–399.

Rodrik, D. (2017). *Populism and economics of globalization.* NBER Working Paper 2017/23559. [pdf] Available at: www.nber.org/papers/w23559.pdf.

Rodrik, D. (2006). Goodbye, Washington consensus, hello, Washington confusion? A review of the world bank's economic growth in the 1990s: Learning from a decade of reform. *Journal of Economic Literature*, 44(4), pp. 973–987.

Rostow, W.W. (1959). The stages of economic growth. *The Economic History Review*, 12(1), pp. 1–16.

Shihata, I. F.I. (1996). The role of law in business development. *Fordham International Law Journal*, 20, pp. 1580–1581.

Singer, H.W. (1949). Economics progress in underdeveloped countries. *Social Research*, 16, pp. 1–11.

Sjursen, H. (2006). The EU as a 'normative power': How can this be? *Journal of European Public Policy*, 13, pp. 235–251.

Trubeck, D.M. and Galanter, M. (1974). Scholars in self-estrangement: Some reflections on the crisis in law and development studies in the USA. *Wisconsin Law Review*, 4, pp. 1062–1103.

Tussie, D. and Saguier, M. (2011). The sweep of asymmetric trade negotiations: Introduction and overview. In: B. Sanoussi, P. Lombaerde, and D. Tussie, eds., *Asymmetric trade negotiations*. London: Routledge, pp. 2–14.

Van der Loo, G. (2015). *Enhancing the prospects of the EU's deep and comprehensive free trade areas in the Mediterranean: Lessons from the eastern partnership*. CEPS Commentary, 2015/06. [online] Available at: www.ceps.eu/ceps-publications/enhancing-prospects-eus-deep-and-comprehensive-free-trade-areas-mediterranean-lessons/.

Wallerstein, I. (1974). The rise and future demise of the world capitalist system: Concepts for comparative analysis. *Comparative Studies in Society and History*, 16, pp. 387–415.

Wetzel, A. (2015). The substance of the EU democracy promotion: Introduction and conceptual framework. In: A. Wetzel and J. Orbie, eds., *The substance of EU democracy promotion: Concepts and cases*. Berlin: Springer, pp. 1–23.

Williamson, J. (1990). What Washington means by policy reform? In: J. Williamson, ed., *Latin American adjustment: How much has happened?* Washington, DC: Institute for International Economics, pp. 7–20.

The World Bank. (1982). *Accelerated development in Sub-Saharan Africa. An agenda for action*. Washington, DC: The World Bank. [pdf] Available at: http://documents.world bank.org/curated/en/702471468768312009/pdf/multi-page.pdf.

The World Bank. (1992). *Development in practice. Governance. The world bank's experience*. Washington, DC: The World Bank. http://documents.worldbank.org/curated/en/711471468765285964/pdf/multi0page.pdf.

The World Bank Group. (2020). *Doing business 2020. Comparing business regulation in 190 economies*. Washington, DC: The World Bank. [pdf] Available at: http://documents.worldbank.org/curated/en/688761571934946384/pdf/Doing-Business-2020-Comparing-Business-Regulation-in-190-Economies.pdf.

The World Bank Group. (n.d.). *Worldwide governance indicators*. [online] Available at: https://info.worldbank.org/governance/wgi/#home.

Zhelyazkova, A., Damjanovski, I., Nechev, Z. and Schimmelfennig, F. (2018). European Union conditionality in the western Balkans: External incentives and Europeanisation. In: J. Džankić, S. Keil, and M. Kmezić, eds., *The Europeanisation of the western Balkans: A failure of EU conditionality?* Berlin: Springer, pp. 15–39.

4 EU rule of law promotion through RTAs in third states

The "regulation" dimension

This chapter proceeds with analyzing specific *mechanisms* through which EU value-promoting RTAs uphold the rule of law components. For the purposes of clarity and in line with our aspiration to explore the coherence of the EU rule of law promotion through RTAs, we apply the "regulation" vs. "action" dichotomy. This chapter will zoom in on the "regulation" dimension or, put differently, look at the substance of the "authoritative public obligations" (Cogan, 2011) which the RTAs with the EU create for states, legal entities and individuals to act or refrain from acting in a certain way. Additionally, according to Black (2002), regulation shall be understood as "the process of controlling, governing and directing" that is exercised, *inter alia*, by supranational bodies (the EU) with respect to other actors through rules, monitoring and sanctioning (p. 4). Although Black (2002) argues that regulation can be exercised through different types of rules (legal, quasi-legal and even market rules), this part of the book explores solely the legal rules under the EU's value-promoting RTAs.

In line with the findings of Chapter 3, Chapter 4 and the subsequent chapters will focus on three categories of RTAs: EU SAAs with Western Balkans, DCFTAs with Eastern Neighbours (as part to the respective AAs) and the Cotonou Agreement and the EPAs with ACP countries (exemplified by the EU-CRIFORUM EPA as the most comprehensive among the EPAs). Given their limited scope, the EU AAs with Southern Neighbours will be seldom addressed. Notably, due to the space limitations, this chapter will cover only selected clauses and disciplines, illustrative of the nature and peculiarities of the RTAs' impact on the rule of law in third states. First, we will discuss the "essential element" conditionality, involving the rule of law, and the challenges its application faces in practice. The second part of this chapter will explore uniquely profound partner states' obligations under the "Transparency" chapters of the EU DCFTAs with "associated" Eastern Neighbours. Third, the study elaborates on the rule of law clauses pertaining to administrative cooperation between the EU and third states under the RTAs. Finally, the analysis will cover public procurement and competition provisions. Since both disciplines in question serve the objective of granting third countries access to the EU Single Market, they presumably provide for numerous rule of law–related obligations partner countries have to fulfil.

EU rule of law: the "regulation" dimension 69

Part 1. "Essential element" clauses in the EU value-promoting RTAs

1. The evolution and design of the "essential element" clauses

As it was briefly discussed in Chapter 2, "essential element" clauses represent the oldest and most well-known instrument the EU uses to channel its values through RTAs. A typical common values conditionality structure entails two elements. First, it contains a clause specifying the core values "the relationships between the parties are founded on" (a substantive "essential element" clause) (Dolle, 2015, p. 214). Second, there is a "suspension clause" that defines the procedure for suspending an agreement or its parts in case of the violation of "essential elements". Such a structure aims at creating the conditions under which human rights violations of a particular scale in partner countries could be qualified as a material breach of the treaty in terms of Art. 60 of the Vienna Convention on Law of Treaties (VCLT) and justify the suspension of the treaty or the application of other counter-measures.[1]

Although it did not include a suspension clause, the 1989 IV Lomé Convention between the Communities and the ACP countries was the first EU instrument to emphasize the parties' attachment to human rights and human dignity.[2] Already since 1995, the EU has implemented a policy of "systematically inserting" a fully-fledged "essential element" clause into all the political framework agreements and economic agreements between the EU and third states.[3] In legal terms, the EU's obligation to include an "essential element" clause into its economic agreements with third states was strengthened pursuant to the extension of the Union's human rights commitments (Art. 21[2][b] TEU) to the CCP. Although Art. 21(2) TEU does not immediately refer to the "essential element" clause, it obliges the EU to promote human rights, democratic principles and the rule of law extraterritorially. In turn, since an "essential element" clause is a critical instrument the EU uses to respond to the violations of fundamental values in partner countries, its inclusion into the EU economic agreements has become the EU's legal obligation, rather than a policy.

2. EU RTAs with Africa: from Lomé IV to the Economic Partnership Agreements

In contrast to the initial 1989 version of the Lomé IV Convention, the 1995 Lomé IV Convention has become the first European Community-ACP countries

---

1 Vienna Convention on the law of treaties, U.N.T.S., 1155, I-18232.
2 Fourth ACP-EEC Convention, signed at Lomé on 15 December 1989. OJ L 229, 17.8.1991, p. 3–286.
3 European Commission, Communication: On the Inclusion of Respect for Democratic Principles and Human Rights in Agreements between the Community and Third Countries, COM 95 (216) final of 23 May 1995.

70 *EU rule of law: the "regulation" dimension*

RTA with a fully-fledged "essential element" clause.[4] In particular, it mentioned the respect for human rights, democratic principles and the rule of law as the principles, "underpinning the relationships between the ACP States and the Community" and constituting "essential elements" thereof.[5] Art. 366 (a)(2) of the Convention stipulated that a party's failure to observe these principles shall lead to the conduct of bilateral consultations. Subsequently, "if in spite of all efforts no solution has been found, or immediately, in the case of urgency or refusal of consultations, the party which invoked the failure to fulfill an obligation may take appropriate steps, including, where necessary, the partial or full suspension" of the Convention.[6] The suspension of the Convention was, however, viewed as "a measure of last resort".[7]

Regarded in literature as a "model" essential element clause, Art. 9 of the Cotonou Agreement (CA) manifests three important differences, compared to the Lomé IV Convention (Hachez, 2015, p. 10). First, it emphasizes "sustainable development, centered on the human person, who is the main protagonist and beneficiary of development" as a core objective of the parties' cooperation.[8] Second, anticipating the conceptual take of the Agenda 2030, Art. 9 CA refers to fundamental values as an integral component of sustainable development. Third, Art. 9(2) CA introduces transparent and accountable governance (also referred to as "good governance") as an "essential element". Notably, as it can be traced from the definition of "good governance" contained in Art. 9(3) CA, good governance shares crucial components (i.e., public accountability, transparency) with substantive rule of law.

In its 2007 Communication regarding the EPAs, the Commission outlined a number of challenges stemming from the CA, such as ensuring the unilateral trade preferences' compliance with the multilateral trade liberalization process and promoting the South-South integration.[9] Hence, the EPAs were designed to complement and reinforce the implementation of the CA through targeting relatively small groups of countries. As it can be exemplified by Art. 2 of the EU-CARIFORUM EPA, the EPAs are based on the "Fundamental Principles, as well as the Essential and Fundamental Principles of the Cotonou Agreement, as set out in Articles 2 and 9, respectively, of the Cotonou Agreement".[10] The two features that make the EPAs' political cooperation provisions different from the ones of the CA, however, are as follows. First, Art.3 of the EU-CARIFORUM EPA

---

4 Agreement amending the Fourth ACP-EC Convention of Lomé, signed in Mauritius on 4 November 1995, OJ L 156/3 of 29 May 1998, Art.5.

5 *Ibid.*

6 *Ibid.*

7 *Ibid.*

8 CA, Art.9(1).

9 European Commission, Communication to the Council and the European Parliament: Economic Partnership Agreements, COM (2007) 635 final of 23 October 2007.

10 Economic Partnership Agreement between the CARIFORUM States, of the one part, and the European Community and its Member States, of the other part, OJ L 289/1/4 of 30 October 2008 (hereinafter referred to as "EU-CARIFORUM EPA").

EU rule of law: the "regulation" dimension   71

distinguishes precise ways through which the parties implement their commitment to sustainable development (e.g. taking an account of the "best interests" of respective populations and future generations). Second, by comparison with the CA, the EPAs are marked by a strong emphasis on regional integration (Merran, 2016). Although the new Agreement between the EU and the ACP countries post-2020 is still being negotiated, the commitment to sustainable development and regional integration promises to remain foundational for EU-ACP relations (e.g. European Parliament, 2020).

Ultimately, "essential element" clauses have been recognized as foundational for the EU relations with the ACP countries since the 1995 revision of the Lomé IV Agreement. The most significant developments since 1995 encompass the expansion of the list of "essential elements" to include good governance, an emphasis on fundamental values as a component of sustainable development and the growing importance of sustainable development and regional integration in the EU-ACP relationship.

3. EU SAAs with Western Balkans

Bilateral Stabilization and Association Agreements (SAAs) between the EU and the Western Balkan countries are part to the Stabilization and Association Process (SAP) that foresees eventual EU membership as a finalité. Due to the complexities of the Yugoslav Wars and the post-conflict settlement, the first SAAs date back to the early 2000s (e.g. the EU-Macedonia SAA), while the most recent EU-Kosovo SAA was only signed in 2015. Since the adherence to common values is a criterion for the EU membership, "essential elements" are necessarily included into each of the SAAs.

As can be traced from the analysis of Art. 2 of the EU SAAs with Montenegro, Albania and Kosovo, the referrals to human rights, democratic principles and the rule of law as "essential elements" exactly follow the formulations contained in the CA and the EPAs.[11] In contrast to the CA, such referrals link fundamental values to the observance of the market economy principle, rather than sustainable development. According to the Document of the CSCE Bonn Conference, referred to by the SAAs, the necessary preconditions of a successful market economy include the "multiparty democracy, based on free, periodic and genuine elections", and the "rule of law and equal protection under the law for all, based

---

11 Stabilization and Association Agreement between the European Communities and their Member States, of the one part, and the Republic of Montenegro, of the other part, OJ L 108 of 29 April 2010 (hereinafter referred to as "EU-Montenegro SAA"); Stabilization and Association Agreement between the European Communities and their Member States, of the one part, and the Republic of Albania, of the other part, OJ L 107/166 of 28 April 2009 (hereinafter referred to as "EU-Albania SAA"); Stabilization and Association Agreement between the European Union and the European Atomic Energy Community, of the one part, and Kosovo, of the other part, OJ L 71 of 16 March 2016, pp. 3–321 (hereinafter referred to as "EU-Kosovo SAA").

72 *EU rule of law: the "regulation" dimension*

on respect for human rights and effective, accessible and just legal system".[12] The Document also mentions a range of components falling within the scope of the previously referred "augmented" Washington Consensus, such as the policies aimed at expanding the free flow of trade, capital and investment, and the protection of private property and IP rights (Rodrik, 2006). Thus, by referring to the Document of the CSCE Bonn Conference, the SAAs both underlined the importance of economic criteria for the successful EU accession and created the bridge between fundamental values and the market economy principles.

Alongside this, the "essential element" clauses in some of the SAAs reflect the EU's continuing preoccupation with the post-conflict settlement in the region. This is, for instance, Art. 2 of the EU-Bosnia and Herzegovina SAA that mentions "full cooperation with the International Criminal Tribunal for the former Yugoslavia (ICTY)" as an "essential element" of the Agreement.[13] Similarly, Art.3 of the EU-Kosovo SAA expands the list of the "essential elements" to include the respect not only for the ICTY, but its residual mechanism and the International Criminal Court (ICC).

As opposed to Art. 96 under the CA, the suspension clauses under the SAAs do not explicitly mention political dialogue or consultations. This would not prevent the parties from engaging into political dialogue or consultations as to any issues, yet, in contrast to the CA and EPAs, such consultations are not obligatory.

In a nutshell, the "essential elements clauses" in SAAs with Western Balkans tend to resemble the peculiarities of the background behind the Agreements. Through emphasizing the adherence to market economy principles as an "essential element", the SAAs do not only reflect their enlargement orientation but implicitly point to the economic dimension of the rule of law.

4. EU AAs with "associated" Eastern Neighbours and Southern Neighbours

The EU AAs with both the "associated" Eastern Neighbours and Southern Neighbours contain the "essential element" clauses. Their scope is, however, highly different, due to the peculiarities of political regimes in the respective countries. Given the prominence of authoritarian regimes in the MENA region, coupled with the Union's being strongly interested in security and stability there, the "essential elements" clauses, included to the Euro-Mediterranean Agreements (EMAs), are formulated in less detail than the ones, contained in the CA, EPAs or SAAs.

Compared with "essential elements" across the whole spectrum of the previously considered Agreements, the common values conditionality under the EU

---

12 Bonn Conference on Economic Cooperation in Europe Document, convened in accordance with the relevant provisions of the Concluding Document of the Vienna Meeting of the Conference on Security and Cooperation in Europe [online]. Available at: www.osce.org/eea/14081?download=true.

13 Stabilization and Association Agreement between the European Communities and their Member States, of the one part, and Bosnia and Herzegovina, of the other part, OJ L 164/2 of 30 June 2015, Art. 59, 92, 108 (hereinafter referred to as "EU-Bosnia and Herzegovina SAA").

AAs with "associated" Neighbours is characterized by several crucial peculiarities. First, the EU RTAs with Ukraine, Moldova and Georgia contain both "hard" conditionality and the principles that "underpin" the relationships between the parties and are "central to enhancing them".[14] The latter include, *inter alia*, the principles of free market economy, sustainable development, effective multilateralism and the fight against corruption and organized crime. Second, under the AAs with "associated" Neighbours, the rule of law and respect for human rights represent not only the "essential elements" but the targets of the "dialogue and cooperation on domestic reform" (e.g. Art. 6 of the EU-Ukraine AA). Third, similar to the SAAs with Western Balkans, the AAs with Eastern Neighbours mention "countering the proliferation of weapons of mass destruction, related materials and their means of delivery" as an "essential element".[15] In light of the ongoing "crisis in and around Ukraine" (OSCE, 2020), the "essential element" clause under the EU-Ukraine AA refers to "the promotion of respect for the principles of sovereignty and territorial integrity, inviolability of borders and integrity".[16] Moreover, the suspension clause, included into the EU-Ukraine AA, specifies the DCFTA-based trade benefits that can be suspended in case Ukraine violates common values[17] and, thus, represents an overlap between the common values and market access conditionality (Van der Loo, 2016, p. 308).

Thus, compared to the EMAs, the "essential element" clauses under the AAs with "associated" Neighbours are more profound and innovative.

5. The problématique of enforcing the "essential element" clauses

It may seem from the preceding legal analysis that the "essential element" clauses represent a promising pathway to promote values through trade liberalization agreements. However, it is the practice of enforcing the "essential element" clauses that challenges such an impression.

The first important criticism in this vein has been the non-inclusion of the "essential element" clauses into a broad range of sectoral trade agreements (e.g. fisheries, steel and textile) that provide for trade liberalization or cooperation only in respect of certain products and services (Hachez, 2015, p. 12). To exemplify this statement, one can refer to the Voluntary Partnership Agreements (VPAs) between the EU and the timber-exporting non-Member States (e.g. Cameroon, Gabon, Liberia, Malaysia).[18] Although the VPAs contain commitments to human rights and sustainable development, they do not include the "essential element" clauses and, therefore, cannot be suspended on the grounds related to the breach of fundamental values. More generally, according to Moberg (2015),

14 E.g. EU-Ukraine AA, Art.2.
15 *Ibid.*
16 *Ibid.*
17 *Ibid.*, Art.478(3).
18 For the background information on VPAs and texts of the Agreements, visit: http://ec.europa.eu/environment/forests/flegt.htm.

74 *EU rule of law: the "regulation" dimension*

including human rights clauses into purely trade agreements that do not contain development aspects is a relatively rare case.

Next, "essential element" clauses tend to be applied rather seldom and in a selective manner (Hachez, 2015, p. 13). Such a practice is determined by two intertwined factors. First, since fundamental values fall within the scope of political cooperation, it is the political choice of the Commission whether to propose the Council to invoke the "essential elements" clause (Moberg, 2015, p. 156). Second, the Commission's flexibility as far as making such proposals is reinforced by the lack of the definition of what constitutes a breach of fundamental values for the purposes of enforcing an "essential element" clause (European Parliament, 2014). Hence, "essential elements clauses" tend to lack legitimacy, since EU institutions tend to criticize human rights violations in third countries without referring to their legal obligations under the RTAs. In this vein, the European Parliament (2014) noted that "the single failure of the EU's policy on human rights and democracy clauses is the failure to invoke them in cases in which they are obviously relevant". On the other hand, an example of the EU's partial suspension of the Cooperation Agreement with Syria following the atrocities of the Syrian Civil War testifies to the fact that the Union can suspend its agreement with a third country, using its sanctions policy, rather than an "essential element" clause.[19]

On various occasions, scholars offered numerous avenues on how to raise the effectiveness of the "essential element" clauses. Such proposals range from introducing a virtually "depoliticized" procedure of enforcing the "essential element" clauses through specific and strict benchmarks (Velutti, 2016) to "leaving it to the Council to assess whether or not it lies in the Union's collective interest to call for consultations in any specific case" (Moberg, 2015, p. 156). There have, however, been no changes in the institutional set-up of the "essential element" clauses' enforcement since 1995, when they started to be streamlined into the majority of the EU RTAs with third states. Therefore, "essential element" clauses shall be regarded as a gateway for political dialogue on values between the EU and a third state, rather than a means to instrumentalize trade for the value-promotion purposes.

Part 2. "Transparency" chapters of the DCFTAs with "associated" Eastern Neighbours and rule of law promotion

The analysis of major value-promoting disciplines under the RTAs (Chapter 3) demonstrates that the parties' obligations in the rule of law domain are usually contained under the umbrella of political association or within specific disciplines. An important exception to this tendency is constituted by the "Transparency" chapters, included into the EU DCFTAs with "associated" Eastern Neighbours. Their uniqueness is determined by two factors. First, they apply to the whole spectrum

---

19 Cooperation Agreement between the European Economic Community and the Syrian Arab Republic, OJ L 269 of 27 September 1987, pp. 2–87; Council Decision 2011/273/CFSP, OJ L 121/11 of 10 May 2011.

EU rule of law: the "regulation" dimension 75

of disciplines under the AAs' trade-related parts. Second, alongside transparency standards, these chapters contain numerous far-reaching rule of law requirements, such as equality and non-discrimination, due process and the right to judicial review. The "deep" and intertwined nature of respective requirements, consonant with an ambitious market integration direction of the AAs/DCFTAs, manifests itself already in the formulations of the "Transparency" chapters' objectives.

1. Objective and context of transparency requirements

According to the DCFTAs, the "Transparency" chapters aim to oblige the parties to ensure a predictable regulatory environment for economic operators, doing business in their territory.[20] The AAs with Ukraine and Georgia specifically mention a predictable business environment for SMEs.[21] As noted earlier in Chapter 1, predictability of the regulatory environment is tightly concerned with the principle of legal certainty, also referred to in the respective provisions. Both the principle of legal certainty and the predictability sub-requirement are recognized in literature as critical for international trade liberalization. Hence, Andersen (2017) argues that the major function of the rule of law within the market economy is "to provide investors with legal certainty and legal expectations concerning their investments" (p. 14). In a similar vein, Van den Bossche and Zdouc (2017) link the very existence of international trade rules to "the need of traders for a degree of security and predictability" (p. 35). Therefore, levelling barriers to trade is not enough for facilitating trade flows in case the parties fail to ensure the transparent and stable regulatory environment in their jurisdictions.

Alongside the predictability principle, important factors that contribute to legal certainty include the transparency-related requirements to publish legislation and court decisions (referred in the DCFTAs as the "measures of general application") and the proportionality principle.[22] In EU law, the proportionality principle is reflected in two dimensions. First, alongside the subsidiarity principle, it governs the exercise of powers by the EU, requiring the content and form of the EU action not to exceed "what is necessary to achieve the objectives of the Treaties".[23] Second, under the settled CJEU case law, the interferences with fundamental rights shall follow the proportionality principle in order to be justified.[24] The proportionality principle is comprised of three sub-principles, namely

---

20 EU-Ukraine AA, Art. 282(1); EU-Moldova AA, Art. 356; Association Agreement between the European Union and the European Atomic Energy Community and their Member States, of the one part, and Georgia, of the other part (hereinafter referred to as "EU-Georgia AA"), Art. 220.
21 EU-Ukraine AA, Art. 282(1); EU-Moldova AA; EU-Georgia AA, Art. 220.
22 See, for instance, EU-Ukraine AA, Art. 283–284.
23 TEU, Art. 5(4).
24 See, for instance, CJEU, Dynamic Medien Vertriebs GmbH/Avides Media, Case C-244/06, AG Opinion of 14.02.2008; CJEU, United Pan-Europe Communications Belgium SA and Others/Belgian State, Case C-250/06, Judgment of 13 December 2017; CJEU, Volker and Markus Schecke GbR (C 92/09) and Hartmut Eifert (C 93/09)/Land Hessen, Case C 92/09, Judgment of 9 November 2010.

76 EU rule of law: the "regulation" dimension

suitability, necessity and proportionality in a narrow sense (optimization with the available legal means) (De Vries, 2013). Both dimensions thereof can be extrapolated to the third states' legal systems. In the cases of unitary states, such as Ukraine, Moldova and Georgia, the proportionality principle may refer to the delimitation of powers between the different levels of authorities. Furthermore, it plays a significant role in the protection of the economic agents' rights (e.g. in the international investment law).

Ultimately, the clauses that specify the objectives of the DCFTAs' "Transparency" chapters already manifest the complex interplay of several rule of law standards (i.e. predictability of the environment for doing business, transparency and proportionality) under the umbrella of a broader legal certainty framework.

2. Rule of law standards in the "transparency" chapters of the DCFTAs

Before we proceed with the analysis of substantive rule of law requirements contained in further clauses under the "Transparency" chapters, two crucial remarks are to be made. The first concerns the scope of application of the respective rule of law requirements and stakeholders that are expected to benefit from them. For the purposes of "Transparency" chapters, the "measures of general application" refer to general and abstract acts (e.g. laws, regulations, judicial decisions) that can impact any issue, covered by the DCFTA.[25] Given the broad scope of the DCFTAs, the "Transparency" chapters are likely to create benefits for both the EU's and domestic businesses. Second, an insight into the rule of law dimension of the DCFTAs' "Transparency" chapters would not be complete without an insight into the scope of the concepts of "regulatory quality" and "good administrative behaviour", referred to by the DCFTAs.[26]

Logically, the DCFTAs' "Transparency" chapters incorporate requirements as to transparency *stricto sensu*. Such requirements are, foremost, channelled through the referrals to the WTO law, such as Art. X GATT "Publication and Administration of Trade Regulations".[27] Art. X GATT contains several types of the transparency requirements. First, Art. X:1 GATT obliges contracting parties to promptly publish laws, regulations, judicial decisions and administrative rulings of general application (e.g. as to the classification or valuation of products for customs purposes), as well as the agreements affecting international trade policy, "in such a manner as to enable governments and traders to become acquainted with them". Moreover, Art. X:3a GATT provides for the uniform, impartial and reasonable administration the "measures of general application". Art. X:3 also goes beyond the requirement of transparency *stricto sensu* to include the due process dimension. In particular, it requires the

---

25 See, for instance, EU-Ukraine AA, Art. 281(1).
26 See EU-Ukraine AA, Art.287; EU-Moldova AA, Art.361; EU-Georgia AA, Art.225.
27 General Agreement on Tariffs and Trade of October 30 1947, 61 Stat. A-11, 55 U.N.T.S.194 (hereinafter referred to as "GATT"), Art. X.

EU rule of law: the "regulation" dimension   77

contracting parties to maintain or institute as soon as practicable judicial, arbitral or administrative tribunals and procedures "for the purpose, inter alia, of the prompt review and correction of administrative action relating to customs matters".[28] Alongside the GATT, the transparency requirements are contained in the WTO TBT, GATS, and TRIPS agreements, referred to in the chapters on the diminution of barriers to trade, establishment and trade in services and the IP rights protection, respectively. Besides the recourse to international trade law, the DCFTAs' chapters in question contain their own norms as to the publication of the measures of general application, the establishment of contact points, the mechanisms for dealing with enquiries and the administration of the respective measures of general application.

In turn, the requirements regarding transparency *stricto sensu* intersect with the ones of the **foreseeability or predictability of regulations**. First, to comply with the publication requirements, "each party shall ensure that measures of general application allow for sufficient time between the publication and the entry into force of such measure except where this is not possible because of an emergency".[29] Second, the predictability of the regulatory environment is supported by the requirements of objectivity, impartiality and reasonability that the DCFTAs stipulate with respect to the administration of the measures of general application.[30] Third, the predictability of the business environment is ensured via the provisions that oblige the parties to "establish appropriate mechanisms for responding to enquiries from any interested person regarding any measures of general application which are proposed or in force",[31] although the answers to such enquiries are not legally binding.

Next, the chapters under study touch upon the **equality and non-discrimination** dimension of the rule of law. For instance, the publication requirements under the AAs, explicitly refer to the non-discriminatory manner in which the measures of general application shall be published. Furthermore, as opposed to the DCFTAs with Moldova and Georgia, the EU-Ukraine AA specifies the principle of non-discrimination, according to which "each party shall apply to the other party transparency standards no less favourable than those accorded to its own interested persons".[32] Within the context of the DCFTAs' "Transparency" chapters, the principle of non-discrimination is inextricably linked to providing stakeholders with the legal pathways to participate in the discussion of the proposed measures of general application and ensure that the respective persons have enough time to realize such opportunities.[33]

Next, in line with the previously mentioned WTO transparency requirements, the DCFTAs provide for **individual rights, directed to ensuring the due**

---

28 *Ibid.*, Art. X:3.
29 EU-Ukraine AA, Art. 283(1)(c); EU-Moldova AA, Art.357(1)(c); EU-Georgia AA, Art.221(1)(c).
30 EU-Ukraine AA, Art.285; EU-Moldova AA, Art.359; EU-Georgia AA, Art.223(1).
31 EU-Ukraine AA, Art.284(1); EU-Moldova AA, Art.358(1); EU-Georgia AA, Art.222(1).
32 EU-Ukraine AA, Art.288.
33 EU-Ukraine AA, Art.283; EU-Moldova AA, Art.357; EU-Georgia AA, Art.221.

78 *EU rule of law: the "regulation" dimension*

process. Foremost, as illustrated by the EU-Ukraine AA, in case of an administrative proceeding, a party shall "endeavour to provide interested persons of the other party that are directly affected by a proceeding and in accordance with the party's procedures, with reasonable notice when a proceeding is initiated".[34] Such a description shall stipulate the nature of the proceeding, the legal basis for the proceeding and the description of controversial issues at stake. Notably, while Art. 285 of the EU-Ukraine AA, as quoted previously, obliges the parties to notify solely the interested persons of *another party*, relevant provisions of the DCFTAs with Moldova and Georgia refer to all interested persons with no regard to the jurisdiction of their operation. Furthermore, as a general rule, interested persons shall be afforded "a reasonable opportunity to present facts and arguments in support of their positions prior to any final administrative action".[35] In terms of the provisions on review and appeal, the parties to the proceedings shall be granted "a reasonable opportunity to support or defend their respective positions".[36] **Due process** is also ensured by a party's right "to the decision based on the evidence or submissions of record, or where required by the party's law, the record, compiled by the administrative authority".[37]

Furthermore, the DCFTAs "Transparency" chapters directly refer to the **principles of independence and impartiality** of the judiciary. For instance, according to the EU-Moldova DCFTA, each party is obliged to "establish or maintain judicial, arbitral or administrative tribunals or procedures for the purpose of the prompt review and, where warranted, the correction of administrative action relating to matters covered by [Title V] (Trade and Trade-related Matters) of this Agreement".[38] Since these broadly formulated obligations do not specifically refer to the physical or legal persons from the other party, they are beyond the doubt directed to promoting the rule of law domestically. Though such broad provisions as to judicial independence and impartiality are conventional for the EU agreement with developed democracies, their implementation is highly likely to constitute a challenge in the context of the DCFTAs (Van der Loo, 2016, p. 310).

As previously noted, analysis of the rule of law dimension of the DCFTAs' "Transparency" chapters would hardly be complete without referring to the concepts of **"regulatory quality"** and **"good administrative behaviour"**. The DCFTAs' "Transparency" chapters stipulate the parties' obligation to "cooperate in promoting regulatory quality and performance".[39] Based on the analysis of numerous definitions of regulatory quality, Di Donato (2015) suggests addressing it as a "meta policy, whose fundamental goal is to establish the environment favourable to stakeholders" (p. 3). As can be seen from this definition, the

---

34 EU-Ukraine AA, Art.285.

35 EU-Ukraine AA, Art.285; EU-Moldova AA, Art. 359; EU-Georgia AA, Art.223.

36 EU-Ukraine AA, Art.286(2)(a); EU-Moldova AA, Art.360(2)(a); EU-Georgia AA, Art.224(2)(a).

37 EU-Ukraine AA, Art.286(2)(b); EU-Moldova AA, Art.360(2)(b); EU-Georgia AA, Art.224(2)(b).

38 EU-Moldova AA, Art.360(1).

39 See EU-Ukraine AA, Art.287; EU-Moldova AA, Art.361; EU-Georgia AA, Art.225.

objective of the regulatory quality is close to the ones the literature attributes to the rule of law and legal certainty in the context of international trade norms. In contrast, the World Bank's "Doing Business" Report links the regulatory quality not to the properties of the legal system as a whole but the regulations and procedures that immediately shape the operation of SMEs (The World Bank, 2020). The criteria encompassed by the Report include, for instance, "procedures, time, cost and paid-in minimum capital to start a business", "procedures, time and cost to transfer a property" and the legal pathways related to the protection of minority shareholders. Moreover, it builds a bridge between the regulatory quality and the quality of the judicial process, in general, and the time and cost of resolving a commercial process, in particular. Subsequently, the Report's approach to regulatory quality is close to the understanding of the rule of law, contained in the "augmented" Washington Consensus, repeatedly referred to in terms of this study (The World Bank, 2020; Rodrik, 2006). Marked by this elusive nature, the concept of regulatory quality integrates selected precepts of the rule of law concept (e.g. legality, legal certainty) and their manifestations within the particular sectors. Such sector-specific emphasis and the non-inclusion of specific rule of law components (e.g. the relationship between international and domestic law) prevents one from equating regulatory quality to the rule of law.

Next, the DCFTAs oblige the parties to observe the principle of good administrative behaviour, as expressed by the CoE Recommendation of the Committee of Ministers to Member States on good administration (Council of Europe Committee of Ministers, 2007). The Preamble to the Recommendation emphasizes the role public authorities play in democratic societies, in particular by affecting the rights and interests of individuals, and recommends the governments of the CoE Members to "promote good administration within the framework of the principles of the rule of law and democracy" (*Ibid.*). Simultaneously, the substance of the soft-law–driven notion of good administrative behaviour refers to numerous components of the rule of law. It encompasses, *inter alia*, the principle of lawfulness ("compliance with domestic law, international law and the general principles of law, governing their organization, functioning and activities"), legal certainty, impartiality (objectivity and non-biased manner), equality before the law and proportionality (*Ibid.*). Along with the principles of good administration, the Recommendation provides for individual rights in administrative proceedings, such as the right to be heard with regard to individual decisions and the right to be involved in certain non-regulatory decisions (*Ibid.*). An emphasis on the public administration context and the non-inclusion of specific rule of law components (e.g. judicial independence, the relationship between domestic and international law) allow for distinguishing between the concepts of good administrative behaviour and the rule of law.

In sum, the "Transparency" chapters under the DCFTAs contain numerous substantive rule of law requirements, going far beyond transparency *stricto sensu*. The instruments the "Transparency" chapters under the DCFTAs use to promote the rule of law are, however, rather limited, and include the imposition of basic standards and the referral to the parties' commitments under international law.

80 *EU rule of law: the "regulation" dimension*

Part 3. The rule of law promotion through administrative cooperation

This part of Chapter 4 explores the EU's external rule of law promotion within the domains of administrative cooperation and customs and trade facilitation.

1. The foundations and scope of the European Administrative Space and EU administrative cooperation with third states

In EU law, the concept of administrative cooperation embraces two dimensions. Internally, the Union is marked by the functioning of the European Administrative Space (EAS), wherein "increasingly integrated administrations jointly exercise powers, delegated to the EU in a system of shared sovereignty" (Hofmann, 2008, p. 663). Hence, the major reason behind the launch of the EAS has been the deepening EU integration and, subsequently, the growing interdependence between the Member States' public administrations (Heidberger, 2011). The legal basis for the administrative cooperation between the EU Member States is constituted by Art. 197 TFEU that, *inter alia*, stresses the importance of such cooperation for the implementation of EU law.

After almost seven decades of European integration, the EAS can be referred to as a *"harmonized synthesis of values"*, shaped by EU institutions and Member States' administrations (Torma, 2011, p. 149). Although the concept of the EAS is to a considerable extent of a metaphoric nature, the experience of the 2004 Enlargement demonstrates that joining the EU presupposes the approximation to the features of the EAS. Such features are marked by the strong linkage to fundamental values (Torma, 2011; Todorova, 2019). They encompass, *inter alia*, political stability and enforcement of the democratic rule of law, increased roles of national administrations, transparency and the democratic nature of the administration, multilevel enforcement of the principles of "European" and "good governance", and the harmonization of procedural systems.

The foundational value of these principles for the EAS determines their validity for EU external administrative cooperation. The legal basis for such cooperation may be constituted by the RTAs between the EU and a third state (e.g. EU-Kosovo SAA, the EU-Ukraine DCFTA) and/or the specific Customs Cooperation and Mutual Administrative Assistance Agreements (e.g. Agreement between the EC and Canada on Customs Cooperation and Mutual Assistance in Customs Matters). The scope of respective provisions conventionally includes the simplification and harmonization of customs procedures, based on WTO or WCO standards, and the exchange of personnel, as well as mutual assistance, exchange of information and institutionalization of customs cooperation. In this vein, it is of particular interest to explore the RTAs' provisions on customs and trade facilitation that ensure the implementation of a barrier-free market access.

In this view, the analysis will proceed with exploring substantive rule of law requirements pertaining to: (i) administrative cooperation *stricto sensu*; (ii) Customs Cooperation and Mutual Assistance Protocols and (iii) cooperation in the field of customs and trade facilitation (as provided for by the DCFTAs).

2. *Administrative cooperation* stricto sensu

The administrative cooperation provisions under the EU value-promoting RTAs can be linked to the rule of law concept in several ways. Most broadly, the exercise of administrative cooperation *stricto sensu* requires the third state's adherence to the EAS principles (that stem from the Union's fundamental values) (Todorova, 2019). In turn, a party's failure to provide administrative cooperation and/or report the customs-related irregularity or fraud can result in the temporary suspension of the preferential treatment.[40] For the purposes of administrative cooperation in a narrow sense, "customs irregularities or fraud" usually concern the deviations from the legality principle (e.g. authorities' failure to verify the originating status of a product or the miscommunication of the results of such verification).[41] The common formulations of breaches in the administrative cooperation domain testify to the RTAs' ambition to strengthen the transparency dimension of the customs' functioning in third states (e.g. "a repeated refusal or undue delay in carrying out/communicating the results of the subsequent verification of the proof of origin", as stipulated by Art. 37[3] of the EU-Ukraine AA). However, in contrast to the "Transparency" chapters of the EU DCFTAs with "associated" Neighbours, the **legality** and **transparency** principles, protected in terms of the administrative cooperation *stricto sensu*, do not go beyond the narrowly defined cooperation domain. Although customs cooperation falls under the scope of the WTO and WCO law, relevant RTA chapters do not contain references to international law norms. This also distinguishes the chapters on administrative cooperation *stricto sensu* from the DCFTA "Transparency" provisions.

Ultimately, the RTA provisions on administrative cooperation *stricto sensu* are, *inter alia*, aimed at promoting the compliance of the customs administrations of EU partner states with particular rule of law standards such as **legality** and **transparency**. The legal instruments used to promote compliance include the sanctions mechanism and consultations with the relevant association bodies, such as the Stabilization and Association Council (EU's SAAs with Western Balkans) or the Trade Committee (EU's DCFTAs with Eastern Neighbours).[42]

3. *Customs Cooperation and Mutual Administrative Assistance Agreements/Protocols*

The EU Customs Cooperation and Mutual Administrative Assistance Agreements usually exist as Protocols to the RTAs.[43] Particular Customs Cooperation and Mutual Administrative Assistance Agreements/Protocols reaffirm the parties' commitment to fundamental values (e.g. the EU-Kosovo SAA, the EU-Ukraine AA), while the Euro-Mediterranean AAs directly proceed with cooperation

---

40 EU-Kosovo SAA, Art.48(4); EU-Ukraine AA, Art.37.

41 *Ibid.*

42 E.g. EU-Kosovo SAA, Art.48(4); EU-Albania SAA, Art. 43(4); EU-Ukraine AA, Art.37(4).

43 For the major characteristics and the list of the EU Agreements on Mutual Administrative Assistance in Customs Matters, please visit https://ec.europa.eu/anti-fraud/about-us/legal-framework/customs_matters_en.

82 *EU rule of law: the "regulation" dimension*

clauses.[44] Despite referring to the promotion of the "gradual rapprochement between the parties based on common values and privileged links"[45], the Agreements/ Protocols between the EU and Western Balkans and Eastern Neighbours are marked with the narrow, customs-specific scope.

The Agreements/Protocols put an emphasis on **legality** in the domain of customs' functioning, aiming to "ensure the correct application of the customs legislation, in particular by preventing, investigating the breaches and combating breaches of such legislation".[46] They target an indefinite range of competent authorities in the customs-related domain, though not referring to the legal consequences of the failure of the parties' authorities to provide the requested information or engage in other forms of cooperation.[47] The **transparency** of the authorities' activities in cooperation terms is ensured through the requirements regarding the delivery of necessary documents and notifications of decisions.[48]

The Agreements/Protocols in question do not create the obligations for the parties to adhere to particular international law norms. However, they still touch upon the issue of **the relationship between international and domestic law** by stipulating the exceptions to the obligation to provide assistance.[49] For instance, the assistance can be refused if it is likely to prejudice the sovereignty of either party or is likely to prejudice public policy, security or other essential interests of the parties (especially with respect to the Justice and Home Affairs domain).[50]

To sum up, since strict observance of customs legislation constitutes both the foundation for an objective of customs cooperation and mutual administrative assistance, the cooperation-related provisions contain the **legality** and **transparency** dimensions of the rule of law. Moreover, the Agreements/Protocols touch upon the **relationship between international and domestic law**.

4. *Cooperation in the field of customs and trade facilitation*

Alongside the conventional provisions regarding administrative cooperation *stricto sensu*, the EU DCFTAs with Eastern Neighbours include "Customs and Trade Facilitation" chapters.[51] According to the WTO definition, trade facilitation refers to the "simplification, modernization and harmonization of export and

---

44 EU-Kosovo SAA, Art.1, Art.104, Protocol IV on Mutual Administrative Assistance in Customs Matters; EU-Ukraine AA, Art.1, Art.81, Protocol II on Mutual Administrative Assistance in Customs Matters; EU-Egypt AA, Art.51–57, Protocol 5 on Mutual Assistance between Administrative Authorities in Customs Matters.

45 See, for instance, EU-Ukraine AA, Art. 1(2)(a).

46 EU-Moldova AA, Protocol No III on Mutual Assistance between Administrative Authorities in Customs Matters, Art.2(1).

47 *Ibid.*

48 *Ibid.*, Art.5, Art.8.

49 *Ibid.*, Art.7(1).

50 *Ibid.*

51 EU-Ukraine AA, Part IV, Chapter 5; EU-Moldova AA, Part IV, Chapter 5; EU-Georgia AA, Part IV, Chapter 5.

import processes" (WTO, 2017). Thus, the concept of "trade facilitation" is much broader than "administrative cooperation" and is applicable to a variety of institutions, engaged into the import and export processes.

"Legitimate trade"

According to the DCFTAs, the "Customs and Trade Facilitation" chapters shall aim to "fulfil the objectives of effective control and support facilitation of legitimate trade, as a matter of principle".[52] In this regard, the concept of *"legitimate trade"* deserves particular attention. Despite being extensively used in the EU DCFTAs with Eastern Neighbours and beyond (e.g. the EU-Vietnam FTA, the proposal for the legal texts of the EU-Indonesia FTA) (European Commission, 2017a, 2018),[53] this concept was never defined in either the EU's policy documents or scholarship. Nonetheless, the teleological analysis of the DCFTA "Customs and Trade Facilitation" chapters testifies to the existence of a tight nexus between "legitimate trade" and the rule of law concept. For instance, according to Art. 193(1)(a) of the EU-Moldova AA, the protection and facilitation of "legitimate trade" requires an "effective enforcement of, and compliance with, legislative requirements". Furthermore, such legislative requirements are to meet a range of the rule of law-inspired standards, such as **transparency, non-discrimination** and the **uniform application of legislation**. Besides, trade can be qualified as "legitimate" if it is free from barriers, arising from a party's (or parties') noncompliance with the international antitrust and IP rights protection standards.

Aiming to fulfil the "legitimate trade" objective, the parties to the DCFTAs have paid considerable attention to trade and customs legislation and procedures. The key rule of law standards, stipulated by the DCFTAs in this regard include: (i) **legality** (comprehensiveness of legislation); (ii) **legal certainty** (stability of the legal framework, predictability of the provisions and procedures; the uniform application of laws and regulations); (iii) **authorities' impartiality** and (iv) **non-discrimination**.[54] The principle of **non-discrimination** is reaffirmed by the parties' commitments "to avoid unnecessary or discriminatory burdens on economic operators", as well as "to ensure the non-discriminatory administration of requirements and procedures applicable to imports, exports and the good in transit".[55] Moreover, the DCFTA clause stipulating the requirements to customs legislation and procedures, contains a specific reference to the principle of **transparency of customs procedures and practices**.[56] Besides, the relevant DCFTAs' chapters

---

52 EU-Ukraine AA, Art.75–76(1); EU-Moldova AA, Art. 192–193(1); EU-Georgia AA, Art.66–67(1).
53 European Commission (2018), EU-Vietnam Trade and Investment Agreements. [online] Available at: http://trade.ec.europa.eu/doclib/press/index.cfm?id=1437; European Commission (2017/2018) The texts proposed by the EU for the trade deal with Indonesia. [online] Available at: http://trade.ec.europa.eu/doclib/press/index.cfm?id=1620.
54 EU-Ukraine AA, Art.76(1); EU-Moldova AA, Art.193(1); EU-Georgia AA, Art. 67(1).
55 See, for instance, EU-Ukraine AA, Art.76(1)(b)(g).
56 E.g. EU-Ukraine AA, Art.76(1)(d)(h)(m).

84 *EU rule of law: the "regulation" dimension*

stipulate an array of rule of law standards, applicable to the working methods of the customs, namely **non-discrimination, transparency, integrity** and the **accountability** of operations.[57]

Customs legislation and procedures

A noteworthy rule of law dimension is also contained in the DCFTA clauses, specifying the peculiarities of the authorities' relations with the business community. In particular, the parties are required "to provide effective, prompt and non-discriminatory procedures, guaranteeing the right of appeal against customs and other authorities' administrative actions, rulings and decisions, affecting the goods submitted to the citizens".[58] They are also obliged to observe **individuals' rights to an effective remedy and to a fair trial** (Ar. 47 CFR), and the **right to good administration** (Art. 44 CFR). Moreover, building on the "Transparency" chapters, the clauses as to relations with business community extend the **transparency** and **public accountability** requirements to the notices of administrative nature and the mode of cooperation between the economic operators and administrations.[59] Amid the tight links between democracy and participatory practices and the rule of law, the "Customs and Trade Facilitation" chapters grant business community a considerable role in the relations with administrations. First, the parties agree "to ensure that their respective customs and customs-related requirements and procedures continue to meet the legitimate needs of the trading community".[60] Furthermore, the "Customs and Trade Facilitation" chapters promote inclusive decision-making by providing for "timely and regular consultations with trade representatives on legislative proposals and procedures related to customs and trade issues".[61] Similar to the rule of law standards, the norms of relations with business community are directed towards ensuring the law-based nature of trade between the EU and its Neighbours.

International standards

As compared to administrative cooperation regulations, the DCFTA "Customs and Trade Facilitation" chapters are marked by numerous international standards. First, they require the parties to apply a range of international instruments in the field of customs and trade, including those developed by the UN, the WTO and the WCO.[62] As exemplified by the WCO Framework of Standards to Secure and Facilitate Global Trade to be applied by the "associated" Neighbours, such documents may contain multiple rule of law standards. They encompass, amongst

---

57 EU-Ukraine AA, Art.76(2); EU-Moldova AA, Art.193(2); EU-Georgia AA, Art.67(2).

58 EU-Ukraine AA, Art.76(2)(c); EU-Moldova AA, Art.193(2)(c); EU-Georgia AA, Art.67(2)(c).

59 EU EU-Ukraine AA, Art.77(a)(c); EU-Moldova AA, Art.194(a)(c); EU-Georgia AA, Art.68(a)(c).

60 EU-Ukraine AA, Art.77(d) EU-Moldova AA, Art.194(d); EU-Georgia AA, Art.68(d).

61 *Ibid.*

62 EU-Ukraine AA, Art.76(1)(h); EU-Moldova AA, Art.193(1)(h); EU-Georgia AA, Art.67(1)(h).

others, the provision of advance electronic information to business, the design of the **transparency mechanisms**, and the promotion of **integrity** within the customs administration (WCO, 2012). Second, the parties agree to apply the European Commission's Customs Blueprints – a soft-law act, specifying "best practices" in the domain of customs (European Commission DG for Taxation and Customs Union, 2015). In turn, the Blueprints require the application of further international law mechanisms, such as the WTO Agreement on Trade Facilitation (TFA). Similar to previously analyzed Art. X GATT, the TFA contains an array of the transparency standards. They include, *inter alia*, the publication and availability of information (Art.1); and ensuring the information's availability through the Internet (Art. 2); procedures for **appeal** or **review** (Art. 4), as well as "other measures to enhance **impartiality, non-discrimination and transparency**" (Art. 5).[63] Third, the international standards are invoked with regard to fostering the relations between administrations and the business community.[64] Ultimately, an indefinite list of international standards concerns "consultations with a view of establishing, where possible, common positions in international organizations" and the exchange of information between the parties.[65]

Cooperation between customs authorities

In the context of the DCFTAs' "Customs and Trade Facilitation" chapters, an important avenue of the rule of law promotion is constituted by advance customs cooperation between the customs authorities of the Member States and of "associated" Neighbours. Such cooperation clause provides for the application of the 2015 European Commission Customs Blueprints as a benchmarking tool (European Commission DG for Taxation and Customs Union, 2015). Alongside multiple requirements as to the application of **international standards**, the Blueprints promote **legality** through setting requirements of the amendment or repeal of the inconsistent or obsolete legislation, and correcting the legislative gaps. Moreover, the Blueprints underline the need for the clear legal definition of the duties, rights and responsibilities of customs officers, reflecting the Guidelines of the WTO and respecting the decisions of the EctHR, CoE and the UN tool (*Ibid.*). They also require the parties to include the precise definition of the "abuse of powers" in the area of customs and ensure the **proportionality** of sanctions (WCO, 2007). Moreover, the cooperation clauses under the "Customs and Trade Facilitation" chapters are capable of advancing **legal certainty** through the parties' obligation to exchange information on customs legislation and procedures.[66] Besides, **legal certainty** and **integrity** are upheld through the parties' obligation to cooperate

---

63 Protocol amending the Marrakesh Agreement establishing the World Trade Organization, Decision WT/L/940 of 27 November 2014 (emphasis added).

64 For the countries' and regional organizations' Memoranda of Understanding (MoU) with the WCO, please visit: www.wcoomd.org/en/about-us/partners/mou-new.aspx.

65 EU-Ukraine AA, Art.80(e) EU-Moldova AA, Art.197(f); EU-Georgia AA, Art.71(f).

66 EU-Ukraine AA, Art.80 EU-Moldova AA, Art.197; EU-Georgia AA, Art.71.

86 *EU rule of law: the "regulation" dimension*

in the planning and delivery of technical assistance and capacity-building meas-ures.[67] Such cooperation between the EU and its "associated" Neighbours is insti-tutionalized through the authorized bilateral Customs Sub-Committees.[68]

Legislative approximation obligations

Similar to other disciplines, critical for the integration of "associated" Neighbours into the Single Market, the "Customs and Trade Facilitation" chapters provide for their numerous legislative approximation obligations.[69] As exemplified by the Union Customs Code, the legislative approximation obligations promote a broad range of the rule of law standards. Hence, the Union Customs Code is, *inter alia*, directed to offering "greater **legal certainty** and uniformity for businesses", ensuring **transparency** through shifting to the fully electronic environment and protecting the economic operators' **right of appeal**.[70] Notably, as opposed to the "Establishment, Trade in Services and Electronic Commerce" and "Public Pro-curement" chapters, the "Customs and Trade Facilitation" chapters do not link legislative approximation to market access conditionality. In other words, the opening of the Single Market for "associated" Neighbours is formally independ-ent on their progress in the domain of customs cooperation and trade facilitation.

In a nutshell, the DCFTA "Customs Cooperation and Trade Facilitation" chapters promote numerous rule of law standards though an array of channels, such as the imposition of substantive standards, references to international standards, coopera-tion between customs authorities and legislative approximation obligations.

Part 4. The rule of law promotion through "deep" disciplines: the case of public procurement

This part of the analysis will zoom in on the rule of law dimension of the public procurement provisions under the EU RTAs. As compared to Parts 1–3 of this chapter, it will pay stronger attention to the EU's strategies and policies in the previously mentioned fields to capture the dynamics of their evolution. Moreover, it will cover the rule of law standards in selected EU secondary law documents, since partner countries' obligations under the relevant chapters of many RTAs are often limited to legislative approximation.

1. The opening of public procurement markets and the rule of law

According to the European Commission's DG "Growth" (n.d.), a considerable part of public investment is spent via public procurement, accounting for €2 trillion a

---

67 *Ibid.*

68 EU-Ukraine AA, Art.83 EU-Moldova AA, Art.200; EU-Georgia AA, Art.74.

69 EU-Ukraine AA, Art.84 EU-Moldova AA, Art.201; EU-Georgia AA, Art.75.

70 Regulation (EU) No 952/2013 of the European Parliament and the Council of 9 October 2013 lay-ing down the Union Customs Code. OJ L 269 of 10 October 2013 (emphasis added).

EU rule of law: the "regulation" dimension   87

year – 14% of the EU's GDP. Public procurement has also played a leading role in the "Europe 2020 Strategy for Smart, Sustainable and Inclusive Growth" as one of the key market instruments to promote growth.[71] The key directions for the public procurement reform over the period 2014–2020 dealt with: (i) increasing the efficiency of public spending; (ii) facilitation of the SMEs' participation in the public procurement process and (iii) "enabling procurers to make better use of public procurement in support of common societal goals".[72]

These directions of the evolution of the EU public procurement policy are complemented by the 2017 European Commission's Public Procurement Strategy, featuring six EU policy priorities in the public procurement domain.[73] In line with the EU commitment to "common societal goals", the EU's top priority is to "ensure wider uptake of innovative, green and social procurement".[74] This priority is to be achieved via streamlining the criteria of innovativeness and conduciveness to sustainable development into the process of making contract award decisions. Further policy priorities, distinguished by the Commission, include: (i) the professionalization of public buyers; (ii) increasing access to procurement markets for SMEs; (iii) promoting the digital transformation of procurement; (iv) improving transparency, integrity and data and (v) promoting the digital transformation of public procurement.[75] Additionally, the Commission has prioritized **transparency**, **integrity** and **data openness**, including the creation of publicly available registers of contracts. It has also emphasized the evolution of the international public procurement in terms of the plurilateral Agreement on Government Procurement (GPA) and "deep" RTAs. As a general rule, public procurement provisions under the EU RTAs follow the UNCITRAL Model Law and the WTO GPA rules (Woolcock, 2008, p. 4).

The implementation of respective policy priorities and the coverage of respective issues in the RTAs requires a clear and elaborate legal framework. According to the Preamble to the Directive 2014/24/EU, the awarding of contracts by the Member States' authorities or on their behalf shall follow the fundamental principles of the Single Market (i.e. free movement of goods, freedom of establishment and the freedom to provide services) and the principles of equal treatment, non-discrimination, mutual recognition and transparency.[76] As stems from our previous insight into the scope of the EU concept of the rule of law in Chapter 1, these principles are consonant with the components of the umbrella rule of law

71 European Commission, Europe 2020. A Strategy for Smart, Sustainable and Inclusive Growth, COM (2010) 2020 final of 3 March 2010.
72 Directive 2014/24/EU of the European Parliament and of the Council of 26 February 2014 on public procurement and repealing Directive 2004/18/EC, OJL94 of 28 March 2014.
73 European Commission, Communication to the European Parliament, the Council, the European Economic and Social Committee and the Committee of the Regions: Making Public Procurement Work in and for Europe, COM (2017) 572 final of 3 October 2017.
74 *Ibid.*
75 *Ibid.*
76 Directive 2014/24/EU of the European Parliament and of the Council of 26 February 2014 on public procurement and repealing Directive 2004/18/EC, OJL94 of 28 March 2014, Preamble.

88 *EU rule of law: the "regulation" dimension*

principle. Furthermore, the EU's ambition to promote international public procurement in terms of the GPA and "deep" RTAs makes it topical to zoom in on the interplay between the international and domestic law in a partner country and its compliance with its international obligations. Nonetheless, the EU strategies and secondary legislation in question tends not to link public procurement and the rule of law as an umbrella concept. The following analysis of the rule of law standards across the public procurement chapters of the EU value-promoting will demonstrate the relevance of looking at the RTAs' public procurement chapters from the rule of law perspective.

2. SAAs with Western Balkans

Concluded in terms of the EU Enlargement policy, the SAAs with Western Balkans represent a crucial instrument of these countries' alignment to the EU *acquis* and progressive Single Market integration. For the time being, all the Western Balkans countries except Kosovo were granted a free trade area with the Union after the respective transitional periods, and are working further on the deepening of economic relations with the EU. Nevertheless, even the most recent SAAs between the EU and Western Balkans (e.g. the EU-Kosovo SAA [2015]) do not include separate chapters regarding "deep" disciplines. Therefore, public procurement and competition regulations are regulated in terms of the titles "Approximation of laws, law enforcement and competition rules".[77] As it can be exemplified by the EU-Albania SAA, the legislative approximation obligations under the SAAs are marked by this dynamic nature so that partner countries are obliged to ensure the compatibility between their future legislation and the *acquis*.[78] Providing for the consistency of the legal system and compliance with the legislation (*inter alia* through the dynamic approximation obligation), the SAA framework legislative approximation norms contribute to the **legality** and **legal certainty** dimensions of the rule of law.

As regards public procurement *per se*, the SAAs recognize "the opening-up of the award of public contracts on the basis of non-discrimination and reciprocity, in particular in the WTO context, to be a desirable objective".[79] Based on this, the SAAs granted companies of the Western Balkan countries access to the EU public procurement market immediately from the date of the respective SAA's entry into force.[80] Candidate countries can, however, benefit from a transitional period (typically up to five years) for conducting respective approximation activities.[81] In this vein, the key sources of the rule of law standards to be transferred to the public procurement legislation of Candidate countries include the WTO's Agreement on Government Procurement (GPA), aimed at the mutual

---

77 See, for instance, EU-Albania SAA, Title VI.
78 *Ibid.*, Art. 70.
79 *Ibid.*, Art.74(4).
80 *Ibid.*, Art.74(2).
81 *Ibid.*, Art.74(3).

EU rule of law: the "regulation" dimension 89

opening of public procurement markets, and the EU's secondary legislation on public procurement.

The GPA

Although all the SAAs refer to the WTO context with regard to the opening of the public procurement market, only Montenegro already joined the GPA, and Albania and Macedonia are presently negotiating their accession (WTO, 2020). Aiming to promote **legal certainty** amid the future market openings, the GPA introduced a range of common definitions of key procurement-related concepts such as "commercial goods and services", "open tendering" and "technical specification" (WTO, 2014). In the **legal certainty** realm, the GPA puts an emphasis on the transparency of public procurement systems. In particular, pursuant to Art. VI(1) GPA, each party is obliged to promptly publish laws, regulations and judicial decisions in the officially designated electronic or paper medium that is widely disseminated and accessible to the public. Art. VII GPA obliges procuring entities to publish notices of intended procurement in specifically designated media, specifying *inter alia* the detailed content of respective notices, as well as "readily accessible" summary notices. Art. XVI GPA provides for the **transparency** of procurement information following the award of contract. Furthermore, Art. VIII GPA contributes to the parties' observance of the **equality** and **non-discrimination** standards through limiting the conditions of participating in procurement to those, "essential to ensure that a supplier has the legal and financial capacities and the commercial and technical abilities to undertake the relevant procurement". The principles of **fairness** and **impartiality** of the procurement process is stipulated in Art. XV GPA. Importantly, Art. XVIII GPA obliges the parties to "provide timely, effective, transparent and non-discriminatory administrative or judicial review", including the **right to appeal**. In sum, the GPA constitutes a crucial legal framework that incorporates numerous rule of law standards in the public procurement domain.

Legislative approximation

Alongside the GPA, a crucial source of the rule of law standards for the Candidate countries is represented by the *acquis communautaire*. EU Directives 2014/24/EU and 2014/23/EU on public procurement and the awarding of concession contracts, respectively, stipulate the principles of **equal treatment, non-discrimination, proportionality, legal certainty** and **transparency,** and numerous mechanisms to implement them.[82] This statement can be exemplified by the provisions of the Directive 2014/24/EU, aimed to ensure equal opportunities of tender participants

---

82 Directive 2014/24/EU of the European Parliament and of the Council of 26 February 2014 on public procurement and repealing Directive 2004/18/EC, OJ L94 of 28 March 2014, Preamble; Directive 2014/23/EU of the European Parliament and of the Council of 26 February 2014 on the award of concession contracts, OJL 94 of 28 March 2014.

90 *EU rule of law: the "regulation" dimension*

and the non-distortion of the competition, such as the norms on preliminary market consultations (Art. 40) and prior involvement of candidates and tenderers (Art. 41). The latter provision stipulates, *inter alia*, the authorities' obligations to communicate information, "exchanged in the context of or resulting from the involvement of the candidate or tenderer in the preparation of the procurement procedure".[83] Naturally, the principles of **equality** and **non-discrimination** lie at the heart of the Directive's provisions as regards the choice of participants and award of contracts (Section 3, Title I, Chapter 1). Art. 25 of the Directive 2014/24/EU prohibits the design of the contract to unduly favour or disadvantage certain economic operators or certain works, supplies or services.

A distinct role in ensuring the observance of **equality** and **non-discrimination** principles belongs to new electronic techniques, such as electronic catalogues, enabling "the organization of information in a manner that is common to all the participating bidders and which lends itself to electronic treatment".[84] In turn, the transparency and **traceability of the decision-making** in public procurement are essential for "ensuring sound procedures, including efficiently fighting corruption and fraud".[85] The fulfillment of these principles is supported via the requirements to publish prior information notices as regards procurements (Art. 48), contract notices (Art. 49) and contract award notices (Art. 51, 53).[86] In Art. 3, the Directive 2014/23/EU stipulates that the contracting authorities and contracting entities "shall act in a transparent and proportionate manner" and ensure the "transparency of the award procedure and of the performance of the contract", especially with respect to balancing transparency and confidentiality requirements (Art. 28 of the Directive 2014/23/EU).

The provisions as to **judicial review** are contained the Council Directive 89/665/EC of 21 December 1989.[87] The Directive obliges the EU Member States to ensure the possibility of the review of contracting authorities' decisions, as rapidly as possible, on the basis of the respective decisions' infringing Community law (and now EU law) or national rules implementing that law. According to the Directive, EU Member States shall extend the **judicial independence** requirement to the administrative bodies, responsible for considering public procurement cases. Additionally, given the limitedness of subjects, capable of submitting a claim under the Directive 89/665/EC, para 122 of the Preamble to the Directive 2014/24/EU grants "citizens, concerned stakeholders, organized or not, and other persons and bodies" an opportunity to indicate the possible violations of the Directive 2014/24/EU, without directly referring to their right to judicial review.[88]

---

83 Directive 2014/24/EU of the European Parliament and of the Council of 26 February 2014 on public procurement and repealing Directive 2004/18/EC, OJL94 of 28 March 2014, Preamble.

84 *Ibid.*

85 *Ibid.*

86 *Ibid.*

87 Council Directive 89/665/EEC of 21 December 1989 on the coordination of the laws, regulations and administrative provisions relating to the application of review procedures to the award of public supply and public works contracts, OJ L 395 of 30 December 1989.

88 Directive 2014/24/EU of the European Parliament and of the Council of 26 February 2014 on public procurement and repealing Directive 2004/18/EC, OJ L94 of 28 March 2014.

EU rule of law: the "regulation" dimension 91

In sum, the liberalization of the Western Balkan counties' public procurement envisages the promotion of numerous rule of law principles, such as **legal certainty**, **equality and non-discrimination**, **transparency**, **the right to judicial review** and the **relationship between domestic and international law** through legislative approximation and the promotion of international standards.

3. DCFTAs with Eastern Neighbours

In contrast to the SAAs, the DCFTAs with "associated" Eastern Neighbours contain distinct "Public Procurement" chapters.[89] According to the DCFTAs, the party shall eventually grant Neighbours' companies "the treatment no less favourable than that accorded to EU Party companies".[90] Therefore, the DCFTAs' "Public Procurement" chapters are regarded as "an unprecedented example of the integration of a non-EEA-Member into the EU Single Market".[91]

Legislative approximation

Similar to the SAAs, legislative approximation represents the key mechanism through which the EU promotes the rule of law in the public procurement domain in the Neighbourhood. In substantive terms, this means the adherence to multiple rule of law standards, such as **legal certainty**, **traceability** and **transparency**, **equality** and **non-discrimination**, **the right to judicial review** and **judicial independence**.[92] In implementation terms, the gradual legislative approximation framework provided for in the DCFTA "Public Procurement" chapters shall be regarded as more ambitious as compared to SAAs for three reasons.

First, the DCFTAs' "Public Procurement" chapters contain their own gradual legislative approximation clause; it provides, *inter alia*, for the development of comprehensive roadmaps to guide the approximation of Neighbours' legislation to *acquis communautaire* in the public procurement domain.[93] Second, the central novelty of the DCFTAs is market access conditionality, immediately linked to legislative approximation. The key reason for introducing market access conditionality into the DCFTA "Public Procurement" chapters deals with the Union being "cautious" to open up its public procurement market "for a third country with a less developed economy and economic capacity than the EEA country" (Van der Loo, 2016, p. 308). Hence, the decision to proceed with the subsequent phase of the market opening shall be based on the assessment of the quality of the adopted legislation and its implementation, conducted by the Association Committee in its

---

89 EU-Ukraine AA, Title IV, Chapter 8; EU-Moldova AA, Title IV, Chapter 8; EU-Georgia AA, Title IV, Chapter 8.

90 E.g. EU-Ukraine AA, Art. 154(3).

91 European Commission, Proposal for a Council Decision on the signing, on behalf of the European Union, and provisional application of the Association Agreement between the European Union and its Member States, of the one part, and Ukraine, of the other part, COM (2013)289 of 15 May 2013.

92 See the previous analysis of the rule of law standards, embedded into the Directive 2014/24/EU of 26 February 2014 and Directive 2014/23/EU, OJL 94 of 28 March 2014.

93 See, for instance, EU-Moldova AA, Art.273.

92 *EU rule of law: the "regulation" dimension*

Trade Configuration.[94] Following the last phase of the gradual approximation, the parties shall consider the complete mutual liberalization of public procurement markets.[95] Third, the quality of the legislative approximation process is reinforced by its dynamic nature and the partner countries' obligation to "take due account" of the CJEU case law and implemented measures adopted by the Commission in terms of the legislative approximation.[96]

Basic standards

In contrast to the SAAs with Western Balkans, the DCFTAs with Eastern Neighbours stipulate in detail basic standards that touch upon various dimensions of the rule of law. Aiming to promote competition and "to allow any interested economic operator to have appropriate access to information regarding the intended procurement", the publication standards contribute to the **equality, non-discrimination, transparency** and **impartiality** standards.[97] Their interconnectedness can be exemplified by Art. 151(5) of the EU-Ukraine AA, stipulating that impartiality shall be "ensured especially by the non-discriminatory description of the subject-matter of the contract, equal access for all economic operators, appropriate time-limits and a transparent and objective approach".

The principles of **transparency** and **non-discrimination** are also emphasized with regard to the cases when the contracting entities are allowed to invite a limited number of applicants to submit an offer or apply the qualification system.[98] Importantly, basic standards require the parties to ensure the transparency of the contract award *per se*, based on the respective tender criteria and applicable procedural rights.[99] Moreover, basic standards under the DCFTA offer "any person, having or having had an interest in obtaining a particular contract and who has been or risks being harmed by an alleged infringement" the right to effective and impartial **judicial review**.[100] With this, the judicial protection clauses under the AAs are inextricably linked to the "Review and Appeal" clauses under the DCFTAs that oblige the parties to establish or maintain courts or other independent tribunals "for the purposes of the prompt review and, where warranted, correction of administrative action in areas covered by this agreement".[101]

Ultimately, the DCFTA "Public Procurement" chapters uphold an array of closely intertwined rule of law standards, such as **equality and non-discrimination, transparency**, authorities' **impartiality** and the **right to judicial review** through basic standards, legislative approximation and market access conditionality clauses.

---

94 *Ibid.*, Art.274.
95 *Ibid.*
96 *Ibid.*, Art.273(2).
97 EU-Ukraine AA, Art.151(1), Art.151(2)(b).
98 *Ibid.*, Art.151(11).
99 *Ibid.*, Art.151(14).
100 *Ibid.*, Art.151(15).
101 *Ibid.*, Art.360(1).

4. EU-CARIFORUM EPA

As it was noted in Chapter 2, the EPAs were to a great extent adopted with a view to increase the flexibility of the EU-ACP relations. Hence, the EU-CARIFORUM EPA is a single EPA that contains an in-detail "Public Procurement" chapter, whose contents follow the voluntary UNCITRAL Model Law and the GPA (Woolcock, 2008, p. 4)

Similar to the SAAs and the DCFTAs, the objectives-related clause of the EU-CARIFORUM EPA links "transparent competitive tendering" to economic development, emphasizing the "special situation of the economies of CARIFORUM states".[102] In this way, the Agreement creates links the EU-CARIFORUM liberalization of public procurement markets and to the partner countries' development-related needs. Such a link is consonant with the GPA's provisions, directed at giving "special consideration to the development, financial and trade needs and circumstances of developing and least developed countries" (WTO, 2014, Art. V). This includes price preference programmes and lingering transitional periods before market liberalization, whose application is, however, conditional on a country's observance of the **transparency** and **non-discrimination** standards. Moreover, the observance of the non-discrimination principle serves as a cornerstone of the facilitation of regional integration – a critical umbrella objective behind the EPAs. At the same time, both the desired economic development and regional integration-related effects of the EPA are being deterred by the fact that the provisions of the public procurement chapter apply solely to the procuring entities, listed in the respective Annex to the EPA and the procurements above the thresholds, established by this Annex.[103]

The central provision as to **transparency** and **non-discrimination** is contained in Art. 168(1) of the EU-CARIFORUM EPA, requiring the parties and signatory states to the EPA to "promptly publish any law, regulation, judicial decision and administrative ruling of general application and procedures, regarding procurement, covered by this Chapter, as well as individual procurement opportunities". The publications are to be made in the appropriate sources, determined by the EPA, and specifically designated electronic media.[104] The provision in question encompasses, *inter alia*, the **legal certainty** dimension that requires the parties to "promptly publish in the same manner" the modifications to these measures of general applications.[105] Moreover, to reinforce the **transparency** and **non-discrimination** standards, Art. 168(2) EPA obliges the parties and signatory states to ensure that their "procuring entities provide for effective dissemination of tendering opportunities", including the set-up and maintenance of an appropriate online facility to meet the above requirements. Furthermore, the principle of **transparency** (also in conjunction with **non-discrimination** and **fairness**) is reflected in the PA's provisions

---

102 EU-CARIFORUM EPA, Art.165.
103 *Ibid.*, Art.167(1).
104 *Ibid.*, Art.168(1).
105 *Ibid.*

94 *EU rule of law: the "regulation" dimension*

on the opening of tenders and awarding of contracts (Art. 176) and the information on contract award (Art.177). In addition, the principles of **transparency** and **non-discrimination** are upheld by the fact that procuring entities are obliged to inform eliminated suppliers about the reasons for the rejection of their tenders and comparative advantages of tenders, submitted by successful suppliers.[106]

The principle of **equality** and **non-discrimination** *per se* is reflected in Art.173 and 174 of the EU-CARIFORUM EPA that concern technical specifications and qualifications of suppliers, respectively. To ensure the equality between eligible suppliers, procuring entities shall be prevented from prescribing technical specifications that "refer to a particular trade mark or trade name, patent, copyright, design or type, specific origin, producer or supplier".[107] Moreover, procuring entities "shall ensure that any conditions and criteria for participating in a public contract award procedure are made known in advance in the notice of intended procurement or tender documents".[108] Such criteria have to be limited to those needed to ensure that a supplier is capable of executing the contract in question, and encompass solely the financial, commercial and technical abilities of a supplier.[109] Subsequently, in view of the **legal certainty**, **equality** and **non-discrimination** standards, a supplier's elimination from the negotiations is only possible in accordance with the evaluation criteria, stipulated in the procurement notice or tender documentation.

A crucial feature of the EU-CARIFORUM EPA "Public Procurement" chapter is constituted by the provisions on "bid challenges", encompassing numerous rule of law standards. Pursuant to Art. 179(1) of the EPA, "the parties and the Signatory CARIFORUM States shall provide **transparent**, timely, **impartial** and effective procedures enabling suppliers to challenge domestic measures implementing this Chapter". In turn, to ensure the appropriate protection of suppliers' rights, each party or signatory state to the EU-CARIFORUM EPA is required to "establish, identify or designate at least one **impartial** administrative or judicial authority", **independent** of procuring entities, to consider respective challenges.[110] There requirements are, however, less profound than the ones under the "Transparency" chapters of the DCFTAs that immediately require "associated" Neighbours to conduct in-depth judicial reforms in line with the independence and impartiality dimensions of the rule of law.

Alongside basic standards, the "Public Procurement" chapter under the EU-CARIFORUM EPA promotes the observance of the rule of law through the cooperation clause. It provides, *inter alia*, for the creation of an online facility, aimed at disseminating information on tendering opportunities and facilitate the companies' awareness about the public procurement process.[111] In contrast to the SAAs

---

106 *Ibid.*, Art.177(2).
107 *Ibid.*, Art.173(5).
108 *Ibid.*, Art.174(1).
109 *Ibid.*, Art.174(3).
110 *Ibid.*, Art.179 (emphasis added).
111 *Ibid.*, Art.182(2)(c).

EU rule of law: the "regulation" dimension 95

and the DCFTAs, respectively, the EU-CARIFORUM EPA neither contains references to the GPA nor the legislative approximation clauses. The lack of direct references to the GPA is "compensated" by the inclusion of detailed basic standards that follow the formulations of the GPA and the voluntary UNCITRAL Model Law. The absence of a legislative approximation clause can be, in turn, explained by the ACP countries' geographical remoteness from the EU and the fact that the EU seeks to promote integration within the region, rather than the partner countries' integration into the Single Market.

Part 5. The rule of law standards in the RTAs' "competition" chapters

The final part of the inquiry will shed light on the promotion of the rule of law dimension of the RTAs' "Competition" chapters that play a critical role in ensuring a third country's genuine barrier-free access to the Single Market.

1. Competition and the rule of law

Competition refers to the rivalry among companies at the marketplace that puts them under continuous pressure to improve the quality of goods and services they provide. The recent era has been marked by the trend to the convergence in the substance, coverage and enforcement of national competition rules (Gerber, 2016). The reasons behind this trend include, *inter alia*, the wide-spread tendency to market liberalization; an emphasis on consumer protection and the strengthening of international cooperation. Given the critical role competition plays in the market economy, competition law reforms and institution-building in this domain represent frequent targets in international development assistance. Such an emphasis on competition laws and policies in the global development agenda is rooted in pronounced political and economic inequalities, peculiar for developing countries, where insiders utilize political power to extract economic rents through limiting newcomers' market entry (Aydin and Büthe, 2016)

Moreover, the appropriate enforcement of competition rules is inextricably linked to the observance of the rule of law standards within the given jurisdiction. For instance, the enforcement of competition rules would be hardly possible under the lack of legal certainty and judicial independence and impartiality. On the other hand, the experience of pre-accession competition law reforms in the Western Balkans illustrates a positive impact the harmonization of national legislation with *acquis communautaire* can exert on the state of the rule of law in a target country, including the quality of enforcement by domestic competition bodies (European Commission, 2017b). Hence, the quality of competition legislation can impact not only financial development and internal economic policies, but the rule of law situation in a state. This is, in turn, crucial for promoting FDI and international trade. The latter determines the fact that, pursuant to the 2015 global estimation, almost 90% of FTAs currently in force contain provisions concerning competition (Laprevote, Frisch and Can, 2015).

96 *EU rule of law: the "regulation" dimension*

Since the EU's shift to the ambitious bilateral trade agenda in 2006, distinct competition chapters with rather detailed provisions have become an essential part of the EU RTAs with third countries.[112] As a general rule, competition clauses aim at preserving the gains of trade liberalization and preventing the strategic enforcement of antitrust rules. However, they can also pursue broader economic development objectives, such as promoting rivalry in the private sector, facilitating the culture of competition and, ultimately, improving consumer welfare (Aydin and Büthe, 2016). In empirical terms, the contributions exploring the attainment of these goals through competition law reforms in various contexts (e.g. Brazil, Korea, Nigeria, Botswana) have touched upon various dimensions of the rule of law, such as **legality, transparency** and **the right to judicial review** (e.g. Stevens, 1995; Kronthaler and Stephan, 2007). Nonetheless, there has been no systematic account of the rule of law component in the competition-related provisions in the EU RTAs with third countries – the lacuna we intend to fill.

2. SAAs with Western Balkans

The norms as to competition are located in the SAA chapters "Competition and other economic provisions". Though considerably less detailed, the SAAs provisions on competition follow the pattern of competition norms, contained in Art. 101–102 TFEU. Hence, the SAAs ban particular forms of behaviour, such as agreements and concerted practices, directed to the "prevention, restriction or distortion of competition" and the abuse of dominant position.[113] In this vein, the observance of **legality** and **legal certainty** standards is ensured by the fact that the SAAs provide for the assessment of respective practices, based on the criteria arising from EU law.[114] This shall also be the case for public undertakings and undertakings to which special and exclusive rights were granted.[115] According to Art. 106 TFEU, such undertakings shall be subject to the rules, contained in the Treaties – in particular, the rules on competition – "in so far the application of such rules does not obstruct the performance, in law or in fact, of the particular tasks, assigned to them". In any case, the key condition is to ensure that the development of trade is not affected to an extent, contradicting the interests of the Union.[116] The application of EU rules to respective cases serves two intertwined objectives: (i) the avoidance of deficiencies and collisions stemming from the adoption of Candidate countries' domestic law and (ii) the creation of a single

---

112 European Commission, Communication to the Council, the European Parliament, the European Economic and Social Committee and the Committee of the Regions: Global Europe, Competing in the World, A Contribution to the EU's Growth and Job Strategy, COM(2006) 567 final of 4 October 2006.

113 Stabilization and Association Agreement between the European Communities and their Member States, of the one part, and the Republic of Serbia, of the other part, OJ L 278 of 18 October 2013 (hereinafter referred to as "EU-Serbia SAA"), Art.71(1).

114 EU-Bosnia SAA, Art.71(2); EU-Serbia SAA, Art.73(2).

115 EU-Bosnia SAA, Art.72; EU-Serbia SAA, Art.74.

116 *Ibid.*

competition law space with Candidate countries and an account of the dynamic nature of competition law enforcement practices in the EU (Penev et al., 2013).

Similar to the SAAs' public procurement provisions, the Agreements oblige Candidate countries to ensure the **independence of authorities**, entrusted with the full application of SAAs' paragraphs related to the prohibited practices of undertakings.[117] In contrast to the public procurement case, the SAAs do not specify Candidate countries' obligations as to ensuring the undertakings' right to judicial review and the independence and impartiality of the responsible judicial or quasi-judicial authorities. There are two possible reasons for such a difference. First, there is no particular EU secondary law act dedicated to the enforcement of competition provisions (on the contrary to the Directive 89/665/EEC on the review procedures in the public procurement domain). Second, given the scale of the EU's support of the rule of law reforms in the Balkans, it could have relied on the positive effects of its unilateral financial and technical assistance (Kmezić, 2018). Alongside the principles of legality, legal certainty and authorities' independence, the SAAs' competition provisions address the **relationship between international and domestic law** by stipulating the absence of conflict between provisions in question and relevant WTO law.[118]

Hence, the EU SAAs with Western Balkans contain virtually identical norms, providing for a significant degree of the partner countries' legislative approximation with the *acquis communautaire*. They refer to **legality**, **legal certainty** and the **relationship between international and domestic law** without, however, addressing the principles of transparency and judicial review. The key avenues, through which the SAAs promote the rule of law standards, include the imposition of basic standards and the obligations regarding the application of Union law (that needs to be distinguished from the legislative approximation obligations).

3. The DCFTAs with "associated" Eastern Neighbours

In contrast to the SAAs, the EU DCFTAs with "associated" Neighbours contain distinct "Competition" chapters. As opposed to the EU-Ukraine DCFTA, the EU DCFTAs with Moldova and Georgia do not provide for the legislative approximation obligations.[119] They contain solely framework norms related to competition that, however, touch upon several dimensions of the rule of law, such as **transparency**, **non-discrimination** and **procedural fairness** (that can be associated with the **procedural dimension of the legality principle**).[120] Given the multiplicity of Ukraine's legislative approximation obligations under the EU-Ukraine AA, it can be distinguished as the most illustrative case of "deep" competition provisions

---

117 See, for instance, EU-Bosnia and Herzegovina SAA, Art.71(3).
118 See, for instance, EU-Bosnia and Herzegovina SAA, Art.71(10). The text of the WTO Agreement on Subsidies and Countervailing Measures is available at: www.wto.org/english/docs_e/legal_e/24-scm.pdf.
119 EU-Moldova AA, Chapter 10; EU-Georgia AA, Chapter 10.
120 See, for instance, EU-Moldova AA, Art.335(3); EU-Georgia AA, Art.204(3).

98   *EU rule of law: the "regulation" dimension*

among the DCFTAs. Pursuant to Art. 254 of the EU-Ukraine AA, "the Parties recognize the importance of free and undistorted competition in their trade relations" and specify a range of practices, inconsistent with the Agreement. Similar to the SAAs, the EU-Ukraine DCFTA defines anticompetitive practices, based on Art.101 and 102 TFEU.[121]

In line with the **legality** principle, the EU-Ukraine DCFTA obliges the EU and Ukraine to maintain competition laws, capable of effectively addressing anticompetitive practices. Furthermore, the DCFTA pays significant attention to the effective enforcement of competition laws, obliging the parties to maintain responsible authorities sufficiently equipped for exercising such enforcement.[122] Among the necessary prerequisites of such enforcement, basic standards under the DCFTA mention legality (**procedural fairness**), **transparency** and **non-discrimination**.[123] Moreover, they emphasize a natural or a legal person's right to be heard and to present evidence within a reasonable time before a competition authority of one of the parties imposes a remedy or sanction.[124] Similar to the basic standards on public procurement under the DCFTAs, the EU-Ukraine DCFTA's norms on competition provide for the **independence of a court or tribunal** that imposes and/or reviews sanctions or remedies against any natural or legal person.[125] In line with the **transparency** standard, the parties are obliged to provide upon request public information concerning enforcement of its competition legislation and adopt and publish a document that explains the principles related to the use of pecuniary sanctions in competition cases and the assessment of horizontal mergers.[126] Unlike the SAAs with Western Balkans, the EU-Ukraine DCFTA provides for partner countries' specific obligations regarding the approximation of their laws and, crucially, the law enforcement practices to the *acquis communautaire*.[127] To acquire an insight into the rule of law dimension of Ukraine legislative approximation under the "Competition" chapter, we will shortly refer to the key relevant EU secondary law act in this domain, starting with the Council Regulation (EC) on the implementation of the rules on competition, laid down in Art. 81–82 of the Treaty (presently Art. 101–102 TFEU).[128]

Aimed at ensuring the uniform application of Art. 101–102 TFEU Union-wide, the Regulation contains numerous manifestations of the **legal certainty** principle, including, *inter alia*, a directly applicable system of exceptions from the prohibition of agreements that distort competition.[129] The uniformity of the national courts' application of EU law is ensured by granting them an opportunity to ask

---

121 EU-Ukraine AA, Art.254.
122 *Ibid.*, Art.255.
123 *Ibid.*, Art.254–257.
124 *Ibid.*, Art.255(3)(a)(b).
125 *Ibid.*, Art.255(3)(b).
126 *Ibid.*, Art.255(6), Art.259–260.
127 *Ibid.*, Art.256.
128 Council Regulation (EC) 1/2003 of 16 December 2002 on the implementation of the rules on competition laid down in Articles 81 and 82 of the Treaty, OJL 1 of 4 January 2003.
129 *Ibid.*, Art.16, para 4 of the Preamble, para 7 of the Preamble.

EU rule of law: the "regulation" dimension 99

the Commission for information or its opinion regarding the application of EU law, and the avoidance of conflicting decisions under the system of parallel powers.[130] Building on that, the Regulation provides for the interplay between Art. 101–102 TFEU, on the one hand, and Member States' national competition laws, on the other hand, and the peculiarities of the Member States' authorities' powers in the competition domain.[131] Moreover, the principles of **legal certainty** and **transparency** pierce the Regulation's norms regarding the exchange of information and cooperation between the Commission and competition authorities of Member States, as well as with national courts.[132]

An emphasis on **legal certainty**, **transparency** and **authorities' independence and impartiality** is also a crucial feature of the EC Merger Regulation.[133] The principle of **legal certainty** is, for instance, referred to with respect to determining the peculiarities of mergers that fall within the scope of Art. 102 TFEU and the Regulation in question; the protection of transactions' validity and the delimitation of competences between the Commission and the national authorities in competition cases.[134] The **transparency** principle guides the relations between the Commission and the national authorities, and is also addressed with respect to the publication of decisions of the Commission and national competition authorities.[135] As opposed to both the Merger Regulation and the Regulation on the agreements between undertakings, the Regulation No 330/210 of 20 April 2010 on the application of Art. 101(3) TFEU to categories of vertical agreements and concerted practices does not refer to either dimensions of the rule of law.[136] Nonetheless, the Regulation doubtlessly contributes to the **legality** and **legal certainty** standards by stipulating the exemptions from the application of Art. 101(1) TFEU to vertical agreements and restrictions concerning the block exemptions benefits.

Furthermore, the "Competition" chapter under the EU-Ukraine DCFTA promotes the observance of the rule of law standards via the provisions as to exchange of information and enforcement cooperation, as well as consultations regarding the matters that may affect trade between the parties.[137] These provisions are of special importance with respect to the **legality** and **legal certainty** principles, since the Agreement urges the parties to exchange information regarding the legislation and enforcement activities and engage in consultations regarding any matter that arises from the application or interpretation of the respective section of the EU-Ukraine AA.[138]

---

130 *Ibid.*, Art.11.
131 *Ibid.*, Art.3.
132 *Ibid.*, Art.12.
133 Council Regulation (EC) No 139/2004 of 20 January 2004 on the control of concentrations between undertakings (the EC Merger Regulation), OJ L 24 of 29 January 2004.
134 *Ibid.*, Art.1, para 34 of the Preamble; Art.21.
135 *Ibid.*, Art.20.
136 European Commission, Regulation No 330/2010 of 20 April 2010 on the application of Art.101(3) TFEU to categories of vertical agreements and concerted practices, OJL 102/1 of 23 April 2010.
137 EU-Ukraine AA, Art.259–260.
138 *Ibid.*

100 *EU rule of law: the "regulation" dimension*

In a nutshell, the DCFTA "Competition" chapters entail numerous dimensions of the rule of law, such as **legal certainty, transparency, non-discrimination** and **the independence and impartiality of the competition authorities**. In contrast to the EU DCFTAs with Moldova and Georgia that contain solely basic standards in the competition domain, the EU-Ukraine DCFTA specifies Ukraine's particular legislative approximation obligations that also necessarily entail the rule of law dimension.

4. EU-CARIFORUM EPA

Although the EPAs were conceived as a framework for the EU's "deep" trade liberalization with the ACP countries, the EU-CARIFORUM EPA is so far a single EPA that contains the "Competition" and "Public Procurement" chapters.

According to Art. 126 of the EU-CARIFORUM EPA, "the Parties recognize the importance of free and undistorted competition in their trade relations". In line with the **legal certainty** principle and similar to the Agreements, addressed previously, the EU-CARIFORUM EPA utilizes the definition of anticompetitive practices as provided for in Art. 101–102 TFEU.[139] Since the EU relations with the ACP countries do not presuppose the partner countries' in-depth integration into the Single Market, the EU-CARIFORUM EPA does not utilize legislative approximation and market access conditionality. Instead, its "Competition" chapter uses basic standards and the parties' obligations as to information exchange and cooperation.

With respect to the **legality** principle, Art. 125(3) of the EU-CARIFORUM EPA specifies the term "competition laws" as applied both to the EU and CARIFORUM countries. Additionally, for the purposes of the fulfillment of the **legality** and **legal certainty** standards, the CARIFORUM states are obliged to inform the EU party about the enactment of further competition laws through the CARIFORUM-EC Trade and Development Committee.[140] Furthermore, the parties to the EU-CARIFORUM EPA and signatories thereto bear an obligation to provide clarifications as to exceptions from the application of the competition legislation.[141] Such an obligation is conducive to **substantive legality**, since the pronounced and uniform rules regarding exceptions and the transparent procedures of their enactment form the necessary part of the legality standard. Moreover, Art. 129 of the EU-CARIFORUM EPA stipulates detailed norms as to the competition rules' applicability to public enterprises and the enterprises, designated with special or exclusive rights. Alongside legality, these rules are directed towards ensuring **equality** between public and private undertakings, as well as **non-discrimination**. Besides, Art. 129(4) contributes to the **relationship between international and domestic law** through obliging the CARIFORUM countries to adjust their domestic legislation to the relevant WTO rules on public enterprises and state

139 EU-CARIFORUM EPA, Art.125.
140 *Ibid.*, Art.123(5)(b).
141 *Ibid.*, Art.127(1).

monopolies. The **transparency** and **accountability** standards are enshrined in Art. 129(5) of the EU-CARIFORUM EPA that provide for the CARIFORUM states' obligation to notify the CARIFORUM-EC Trade and Development Committee about: (i) sectoral rules that condition the non-application of competition legislation to public enterprises and (ii) the progress in adjusting domestic legislation to the relevant WTO rules.

In contrast to the SAAs and the DCFTAs, the EU-CARIFORUM EPA stresses the importance of technical assistance and capacity-building in the attainment of the competition-related objectives.[142] Many of the envisaged assistance forms (e.g. assistance in drafting guidelines, manuals and, when needed, the legislation; Twinning projects) are of high relevance for promoting the observance of legality standard and further dimensions of the rule of law). As compared to previous agreements in question, the EU-CARIFORUM EPA makes a relatively strong emphasis on the **legality** dimension of the rule of law. In instrumental terms, it utilizes the imposition of substantive obligations and basic standards, information exchange, enforcement cooperation and the referral to the WTO obligations to promote the rule of law.

Conclusion

This chapter aimed at exploring the legal mechanisms through which the EU RTAs can promote the rule of law.

Foremost, the analysis revealed a significant variation in the number and degree of detail of the rule of law-related clauses across the value-promoting RTAs under study. In contrast to the EU early AAs with third countries, the latest generation of the EU value-promoting RTAs (e.g. the DCFTAs with Eastern Neighbours) demonstrates a surge in both the rule of law standards and the instruments of promoting them (e.g. market access conditionality). Such a phenomenon can be explained by two factors: (i) a rapid evolution of the EU ambitious bilateral and plurilateral "deep" trade agenda due to the deadlock of the WTO Doha Round and (ii) the DCFTAs' orientation on the integration of "associated" Neighbours into the EU Single Market. Hence, the scope of integration, envisaged by an RTA, constitutes a crucial factor, determining the reach of the rule of law obligations.

With respect to the "essential element" clauses, it was established that, in view of the VCLT, trade liberalization could potentially represent a useful framework for locating the "essential elements" clauses. Nonetheless, the highly politicized and selective nature of the EU's application of the "essential elements" clauses prevents one from considering the "essential element" clauses a legitimate and efficient legal instrument of the rule of law promotion through trade liberalization. Presently, "essential elements" clauses can be rather viewed as a gateway for political dialogue on the observance of fundamental values with non-Member

---

142 *Ibid.*, Art.130(1).

102 *EU rule of law: the "regulation" dimension*

States and, in particular cases, as a legal basis for the suspension of the Union's financial aid to third countries.

The DCFTA "Transparency" chapters, and the provisions regarding administrative cooperation across all the RTAs in question encompass numerous rule of law-related standards. They include legality, legal certainty (e.g. stability of the legal system, predictability of the legal environment for economic operators), the right to judicial review, independence and impartiality of the judiciary and administrative bodies (e.g. public procurement and competition authorities), equality and non-discrimination and the relationship between the domestic and international law (most commonly, the WTO rules). The introduction of basic standards and legislative approximation obligations represent the key avenues through which the value-promoting RTAs promote the rule of law. Amid the Agreements' ambitious market integration objectives, the EU may use market access conditionality as a means to facilitate legislative approximation and, subsequently, the implementation of respective rule of law obligations. Simultaneously, an insight into administrative cooperation chapters across the whole spectrum of the agreements in question and the DCFTAs' "Customs and Trade Facilitation" clauses has demonstrated the importance of cooperation in the external projection of the EU values. This statement can be, *inter alia*, exemplified by the legal certainty and transparency regarding the administrative framework of cooperation and information exchange, as provided for in the DCFTAs with "associated" Eastern Neighbours and the EU-CARIFORUM EPA. Moreover, the RTAs promote the rule of law standards through reaffirming the parties' obligations under the relevant international law acts, such as the TBT and GPA, and referring to "soft" international law rules (e.g. the UNCITRAL Model Law). Pointing to the nexus between the "regulation" and "action" dimensions of value promotion, the EU-CARIFORUM EPA emphasizes technical assistance in the law-making domain and institutions' capacity-building.

Last, but not least, the analysis demonstrated considerable differences in the reach and potential spillover effects among various categories of the rule of law clauses under study. The broadest and allegedly the most far-reaching rule of law clauses have been detected in the "Transparency" chapters of the EU's DCFTAs with Eastern Neighbours, requiring the latter to establish or maintain independent and impartial tribunals for the correction of administrative action in the domains covered by the Agreement. Although such a requirement has been designed to exert a profound impact on the legal system of a country as a whole, its implementation would to a great extent depend on the political will and enforcement capacity of a partner country. As compared to the DCFTAs' "Transparency" chapters, its provisions regarding administrative cooperation and customs cooperation and trade facilitation are marked by a narrower scope of application. Nonetheless, following the neo-functionalist logic, a third country's advanced cooperation with the EU in particular domains, requiring the observance of the rule of standards, can generate spillovers to other cooperation domains. For instance, due to the importance of functioning competition and public procurement rules for

EU rule of law: the "regulation" dimension   103

private sector development, the strengthening of the rule of law standards in these domains can contribute to the improvement of state-business relations and the environment for doing business in target countries. Once again, the depth and sustainability of the respective impact would, to a great extent, depend on both the efforts of target countries and external donors' support. Hence, the EU value-promoting RTAs have a considerable potential to promote the rule of law standards both within strictly distinguished domain and beyond them through spillover effects. The actual effects of the respective norms would, however, be determined by the domestic strategies of value-promoting RTAs' implementation and political will and reforms' design, as well as the design of the EU's unilateral assistance instruments to be considered in Chapter 5.

References

Andersen, H. (2017). WTO anti-dumping jurisprudence and the rule of law challenges. In: P. Rendahl, M. Tjenberg, and H. Wenander, eds., *Festkrift till Christina Modell*. Lund: Juristförlaget I Lund, pp. 11–33.

Aydin, U. and Büthe, T. (2016). Competition law and policy in developing countries: Explaining variations in outcomes: Exploring possibilities and limits. *Law and Contemporary Problems*, 79, pp. 1–36.

Black, J. (2002). Critical reflections on regulation. *Australian Journal of Philosophy*, 27, pp. 1–35.

Cogan, J.K. (2011). The regulatory turn in international law. *Harvard International Law Journal*, 52(2), 322–372.

Council of Europe Committee of Ministers. (2007). *Recommendation CM/Rec (2007)7 to member states on good administration*. [online] Available at: https://rm.coe.int/ 16807096b9.

De Vries, S.A. (2013). Balancing fundamental rights with economic freedoms according to the European court of justice. *Utrecht Law Review*, 9, pp. 169–192.

Di Donato, L. (2015). The regulatory quality in the European Union. *Amministrazione in Cammino*, 12, pp. 1–12.

Dolle, T. (2015). Human rights clauses in EU trade agreements: The new European strategy in free trade agreement negotiations focuses on human rights – Advantages and disadvantages. In: N. Weiß and J.M. Thouvenin, eds., *The influence of human rights on internal law*. London: Routledge, pp. 213–228.

European Commission. (2017a). *The texts proposed by the EU for the trade deal with Indonesia*. [online] Available at: http://trade.ec.europa.eu/doclib/press/index.cfm?id=1620.

European Commission. (2017b). *Competition and the rule of law. Speech at the Romanian competition council anniversary event*. [online] Available at: https://ec.europa.eu/commis sion/commissioners/2014-2019/vestager/announcements/competition-and-rule-law_en.

European Commission. (2018). *EU-Vietnam trade and investment agreements*. [online] Available at: https://ec.europa.eu/trade/policy/in-focus/eu-vietnam-agreement/.

European Commission DG "Growth". (n.d.). *Public procurement*. [online] Available at: https://ec.europa.eu/growth/single-market/public-procurement_en.

European Commission DG for Taxation and Customs Union. (2015). *Customs blueprints. pathways to better customs*. [online] Available at: https://op.europa.eu/en/publication-detail/-/publication/ad5f6272-7687-11e5-86db-01aa75ed71a1.

104   *EU rule of law: the "regulation" dimension*

European Parliament. (2014). *The European parliament's role in relation to human rights in trade and investment agreements.* European Parliament. [pdf] Available at: www.euro parl.europa.eu/RegData/etudes/etudes/join/2014/433751/EXPO-JOIN_ET(2014) 433751_EN.pdf.

European Parliament. (2020). *Legislative train 05.2020.* [online] Available at: www.euro parl.europa.eu/legislative-train/theme-development-deve/file-signature-of-the-new-eu-acp-agreement-(%E2%80%98-post-cotonou-%E2%80%98).

Gerber, D.J. (2016). Global competition law convergence: Potential roles for economics. In: T. Eisenberg and G.B. Ramello, eds., *Comparative law and economics.* Cheltenham: Edward Elgar, pp. 206–235.

Hachez, N. (2015). *"Essential elements" clauses in EU trade agreements making trade work in a way that helps human rights?* Leuven Centre for Global Governance Studies Working Paper 2015/158. [pdf] Available at: https://ghum.kuleuven.be/ggs/publications/ working_papers/2015/158hachez.

Heidberger, E.G. (2011), Structuring the European administrative space: Policy instruments of multi-level administration. *Journal of European Public Policy,* 5, pp. 709–727.

Hofmann, H.C. (2008). Mapping the European administrative space. *West European Politics,* 31(4), pp. 662–676.

Kmezić, M. (2018). EU rule of law conditionality: Democracy or "stabilitocracy" promotion in the Western Balkan. In: J. Džankić, S. Keil, and M. Kmezić, eds., *The Europeanization of the Western Balkans.* Berlin: Springer, pp. 87–109.

Kronthaler, F. and Stephan, J. (2007). Factors accounting for the enactment of a competition law: An empirical analysis. *The Antitrust Bulletin,* 52, pp. 137–168.

Laprevote, F., Frisch, S. and Can, B. (2015). *Strengthening the global trade and investment system for sustainable development.* The E15 Initiative. [pdf] Available at: http://e15initiative.org/wp-content/uploads/2015/07/E15-Competition-Laprevote-Frisch-Can-FINAL.pdf.

Merran, H. (2016). *Economic partnership agreements: Implications for regional governance and EU-ACP development cooperation.* German Development Institute 12/2016. [online] Available at: www.die-gdi.de/en/briefing-paper/article/economic-partnership-agreements-implications-for-regional-governance-and-eu-acp-development-cooperation/.

Moberg, A. (2015). Can the European Union use agreements to even out the global imbalances in the protection of human rights? In: A. Bakardjieva-Engelbrekt, M. Martensson, L. Oxelheim, and T. Persson, eds., *The EU's role in fighting global imbalances.* Cheltenham: Edward Elgar Publishing, pp. 138–164.

OSCE. (2020). *OSCE responds to crisis in and around Ukraine.* OSCE. [pdf] Available at: www.osce.org/files/f/documents/d/6/126167.pdf.

Penev, S., Marušić, A., Milović, N., Čaušević, F. and Hyseni, D. (2013). *Competition policy in Western Balkan countries.* Westminster Foundation for Democracy (WFD). [online] Available at: www.npcbalkan.net/admin/doc/Competition_Policy_in_Western_Balkan_Countries.pdf.

Rodrik, D. (2006). Goodbye, Washington consensus, hello, Washington confusion? A review of the world bank's economic growth in the 1990s: Learning from a decade of reform. *Journal of Economic Literature,* 44(4), pp. 973–987.

Stevens, D. (1995). Framing competition law within an emerging economy: The case of Brazil. *The Antitrust Bulletin,* 40, pp. 929–972.

Todorova, E. (2019). Public administration reform in post-communist countries as a requirement for EU membership: Towards the European administrative space. *Revue de Sciences Politiques,* 63, pp. 22–33.

Torma, A. (2011). The European administrative space. *European Integration Studies*, 9, pp. 149–161.

Van den Bossche, P. and Zdouc, W. (2017). *The law and policy of the world trade organization. Text, cases and materials*, 4th ed. Cambridge: Cambridge University Press.

Van der Loo, G. (2016). *The EU-Ukraine association agreement and deep and comprehensive free trade area.* Leiden: Brill.

Velutti, S. (2016). The promotion and integration of human rights in EU external trade relations. *Utrecht Journal of International and European Law*, 32, pp. 41–68.

WCO. (2007). *Compendium of integrity. Best practices.* [online] Available at: www.wcoomd. org/en/topics/integrity/~/media/F8980A7CB73A4F2E80A137967AF75CA8.ashx.

WCO. (2012). *SAFE framework of standards to secure and facilitate global trade.* [online] Available at: www.wcoomd.org/en/topics/facilitation/instrument-and-tools/tools/~/media/55F00628A9F94827B58ECA90C0F84F7F.ashx.

Woolcock, S. (2008). *Public procurement and the economic partnership agreements: Assessing the potential impact on ACP procurement policies.* London School of Economics Working Paper. London School of Economics. [Online] Available at: www.lse.ac.uk/internationalrelations/centresandunits/itpu/docs/woolcockpublicprocurement.pdf.

The World Bank. (2020). *Doing business report 2020. Comparing business regulation in 190 economies.* The World Bank. [pdf] Available at: http://documents.worldbank.org/curated/en/688761571934946384/pdf/Doing-Business-2020-Comparing-Business-Regulation-in-190-Economies.pdf.

WTO. (2014). *Revised agreement on government procurement.* [online]Available at: www.wto.org/english/docs_e/legal_e/rev-gpr-94_01_e.htm.

WTO. (2017). *Trade facilitation.* [online] Available at: www.wto.org/english/tratop_e/tradfa_e/tradfa_e.htm.

WTO. (2020). *Agreement on government procurement. Parties, observers and accessions.* [online]. Available at: www.wto.org/english/tratop_e/gproc_e/memobs_e.htm.

5 EU rule of law promotion through RTAs in third states

The "action" dimension

As highlighted previously, this book juxtaposes the "regulation" and "action" dimensions of the EU rule of law promotion through trade liberalization. As compared to "regulation", immediately exercised through the RTA rules, the term "action" refers to the EU's unilateral application of rule of law promotion instruments. Hence, "action" usually takes place outside the scope of the contractual relations between the EU and a partner country and, thus, may lack the legal basis for a partner country's rule of law obligations.

In EU Studies scholarship, there have been numerous attempts to explore the mechanisms and impact of the EU's external value-promotion. However, only a few authors offered a comprehensive mapping of policy and legal instruments the EU utilizes to project values beyond its borders. Based on their insight into the EU's external democratization and human rights promotion, Keukeleire and Delreux (2014) conditionally distinguished four sets of relevant instruments (toolboxes). The first set encompasses the instruments of the EU Common Foreign and Security Policy (CFSP), such as the CFSP statements and declarations,[1] decisions under the CFSP (e.g. leading to the application of sanctions), human rights guidelines[2] and bilaterally or multilaterally adopted "soft" documents, such as summit declarations. The second group features political framework agreements (mostly, the AAs) and related geographical development cooperation instruments (e.g. the European Development Fund [EDF]). Third, the EU promotes democracy and human rights through thematic instruments, such as the European Instrument for Democracy and Human Rights (EIDHR). Finally, Keukeleire and Delreux (2014), as well as Cardwell (2011), emphasize the role of internal policies with the external dimension (e.g. fight against the trafficking in human beings). A less comprehensive yet practical mapping of the EU external rule of law promotion was suggested by Pech (2012/2013). In his mapping, Pech (2012/2013) uses three categories:

---

1 Statements and declarations involve the declarations of the High Representative on behalf of the EU (agreed with all Member States of the EU); statements on the own behalf of the High Representative, as well as the statements by the spokesperson of the High Representative and local EU statements.

2 EU human rights guidelines represent non-binding pragmatic instruments of the EU Human Rights Policy, highlighting the Union's priorities in the field of human rights.

EU rule of law: the "action" dimension 107

- "Soft" (diplomatic) instruments (e.g. conclusions, resolutions and public declarations).
- Unilateral trade, financial and technical assistance instruments.
- Bilateral instruments (e.g. the AAs).

This chapter will utilize the components of both mappings, adapting them to the design of this study. First, we will accommodate the "regulation"–"action" dichotomy by not bringing together bilateral agreements and the unilateral development cooperation instruments (toolbox 2, according to Keukeleire and Delreux [2014]). At the same time, we will use a broad category of "unilateral trade, financial and technical assistance instruments", suggested by Pech (2012/2013) and apply it to policy contexts in question (i.e. the EU Enlargement, Neighbourhood and Development policies). It is also suggested to consider the institutional architecture of the EU rule of law promotion in third countries, paying particular attention to the scope of their mandates. Nevertheless, since the external dimension of the EU's internal policies does not necessarily deal with the EU's intentional projection of fundamental values, the analysis will solely focus on external policies, specifically designed to promote values. In sum, the types of the EU's "action" instruments to be considered in this chapter are as shown in Table 5.1.

Part 1. Enlargement

The EU state-building engagement in the Balkans is rooted in the Stability Pact for South-Eastern Europe that gave rise to the Stabilization and Association Process (SAP), provided for in the "Promotion of Free Trade Agreements" working table (European Commission, 1999). Alongside the conclusion of the SAAs with Western Balkans, the SAP covered the application of the EU autonomous trade measures, financial and technical assistance and the stabilization-specific measures. The Final Declaration of the 2000 EU-Western Balkans Zagreb Summit welcomed opened up the way for regional reconciliation and cooperation, emphasizing the impetus given to the policy of the "new neighbourliness", and the launch of the SAP as a means to implement the accession perspective for the

Table 5.1 EU "Action" Instruments

"Soft" diplomatic instruments	Unilateral trade, financial and technical assistance instruments	EU rule of law promotion missions and projects on the spot
Decisions, declarations, bilateral and multilateral summit declarations	– Those immediately supporting the implementation of value-promoting RTAs – Other unilateral trade, financial and technical assistance instruments	e.g. EULEX in Kosovo

108 *EU rule of law: the "action" dimension*

Western Balkans.[3] Since that time, the application of unilateral trade, financial and technical assistance instruments constitutes a crucial pillar of the EU's policy *vis-à-vis* Western Balkans, including the rule of law promotion.

1. *"Soft" documents*

The rule of law has been repeatedly emphasized as a priority in the EU-Western Balkans relations, both on multilateral and bilateral levels. In particular, it has been seen as both a driver and a desired outcome of Western Balkans' Europeanization, i.e. a politically driven top-down process through which EU norms, policy-making processes and institutions impact norms, policy-making processes, institutions and the formation of collective identity beyond EU borders (Anastasakis, 2005; Džankić, Keil and Kmezić, 2019). Most recently, the attention to the rule of law in the EU-Western Balkans relations was reinforced by the EU's experiences of dealing with the rule of law crises in Poland and Hungary (Kochenov and Bárd, 2018) and the rule of law backsliding in the Western Balkans *per se* (Kmezić, 2019). As it will be demonstrated further, complex dynamics of domestic change in the Western Balkans and the EU policy learning has determined a variety of connotations and emphases related to the rule of law in the diplomatic documents in question. Although the nexus between the rule of law and economic development has become stronger over the history of the EU-Western Balkans diplomatic relations, the "soft" documents in question barely ever construed bridges between the rule of law and trade liberalization cooperation priorities.

Early "soft" documents (2005–2008)

Due to the legacy of the Yugoslav Wars, early programmatic documents of the pre-accession process tended to link the promotion of fundamental values, including the rule of law to the objectives of peace, stability (stabilization) and "building fully functioning states" (European Commission, 2003a, p. 15). In the latter context, the 2003 Thessaloniki Agenda viewed the rule of law reform as an essential task alongside countering corruption, organized crime and illegal migration (European Commission, 2003b). The 2006 Commission's Communication, aimed to reflect on the EU's stabilization efforts in the Western Balkans and consolidate the way forward, similarly addressed the rule of law in the context of the fight against corruption and organized crime.[4] Affirming the EU's "full support for the European perspective of the Western Balkans", the 2008 Council Presidency Conclusions did not immediately mention the rule of law, yet referring to the fight against corruption, the consolidation of institutions and judicial reform.[5]

---

3 The Final Declaration of Zagreb Summit, 24 November 2000. [online] Available at: www.con silium.europa.eu/ueDocs/cms_Data/docs/pressdata/en/er/Declang4.doc.html.

4 European Commission, Communication: The Western Balkans on the Road to the EU: Consolidating Stability and Raising prosperity, COM(2006) 27 final of 27 January 2006.

5 Council of the European Union, Presidency Conclusions, 11018/1/08 REV1 of 17 July 2008, p. 14.

EU rule of law: the "action" dimension 109

Although the whole spectrum of these "soft" documents contain separate parts related to EU-Western Balkans economic cooperation and trade, the linkages between the rule of law, of the one part, and economic cooperation or trade liberalization, of the other part, remained highly limited. For instance, the 2003 Thessaloniki Agenda referred to promoting the principles of **transparency** and **accountability** in the public sector as a prerequisite for undertaking structural reforms and the reforms in the domain of tax administration and policy (European Commission, 2003b). These rule of law standards, and the notion of "good governance" were also addressed in the context of the financial sector reform and fostering the environment, conducive to business development (*Ibid.*). Notably, the Thessaloniki Agenda provided for numerous avenues to facilitate trade between the EU and Western Balkans in terms of the SAP (e.g. technical assistance, the extension of pan-European diagonal cumulation of origin). It did not, however, refer to either of the "deep disciplines" (e.g. public procurement, competition) or the rule of law standards to be advanced. As compared to the Thessaloniki Agenda, the 2006 Commission's Communication "The Western Balkans on the Road to the EU" demonstrated stronger awareness about the "added value" of SAAs as a framework for the "alignment on the main non-trade-related aspects of the acquis, especially on the customs, industrial, sanitary, phytosanitary and veterinary standards" and strengthening the Candidate countries' administrative capacity.[6]

The Berlin Process

As highlighted in the Europeanization scholarship, the period from 2008–2014 was marked by a relative "diplomatic silence" in EU-Balkans relations (Börzel, 2011) The key challenges the EU had been facing over this period included the differential impact of the EU conditionality, lacking institutional capacities in the partner countries and the sustaining legacies of inter-ethnic conflicts (Börzel, 2011; Noutcheva, 2009; Anastasakis, 2008). Aiming to tackle these challenges, German Chancellor Angela Merkel launched the 2014 Conference on the Western Balkan States. Pursuant to the Berlin Conference Declaration, the parties agreed that the years 2014–2018 would be "four years of real progress" in political and economic reforms, reconciliation and the facilitation of regional cooperation.[7] In contrast to earlier "soft" documents, the Berlin Process declarations were marked by a stronger nexus between the rule of law and economic development. Hence, both the 2015 Vienna and the 2017 Trieste Declarations addressed the **rule of law as a prerequisite for economic development** ("building a sound economic fabric"*).* According to the 2017 Trieste Declaration, the key junctures between the

---

6 European Commission, Communication: The Western Balkans on the Road to the EU: Consolidating Stability and Raising prosperity, COM(2006) 27 final of 27 January 2006.

7 Conference on the Western Balkans, Final Declaration by the Chair of 28 August 2014. [online] Available at: https://archiv.bundesregierung.de/archiv-de/meta/startseite/final-declaration-by-the-chair-of-the-conference-on-the-western-balkans-754634.

110 *EU rule of law: the "action" dimension*

economic development and the rule of law included the lessening of the negative impact of corruption, avoiding mismanagement of public finances and creating the conditions for market competitiveness.[8] Building on this, the Italian Chair suggested the parties to focus on five major issues at the crossroads of the rule of law and economic development, such as preventing corruption, preventing conflict of interest, transparency and public procurement. Despite some points of intersection with the SAP (e.g. developing the public procurement market), the Berlin Process was intentionally designed as formally disentangled from the SAP. Such an intention, coupled with the Process' "focus on a limited number of specific themes"[9], explains the lack of referrals to the rule of law in the political and stabilization-related context in the Berlin Process realm

The 2018 Communication "A Credible Enlargement Perspective for and Enhanced EU Engagement with the Western Balkans"

Most recently, both the political and economic dimensions of the rule of law were addressed in the 2018 Commission's Communication "A Credible Enlargement Perspective for and Enhanced EU Engagement with the Western Balkans".[10] In the Communication, the Commission reaffirmed the EU's "unequivocal support" for the European perspective of the region, yet claimed that neither of the Western Balkan countries so far meets the Copenhagen criteria.[11] The document called for further strengthening the rule of law in the region, stressing the **independence, quality and efficiency of the judiciary, accountability of governments and administrations**, and **combating state capture and organized crime**.[12] The Communication did not explicitly link the rule of law and economic development. Nonetheless, the "Strengthening the Economy" part of the Communication mentions several critical "junctures" between the rule of law and economic development, such as the **transparency** of public procurement and public finances, and **transparency** and **legal certainty** with respect to privatization.[13] Notably, the 2018 Communication strictly delimits between values and *acquis* conditionality, making it difficult to ensure the interplay between the promotion of the rule of law

---

8 Trieste Western Balkans Summit Declaration by the Italian Chair of 7 December 2007. [online] Available at: www.esteri.it/mae/en/sala_stampa/archivionotizie/approfondimenti/trieste-western-balkan-summit-declaration.html.

9 Final Declaration of the Chair of the Paris Western Balkans Summit of 4 July 2016. [pdf] European Commission. Available at: https://ec.europa.eu/neighbourhood-enlargement/sites/near/files/pdf/policy-highlights/regional-cooperation/20160713-01.final-declaration-by-the-chair-of-the-paris-western-balkans-summit.pdf.

10 European Commission, Communication to the European Parliament, the Council, the European Economic and Social Committee and the Committee of the Regions: A Credible Enlargement Perspective for and Enhanced EU Engagement with the Western Balkans, COM (2018)65 final of 6 February 2018.

11 *Ibid.*, p. 1.

12 *Ibid.*

13 *Ibid.*, pp. 4–5.

as a political value and of particular rule of law standards, as embedded into the provisions of the SAAs (e.g. in the considered domains of administrative cooperation, public procurement and competition).

In sum, while early "soft" documents related to the EU-Western Balkans relations considered the rule of law solely as a part of the political stabilization agenda, the Berlin Process gave a considerable impetus to the rule of law–economic development nexus. Nevertheless, the "soft" documents in question barely construed bridges between the rule of law and trade liberalization, most probably due to several conceptual demarcation lines:

- Between the political and economic cooperation under the SAP.
- Between the SAP (involving trade liberalization) and the Berlin Process (stipulating the rule of law–economic development nexus).
- Last, but not least, between the values and *acquis* conditionality.

2. Autonomous trade measures

EU–Western Balkans relations since 2000 have been marked by the EU's continuous application of "exceptional trade measures for countries and territories participating in or linked to the European Union's Stabilization and Association Process".[14] We argue that, in contrast to "soft" documents, autonomous trade preferences represent a strong nexus between trade liberalization and the rule of law promotion.

By analogy with the "essential element" clauses, the initial Council Regulation No 2007/2000 linked the granting of autonomous trade measures to partner countries' respect for fundamental principles of democracy and human rights, and their efforts to promote regional economic integration and "engage into effective economic reforms".[15] Although the instrument in question did not immediately refer to the rule of law, it implicitly addresses several aspects this concept.

First, for the Western Balkan countries to be eligible for trade benefits, Art. 2 of the Regulation obliged them to possess customs administration and get involved into active administrative cooperation with the Union. In turn, an active involvement into administrative cooperation with the EU requires that partner countries adhere to the standards, underpinning the EAS. Such standards include, *inter alia*, **legality** (as opposed to the arbitrariness of administrative decisions), **legal certainty** (decisions' **predictability, respect of individuals' legitimate expectations**), **transparency** and administrations' **accountability** to further authorities (Cardona, 2009; Elbasani and Šabić, 2018). Second, the granting of autonomous

---

14 Council Regulation (EC) No 2007/2000 of 18 September 2000 introducing exceptional trade measures for countries and territories participating in or linked to the European Union's Stabilization and Association Process, amending Regulation (EC) No 2820/98 of 21 December 1998, and repealing Regulations (EC) No 1763/1999 of 29 July 1999 and (EC) No 6/2000 of 7–9 December 2000, OJL 240 of 23 September 2000.

15 *Ibid.*, Art. 12.

112 EU rule of law: the "action" dimension

trade measures was made conditional on the beneficiaries' compliance with the GATT 1994 and other relevant WTO provisions.[16] It is, however, impossible to comply with the WTO rules without fulfilling numerous intertwined rule of law standards, such as **legal certainty, transparency, judicial review** and **due process.** Furthermore, the observance of the WTO standards *per se* contributes to fostering the **relationship between domestic and international law.**

Later on, the conditionality model, stipulated by the Council Regulation No 2007/2000, was included into the Regulation 1946/2005 that prolonged the validity of autonomous trade measures until 2010.[17] The Council's subsequent Regulations on autonomous trade measures 1215/2009 and 1336/2011, however, did not include an "essential element" clause.[18] Nonetheless, already the Regulation 2015/2423 stressed the need for the EU to have a possibility to temporarily suspend the application of exceptional trade measures in the event of "serious and systemic violations of human rights, including core labour rights, of fundamental principles of democracy and the rule of law".[19] Thus, under the 2015 Regulation, the rule of law acquired the legal status of an "essential element". Moreover, Regulation 2015/2423 is of interest for the present research since it provides for applying the suspension clause to Bosnia and Herzegovina due to its failure to grant trade concessions to Croatia under the CEFTA. Though not concerned with the rule of law requirement, this case illustrates a strong link between the partner country's compliance with the essentials of the SAP and its eligibility for trade preferences, unilaterally granted to it by the Union. While such a link enables the Commission to suspend autonomous trade measures in response to the rule of law violations in the Balkans, the Commission in practice may opt for measures that less impede trade.

In sum, immediately linked to the partner country's observance of the EAS and the WTO standards, autonomous trade measures represent a vital connecting element between trade liberalization and the rule of law agendas.

---

16 *Ibid.*, Preamble, Art. 2.
17 Council Regulation (EC) No 1946/2005 of 14 November 2005 amending Regulation No 2007/2000 of 18 November introducing exceptional trade measures for countries and territories participating in or linked to the European Union's Stabilization and Association Process, OJL 312 of 29 November 2005.
18 Council Regulation (EC) No 1215/2009 of 30 November 2009 introducing exceptional trade measures for countries and territories, participating in or linked to the European Union's Stabilization and Association Process, OJ L 328/1 of 15 December 2009; Regulation (EU) No 1336/2011 of the European Parliament of 13 December 2011 and of the Council of 13 December 2011 amending Council Regulation (EC) No 1215/2009 of 30 November 2009 introducing exceptional trade measures for countries and territories participating in or linked to the European Union's Stabilization and Association Process, OJL 347 of 30 December 2011.
19 Regulation (EU) No 2015/2423 of the European Parliament and of the Council of 16 December 2015 amending Council Regulation (EC) No 1215/2009 of 30 November 2009 introducing exceptional trade measures for countries and territories participating in or linked to the European Union's Stabilization and Association Process and suspending its application with regard to Bosnia and Herzegovina, OJL 341 of 24 December 2015.

3. Financial and technical assistance

The key legal frameworks the EU has applied to channel its financial and technical assistance to the Western Balkan countries over the last two decades were the CARDS assistance programme (2000–2006), the Instrument for Pre-Accession Assistance (IPA I, 2007–2013) and the IPA II (2014–2020).[20] We argue that, although all the instruments in question have supported multiple measures at the crossroads between trade liberalization and the rule of law, a strong delimitation between the values and *acquis* conditionality (Trauner, 2009; Kochenov, 2008) and the political and economic cooperation agendas prevented the EU from systemizing and synergizing such links.

CARDS Assistance programme (2000–2006)

Launched in 2000, the Community Assistance for Reconstruction, Development and Stabilization (CARDS) programme declared an umbrella goal of facilitating the Western Balkans' participation in the SAP.[21] As well as the Thessaloniki Agenda, the Regulation 2666/2000 did not provide for specific links or synergies between the objectives of "creation of the institutional and legislative framework to underpin democracy, the rule of law and human and human and minority rights" and the support of SAAs implementation.

However, at the regional programme level, both the rule of law promotion and the support of SAAs implementation fell under the "Institution-Building" funding priority. The key rule of law initiative, conducted under this priority, has been the project "Regional Cooperation among Judicial, Police and other Law Enforcement Agencies" that primarily linked the rule of law to the security and public order issues, such as countering organized crime and illegal migration.[22] The rule of law dimension was also relatively strong under the programme facilities related to the SAAs' implementation: the General Support Facility (GSF) and the Intellectual Property Rights Facility.[23] The former facility was directed "to transpos[ing], implement[ing] and enforc[ing] policies and legislation that is approximated to the EU acquis in key areas arising from the SAP" and, subsequently, tackled a

---

20 The pre-CARDS EU support of the respective countries was channeled through the ECHO, Obnova and PHARE financial instruments.

21 Council Regulation (EC) No 2666/2000 on assistance for Albania, Bosnia and Herzegovina, Croatia, the Federal Republic of Yugoslavia and the former Yugoslav Republic of Macedonia, repealing Regulation (EC) No 1628/96 and amending Regulations (EEC) No 3906/89 and (EEC) No 1360/90 and Decisions 97/256/EC and 1999/311/EEC, OJ C 332E of 27 November 2001.

22 European Commission Directorate Western Balkans (2001). CARDS Assistance Programme to the Western Balkans, Regional Strategy Paper 2002–2006. [pdf] Available at: https://ec.europa.eu/ neighbourhood-enlargement/sites/near/files/pdf/financial_assistance/cards/publications/regional_ strategy_paper_en.pdf, p. 40.

23 European Commission Directorate Western Balkans (2002). CARDS Regional Annual Programme, Financing Proposal. European Commission. [pdf] Available at: https://ec.europa.eu/ neighbourhood-enlargement/sites/near/files/pdf/financial_assistance/cards/publications/regional_ programme_2002_en.pdf, pp. 5–10.

114 EU rule of law: the "action" dimension

broad array of the rule of law standards, included into the SAAs.[24] The latter facility aimed at "the adaptation of national legal frameworks to TRIPS in all fields of intellectual property rights protection".[25] As well as other WTO agreements, considered in Chapter 4, the WTO TRIPS Agreement encompasses numerous clauses related to **legality** and **legal certainty** (e.g. by establishing "standards concerning the availability, scope and use of IP rights" in Part II), as well as **transparency** and **due process** (Part III "Enforcement of IP Rights").[26] Furthermore, compliance with the WTO rules contributes to the **relationship between domestic and international law**.

According to the Regulation (EC) No 2666/2000, the long-term objectives of assistance and priority action fields at the country level are to be determined based on country strategic papers, Multiannual Indicative Programmes and Annual Action Programmes.[27] For the purposes of this part of the book, we looked at respective documents concerning three randomly selected countries: North Macedonia (referred to as Former Yugoslav Republic of Macedonia [FYROM]), Albania and Bosnia and Herzegovina. In all country contexts, the EU linked the rule of law to divergent reform agendas: democracy and good governance (FYROM); strengthening public order, the fight against organized crime, fraud and corruption, legal security and appropriate law enforcement (Albania) and "creating a physically and legally secure environment" (Bosnia and Herzegovina).[28] Nonetheless, the EU's CARDS-based rule of law action in countries in question tended to focus solely on the reforms of the judiciary and law enforcement agencies.[29] As well as at the programme's regional level, a relatively strong nexus between the rule of law and trade liberalization was reflected in the programming of assistance related to "deep disciplines". Hence, the programming for FYROM and Albania

---

24 *Ibid.*, p. 5.

25 *Ibid.*, p. 10.

26 Agreement on Trade-Related Aspects of Intellectual Property Rights, 15 April 1994, Marrakesh Agreement Establishing the World Trade Organization, Annex 1C, The Legal Texts: The Results of the Uruguay Round of Multilateral Trade Negotiations 320 (1999), 1869 U.N.T.S.299, 33 I.L.M. 1197 (1994).

27 Council Regulation (EC) No 2666/2000, OJ C 332E of 27 November 2001, Art.3(a)(b).

28 European Commission Directorate Western Balkans (2002) CARDS Assistance Programme, Former Yugoslav Republic of Macedonia 2002–2006. [pdf] European Commission. Available at: https://ec.europa.eu/neighbourhood-enlargement/sites/near/files/pdf/financial_assistance/cards/publications/fyrom_strategy_paper_en.pdf, p. 33 (hereinafter referred to as "CARDS Assistance Programme FYROM"); European Commission Directorate Western Balkans (2001). CARDS Assistance Programme, Albania 2002–2006. [pdf] European Commission. Available at: https://ec.europa.eu/neighbourhood-enlargement/sites/near/files/pdf/financial_assistance/cards/publications/albania_strategy_paper_en.pdf, p. 24 (hereinafter referred to as "CARDS Assistance Programme Albania"); European Commission Directorate Western Balkans (2004). CARDS Assistance Programme Bosnia and Herzegovina 2005–2006. [pdf] European Commission. Available at: https://ec.europa.eu/neighbourhood-enlargement/sites/near/files/pdf/bosnia_and_herzegovina/mip_2005_2006_bih_en.pdf, pp. 27–28.

29 CARDS Assistance Programme FYROM, p. 27; CARDS Assistance Programme Albania, pp. 24–26; CARDS Assistance Programme Bosnia and Herzegovina, pp. 13–15.

EU rule of law: the "action" dimension   115

envisaged contributing to the following rule of law standards with respect to competition and state aid, public procurement and IP rights:

- **Legality** (the focus on the contents of legal frameworks in the above domains, and institutions' compliance with respective laws).
- **Legal certainty** (promotion of the uniform application of respective legislation, foreseeability of such implementation).
- **Independence and impartiality** of public procurement, competition and IP rights institutions.
- **Judicial review** in the relevant domains.
- **Transparency** of the flow of information on respective reforms.[30]

Among the implementing instruments, utilized by the EU at both the regional and country levels, one can distinguish:

- The coordination of national authorities' cooperation (e.g. between the judiciary and the law enforcement agencies).
- Capacity-building (e.g. trainings for judges and law enforcement agencies' employees).[31]
- TAIEX (Technical Assistance and Information Exchange Instrument), aimed at supporting public administrations with respect to the approximation, application and enforcement of the *acquis communautaire* through workshops, expert missions and study visits.[32]
- Twinning programme, aimed at promoting targeted administrative cooperation between beneficiary countries and the Member States, as well as building long-term relationships between the old and new Member States, and Candidate countries.[33]

Besides, the achievement of the CARDS goals was assisted by the conditionality, functioning at the levels of the SAP as a whole, as well as the programme and project levels (defined via the Financing Memoranda). Such multilevel conditionality structures were, however, extensively criticized in scholarship due to the tendency to overlook partner countries' priorities and, subsequently, the inability to generate local consensus about the reforms (Anastasakis and Bechev, 2003; Pridham, 2010). Furthermore, by introducing conditionality at both the regional and the

---

30 CARDS Assistance Programme FYROM, pp. 9–18, 33–60; CARDS Assistance Programme Albania, pp. 9–17, 22–29.

31 European Commission Directorate Western Balkans (2001). CARDS Assistance Programme to the Western Balkans, Regional Strategy Paper 2002–2006. [pdf] European Commission. Available at: https://ec.europa.eu/neighbourhood-enlargement/sites/near/files/pdf/financial_assistance/cards/publications/regional_strategy_paper_en.pdf, pp. 20.46.

32 For general information about TAIEX Instrument, please visit https://ec.europa.eu/neighbourhood-enlargement/tenders/taiex_en.

33 For general information about Twinning projects, please visit https://ec.europa.eu/neighbourhood-enlargement/tenders/twinning_en.

116 *EU rule of law: the "action" dimension*

country level, the EU was found to generate the climate of suspicion about it unfairly favouring weaker countries (Anastasakis and Bechev, 2003). Not surprisingly, these issues influenced the results of the CARDS' implementation at both levels of operation. Pursuant to the 2008 *ad hoc* evaluation of the programme, its regional-level impacts were in line with the initial objectives of the CARDS, but beneficiary countries were not yet ready to cooperate on the regional level without the Union's assistance.[34] "The process of harmonization of the legal bodies to acquis communautaire has proven to be extremely burdensome and time-consuming", largely due to the fact that the Western Balkans countries had different starting levels of the respective legislation's development.[35] Similarly, at the bilateral level, "the CARDS assistance has had planned effects, but has been affected by the lack of capacity and commitment".[36]

Ultimately, despite the challenges it faced, the CARDS constituted a crucial framework of the EU's support of the SAP. In this section, we showed that the CARDS had been advancing an array of rule of law standards in the Balkans through supporting legislative approximation and the enforcement of the EU *acquis* in public procurement, competition and state aid domains.

Instrument for Pre-Accession Assistance (IPA I) 2007–2013

The IPA I was introduced in 2007 as an umbrella legal framework, targeting two beneficiaries' groups, namely EU Candidate countries (Turkey, Albania, Serbia and North Macedonia) and Potential Candidate countries (Bosnia and Herzegovina and Kosovo).[37] The assistance objectives under the IPA I were largely similar to the ones under the CARDS (i.e. strengthening of democratic institutions and the rule of law, economic reforms, social inclusion). The structure of aid was consolidated to distinguish between transition assistance and institution-building, on the one hand, and different aspects of cross-border cooperation (i.e. regional development, human resources development and rural development). These components served as a foundation for multiannual and annual planning of assistance. As in the case of CARDS, this section of the analysis will zoom in on the interplay of the rule of law promotion and support of the implementation of SAAs' "deep" disciplines in the programming of the assistance for previously considered countries, namely North Macedonia (FYROM), Albania and Bosnia and Herzegovina.

---

34 European Commission Directorate Western Balkans, CARDS Assistance Programme to the Western Balkans, Regional Strategy Paper 2002–2006 of 18 October 2001. European Commission. [pdf] Available at: https://ec.europa.eu/neighbourhood-enlargement/sites/near/files/pdf/financial_assistance/cards/publications/regional_strategy_paper_en.pdf, p. 2.

35 *Ibid.*

36 European Commission DG Elarg (2008). Ad Hoc Evaluation of the CARDS Regional Programmes in Western Balkans, 2008. European Commission. [pdf] Available at: https://ec.europa.eu/neighbourhood-enlargement/sites/near/files/pdf/financial_assistance/phare/evaluation/final_report_181208_en.pdf, p. 2.

37 Council Regulation (EC) No 1085/2006 of 17 July 2006 establishing an Instrument for Pre-Accession Assistance (IPA), OJ L 210 of 31 July 2006, Annex I, Annex II.

EU rule of law: the "action" dimension   117

We demonstrate that the impact on the IPA I on the interplay between the EU's "action" in the rule of law and trade liberalization domains has been controversial. On the one hand, particularly the multiannual programmes for FYROM and Albania[38] formalized the demarcation line between the values and *acquis* conditionality, discussed previously. On the other hand, the programming's focus on the enforcement of legal rules and strengthening institutions can be regarded as a "cross-cutting element", linking the trade liberalization and the rule of law promotion agendas.

As reflected in the multiannual indicative programmes (MIPDs) for FYROM and Albania and annual financing plans for Bosnia and Herzegovina, the reform of judiciary and law enforcement agencies continued to represent the key dimensions of the rule of law.[39] While the MIPDs for FYROM and Albania explicitly addressed the rule of law as a part of values conditionality, the annual plans for Bosnia and Herzegovina continued regarding it as one of many funding priorities. Nonetheless, the planning for all three countries in question demonstrates two crucial differences, as compared to the CARDS. First, following the adoption of required legal framework in partner countries, the EU put a stronger emphasis on its enforcement and ensuring sufficient capacities of public administration. This difference can be exemplified by the MIPDs for FYROM and Albania that regarded public administration reform as a part of a broader rule of law agenda, with the focus made on **legal certainty** and **transparency** aspects (e.g. the introduction of professional career development criteria, specified procedures for recruitment, appraisal, promotion and dismissal of public servants).[40] Second, the IPA I linked the rule of law to an array of economic issues, such as the enhancement of financial management and control procedures, overcoming institutional weaknesses and improving business climate. However, the MIPDs did not explicitly refer to these issues as "cross-cutting", unequally "distributing" them among political, economic and *acquis*-related strategic objectives and programmes.

Pursuant to the delimitation between the values and *acquis* conditionality, the MIPDs for FYROM and Albania consider the promotion of "deep" disciplines under the heading "Ability to assume the obligations of membership". The relevant part of the EU MIPD for Albania under the IPA I exemplifies the EU's focus

---

38 European Commission, Decision on a Multi-annual Indicative Planning Document (MIPD) 2007–2009 for the former Yugoslav Republic of Macedonia, C(2007) 1853 of 30 April 2007; European Commission, Decision on a Multi-annual Indicative Planning Document (MIPD) for Albania 2008–2010, C(2007)2245 of 31 May 2007.

39 *Ibid.*; European Commission Decision adopting a National Programme (Part I) for Bosnia and Herzegovina under the IPA-Transition Assistance and Institution-Building Component for 2008, C(2008) 5659/2 of 9 October 2008. See also: European Commission, Implementing Decision on adopting a National Programme for Albania under the IPA Transition Assistance and Institution-Building Component for the year 2012, C(2012)8208 final of 9 November 2012, p. 3.

40 European Commission, Decision on a Multi-annual Indicative Planning Document (MIPD) 2007–2009 for the former Yugoslav Republic of Macedonia, C(2007) 1853 of 30 April 2007, p. 15; European Commission, Decision on a Multi-annual Indicative Planning Document (MIPD) for Albania 2008–2010, C(2007)2245 of 31 May 2007, p. 17.

118 *EU rule of law: the "action" dimension*

on the implementation/enforcement of national legislation in line with the *acquis* (following its transposition, supported under the CARDS) and capacity-building of institutions.[41] Though the objectives of the "Ability to assume the obligations of membership" sections of the MIPDs do not explicitly refer to the rule of law, the "action" they envisage still implies specific rule of law standards. For instance, in line with the **institutional dimension of legality** (institutions' compliance with legislation), the MIPD for Albania 2008–2010 expects "smooth application of public procurement procedures, with a reduced number of controversial cases and complaints".[42] Another noteworthy example is an immediate referral to advancing **legality** and **legal certainty** in the field of Movement of Capital and Payments and Financial Services under the 2007–2010 MIPD for FYROM.[43]

The IPA I implementing instruments included, *inter alia*, institutions' capacity-building, the facilitation of inter-institutional cooperation, the application of TAIEX and Twinning instruments, and conditionality. As well as in the era of the CARDS, the scholarship on political conditionality under the IPA was marked by pessimism about "fake, partial and imposed compliance" (Noutcheva, 2009) and "building impossible states" (Bieber, 2011). Expectedly, the 2013 Commission's progress reports demonstrated mixed results both in domains of the rule of law and "deep disciplines", acknowledging the absence of progress or limited progress in many areas (e.g. the independence and enforcement capacity of competition and state aid bodies in all the countries in question).[44]

Instrument for Pre-Accession Assistance (IPA II) 2014–2020

Continuing the IPA I pre-accession assistance logics, IPA II assistance followed the structure of the Copenhagen criteria, with the rule of law addressed as a component of the "support for political reforms".[45] The key novelty of the IPA II has been the integration of the beneficiaries' own development and reform strategies within the long-term indicative Country Strategy Papers (CSPs) (European Commission, n.d.). We show that, as opposed to the programming under CARDS and the IPA I, the IPA II programming was marked by an emphasis on cross-cutting themes and the rule of law aspects of economic governance.

---

41 European Commission, Decision on a Multi-annual Indicative Planning Document (MIPD) for Albania 2008–2010, C(2007)2245 of 31 May 2007, pp. 19–22.

42 *Ibid.*, p. 21.

43 European Commission (2007). Decision on a Multi-annual Indicative Planning Document (MIPD) 2007–2010 for the former Yugoslav Republic of Macedonia. [pdf] European Commission. Available at: https://ec.europa.eu/neighbourhood-enlargement/sites/near/files/pdf/mipd_fyrom_2008_2010_en.pdf, pp. 6–7.

44 See, for instance, European Commission, Commission Staff Working Document – The Former Yugoslav Republic of Macedonia 2013 Progress Report, SWD(2013) 411 final, pp. 5–12; European Commission, Commission Staff Working Document – Bosnia and Herzegovina 2013 Progress Report, SWD(2013) 415 final, pp. 6–15.

45 Regulation (EU) No 231/2014 of the European Parliament and of the Council of 11 March 2014 establishing an Instrument for Pre-accession Assistance (IPA II), OJL 77/1 of 15 March 2014, Art. 2(1).

As well as the programming under the CARDS and the IPA I, the CSPs under study extensively referred to the rule of law standards with respect to the justice (e.g. independence, impartiality and integrity of the judiciary, fair system of bailiffs, compliance with international standards in the penitentiary field).[46] Additionally, the Strategy Paper for Albania emphasized the advancement of the system of property rights management as one of the key reform directions, lying at the crossroads of the political and economic Copenhagen criteria.[47] Similarly to the IPA I, the IPA II programming dedicated considerable attention to the institutional design and capacities of state administrations (with a focus on the **accountability** and **transparency** dimensions of the rule of law).[48] Furthermore, in their parts devoted to political criteria ("democracy and governance"), the IPA II CSPs elaborated on strengthening the policy-making and legal dimensions of economic governance and ensuring a favourable environment for doing business.[49] These efforts were mainly aimed at "improving legal predictability and enforcement of laws and courts' decisions".[50] In sharp contrast to the programming under CARDS and IPA I, the "Democracy and Governance" parts of the CSPs referred to several aspects of the *acquis'* transposition into the domestic legal system (e.g. the functioning of tax and customs administrations).[51]

Addressing the implementing instruments under the IPA II, it is crucial to underline the shift from pessimistic accounts of the application of conditionality to reassessing the EU's effort to Europeanize and democratize Western Balkans (e.g. Börzel and Grimm, 2018). In particular, a number of influential studies reaffirmed the EU's contribution to stabilization and democratization in the region, distinguishing aid and conditionality, rather than trade liberalization, as a crucial engine of successes (Börzel and Grimm, 2018; Grimm and Mathis, 2015). However, the EU was extensively criticized for prioritizing stability over democracy in its support for the Western Balkans and insufficient successes in the domains of the rule of law and countering corruption (Grimm and Mathis, 2015; Vachudova, 2018).

---

46 *Ibid.*
47 Commission Implementing Decision amending Commission Decision C(2014)5770 of 18 August 2014 adopting the Indicative Strategy Paper for Albania for the period 2014–2020, C(2018)5027 final of 3 August 2018, pp. 6–7.
48 See, for instance, Commission Implementing Decision amending Commission Decision C(2014)5770 of 18 August 2014 adopting the Indicative Strategy Paper for Montenegro for the period 2014–2020, C(2018)5027final of 3 August 2018, pp. 12–13; Commission Implementing Decision amending Commission Decision C(2014)5770 of 18 August 2014 adopting the Indicative Strategy Paper for Albania for the period 2014–2020, C(2018)5027final of 3 August 2018, p. 13; Commission Implementing Decision amending Commission Decision C(2014)8561 of 19 August 2014 adopting the Indicative Strategy Paper for the former Yugoslav Republic of Macedonia for the period 2014–2020, C(2018) 524 final of 3 August, pp. 13–16.
49 *Ibid.*
50 See, for instance, Commission Implementing Decision amending Commission Decision C(2014)5770 of 18 August 2014 adopting the Indicative Strategy Paper for Albania for the period 2014–2020, C(2018)5027 final of 3 August 2018, p. 14.
51 *Ibid.*

120 *EU rule of law: the "action" dimension*

Despite lesser attention to the previously mentioned cross-cutting themes, country reports, produced by the Commission in line with the 2018 Communication on EU Enlargement policy, extensively dealt with rule of law standards in the legislative approximation context. Having stipulated the partner countries' "moderate preparedness" in numerous sectors pertaining to the *acquis*, the reports for North Macedonia and Albania pointed to the challenge of completing the rule of law reforms, necessary to ensure authorities' compliance with the *acquis*. In particular, the report for Albania referred to the insufficient observance of numerous rule of law standards (e.g. **procedural legality**, **authorities' independence and impartiality**, and **accountability**) as an obstacle to Albania's readiness to assume the obligations of membership.[52] Given Bosnia and Herzegovina's Potential Candidate status, the report adopted the "fundamentals first" approach and referred to cross-cutting issues (policy-makers' accountability, transparency of public finances' management), rather than the *acquis*-specific issues.[53]

Ultimately, compared to the CARDS and the IPA I, the IPA II was marked by a stronger bridge between the values and *acquis* conditionality and an emphasis on cross-cutting themes, such as public finance management, improving the environment for doing business and economic governance.

4. Institutional dimension: the EULEX mission to Kosovo

The EULEX (European Union Rule of Law Mission to Kosovo) is a single EU CSDP mission, operating across the Western Balkans, "mandated to enforce the rule of law in Kosovo") (Grasten, 2016). It is "a technical mission, which mentors, monitors and advises whilst retaining a number of limited executive powers" (European Union Office in Kosovo, 2016). We argue that, although the EULEX is a CSDP mission, and its rule of law focus is strongly linked to the stabilization agenda, its mandate is also supportive to the SAAs' implementation.

Pursuant to the initial[54] mission statement, stipulated in Art.2 of the Council Joint Action of 4 February 2008, the EULEX "shall assist Kosovo institutions, judicial authorities and law enforcement agencies in their progress towards sustainability and accountability".[55] It shall also: (i) promote the development of multi-ethnic police, justice system and customs services, free from political interference; (ii) contribute to the fight against corruption, fraud and organized crime and (iii) take part in the implementation of the Kosovo Anti-Corruption Strategy and Anti-Corruption Action Plan.[56] Subsequently, the Mission's activities

---

52 European Commission, Commission Staff Working Document – Albania 2018, SWD(2018) 151 final, pp. 57–63.

53 European Commission, Commission Staff Working Document – Bosnia and Herzegovina 2018 Report, SWD(2018)155 final, pp. 4–6, pp. 30–36.

54 The current mandate of the EULEX is defined in the Council Decision amending Joint Action 2008/124/CFP on the European Union Rule of Law Mission in Kosovo (EULEX Kosovo), 2018/856 of 8 June 2018.

55 Council Joint Action on the European Union Rule of Law Mission in Kosovo (EULEX Kosovo), 2008/124/CFSP of 4 February 2008, Art.2.

56 *Ibid.*, Art.3.

concern numerous rule of law standards, such as **legality** (adherence to recognized international and European standards; institutions' compliance with the legislation); **authorities' impartiality** (freedom from political interference); **transparency** and **accountability**; and the **relationship between domestic and international law**. The EULEX mandate does not, however, refer to strengthening the rule of law in previously considered domains related to implementation of the SAAs.

Nevertheless, the EULEX activities are still capable of influencing the rule of law standards, as contained in the trade-related parts of the SAAs. First, by promoting the **judiciary's and law enforcement agencies' independence on political interference and public accountability**, the EULEX strengthens the prospects of **authorities' compliance with domestic law and international law**, including the SAAs. Moreover, the judicial independence and efficiency promoted by the EULEX constitute necessary institutional prerequisites for the Western Balkans' successful integration to the Internal Market. In turn, authorities' compliance with the legislation is essential to safeguard other dimensions of the rule of law, such as **procedural legality** and **legal certainty**. Potentially, this testifies to the complex "two-way-road" interplay between the rule of law standards, as promoted by the EU missions and projects via the unilateral financial and technical assistance, and the ones contained in the SAAs. Such interplay will be explored in more detail in Chapter 7.

Coming back to the EULEX mandate and operation, it has to be mentioned that the judicial-executive part of the Mission was finalized on 8 June 2018, and its mandate was adapted accordingly (European Council and Council of the European Union, 2018). Since 14 June 2018, the key dimensions of the EULEX operation encompass the monitoring of selected cases and trials in criminal and civil justice institutions in Kosovo; "monitoring, mentoring and advising" concerning the correctional service and the facilitation of Serbia-Kosovo agreements regarding the normalization of relationships.[57] Although the executive mandate of the Mission came to an end, the EULEX can still exert on-site diplomatic influence on Kosovo institutions with the help of its "monitoring, mentoring and advising" mandate.

Ultimately, although the EULEX is a CSDP mission, it also has the capability to contribute to the rule of law standards, as provided for in the trade-related parts of the SAAs.

Part 2. Eastern dimension of the ENP ("associated" Neighbourhood)[58]

The first contractual link between the EU and the region, presently addressed as "Eastern Neighbourhood" is constituted by the 1989 EEC-Soviet Union Trade

---

57 *Ibid.*

58 Since the EU's AAs with Southern Neighbours do not contain "deep disciplines" chapters and encompass a highly limited number of the rule of law standards, this part of the thesis will only consider the action dimension of the EU's rule of law promotion through trade in the "associated" Neighbourhood.

122 *EU rule of law: the "action" dimension*

and Cooperation Agreement (TCA).[59] Following the disintegration of the Soviet Union at the end of 1991, the Union started negotiating new agreements with the former Soviet countries, based on the EEC-Soviet Union TCA. Automatically replacing the TCA, upon their entry into force, the Partnership and Cooperation Agreements (PCAs) did not provide for free trade between the Union and the former Soviet countries but covered general principles of cooperation, current payments, IP rights protection and mutual assistance in customs matters (European Commission, 2020). After the EU borders shifted eastwards as a result of the 2004 "Big Bang" enlargement, the EU launched the ENP as a framework to deal with new Eastern and Southern Neighbours. In bilateral terms, one of the crucial objectives of the Eastern dimension of the ENP has been the conclusion of "deep" AAs that would replace existing PCAs.[60]

As a result of policy differentiation due to Belarus and Armenia joining the Russia-led Eurasian Customs Union (EACU) and Azerbaijan's refusal to sign the AA, the AAs including previously researched DCFTAs were only signed by the EU with Ukraine, Moldova and Georgia. This section of the book will examine the "action" dimension of the EU's rule of law promotion through DCFTAs in the Eastern Neighbourhood, also taking stock of the instruments that were signed during the preparation to signing the DCFTAs.

1. *"Soft" (diplomatic) instruments*

Given the plenitude of "soft" documents, adopted under the ENP umbrella, this part of the analysis will draw on two groups of documents, the EU Action Plans for future "associated" Neighbours 2004 and Eastern Partnership summits declarations (2009–2017). We chose these groups of documents for two reasons. First, we chose to focus on early Action Plans, because since the launch of the European Neighbourhood and Partnership Instrument (ENPI), the programming of assistance predominantly took place within the realm of the unilateral financial and technical assistance instruments, rather than "soft" documents. Second, by looking at the 2004–2007 Action Plans, we seek to embrace both the bilateral and multilateral aspects of the EU's relations with Eastern Neighbours.

2004 EU Action Plans for future "associated" Neighbours

The first political documents, agreed between the EU and its "associated" Neighbours (Ukraine, Moldova and Georgia), following the 2004 "Eastern" enlargement, have been the 2004 Action Plans. We demonstrate that, three years prior to the official start of the AAs' negotiations, the EU and Eastern Neighbours agreed

---

59 Agreement between the European Economic Community and the European Atomic Energy Community and Union of Soviet Socialist Republics on trade and commercial and economic cooperation, OJ L 068 of 15 March 1990.
60 Commission of the European Communities, European Neighbourhood Policy – Strategy Paper, COM (2004)373 final of 12 May 2004, p. 3.

EU rule of law: the "action" dimension   123

upon an ambitious reform agenda that encompassed numerous issues at the cross-roads of economic development, "deep" disciplines and the rule of law.

Naturally, all three country-specific Action Plans mentioned the rule of law among priorities for action as part of "Political Dialogue and Reform" action pillar.[61] Moreover, following the pattern of the EU-Western Balkans relations, the Action Plans for Moldova and Ukraine referred to the strengthening of the rule of law as a prerequisite for stability.[62] In contrast to rather vague referrals to the rule of law in the early EU-Western Balkans "soft" documents, the Action Plans in question immediately addressed the substance of the envisaged rule of law reforms. For instance, the planned judicial reform in Georgia should have addressed numerous rule of law standards, such as **legality** (institutions' compliance with laws), **legal certainty** (e.g. through the establishment of the legal aid system), **judicial independence** and **impartiality**, and the **relationship between domestic and international law** (compliance with international and European human rights standards). Alongside the judicial reform, the Action Plans provided for improving the quality and transparency of the law-making processes (Ukraine, Moldova), reforms of the law enforcement agencies (all three countries) and public service (Georgia).

Alongside the general aspects of the rule of law reforms, the Action Plans zoomed in on numerous areas lying at the crossroads between the rule of law and economic development. For instance, the "development and implementation of a comprehensive business climate improvement programme" envisaged by the EU-Georgia Action Plan provides for strengthening of the **legality** and **legal certainty** dimensions of the rule of law (e.g. in the domains of contract enforcement and investor protection).[63] Under the EU-Ukraine Action Plan, fostering business development was also recognized to be linked to the specific aspects of **legality** (the simplification of the relevant legislation), **legal certainty** (predictability of the business environment) and the **relationship between domestic and international law** (adherence to the WTO rules). Besides, all three Action Plans emphasized the **transparency** dimension of the rule of law, i.e. with respect to the functioning of tax and customs administrations, privatization and notifying economic operators about regulatory changes.

The Action Plans also referred to specific rule of law standards in the context of "deep" disciplines. For instance, the competition provisions of the Action Plan for Moldova envisage specific measures to advance the **legality**, **equality** and **non-discrimination** and **transparency** dimensions of the rule of law.[64] It also made a specific reference to the institutional dimension of competition laws enforcement[65] that similarly falls within the umbrella **legality** dimension of the rule of law. Furthermore, the "deep disciplines"-related parts of all three Action Plans

---

61 See, for instance, EU-Moldova Action Plan 2004, pp. 3–6.
62 EU-Moldova Action Plan 2004, p. 5; EU-Ukraine Action Plan 2004, p. 5.
63 EU-Georgia Action Plan 2004, pp. 5–6.
64 *Ibid*, p. 22.
65 *Ibid*.

124 *EU rule of law: the "action" dimension*

in question emphasized an individual's **right to review** to be ensured both via institutional action in the relevant domains (e.g. competition, public procurement) and judicial reforms.

Ultimately, in contrast to rather vague SAP framework documents, the 2004 EU Action Plans were marked by an emphasis on the substance of envisaged legal reforms. As discussed in Chapter 6, this testifies to the parties' intention to ensure coherence between the EU Neighbourhood cooperation on domestic reforms prior to the AAs' conclusion and the contents of the AAs.

Eastern Partnership summits' declarations (2009–2017)

The EaP was launched in late 2008 as a joint policy, aimed at promoting regional cooperation between the EU, its Member States and Eastern Neighbours. An important peculiarity of the EaP has been a combination of the EU's bilateral cooperation with each of the Neighbours and the "multilateral track", serving as a new framework of cooperation between the EU, Member States and Neighbours. To complement the findings of the previous analysis and the analysis of the assistance programming as follows, this sub-section will pay particular attention to the multilateral aspects of the EaP. We show that, despite numerous specific initiatives, lying at the crossroads between the rule of law and economic development, the EaP Summits' declarations are marked by a strict demarcation line between political cooperation and measures to advance economic development and trade.

To start, it shall be stressed that the 2008 Commission's Communication on the EaP distinguished the rule of law and the facilitation of the EU-EaP free trade and economic integration as a key "mutual commitment" and a flagship cooperation area, respectively.[66] Calling for the creation of the "Neighbourhood Economic Community, taking inspiration from the European Economic Area", the Communication pointed to the harmonization of Neighbours' legislation with *acquis communautaire* as an important aspect of facilitating the multilateral policy track.[67] Nevertheless, the conceptualization of the "Economic Integration and Convergence with EU Policies" EaP thematic platform did not refer to either the rule of law concept or cross-cutting issues concerning both the rule of law and the functioning market economy.[68]

A similar trend can be distinguished based on the analysis of the joint declarations, adopted at the 2009 Prague EaP Summit and the 2011 Warsaw EaP Summit.[69] The former broadened mutual commitments, specified in the 2008 Commission

---

66 European Commission, Communication to the European Parliament and the Council: Eastern Partnership, COM(2008) 823/4 of 3 December 2008, p. 3.

67 *Ibid.*

68 *Ibid.*, p. 11.

69 European Commission/High Representative of the European Union for the Common and Security Policy Communities, Joint Declaration of the Prague Eastern Partnership Summit, 8435/09 of 7 May 2009; Council of the European Communities, Joint Declaration of the Warsaw Eastern Partnership Summit, 14983/11 of 30 September 2011.

Communication, to include the respect for the principles of international law and good governance.[70] At the same time, it only referred to the rule of law as a "fundamental value" and "mutual commitment", without linking the concept to "regulatory approximation leading to convergence with EU laws and standards"[71] under the umbrella of free trade. In turn, the Warsaw EaP Summit Declaration emphasized the rule of law as a cooperation and coordination area, tightly connected to the development of democracy and human rights.[72] Welcoming progress as to the EU-Neighbours trade liberalization, the Warsaw Summit Declaration stressed institution-building, rather than legislative approximation and regulatory, as a key cross-cutting area between free trade and the promotion of values.[73]

The 2013 Vilnius Summit Declaration also barely changed the pattern of a strict demarcation line between the rule of law and trade liberalization/economic integration.[74] Similar to the 2011 Warsaw Summit Declaration, the Vilnius Summit Declaration distinguished the rule of law as a foundational policy "mutual commitment" and cooperation area, stressing the need for reforming judiciary and law enforcement agencies in the Neighbourhood.[75] Though introducing the "business dimension of the EaP", the Vilnius Declaration did not link the improvement of business environment in the region to advancing specific rule of law standards. However, already the 2015 Riga Summit Declaration emphasized the rule of law and **legal certainty** as the means to maximize benefits the parties gain in the context of the "business dimension" of the EaP and implementation of the AAs/DCFTAs.

In contrast to the vast majority of the previously analyzed documents, the 2017 Joint Declaration of the Brussels EaP Summit introduced an in-detail list of the rule of law initiatives to be pursued in the region.[76] They included, *inter alia*, the establishment of effective systems of the declaration of assets and conflict of interest; the implementation of international standards regarding party funding and the creation of independent anti-corruption bodies.[77] The 2017 version of the EaP "20 Deliverables for 2020" also tended to suggest "action" at the crossroads of the rule of law, on the one hand, and countering corruption and money laundering, on the other hand (e.g. the creation of public registries of beneficial ownership of legal entities, the establishment of the offices for the recovery and management of assets). Since respective initiatives immediately concern the **legal certainty** and **transparency** dimensions of the rule of law, their implementation is conducive to

---

70 Council of the European Communities, Joint Declaration of the Prague Eastern Partnership Summit 8435/09 of 7 May 2009.

71 *Ibid.*

72 Council of the European Union, Joint Declaration of the Warsaw Eastern Partnership Summit, 14983/11 of 30 September 2011.

73 *Ibid.*

74 Council of the European Union, Joint Declaration of the Vilnius Eastern Partnership Summit "Eastern Partnership – the Way Ahead", 17130/13 of 29 November 2013.

75 *Ibid.*

76 Council of the European Union, Joint Declaration of the Eastern Partnership Summit, 14821/17 of 24 November 2017.

77 *Ibid.*

126 *EU rule of law: the "action" dimension*

improving business environment in the region. Nonetheless, the "20 Deliverables for 2020" did not connect them to the Priority I "Economic Development and Market Opportunities" aimed at improving regulatory environment for business.

Ultimately, these "soft" documents reflect a turbulent history of the rule of law and its connection to economic development and trade agenda in the EaP context. Despite suggesting specific rule of law initiatives that could potentially complement partners' efforts in the domains of economic development and trade, even the most recent declarations strictly delimit between the cooperation on values and economic development. This differentiates the documents in question from the 2004 Action Plans for Moldova, Ukraine and Georgia. Although the 2004 Action Plans stress multiple cross-cutting issues, both categories of the documents under study view the rule of law-economic development nexus as a "one-way road" relationship, whereby the rule of law is conducive to trade liberalization, doing business and integrating economies.

2. *Unilateral trade measures*

Compared to the SAP, the EU's application of autonomous trade measures in its relations with Eastern Neighbours has been highly limited. This difference may be predominantly attributed to the contextual differences, i.e. relative stability of the situation in the Eastern Neighbourhood before 2014. Hence, the EU only applied temporary autonomous trade measures as a reaction to the outbreak of the Ukraine crisis. According to the 2014 statement by the EU Trade Commissioner Karel de Gucht, the Union's unilateral "opening its doors for exports from Ukraine" has been a part of the comprehensive aid package, delivered by the EU to Ukraine in March 2014 (European Commission, 2014).

Notwithstanding "unprecedented security, political and economic challenges faced by Ukraine", Regulation No 374/2014 required Ukraine to adhere to a number of conditions to make use of the preferential arrangements.[78] Apart from promoting the rule of law via the conventionally designed "essential elements" clause, the Regulation stipulated Ukraine's obligation to participate in "effective administrative cooperation with the Union".[79] As noted earlier, fulfilling such an obligation requires strengthening of the **legal certainty**, **transparency**, and **equality** and **non-discrimination** dimensions of the rule of law.[80] Moreover, Art. 2 of the Regulation No 374/2014required Ukraine's "compliance with the methods of administrative cooperation", set in Art. 121–122 of the Regulation (EEC) 2454/93.[81] The legal analysis of relevant provisions demonstrates their

---

78 Regulation (EU) No 374/2014 of the European Parliament and of the Council of 16 April 2014 on the reduction or elimination of customs duties on goods originating in Ukraine, OJ L 118 of 22 April 2014.

79 *Ibid.*

80 *Ibid.*, Art.2.

81 Commission Regulation (EEC) No 2454/93 of 2 July 1993 laying down the provisions for the implementation of Council Regulation (EEC) No 2913/92 establishing the Community Customs Code, OJ L 253 of 11 October 1993.

relatedness to the **legality** (the substance of customs rules and procedures), **legal certainty** and **transparency** (the design of customs procedures) dimensions of the rule of law.

The set of conditions for Ukraine to be eligible for continued access to the EU market was significantly broadened after the entry into force of the Regulation 2017/1566 supplementing the trade concessions under the EU-Ukraine AA.[82] In particular, the "essential element" clause was supplemented by the requirement of "continued and sustained efforts with regard to the fight against corruption and illegal activities under Art.2, 3 and 21 of the EU-Ukraine AA".[83] Moreover, the Regulation introduced the additional conditions of Ukraine's "continued compliance with obligations to cooperate" in the domains of trade and sustainable development (Chapter 13 of Title IV of the AA) and employment, social policy and equal opportunities.[84] In our view, the introduction of these additional conditions testifies to the EU's ambition to use autonomous trade measures as an instrument to both assist Ukraine under severe security and socio-economic challenges it presently faces and strengthen Ukraine's compliance with fundamental values and obligations to cooperate under the AA.

In a nutshell, autonomous trade measures represent a flexible instrument the Union can use to react to a broad range of developments with respect to Ukraine's compliance with fundamental values and its obligations to cooperate, stemming from the EU-Ukraine AA.

3. *Unilateral financial assistance instruments*

European Neighbourhood and Partnership Instrument (ENPI) 2007–2013

The ENPI has been the key framework for the EU's financial and technical assistance to Eastern Neighbours since 2007 up to the signing of the AAs in 2013/2014. We show that, similar to the CARDS and IPA I programming, the ENPI programmes tend to draw a strict borderline between the promotion of the rule of law and legislative and regulatory approximation required for Single Market integration.[85]

According to Art.7 of the ENPI Regulation, financial and technical assistance under the ENPI shall be implemented through the country, multi-country and cross-border cooperation programmes. Since the ENPI cross-border component does not relate to either the promotion of fundamental values or the preparation

---

82 Regulation (EU) 2017/1566 of the European Parliament and of the Council of 13 September 2017 on the introduction of temporary autonomous trade measures for Ukraine supplementing the trade concessions under the Association Agreement, OJ L 254/1 of 30 September 2017.

83 *Ibid.*

84 *Ibid.*

85 Regulation (EC) No 1638/2006 of the European Parliament and of the Council of 24 October 2006 laying down the general provisions establishing a European Neighbourhood and Partnership Instrument, OJ L 310/1 of 9 November 2006, Art. 2 (hereinafter referred to as "ENPI Regulation").

128 *EU rule of law: the "action" dimension*

for the implementation of AAs/DCFTAs,[86] the subsequent analysis will focus on the single-country multiannual programmes. According to the 2007–2010 indicative country programmes for Ukraine, Moldova and Georgia, the rule of law reform in the Neighbourhood had to embrace the judicial reform, reform of law enforcement agencies, the simplification of legal procedures and enhanced management of migration and border security.[87] In turn, the country programmes stressed legislative approximation as a stand-alone priority in the context of the support for economic development and trade.[88] In contrast to the 2004 Action Plans for Neighbours, the sub-priorities under this priority point to specific tasks to be conducted (e.g. tax reform, reforms in the employment and social area),[89] rather than the rule of law standards to be achieved. Moreover, neither of the sub-priorities in question has addressed cross-cutting issues concerning both "deep" disciplines and the rule of law.

Analysis of the indicative country programmes 2011–2013 demonstrates a slight change regarding the contextualization of the rule of law. Hence, alongside the judicial and public administration reforms, the 2011–2013 indicative programmes for Moldova and Ukraine pointed to the connection between the rule of law and the improvement of business and investment climate.[90] In this vein, the programmes distinguished specific tasks to be completed, such as improving the efficiency and **impartiality** of administrative and business courts, and the enforcement of their decisions.[91] Furthermore, by analogy with the IPA I and IPA II, the 2011–2013 ENPI programmes paid significant attention to public administration reforms and institution-building.[92] Moreover, the "deep" disciplines-related priorities under the 2011–2013 programming referred to specific rule of law standards, such as **legal certainty**, **transparency**, **equality** and **non-discrimination** in the

---

86 European Commission DG "NEAR" (2018). Cross-Border Cooperation. [online] Available at: https://ec.europa.eu/neighbourhood-enlargement/neighbourhood/cross-border-cooperation_en.

87 European Commission DG "External Relations" (2007). Ukraine: National Indicative Programme 2007–2010 [online]. Available at: https://library.euneighbours.eu/content/ukraine-national-indicative-programme-2007-2010; European Commission DG "External Relations" (2007). Moldova: National Indicative Programme 2007–2010. Available at: https://library.euneighbours.eu/content/moldova-national-indicative-programme-2007-2010; European Commission DG "External Relations" (2007). Georgia: National Indicative Programme 2007–2010. Available at: https://publications.europa.eu/en/publication-detail/-/publication/14729e8f-6edb-448c-b1c3-a05a60c30c7e/language-en.

88 See, for instance, European Commission DG "External Relations" (2007). Georgia: National Indicative Programme 2007–2010, pp. 9–12.

89 *Ibid.*

90 European Commission DG "External Relations" (2010). Ukraine: National Indicative Programme 2011–2013. [pdf] European Commission. Available at: http://eeas.europa.eu/archives/docs/enp/pdf/pdf/country/2011_enpi_nip_ukraine_en.pdf, pp-10–11; European Commission DG "External Relations" (2010). Moldova: National Indicative Programme 2011–2013. [pdf]. European Commission. Available at: https://ec.europa.eu/europeaid/sites/devco/files/nip-moldova-2011-2013_en.pdf, pp. 13–15.

91 European Commission DG "External Relations" (2010). Moldova: National Indicative Programme 2011–2013, pp. 13–15.

92 *Ibid.*, p. 16.

EU rule of law: the "action" dimension   129

public procurement and competition domains.[93] Nonetheless, the formulations of respective priorities were not meant to bridge the gap between the rule of law, as a part of the political cooperation agenda, and legislative approximation, required to promote trade and economic development.

Ultimately, the evolution of country programming under the ENPI is illustrative of the transfer from the strict delimitation between political and economic cooperation-related priorities to the emerging emphasis on cross-cutting domains of cooperation. Notwithstanding this, the ENPI programming and respective reports are marked by the non-integration of tasks under the rule of law and trade development-related aspects of indicative programmes.

European Neighbourhood Instrument (ENI) 2014–2020

Adopted in 2014, the ENI was marked by considerable differentiation among partner countries[94] and the pronounced "more-for-more" principle.[95] Pursuant to Annex II to the ENI Regulation, the Union's rule of law assistance under the ENI focused on the reforms of justice, public administration and the security sector. The achievement of progressive integration into the Single Market through legislative approximation and regulatory convergence towards the EU was recognized as a self-standing objective of the EU's support of Neighbours.[96] Despite strictly delimiting between the rule of law and trade-related objectives, the country-level strategies and programming under the ENI embrace several crucial cross-cutting elements, such as institution-building and the improvement of regulatory environment for business.

According to the Regional East Strategy Paper (2014–2020) and Multiannual Indicative Programme (MIP) (2014–2020), the rule of law remained a "critical priority" across the Eastern Neighbourhood for the period 2014–2020.[97] While referring to the rule of law promotion as a part of the "political association" (alongside democracy and human rights), the Strategy Paper also emphasized the creation of a "reliable regulatory framework that is enforced under the primacy of the rule of law" in its economic development-related part.[98] Furthermore, the economic part of the Strategy mentioned several cross-cutting themes, such as "the improvement of the business environment to attract investments", institution-building and countering policy and legal obstacles to entrepreneurship.[99] Such

---

93 *Ibid.*, pp. 24–25.
94 Regulation (EU) No 232/2014 of the European Parliament and the European Council of 11 March 2014 establishing a European Neighbourhood Instrument, OJ L 77/27 of 15 March 2014, Art.4 (hereinafter referred to as "ENI Regulation").
95 *Ibid.*, Art.3(2).
96 *Ibid.*, Art.2(2)(b).
97 European External Action Service (2014). Programming of the European Neighbourhood Instrument (ENI) 2014–2020: 2014–2020 Regional East Strategy Paper and Multiannual Indicative Programme (2014–2017). Available at: https://library.euneighbours.eu/content/programming-european-neighbourhood-instrument-eni-2014-2020-regional-east-strategy-paper-201, p. 2.
98 *Ibid.*, p. 5.
99 *Ibid.*

130 *EU rule of law: the "action" dimension*

cross-cutting themes, however, lacked a coherent reflection in both the Sector of Intervention Framework, included into the respective Strategy, and the country-specific action programmes.

The Annual ENI Action Programmes for Moldova and Ukraine tended to link the rule of law to countering corruption and reforming police forces (Moldova) and support of justice sector and law enforcement agencies (Ukraine).[100] The 2017 and 2018 Action Programmes for the Republic Georgia were, however, explicitly located at the crossroads of the rule of law and trade/economic integration.[101] For instance, the Annual Action Programme 2017 for Georgia provided for "facilitating fairer and faster litigations in commercial matters".[102] This broad cooperation target encompassed, *inter alia*, the evolution of mediation and arbitration, changes to be made into company law and the legislation on insolvency and the enforcement of judicial decisions.[103] In 2018, the Annual Action Programme was dedicated to the reinforcement of economic governance, accountability and transparency mainly in the domains of public finance and fiscal law.[104] Hence, at the programming level, Georgia has been a single case of the EU's application of the ENI funds to the support of reforms, immediately lying at the crossroads between the rule of law and economic development.

Simultaneously, on the project level, the EU has been implementing several initiatives in Ukraine, Moldova and Georgia, tailored to support the implementation of the DCFTAs' "deep disciplines" chapters. Among such initiatives (to be further analyzed in Chapter 6), one can mention the "Implementation of the National Competition and State Aid Programme" (Moldova), "Harmonization of Public Procurement System of Ukraine with EU Standards" (Ukraine) and "Support to the Establishment of the State Aid Control System in Ukraine" (Ukraine).[105] Although neither of these respective projects' descriptions referred to the rule

---

100 See, for instance, European Commission, Implementing Decision on the Annual Action Programme 2015 in favour of the Republic of Moldova to be financed from the general budget of the European Union, C(2015)7150 final of 16 October 2015, Art. 1; European Commission Action Document for Support to Rule of Law Reforms in Ukraine (PRAVO), COM(2016) 8266 final of 12 December 2016, Art. 1.

101 European Commission, Implementing Decision of the Annual Action Programme 2017 in favour of Georgia to be financed from the general budget of the Union, C(2017) 8575 final of 11 December 2017; European Commission, Implementing Decision on the Annual Action Programme in favour of Georgia for 2018, C(2018) 8064 final of 28 November 2018.

102 European Commission, Implementing Decision of the Annual Action Programme 2017 in favour of Georgia to be financed from the general budget of the Union, C(2017) 8575 final of 11 December 2017, p. 2.

103 *Ibid.*

104 European Commission, Implementing Decision on the Annual Action Programme in favour of Georgia for 2018, C(2018) 8064 final of 28 November 2018, pp. 1–4.

105 For more information about the projects, see Competition Council of the Republic of Moldova (2017). Implementation of the National Competition and State Aid Programme. [online] Available at: https://competition.md/libview.php?l=en&idc=38&id=6177&t=/Press/News/Implementation-of-the-National-Competition-and-State-Aid-Program; Crown Agents (n.d.) Harmonization of Public Procurement System of Ukraine with EU Standards. Available at: http://eupublicprocurement.org.ua; Institutional Strengthening Risk Managing Sustainable Development (AETS)

of law, the project activities could have tackled specific rule of law standards, as provided for in the DCFTAs and analyzed in the previous chapter.

Concluding, compared to the ENPI, the ENI strategy and multiannual programming makes a stronger emphasis on the rule of law–economic development nexus. On the annual programme level, however, the respective nexus was less visible, with Georgia being the only country among the "associated" Neighbours where the EU funded programmes, lying at the crossroads of the rule of law and economic development. On the project level, the Union funded an array of initiatives, directed to support of the implementation of "deep disciplines"-related chapters of DCFTAs in Moldova and Ukraine that were not positioned as the EU's rule of law assistance to the Neighbourhood.

4. EU Rule of law missions to Georgia and Ukraine

Over the history of the ENP, the EU deployed several missions, mandated to promote the rule of law in Georgia (EUJUST THEMIS) and Ukraine (EUAM, EU project "PRAVO-JUSTICE"). Although such missions predominantly focused on the rule of law as a part of political association, an insight into their mandates allows revealing activities, capable of both advancing the rule of law, and contributing to economic development and trade liberalization.

Based on the Council Joint Action 2004/523/CFSP, the EUJUST THEMIS advisory mandate focused on the domains of the judiciary, criminal law and criminal justice, countering corruption and the support of international and regional cooperation in the field of criminal justice.[106] The EUJUST THEMIS activities were not directed to supporting the execution of legislative and regulatory convergence-related tasks under the 2004 Action Plan for Georgia.

The non-executive EU Advisory Mission to Ukraine (EUAM) was launched in 2014 to assist Ukrainian authorities to implement the sustainable civilian sector reform.[107] It has been a complex institution-building project, targeting the Ministry of Internal Affairs, National Police, Security Service of Ukraine, local courts and anti-corruption bodies.[108] Though contributing to the **transparency** and **accountability** of the stated agencies, the EUAM's activities are not immediately linked to the economic development/trade liberalization domain. Nonetheless, similar to the previously considered case of EULEX, EUAM-led institution-building (e.g. with regard to the functioning of anti-corruption bodies and local courts) can be conducive to the promotion of the rule of law standards contained in the DCFTA.

(n.d.) Support to the Establishment of State Aid Control System in Ukraine. [online]. Available at: www.aets-consultants.com/en/news,147.

106 Council of the European Union, Joint Action of 28 June 2004 on the European Union Rule of Law Mission in Georgia, EUJUST THEMIS, OJ L 228 of 29 June 2014, p. 21.

107 European Union Advisory Mission (EUAM) (2018). Our Mission. [online] EUAM. Available at: www.euam-ukraine.eu/our-mission/about-us/.

108 *Ibid.*

132 *EU rule of law: the "action" dimension*

Alongside the EUAM, an important instrument of the EU's rule of law promotion in Ukraine had been its on-site project "Support to Justice Sector Reforms in Ukraine" (2014–2017).[109] It was designed to support the design and implementation of the comprehensive justice sector reform strategy and the "division of labour" between Ukrainian actors, involved into the operation of the justice system.[110] In contrast to the "Support to Justice Sector Reforms in Ukraine" that tackled the justice sector from the strategic perspective, its successor project "PRAVO-JUSTICE" includes a focus area "Property Right Protection and Ease of Business".[111] In terms of this focus area, the project tackles a variety of issues, such as support of new private enforcement service, improvement of the functioning of notary service and the enhancement of bankruptcy legislation.[112] Nonetheless, neither the "PRAVO-JUSTICE" itself nor its "joint vision of justice as a chain" offered a coherent vision of the rule of law as an economic concept or linked it to the problématique of implementation of the AAs/DCFTAs.

Hence, as well as the ENP and ENI programming, the institutional dimension of the rule of law promotion under the ENP has lacked a systemic nexus between the rule of law, on the one hand, and economic development and trade liberalization, on the other hand.

Part 3. Development

As noted earlier, the history of EU-Africa relations dates back to the signing of the Yaoundé Convention between the EEC and the Associated African States and Madagascar (AASM) in 1963.[113] Apart from liberalizing the EU-AASM trade, the Convention was the first one to launch numerous financial and technical assistance schemes in favour of the AASM, including the European Development Fund (EDF).[114] Subsequently, the EU-ACP Lomé Conventions (1975, 1979, 1985 and 1989) and the Cotonou Agreement (CA) (2000) served as a legal framework for both the EU-ACP trade liberalization and channelling the EU's financial and technical assistance to the ACP countries.

Under the CA, the parties agreed to conclude new WTO-compatible trade arrangements, "removing progressively barriers to trade between them and enhancing cooperation in all areas relevant to trade".[115] Based on the WTO con-

---

109 Delegation of the European Union to Ukraine (n.d.). Project to Support Justice Sector Reforms in Ukraine. [online] Available at: https://eeas.europa.eu/delegations/ukraine/27521/project-support-justice-sector-reforms-ukraine_en.
110 *Ibid.*
111 PRAVO-JUSTICE (2018). European Justice for Ukraine. [online] Available at: https://eeas.europa.eu/delegations/ukraine/27521/project-support-justice-sector-reforms-ukraine_en.
112 *Ibid.*
113 European Community Information Service (1966). Partnership in Africa: the Yaoundé Association. Community Topics 26. [pdf] European Community. Available at: http://aei.pitt.edu/34505/1/A674.pdf.
114 *Ibid.*, pp. 8–14.
115 CA, Art.36.

cept of "special and differentiated treatment", the EPAs provided for the ACP countries' gradually liberalizing their markets for imports from the EU (Conconi and Perroni, 2015). This process is, however, impeded by the fact that many EPAs are not yet applied even provisionally (e.g. EPAs with Central Africa, Eastern and Southern Africa [ESA]), as well as the continuing post-Cotonou negotiations (European Commission, 2018). Since the preferential trade arrangements for goods, originating in the ACP region, are embedded into the CA and the EPAs, the EU has not utilized autonomous trade measures in favour of the ACP countries. Therefore, the subsequent analysis will only focus on "soft" documents and the EU's financial and technical assistance in its relations with CARIFORUM (the EU-CARIFORUM EPA is the only EPA currently in force that contains "deep" disciplines chapters).

1. "Soft" (diplomatic) instruments

The first EU-Latin America and the Caribbean (EU-LAC) Summit took place in 1999 in Rio de Janeiro. As a result, the parties agreed to reinforce institutional dialogue between the two regions, promote democracy and human rights, and jointly contribute to the strengthening of the multilateral system, regionalism and trade liberalization.[116] We argue that, prior to the adoption of the 2016 Joint Communication on a Renewed Partnership with the ACP Countries, "soft" documents pertaining to the EU-CARIFORUM relations have been lacking a coherent emphasis on the rule of law and its linkage to trade liberalization/economic development.

Similar to the Final Document of the Rio Summit, the 2005 Commission's framework document "The European Union, Latin America and the Caribbean: A Strategic Partnership" did not mention the rule of law among the parties' political commitments.[117] Emphasizing the creation of "a climate favourable to trade and investment", the Strategy mentioned several issue areas at the crossroads between the rule of law and the promotion of trade liberalization, such as conducting dialogue on barriers to trade and investment and improving the business environment in partner countries.[118] Nevertheless, largely due to the framework nature of the document, it did not mention specific legal and regulatory steps to be taken by Latin American and Caribbean countries. In contrast to the previously mentioned Strategy, the joint Communiqué of the 2006 Vienna EU-CARIFORUM Summit affirmed the parties' commitments to the rule of law, good governance and sound economic policies.[119] Welcoming the launch of the CARICOM

---

116 On the results of the 1999 Rio Summit, see European Commission, Communication to the Council and the European Parliament: Follow-Up to the First Summit between Latin America, the Caribbean and the European Union, COM(2000) 670 final of 31 October 2000.

117 European Commission (2005). The European Union, Latin America and the Caribbean: A Strategic Partnership. [pdf] European Commission. Available at: http://eeas.europa.eu/archives/docs/la/docs/guadal_04_en.pdf.

118 *Ibid.*, p. 30.

119 Council of the European Communities, EU-CARIFORUM Summit Joint Communiqué, 9338/06 of 13 May 2006.

134 *EU rule of law: the "action" dimension*

Single Market, neither the 2006 Vienna Summit Communiqué nor the 2008 Lima Summit Declaration referred to the previously mentioned region-to-region dialogue on barriers to trade and investment and the improvement of the business climate.[120] Similarly, the 2010 Madrid Declaration and 2012 Joint Caribbean-EU Partnership Strategy stressed intra-regional integration and mentioned business development without referring to cooperation areas, lying at the crossroads of trade liberalization and the rule of law promotion.[121]

Following an emphasis on peace, governance and the rule of law in the Agenda 2030 and the new European Consensus on Development, the 2016 Joint Communication on a Renewed Partnership with the ACP Countries distinguished the "promotion of peaceful and democratic societies, good governance and human rights for all" as a crucial cooperation priority.[122] In contrast to these documents, the 2016 Communication stressed the role of the rule of law as a foundation for sustainable development and linked it to creating a conducive business environment and ensuring justice for business.[123] In its part related to the promotion of inclusive growth and decent jobs for all, the Communication also referred to several dimensions of an umbrella rule of law concept, such as **transparency** and the **relationship between domestic and international law (WTO law and EPAs)**.[124] Besides, it underlined the importance of an EU-Caribbean consultation procedure on sensitive issues relating to fundamental values, capable of supplementing the "essential element" clause and envisaging full or partial suspension of relations as a measure of last resort.[125]

Ultimately, prior to the adoption of the 2016 Joint Communication, "soft" documents concerning EU-LAC relations have been lacking a coherent approach to linking the rule of law, on the one hand, and economic development or trade liberalization, on the other hand.

2. *Financial and technical assistance*

9th European Development Fund (EDF) 2000–2007

Established by the 1957 Treaty of Rome and launched in 1959, the EDF represents the pivotal instrument of the EU's aid delivery to ACP countries. Compared

---

120 *Ibid.*; Council of the European Communities, CARIFORUM EU Troika Summit Joint Communique, C/08/129 of 17 May 2008.
121 Council of the European Union, EU-LAC Summit Declaration, Madrid Action Plan 2010–2012, 10449/1/10 REV1 of 15 November 2010; Council of the European Union (2012). Council Conclusions on the Joint Caribbean-EU Partnership Strategy, 3199th Foreign Affairs Council meeting of 19 November 2012. [pdf] Council of the European Union. Available at: https://eeas.europa.eu/sites/eeas/files/partnership_strategy.pdf.
122 European Commission, Communication to the European Parliament and the Council: A Renewed Partnership with the Countries of Africa, the Caribbean and the Pacific, JOIN(2016) 52 final of 22 November 2016, pp. 19–20.
123 *Ibid.*, p. 15.
124 *Ibid.*, pp. 19–20.
125 *Ibid.*, p. 16.

to the Development Cooperation Instrument (DCI), briefly analyzed in Chapter 2, the EDF is marked by the fact that it is funded outside the EU budget through Member States' voluntary contributions.[126] According to Annex I to the CA "Financial Protocol", the Community's financial assistance under the 9th EDF accounted for €13.5 million, with €10 million reserved for an "envelope for support for long-term development" based on national indicative programmes (NIPs) and €1.3 million for financing of support of regional cooperation and integration among the ACP states.[127] An insight into the regional and country indicative programmes under the 9th EDF demonstrates that while pursuing development objectives in the region, the EU did not engage in value-promotion activities, including the rule of law promotion.

The region-level programmes, financed in the Caribbean under the 9th EDF, predominantly aimed at establishing the institutional infrastructure of regional integration in the ACP, including the Caribbean Single Market and Economy (CSME).[128] Similarly, under the 9th EDF, CSPs, NIPS and related programme reports tended not to refer to the rule of law concept, and barely referred to political and legal development-related problématique.[129] Hence, the 9th EDF programmes in Antigua and Barbuda, Barbados, Jamaica, Grenada and St. Lucia predominantly focused on the objectives related to poverty eradication, social infrastructure, education, health, road infrastructure, rural development and water management.[130] The 2002–2007 CSP for Trinidad and Tobago has been the only country programmatic document produced under the 9th EDF to refer to the concept of good governance and address compliance with the government's policies

---

126 European Commission (n.d.). European Development Fund. [online] Available at: https://ec.europa.eu/europeaid/funding/funding-instruments-programming/funding-instruments/european-development-fund_en.

127 *Ibid.*

128 See, for instance, Delegation of the EU in Barbados and the Eastern Caribbean (2003). Cooperation between the EU and Antigua and Barbuda – Annual Report 2002. [pdf] Delegation of the EU in Barbados and the Eastern Caribbean. Available at: http://edz.bib.uni-mannheim.de/daten/edz-ma/gdex/03/ag_review_2003_en.pdf.

129 See, for instance, Delegation of the EU in Trinidad and Tobago, Ministry of Integrated Planning and Development of Trinidad and Tobago (2001). Country Strategy Paper for 2002–2007. [pdf] Delegation of the EU in Trinidad and Tobago. Available at: http://eeas.europa.eu/archives/delegations/trinidad/documents/eu_trinidad/9th_edf_country_strategy_paper.pdf; Delegation of the EU in Jamaica (2007). Joint Action Report, Cooperation between the European Union and Jamaica [pdf] Delegation of the EU in Jamaica. Available at: https://ec.europa.eu/europeaid/sites/devco/files/joint-annual-report-07-cooperation-eu-jamaica-200806_en.pdf.

130 See, for instance: Delegation of the European Commission in Barbados and the Eastern Caribbean, Office of the National Authorizing Officer in Antigua and Barbuda (2008). Joint Action Report for Antigua and Barbuda. [pdf] Delegation of the European Commission in Barbados and the Eastern Caribbean. Available at: https://ec.europa.eu/europeaid/sites/devco/files/joint-annual-report-08-cooperation-eu-antigua-barbuda-20091013_en.pdf; Delegation of the European Commission in Barbados and the Eastern Caribbean (2007). Joint Action Report: Cooperation between the European Union and Grenada. [pdf] Delegation of the European Commission in Barbados and the Eastern Caribbean. Available at: https://ec.europa.eu/europeaid/sites/devco/files/joint-annual-report-07-cooperation-eu-grenada-2008_en.pdf.

136 *EU rule of law: the "action" dimension*

in the domains of education and health.[131] Furthermore, despite an emphasis on economic integration at the regional level, neither of the country programmes or reports distinguished economic development or intensification of trade as a focal area of cooperation. Actually, the NIP for Jamaica was the only programmatic document under the 9th EDF referring to private sector development as a focal cooperation area.[132]

Almost complete absence of the rule of law and the promotion of trade on the country development agenda can be attributed to several phenomena. First, inspired by the Millennium Development Goals (MDGs), then EU development policy focused on poverty eradication rather than economic development, and did not encompass any peace, governance or rule of law–related issues.[133] Second, relevant EU primary law (i.e. the Treaty of Amsterdam and the Treaty of Nice) did not distinguish the promotion of fundamental values as the EU's foreign policy objective. Third, the non-inclusion of trade liberalization and economic development objectives into the country programming may stem from the region-to-region nature of the CA that served as a foundation for the 9th EDF.

In a nutshell, the EU's assistance to CARIFORUM under the 9th EDF prioritized regional economic integration without distinguishing economic development and trade intensification into country-level strategies and programmes. Not recognized as either a foreign policy objective or a development policy objective, the rule of law was absent from the agenda of the 9th EDF.

10th European Development Fund (EDF) 2008–2013

Adopted in the context of the 2005 EU Strategy for the Caribbean and the 2006 European Consensus for Development, the 10th EDF contained a stronger emphasis on fundamental values and governance, compared to the 9th EDF.[134] Nonetheless, both the rule of law promotion and the support of trade liberalization have been seldom targets under both the regional and country dimensions of the 10th EDF.

The 2008–2013 Regional Strategy Paper distinguished the focal area of cooperation "Regional Economic Integration and Cooperation" and three non-focal cooperation areas "Crime and Security", "Civil Society Participation" and

---

131 Delegation of the EU in Trinidad and Tobago, Ministry of Integrated Planning and Development of Trinidad and Tobago (2001). Country Strategy Paper for 2002–2007. [pdf] Delegation of the EU in Trinidad and Tobago. Available at: http://eeas.europa.eu/archives/delegations/trinidad/documents/eu_trinidad/9th_edf_country_strategy_paper.pdf, p. 18.

132 EU Delegation in Jamaica (2007). Joint Action Report. Cooperation between the European Union and Jamaica. [pdf] EU Delegation in Jamaica. Available at: https://ec.europa.eu/europeaid/sites/devco/files/joint-annual-report-07-cooperation-eu-jamaica-200806_en.pdf, Annex b.

133 UN General Assembly Resolution, United Nations Millennium Declaration, A/Res/55/2 of 18 September 2000.

134 ACP-EC Council of Ministers, Decision No 1/2006 specifying the multiannual framework for the period 2008 to 2013 and modifying the revised ACP-EU Partnership, OJ L247/22 of 9 September 2006.

EU rule of law: the "action" dimension 137

"Institutional Support/Programme Implementation". Similar to the regional level programming under the 9th EDF, neither of these focal/non-focal cooperation areas encompassed the promotion of the rule of law.[135] Simultaneously, the focal cooperation area "Regional Economic Integration and Cooperation" has encompassed multifaceted support of the EPAs' implementation, targeting fiscal reform and adjustment, and phytosanitary legislation, technical barriers to trade, legislative and regulatory frameworks for services sector and raising the CARIFORUM countries' institutional and implementation capacity.[136] Although the implementation of this programme was concerned with numerous changes to partner countries' legal and regulatory systems, its description did not refer to either the rule of law components or the concept as a whole.[137]

Compared to the country programming under the 9th EDF, many more 10th EDF-based CSPs and NIPs underlined governance-related improvements as a focal cooperation area. For instance, the 2003–2009 CSP and NIP for Jamaica included "support for governance reform (justice and security)" as a part to its Envelope I assistance for Jamaica.[138] In this vein, these documents tended to link the rule of law to reduced organized crime rates, promoting public confidence in law enforcement, as well as the improvement of access to justice and human rights.[139] While not linking the envisaged governance reform to the implementation of the EPA, the CSP for Jamaica introduced a country-level facility to assist the government in the EPA's implementation.[140] "Good and Effective Governance" was also distinguished as a non-focal cooperation priority in the EU CSP and NIP for Trinidad and Tobago, encompassing the improvement in the criminal justice system, improved efficiency and effectiveness of the police, judicial and prison systems, as well as the promotion of security.[141] Moreover, in contrast to the previously considered CSPs and NIPs under the 9th and 10th EDFs, the CSP for Trinidad and Tobago linked the rule of law/good governance reforms and the promotion of trade/economic development through aiming "to create a business climate that attracts investors and encourages competitive business to

---

135 European Commission (2007). CARIFORUM – Regional Strategy Paper and Regional Indicative Programme 2008–2013. European Commission. [pdf] Available at: https://eulacfoundation.org/en/system/files/EUROPEAN%20COMMUNITY%20_%20CARIBBEAN%20REGION%20%20REGIONAL%20STRATEGY%20PAPER.pdf, p. 37.

136 *Ibid.*, pp. 37–40.

137 *Ibid.*

138 European Commission, Government of Jamaica (2007). Country Strategy Paper and National Indicative Programme for Jamaica for the period 2008–2013. [pdf] European Commission. Available at: https://ec.europa.eu/europeaid/sites/devco/files/csp-nip-jamaica-2008-2013_en.pdf, pp. 22–24.

139 *Ibid.*, pp. 31–32.

140 *Ibid.*, p. 33.

141 European Commission, Government of Trinidad and Tobago (2007). Country Strategy Paper and National Indicative Programme for Trinidad and Tobago 2008–2013. [online] Available at: https://eeas.europa.eu/delegations/tunisia/3721/trinidad-and-tobago–country-strategy-paper-and-national-indicative-programme-2008-2013_en, pp. 24–25.

138 *EU rule of law: the "action" dimension*

start and grow".[142] Nonetheless, many CSPs and NIPs for CARIFORUM countries (e.g. Bahamas, Belize, Grenada) concentrated solely on development issues (e.g. poverty reduction, road infrastructure, human settlement), rather than governance/the rule of law reforms and support of the implementation of the EU-CARIFORUM EPA.[143] Such a difference between the EU's assistance priorities across the CARIFORUM countries can be explained by the EU's efforts to tailor its assistance to the partner countries' development strategies.

Ultimately, the adoption of the 2005 EU Strategy for the Caribbean and the 2006 European Consensus for Development gave an important impetus to the promotion of fundamental values and governance reforms under the CSPs and NIPs across the Caribbean. Nonetheless, as well as both the regional and country dimensions of assistance under the 9th EDF, the 10th EDF programming did not create a systemic link between the rule of law promotion and the support of EPAs' implementation.

11th European Development Fund (EDF) 2015–2020

The 11th EDF was launched by the intergovernmental agreement that was signed in 2013 and entered into force in 2015. To ensure the continuity of EU programmes' funding in the ACP region, a "Bridging Facility" was utilized by the Union over the period from December 2013 (end of the 10th EDF) to March 2015 (start of the 11th EDF).[144] Following the adoption of the 11th EDF, the EU continued its support for the implementation of the EU-CARIFORUM EPA predominantly on the regional level, not linking it to the problématique of security and the rule of law promotion. Moreover, we show that the objectives of the rule of law promotion and the support for the EU-CARIFORUM EPA implementation have remained disconnected under country-level programming.

Similar to the EU's region-level strategy for the Caribbean under the 10th EDF, the Caribbean Regional Indicative Programme (CRIP) under the 11th EDF distinguished the support of the implementation of the EU-CARIFORUM EPA as a focal cooperation priority.[145] Building on the democracy-security-rule of law

---

142 *Ibid.*, p. 34.

143 The Commonwealth of the Bahamas, European Community (2008). Country Strategy Paper and National Indicative Programme for the Bahamas for the period 2008–2013. [pdf] European Community. Available at: https://ec.europa.eu/europeaid/sites/devco/files/csp-nip-bahamas-2008-2013_en.pdf; Belize, European Community (2008). Country Strategy Paper and National Indicative Programme for Belize for the period 2008–2013. [pdf] European Community. Available at: https://ec.europa.eu/europeaid/sites/devco/files/csp-nip-belize-2008-2013_en.pdf; Grenada, European Community (2008). Country Strategy Paper and National Indicative Programme for Grenada for the period 2008–2013. [pdf] European Community. Available at: https://ec.europa.eu/europeaid/sites/devco/files/csp-nip-grenada-2008-2013_en.pdf.

144 Council Decision of 12 December 2013 regarding transitional EDF management measures from 1 January 2014 until the entry into force of the 11th European Development Fund, 2013/759/EU, OJ L 335/48 of 14 December 2003.

145 European Commission, CARIFORUM (2015). Caribbean Regional Indicative Programme under the 11th European Development Fund. [pdf] European Commission. Available at: https://ec.europa.eu/europeaid/sites/devco/files/rip-edf11-caraibes-2014-2020_en.pdf, pp. 19–30.

EU rule of law: the "action" dimension 139

nexus under the 2011 Agenda for Change, the CRIP linked the rule of law promotion to crime prevention, restorative justice and the improvement of compliance with international norms regarding financial crimes, financing of terrorism and corruption.[146] Nonetheless, the CRIP did not provide for the interplay between the priorities of supporting the implementation of the EU-CARIFORUM EPA and the rule of law promotion.

The analysis of 2014–2020 NIPs reveals the similarity to the NIPs under the 10th EDF: only some of the CSPs/NIPs referred to governance reform/promotion of the rule of law and support of economic development, in general, and the implementation of the EU-CARIFORUM EPA, in particular.[147] For instance, the NIP for Jamaica continued referring to justice as a focal cooperation area with a particular emphasis on the observance of **accountability**, **transparency**, **equality** and **non-discrimination** dimensions of the rule of law.[148] The 2014–2020 NIP for Trinidad and Tobago extended the EU's assistance's previous focus on "building a competitive and innovative economy".[149] Though supporting the reform of governance structures (e.g. IP rights protection, economic governance, innovation governance), the 2014–2020 NIP for Trinidad and Tobago did not link such a reform to any of the rule of law components or the concept as a whole.[150] Similar to the 10th EDF, numerous CSPs and NIPs under the 11th EDF did not cover either governance/the rule of law or support of the implementation of the EU-CARIFORUM EPA, stressing energy efficiency, healthcare, education and human resource development (e.g. NIPs for Barbados, Belize, Saint Kitts and Nevis).[151]

To conclude, the programming of the EU's assistance to the Caribbean under the 11th EDF did not include a systemic rule of law agenda (despite the emphases on the rule of law under the 2011 Agenda for Change and the 2017 new

---

146 European Commission, Communication to the European Parliament, the Council, the European Economic and Social Committee and the Committee of the Regions: Increasing the Impact of EU Development Policy: An Agenda for Change, COM (2011) 637 final of 13 October 2011; European Commission, CARIFORUM: Caribbean Regional Indicative Programme under the 11th European Development Fund of 2015, p. 27.

147 See, for instance, European Commission, the Government of Jamaica (2014). 11th EDF National Indicative Programme (2014–2020) for cooperation between the European Union and Jamaica. [pdf] European Commission. Available at: https://eeas.europa.eu/sites/eeas/files/nip_jamaica_signed.pdf, pp. 13–15.

148 *Ibid.*, pp. 13–15.

149 European Commission, the Government of the Republic of Trinidad and Tobago (2014). 11th EDF National Indicative Programme (2014–2020) for cooperation between the European Union and the Republic of Trinidad and Tobago. [pdf] European Commission. Available at: https://eeas.europa.eu/sites/eeas/files/trinidad_national_indicative_programme_11th_edf.pdf, pp. 9–12.

150 *Ibid.*

151 European Commission, the Government of Barbados (2014). The EU: 11th EDF National Indicative Programme (2014–2020) for cooperation between the European Union and Barbados. [pdf] European Commission. Available at: https://ec.europa.eu/europeaid/sites/devco/files/nip-edf11-barbados-2014-2020_en.pdf; European Commission, the Government of Belize (2014); European Commission, the Government of St. Kitts and Nevis (2014). The EU: National Indicative Programme for cooperation between St. Kitts and Nevis and the EU, 2014. [pdf] European Commission. Available at: https://ec.europa.eu/europeaid/sites/devco/files/nip-edf11-st-kitts-navis-2014-2020_en.pdf.

140 *EU rule of law: the "action" dimension*

European Consensus on Development). It also did not provide for the linkage between the rule of law promotion and the support of the implementation of the EU-CARIFORUM EPA, through such a linkage was stressed by Agenda 2030 and the new European Consensus on Development.

Conclusion

The objective of this chapter has been to explore action that the EU undertakes to promote the rule of law and support the implementation of value-promoting RTAs in the Enlargement, Neighbourhood and Development policy contexts.

Across all foreign policy contexts in question, the EU tended to predominantly link the rule of law to the reforms of the judiciary and law enforcement agencies, and countering corruption and organized crime. Given the Single Market integration aspirations of both SAAs and DCFTAs, an array of "soft" and binding instruments that the EU utilized in the Balkans and the "associated" Neighbourhood dedicated much attention to the transposition of *acquis communautaire* to partner countries' legal systems and its enforcement. This statement is highly relevant for "deep" disciplines that can be viewed as a crucial "juncture" between the EU's support of the RTAs' implementation and the promotion of the rule of law standards. The EU's focus on a number of such "junctures" can be exemplified by the CARDS multi-country programmes in the Balkans and 2004 EU Action Plans for Ukraine, Moldova and Georgia that supported, *inter alia*, legal and institutional changes in the domains of public procurement, competition and IP rights. The programming in question did not, however, coherently link the rule of law promotion to the transposition of the relevant *acquis communautaire*. Most probably, the reason for this has been the strict delimitation between values and *acquis* conditionality in the design of both Neighbourhood and Enlargement policies. Additionally, crucial "junctures" between the objectives of the rule of law and trade liberalization in the Enlargement and Neighbourhood contexts include "economic governance" and "the creation of the environment, conducive to business development". Though referring to specific rule of law standards (e.g. transparency, accountability, the observance of the international law standards), the parts of the programmes in question did not refer to the rule of law as a whole.

The EU-CARIFORUM relations are marked by the fact that, despite significant aid volumes under the 9th–11th EDFs, relevant programmes seldom referred to the rule of law or the rule of law–trade liberalization nexus. Such a situation can be attributed to at least three reasons: (i) the lack of ambitions regarding Single Market integration in EU–CARIFORUM relations; (ii) the EU's reliance on national development strategies in its relations with CARIFOUM and (iii) the peculiarities of framing "development" in the EU development policy and national development strategies of the CARIFORUM countries. Founded on the Agenda 2030, the 2016 Commission's and High Representative's Joint Communication regarding the "renewed partnership" with the ACP countries introduced a crucial shift into the EU's policy towards the Caribbean by prioritizing the rule of law and conceptualizing it as a means of sustainable development. Nonetheless,

EU rule of law: the "action" dimension 141

since the 2014–2020 region-wide and country-wide programmes for the Caribbean were adopted prior to the "renewed partnership", it is so far impossible to establish whether the Union would significantly change its aid priorities *vis-à-vis* the Caribbean.

This demonstrates that the EU's unilateral "action" instruments barely conceptualize the nexus between the rule of law, on the one hand, and trade liberalization and economic development, on the other hand. While several considered policy documents tangentially referred to the rule of law and its components as a *means* that support the implementation of RTAs, neither of them stressed the opportunities that the implementation of "deep" RTAs provides for the support of the rule of law. Keeping this takeaway in mind, the book will proceed with exploring the problématique of coherence of the EU's rule of law promotion through trade liberalization.

References

Anastasakis, O. (2005). The Europeanization of the Balkans. *Brown Journal of World Affairs*, 12, pp. 77–87.

Anastasakis, O. (2008). The EU political conditionality in the Western Balkans: Towards a more pragmatic approach. *Southeast European and Black Sea Studies*, 8, pp. 365–377.

Anastasakis, O. and Bechev, D. (2003). *EU conditionality in South-East Europe: Bringing commitment to the process, South-Eastern European studies programme (University of Oxford)*. Working Paper. St Antony's College University of Oxford. [pdf] Available at: www.sant.ox.ac.uk/sites/default/files/euconditionality.pdf.

Bieber, F. (2011). Building impossible states? State-building strategies and EU membership in the Western Balkans. *Europe-Asia Studies*, 63, pp. 1783–1802.

Börzel, T.A. (2011). *When Europeanization hits limited statehood: The Western Balkans as a test case of the transformative power of Europe, KFG "the transformative power of Europe*. Working Paper 2011/30. Freie Universität Berlin. [pdf] Available at: http://userpage.fu-berlin.de/kfgeu/kfgwp/wpseries/WorkingPaperKFG_30.pdf.

Börzel, T.A. and Grimm, S. (2018). Building good (enough) governance in post-conflict societies and areas of limited statehood: The European Union and the Western Balkans. *Daedalus*, 147, pp. 116–127.

Cardona, F. (2009). *Integrating national administrations into the European administrative space*. SIGMA Conference on Public Administration Reform and European Integration. [pdf] Available at: www.sigmaweb.org/publicationsdocuments/42747690.pdf.

Cardwell, P.J. (2011). Mapping out EU external democracy promotion in the EU's external relations. *Foreign Affairs Review*, 16, pp. 21–40.

Conconi, P. and Perroni, C. (2015). Special and differential treatment of developing countries in the WTO. *World Trade Review*, 14, pp. 67–86.

Džankić, J., Keil, S. and Kmezić, M. (2019). Introduction: The Europeanisation of the Western Balkans. In: J. Džankić, S. Keil, and M. Kmezić, eds., *The Europeanisation of the Western Balkans. A failure of the EU conditionality?* Basingstoke: Palgrave Macmillan, pp. 1–14.

Elbasani, A. and Šabić, S. (2018). Rule of law, corruption and democratic accountability in the course of EU enlargement. *Journal of European Public Policy*, 25, pp. 1317–1335.

European Commission. (1999). *Stabilization and association process*. [online] Available at: https://ec.europa.eu/neighbourhood-enlargement/policy/glossary/terms/sap_en.

142   *EU rule of law: the "action" dimension*

European Commission. (2003a). *2518th Council meeting – external relations – Luxembourg*, 16 June 2003. [online] Available at: https://ec.europa.eu/commission/presscorner/detail/en/PRES_03_166.

European Commission. (2003b). *EU-Western Balkans summit Thessaloniki*, 21 June 2003. [online] Available at: https://ec.europa.eu/commission/presscorner/detail/en/PRES_03_163

European Commission. (2014). *European Commission proposes temporary tariff cuts for Ukrainian exports to the EU*. [online] Available at: https://ec.europa.eu/commission/presscorner/detail/en/IP_14_250.

European Commission. (2018). *Overview of economic partnership agreements*. European Commission. [pdf] Available at: http://trade.ec.europa.eu/doclib/docs/2009/september/tradoc_144912.pdf.

European Commission. (2020). *Partnership and Cooperation Agreements (PCAs): Russia, the South Caucasus and Central Asia*. [online] Available at: https://eur-lex.europa.eu/legal-content/EN/TXT/?uri=LEGISSUM%3Ar17002.

European Commission. (n.d.). *European neighbourhood policy and enlargement negotiations, overview – Instrument for pre-accession assistance*. [online] Available at: https://ec.europa.eu/neighbourhood-enlargement/instruments/overview_en.

European Council and Council of the European Union. (2018). *EULEX Kosovo: New role for the EU rule of law mission*. [online] Available at: www.consilium.europa.eu/en/press/press-releases/2018/06/08/eulex-kosovo-new-role-for-the-eu-rule-of-law-mission/.

European Union Office in Kosovo. (2016). *An overview of relations between the EU and Kosovo*. [online] Available at: https://eeas.europa.eu/delegations/kosovo_en/1387/Kosovo%20and%20the%20EU.

Grasten, M. (2016). Whose legality? Rule of law missions and the case of Kosovo. In: N.M. Rajkovic, T. Allaberts, and T. Gammeltoft-Hansen, eds., *The power of legality: Practices of international law and their politics*. Cambridge: Cambridge University Press, pp. 320–342.

Grimm, S. and Mathis, O.L. (2015). Stability first, development second, democracy third: The European Union's policy towards the post-conflict Western Balkans 1991–2010. *Europe-Asia Studies*, 67, pp. 916–947.

Keukeleire, S. and Delreux, T. (2014). *The foreign policy of the European Union*, 2nd ed. Basingstoke: Palgrave Macmillan.

Kmezić, M. (2019). EU rule of law conditionality: Democracy or "stabilitocracy" promotion in the Western Balkans. In: J. Džankić, S. Keil, and M. Kmezić, eds., *The Europeanisation of the Western Balkans. A failure of the EU conditionality?* Basingstoke: Palgrave Macmillan, pp. 87–109.

Kochenov, D. (2008). The ENP conditionality: Pre-accession mistakes repeated. In: L. Delcour and E. Tulmets, eds., *Pioneer Europe? Testing EU foreign policy in the neighbourhood*. Baden-Baden: Nomos, pp. 105–120.

Kochenov, D. and Bárd, P. (2018). *Rule of law crisis in the new member states of the EU. The pitfalls of overemphasizing enforcement*. RECONNECT Working Paper 2018/1. [pdf] Available at: https://reconnect-europe.eu/wp-content/uploads/2018/07/RECONNECT-KochenovBard-WP_27072018b.pdf.

Noutcheva, G. (2009). Fake, partial and imposed compliance: The limits of the EU's normative compliance in the Western Balkans. *Journal of European Public Policy*, 16, pp. 1065–1084.

Pech, L. (2012/2013). *The rule of law as a guiding principle of the European Union's external action*. CLEER Working Papers, 2012/2013. T.M.C. ASSER INSTITUUT. [pdf] Available at: www.asser.nl/media/1632/cleer2012-3web.pdf.

Pridham, G. (2010). Change and continuity in the European Union's political conditionality: Aims, approaches and priorities. *Democratization*, 14, pp. 446–471.

Trauner, F. (2009). From membership conditionality to policy conditionality: EU external governance in South-Eastern Europe. *Journal of European Public Policy*, 16, pp. 774–790.

Vachudova, M.A. (2018). EU enlargement and state capture in the Western Balkans. In: J. Džankić, S. Keil, and M. Kmezić, eds., *The Europeanisation of the Western Balkans. A failure of the EU conditionality?* Basingstoke: Palgrave Macmillan, pp. 63–85.

6 Coherence between the "regulation" and "action" dimensions of rule of law promotion through RTAs (internal coherence)

The central research question under Chapter 6 is as follows: to what extent are the previously explored "regulation" and "action" dimensions of the EU rule of law promotion through RTAs coherent with each other? Simultaneously, we seek to map the room for strengthening the interplay between the "regulation" and "action" aspects of the EU's activities. To start, the introductory part of this chapter will zoom in on the evolution and problématique of coherence in the EU. This analysis is also relevant for Chapter 7 that will use the case of justice sector reforms to investigate the coherence between EU rule of law promotion through trade liberalization and other aspects of the EU's rule of law promotion.

The principle of policy coherence has been continuously debated in external relations of the EEC and, later on, the EU since the 1974 Paris Meeting of the Heads of State or Government of the Nine. Hence, the Final Communiqué of the Meeting stressed the need for "an overall approach to the internal problems involved in achieving European unity and the external problems facing Europe".[1] The key source of assumed inconsistency had been the potential overlap between the EEC's external activities and the European Political Cooperation (EPC) that functioned outside the Treaties.[2] Similarly, the 1986 Single European Act (SEA) linked consistency and cohesiveness to the relationship between the external activities of the Community and the EPC,[3] seeking to ensure that they do not "contaminate" each other (Duke, 1999, p. 7). Having introduced the EU-s three-pillar structure, the TEU(M) highlighted two aspects of consistency: (i) between the CFSP and the EU's external policies and (ii) between the policies of the EU and the ones of the Member States.[4] Simultaneously, the TEU(M) had been the first EU primary law document to stress the horizontal dimension of coherence, i.e. "the consistency of its [the EU's] external activities, as a whole in the context of its external relations, security, economic and development policies".[5]

---

1 Final Communique of the meeting of heads of governments of the Community (Paris, 9–10 December 1974) of 23 October 2012. [pdf] CVCE. Available at: www.cvce.eu/content/publication/1999/1/1/2acd8532-b271-49ed-bf63-bd8131180d6b/publishable_en.pdf, p. 2.
2 *Ibid.*
3 European Communities, Single European Act, OJ L 169/1 of 29 June 1987, Art. 30(3)(b)(c).
4 TEU(M), Art. C.
5 *Ibid.*

Internal coherence 145

The attention to the interplay between various external policies of the Union, and their impact on development cooperation was reinforced by the adoption of Millennium Development Goals (MDGs) in 2000. In this vein, the 2006 European Consensus on Development affirmed the EU's commitment to policy coherence for development (PCD), meaning the EU's obligation "to take account the objectives of development cooperation in all policies that it implements, which are likely to affect developing countries and that these policies support development objectives".[6] Importantly, the PCD concept understands coherence for development as a means to *synergize* EU policies in the development context, rather than solely avoid contradictions between the policies. As it is demonstrated by the 2020 PCD Report, the PCD embraces not only the horizontal interplay between the policies but the issues pertaining to vertical coherence (e.g. the institutionalization of the PCD within different formations of the Council and in the realm of Commission-Council cooperation).[7]

The Lisbon Treaty that entered into force on 1 December 2019 introduced an array of crucial novelties related to vertical coherence, horizontal coherence and the PCD, seeking to create a more straightforward and effective architecture of EU external policy-making.[8] Its key institutional innovations include the launch of the positions of the President of European Council and the High Representative of the Union for Foreign Affairs and Security Policy.[9] In horizontal terms, the TEU(L) is marked by having introduced an array of "general" or "overarching" objectives of the Union's external action, including the external dimension of the Area of Freedom, Security and Justice (Part V TFEU). Finally, in line with Art. 208(2) TFEU, the PCD acquired the status of the legally binding principle of the EU's external action.

The co-existence of the "different faces" of coherence in the realm of the EU's external relations and their changing substance determines the variation in the concept's application in the literature on the Enlargement, Neighbourhood and Development policies, as well as on the rule of law promotion, irrespective of the policy context. Thus, alongside numerous contributions on the Commission-Council relations, the scholarship on Western Balkans tends to link coherence to the EU's lack of strategic vision of action in the region that would bring together integration, security and the promotion of fundamental values (e.g. Gross and Rotta, 2011; Juncos, 2017, p. 39). Regarding the ENP, scholars' key concern has been the lack of horizontal coherence between the EU's support for security/stability and its promotion of fundamental values ("values-interests dilemma") (e.g. Ghazaryan, 2014, pp. 29–30; Börzel and Van Hüllen, 2014). In this vein,

---

6 The Council, the representatives of the governments of Member States meeting within the Council and the European Parliament and the Commission, Joint Statement on European Union Development Policy: "The European Consensus", 2006/C46 of 24 February 2006, p. 27.

7 European Commission, Commission Staff Working Paper – EU Report on Policy Coherence for Development, COM(2007) 545 final of 20 September 2007, p. 19.

8 Treaty of Lisbon amending the Treaty on European Union and the Treaty establishing the European Communities, signed at Lisbon of 13 December 2007, OJ36, 17.12.2007.

9 This position was introduced to merge the positions of High Representative for the CFSP and European Commissioner for External Relations.

146 *Internal coherence*

the contributions on both the Western Balkans and the Eastern Neighbourhood pointed to the EU's incoherent application of political conditionality and funding instruments that may even strengthen autocracies through building the capacity of bureaucratic institutions (Wetzel and Orbie, 2012). Expectedly, the development policy research has predominantly focused on the PCD and the implementation of the EU's development policy in light of its foreign policy objectives. Finally, there had been only a limited number of contributions that applied the concept of coherence to the EU's global effort to promote the rule of law (Pech, 2016; Magen, 2016; Mendelski, 2015). As argued by Pech (2016), the key obstacles to the EU's coherent rule of law promotion encompass: (i) uncertainty as to the substance of the EU rule of law and (ii) the lack of a unified strategy to assess/measure the rule of law performance in target countries.

Keeping in mind a rather flexible application of the concept of "coherence" as a takeaway, we will proceed with analyzing the interplay between the "regulation" and "action" of the EU's rule of law promotion through trade. Due to the space limitations, the chapter will only briefly refer to the reflection of the RTAs in the relevant "soft" documents, dedicating most of the attention to "collating" the rule of standards across RTAs' disciplines/cooperation areas in question with the provisions of the unilateral trade, financial and technical assistance instruments.

Part 1. Enlargement (Western Balkans)

1. Stabilization and Association Process (SAP) in soft documents

The analysis of the SAP's reflection pertaining to the "soft" documents demonstrated partial coherence.

The key "juncture" between the "soft" documents, underlying EU-Balkans relations, and the SAP has been the multidimensional conditionality system. Its foundations include, *inter alia*, the Copenhagen criteria, the 1997 EU's "Regional Approach" to Southeastern Europe, the 1990 SAP and the relevant peace agreements and political deals (e.g. the Dayton, Ohrid and Belgrade agreements)[10] (Anastasakis and Bechev, 2003, p. 8). Pursuant to the 1993 Copenhagen Council Presidency Conclusions, "membership requires that the candidate country has achieved stability of institutions guaranteeing democracy, the rule of law".[11] Not

---

10 European Commission (1998). Regional Approach, MEMO/98/76. [online] Available at: https://ec.europa.eu/commission/presscorner/detail/en/MEMO_98_76; European Commission (1999). Stabilization and Association Process (SAP). [online] Available at: https://ec.europa.eu/neighbourhood-enlargement/policy/glossary/terms/sap_en; The General Framework Agreement for Peace in Bosnia and Herzegovina, initialed in Dayton on 21 November 1995 and signed in Paris on 14 December 1995. [pdf] OSCE. Available at: www.osce.org/files/f/documents/e/0/126173.pdf; Framework Agreement (Ohrid Agreement) of 13 August 2001. [pdf]. UN Peacemaker. Available at: https://peacemaker.un.org/fyrom-ohridagreement2001; Starting Points for the Restructuring of Relations between Serbia and Montenegro. [pdf] UN Peacemaker. Available at: https://peacemaker.un.org/montenegro-belgradeagreement2002.

11 Copenhagen European Council, Presidency Conclusions (21–22 June 1993). [online] Available at: www.europarl.europa.eu/enlargement/ec/pdf/cop_en.pdf.

Internal coherence 147

immediately referring to the rule of law, the 1997 "Regional Approach" and the 1999 Stability Pact mentioned partner countries' "credible commitment to engage in democratic reforms" as one of the conditions, underlying the EU-Western Balkans contractual relations.[12] Simultaneously, as described in Chapter 4 and Chapter 5, both the SAAs and the EU's autonomous trade measures in favour of the Western Balkans referred to fundamental values as "essential elements", thus creating the bridge to the previously mentioned "soft" norms.

Second, given the accession finalité of the SAP, the SAAs provide for legislative approximation that, as shown in Chapter 4, represents a viable avenue of the rule of law promotion. Not referring to specific rule of law standards, relevant "soft" documents (e.g. the 2006 Commission's Communication "The Western Balkans on the Road to the EU: Consolidating Stability and Raising Prosperity") were stressing the Western Balkans' legislative approximation to the SAAs as a key task in the realm of accession.

Third, the "junctures" may include specific rule of law standards or cooperation areas. The former part of the statement can be exemplified by the standards of judicial independence and impartiality, as well as authorities' accountability. The SAAs provide for the observance of these standards, amongst others, in the contexts of EU-Balkans administrative cooperation and the enforcement of the WTO GPA and public procurement *acquis* (Directive 89/665/EC). Simultaneously, the reforms of judiciary and the public administration were systematically stressed in EU-Western Balkans diplomatic documents as the key component of the rule of law promotion (e.g. 2000 Zagreb Summit Declaration, 2003 Thessaloniki Agenda, 2008 Council Presidency Conclusions).[13] An emphasis on cooperation areas, lying at the crossroads between the rule of law promotion and economic development, is particularly visible in the diplomatic documents, adopted in terms of the Berlin Process, such as the 2017 Trieste Declaration and the 2018 Communication "A Credible Enlargement Perspective for and Enhanced EU Engagement with Western Balkans".[14] Simultaneously, a broad objective of creating the "dynamic business environment"[15] stipulated in both documents is hardly implementable without partner countries' observance of the rule of law standards, included into

---

12 European Commission (1998). Regional Approach, MEMO/98/76. [online] Available at: https://ec.europa.eu/commission/presscorner/detail/en/MEMO_98_76; European Commission (n.d.) Stability Pact for Southeastern Europe. [online] Available at: https://ec.europa.eu/neighbourhood-enlargement/policy/glossary/terms/stability-pact_en.

13 The Final Declaration of Zagreb Summit of 24 November 2000; European Commission, EU-Western Balkans Summit Declaration, The Thessaloniki Agenda for the Western Balkans: Moving towards European Integration, June 2003. [online] Available at: http://europa.eu/rapid/press-release_PRES-03-163_en.pdf; European Union, Brussels European Council Presidency Conclusions, 11018/1/08, REV1of 17 July 2008, p. 14.

14 Trieste Western Balkans Summit Declaration by the Italian Chair of 7 December 2007. [online] Available at: www.esteri.it/mae/en/sala_stampa/archivionotizie/approfondimenti/trieste-western-balkan-summit-declaration.html; European Commission, Communication to the European Parliament, the Council, the European Economic and Social Committee and the Committee of the Regions: A Credible Enlargement Perspective for and Enhanced Engagement with the Western Balkans", COM (2018) 65 final of 6 February 2018.

15 *Ibid.*

148 *Internal coherence*

the SAAs (e.g. legal certainty, authorities' independence and impartiality). In this vein, the 2018 Communication specifically referred to the need for "substantial increase" of transparency, competitiveness and fairness dimensions of public procurement procedures.[16] This call for action can, in turn, be seen as reinforcing the implementation of numerous transparency and fairness provisions, contained in Directives 2014/24/EU and 89/665/EC that the Western Balkan countries are obliged to transpose in accordance with the SAAs.[17]

Besides, one can mention at least four instances of incoherence between the "soft" documents related to the EU-Western Balkans cooperation.

To start, as stressed in Chapter 5, relevant "soft" documents predominantly refer to the rule of law as a part of the EU-Western Balkans political cooperation agenda. The key reason for this has been a strict delimitation between the values and *acquis* conditionality, stemming from the structure of the Copenhagen criteria. This delimitation and the referral to the rule of law solely in the political cooperation realm determines the lack of a systemic connection between values conditionality, *acquis* conditionality and partner countries' implementation of the rule of law standards, as contained in the SAAs (Kochenov, 2009).

Next, systemically emphasizing the political dimension of the rule of law, the majority of the "soft" documents seldom referred to either the dynamics of trade liberalization between the parties or, more specifically, their progress in harmonizing domestic legislation with the *acquis*. Hence, the 2006 Commission's Communication "The Western Balkans on the Road to the EU: Consolidating Stability and Raising Prosperity" was the only pre-Berlin Process document that called for reinforcing the partner countries' "alignment on the main trade-related areas of the acquis, especially on customs and industrial, sanitary, phytosanitary and veterinary standards",[18] yet not referring to specific rule of law standards. While the 2018 Communication "A Credible Enlargement Perspective for and Enhanced EU Engagement with Western Balkans" stressed the importance of harmonizing domestic public procurement legislation with the *acquis*, it neither mentioned other "deep" disciplines or specific rule of law standards.

Furthermore, it shall be pointed to the implicit nature of the links between the observance of rule of law standards, embedded into the SAAs, and economic development in the areas, previously referred to as "cross-cutting" (e.g. creation of the environment, conducive to business development; private sector development or economic governance). The functioning of each of these domains depends on the observance of the rule of law standards, promoted via the SAAs (i.e. legal

---

16 *Ibid.*, p. 4.
17 Directive 2014/24/EU of the European Parliament and of the Council of 26 February 2014 on public procurement and repealing Directive 2004/18/EC, OJ L94 of 28 March 2014; Council Directive 89/665/EEC of 21 December 1989 on the coordination of the laws, regulations and administrative provisions relating to the application of review procedures to the award of public supply and public works contracts, OJ L 395 of 30 December 1989.
18 European Commission, Communication: The Western Balkans on the Road to the EU: Consolidating Stability and Raising Prosperity, COM(2006) 27final of 27 January 2006.

certainty, transparency, the availability of judicial review). Nonetheless, neither of the examined "soft" documents presented respective cooperation areas as lying at the crossroads between values and *acquis* conditionality. Thus, the inclusion of these cooperation areas into the framework policy documents creates an explicit bridge only between the political and economic aspects of values conditionality, leaving its interplay with the *acquis* conditionality in the shadow and letting it be further operationalized in unilateral trade, financial and technical assistance instruments.

Ultimately, "soft" documents serve as a crucial framework for the implementation of the SAAs, the application of "essential element" clauses and the harmonization of domestic legislation with *acquis communautaire*. Nonetheless, such "soft" documents were found to strictly delimit between the values and *acquis* conditionality, even with respect to the cooperation areas, lying at the crossroads between the rule of law promotion and the support of economic development. They also lack coherent referrals to the dynamics of the EU-Western Balkans trade liberalization and the implementation of related rule of law standards. This testifies to the fact that, at the framework policy level, the EU has not strategized the rule of law effects of the SAAs' trade-related chapters.

2. Rule of law standards in the SAAs and unilateral trade, financial and technical assistance instruments

This part of the analysis seeks to distinguish the key "junctures" of (in)coherence between the rule of law requirements contained in the SAAs, and conditionality structures/cooperation priorities under the respective unilateral trade, financial and technical assistance instruments (with a focus on those, immediately supporting the observance of SAAs). The analysis will once again refer to the multidimensional conditionality system in the EU-Western Balkan relations, as well as the EU's unilateral support for developing the EU-Western Balkans administrative cooperation and implementing the SAAs' "deep" disciplines chapters.

Multidimensional conditionality

First, as previously mentioned, both the SAAs and the vast majority of the EU's autonomous trade measures in favour of the Western Balkans recognize the rule of law as an "essential element" of EU-Western Balkans relations.[19] Pursuant to the classification of conditionality under EU-Western Balkans relations, introduced by Noutcheva (2006), the rule of law conditionality is the part of the "overarching conditionality", linked to progress in the pre-accession process (the SAP). In turn, the rule of law requirement, stipulated under the "overarching" conditionality, is also complemented by sector-specific conditions (including those contained in

19 See, for instance, EU-Serbia SAA, Art. 2; EU-Bosnia SAA, Art. 2; Regulation (EU) No 2015/2423 of the European Parliament and of the Council of 16 December 2015 amending Council Regulation (EC) No 1215/2009 of 30 November 2009 introducing exceptional trade measures.

150 *Internal coherence*

Single Market, Justice and Home Affairs [JHA], and Sectoral Policy *acquis*, and those linked to specific projects [Noutcheva, 2006, p. 41]).

The analysis of the legislative approximation requirements under the SAAs' chapters "Approximation of laws, law enforcement and competition rules" demonstrates that the Single Market *acquis* complements the above vague rule of law requirement by referring to specific rule of law standards.[20] Similarly, dependent on the nature of a funded project, the observance of particular rule of law standards was repeatedly envisaged as a funding condition under CARDS, IPA I and IPA II (e.g. CARDS regional-level programme in support of industrial IP rights and the implementation of the TRIPS Agreement).[21] Hence, the rule of law-related conditions under the SAAs, autonomous trade measures and the programming of financial and technical assistance form the multidimensional conditionality system that is, *inter alia*, directed to the rule of law promotion. Within the system, the relationship between the "overarching" and the sector-specific *acquis* can be viewed as mutually reinforcing, where the former serves as a framework for the latter.

The described system, however, entails an important instance of incoherence between the "regulation" and "action" dimensions of the EU's rule of law promotion through SAAs. It lies in the fact that, reinforcing the implementation of SAAs, neither the "overarching" nor sector-specific (Single Market *acquis*) conditionality encompasses or at least speaks to the rule of law standards the Union promotes through the SAAs beyond legislative approximation obligations. In other words, neither the EU's unilateral "soft" documents nor the "hard" assistance regulations have systemically referred to the partner countries' rule of law obligations, stipulated by the SAAs as basic standards or cooperation requirements. This reflects the previously highlighted challenge of a strict delimitation between the values and *acquis* conditionality in the EU-Western Balkans relations and contributes to the "politics-only" understanding of the rule of law concept.

Administrative cooperation

According to the findings of Chapters 4–5, joining the European Administrative Space (EAS) is concerned with fulfilling numerous rule of law requirements, such as **legality**, **legal certainty**, **accountability** and **transparency** (e.g. Olsen, 2011; Hofmann, 2008; Karadjoski, Memeti and Dimeski, 2019). At the same time, Council Regulations 2007/2000 and 1946/2005 distinguished the functionality of partner countries' customs administrations and their "active engagement" into the administrative cooperation with the EU as crucial preconditions of benefiting from autonomous trade measures.[22]

---

20 See Chapter 4, Part 1.

21 See, for instance, European Commission Directorate Western Balkans (2001). CARDS Assistance Programme to the Western Balkans, Regional Strategy Paper 2002–2006. [pdf] European Commission. Available at: https://ec.europa.eu/neighbourhood-enlargement/sites/near/files/pdf/finan cial_assistance/cards/publications/regional_strategy_paper_en.pdf, pp. 24–26.

22 Council Regulation (EC) No 2007/2000 of 18 September 2000 introducing exceptional trade measures for countries and territories participating in or linked to the European Union's Stabilization

Moreover, the 2002–2006 CARDS Regional Strategy Paper addressed "national trade facilitation" (including the support of efficient customs administration) as the priority under both regional and national level CARDS programming.[23] To this end, the Regional Strategy Paper envisaged region-level and country-specific institution-building measures for customs administrations.[24] Capacity-building in the field of administrative cooperation was also prioritized under the IPA I Regulation that distinguished "administrative cooperation measures for the purpose of training and information exchange involving publicsector experts dispatched from Member States and international organizations in particular through Twinning, Twinning Light and TAIEX".[25] The IPA I was also utilized to fund a large-scale region-wide programme "Technical Assistance to Tax and Customs Administrations in the Western Balkans" (TACTA) (Studiare Sviluppo, 2008/2009). This programme focused on three crucial dimensions of the rule of law: **legality** (alignment of customs and indirect tax legislation and procedures to *acquis communautaire*), **legal certainty** (focus on the application of customs and indirect tax legislation) and **transparency** (facilitation of information exchange and the "enforcement of measures preventing the avoidance or evasion of duties and taxes") (*Ibid.*). As it can be exemplified by MIPDs for Albania 2008–2010 and FYROM 2007–2009, IPA I tended to promote these countries' domestic capacities for fruitful administrative cooperation through targeting specific institutions (e.g. Directorate-General of Customs, Ministry for Finance of Albania).[26] Under the IPA II, capacity-building in the administrative cooperation domain remained to be targeted under broader cooperation priorities, such as "public administration reform" and "institution-building".[27]

Despite the EU's extensive unilateral support for the development of the EU-Western Balkans administrative cooperation, the EU's unilateral documents,

---

and Association Process, amending Regulation (EC) No 2820/98 of 21 December 1998, and repealing Regulations (EC) No 1763/1999 of 29 July 1999 and (EC) No 6/2000 of 7–9 December 2000, OJ L 240 of 23 September 2000; Council Regulation (EC) No 1946/2005 of 14 November 2005 amending Regulation No 2007/2000 of 18 November introducing exceptional trade measures for countries and territories participating in or linked to the European Union's Stabilization and Association Process, OJ L 312 of 29 November 2005.

23 See, for instance, European Commission Directorate Western Balkans (2001). CARDS Assistance Programme to the Western Balkans, Regional Strategy Paper 2002–2006. [pdf] European Commission. Available at: https://ec.europa.eu/neighbourhood-enlargement/sites/near/files/pdf/financial_assistance/cards/publications/regional_strategy_paper_en.pdf, pp. 24–26, p. 31.

24 *Ibid.*

25 Council Regulation (EC) No 1085/2006 of 17 July 2006 establishing an Instrument for Pre-Accession Assistance (IPA), OJ L 210 of 31 July 2006, para 21 of the Preamble.

26 See, for instance, European Commission, Decision on a Multi-annual Indicative Planning Document (MIPD) for Albania 2008–2010, C(2007)2245 of 31 May 2007, pp. 16–17; European Commission, Decision on a Multi-annual Indicative Planning Document (MIPD) 2007–2009 for the former Yugoslav Republic of Macedonia, C(2007) 1853 of 30 April 2007, pp. 15–16.

27 See, for instance, Commission Implementing Decision amending Commission Decision C(2014)5770 of 18 August 2014 adopting the Indicative Strategy Paper for Montenegro, C(2018)5027final of 3 August 2018, p. 2.; Commission Implementing Decision amending Commission Decision C(2014)5770 of 18 August 2014 adopting the Indicative Strategy Paper for Albania, C(2018)5027 final of 3 August 2018, pp. 2–4.

152 *Internal coherence*

analyzed previously (as well as the SAAs) have not explicitly connected administrative cooperation to the rule of law concept. Nonetheless, the field is marked by the EU's coherent long-term support for partner countries' implementation of the SAAs' rule of law requirements (**legality**, **legal certainty** and **transparency**) through autonomous trade measures, as well as financial and technical assistance instruments.

"Deep" disciplines competition and public procurement

As demonstrated in Chapter 4, both the mutual opening of public procurement markets and ensuring fair competition between economic agents is hardly possible without the observance of the rule of law. Not surprisingly, the scope of legislative approximation, envisaged in the SAA provisions "Approximation of laws, law enforcement and competition rules" encompasses numerous rule of law standards, such as **legality**, **legal certainty** (including foreseeability of regulations and meeting legitimate expectations of economic operators), **access to judicial review** and **equality and non-discrimination among economic operators**. We show that, although the EU's unilateral instruments assisted the Western Balkans in fulfilling the conditions related to the Single Market *acquis*, the public procurement and competition fields are marked by the lack of interplay between the "regulation" and "action" dimensions of the rule of law promotion through SAAs.

Hence, the General Support Facility under the CARDS had been directed to "transposing, implementing and enforcing policies and legislation that is approximated to the EU acquis in key area, arising from the SAP" and raising awareness about the respective policies and legislation.[28] Moreover, the approximation of legislation in public procurement and competition domains had been the focal area of the EU's cooperation with FYROM and Albania under the CARDS programming.[29] In turn, the CARDS national programmes touched upon numerous rule of law standards, such as **legality** (focusing on both contents of laws and institutions' compliance with them); **legal certainty** (foreseeability of the implementation of *acquis*) and **transparency** (including support of the launch of e-procurement systems).[30] However, neither the region-level nor the country-level programming

---

28 European Commission Directorate Western Balkans (2002). CARDS Regional Annual Programme, Financing Proposal of 26 June 2002. [pdf] European Commission. Available at: https://ec.europa.eu/neighbourhood-enlargement/sites/near/files/pdf/financial_assistance/cards/publications/regional_programme_2002_en.pdf, p. 5.

29 See, for instance, European Commission Directorate Western Balkans (2001). CARDS Assistance Programme, Albania 2002–2006. [online] Available at: https://ec.europa.eu/neighbourhood-enlargement/sites/near/files/pdf/financial_assistance/cards/publications/albania_strategy_paper_en.pdf, pp. 40–41; European Commission Directorate Western Balkans (2002). CARDS Assistance Programme. Former Yugoslav Republic of Macedonia 2002–2006. [online] Available at: https://ec.europa.eu/neighbourhood-enlargement/sites/near/files/pdf/financial_assistance/cards/publications/fyrom_strategy_paper_en.pdf, p. 37.

30 *Ibid.*

Internal coherence 153

under the CARDS explicitly utilized the rule of law concept for assessing partner countries' progress related to the transposition and implementation of the Single Market *acquis*.

In contrast to the CARDS, the IPA I programming shifted the emphasis of the EU's assistance from the transposition of the *acquis*to building the capacity of national institutions, responsible for implementing or enforcing national legislation in the relevant domains. While the IPA I programming referred to the rule of law components in "Expected results and indicators" sections, it did not use the concept to assess or measure partner countries' performance.[31] The same applies to the IPA II programming that demonstrates an even stronger emphasis on institution-building, rather than the support of the transposition/implementation of the respective *acquis*.[32] The shift of the Commission's attention from institutions' capacity-building to the actual state of observance of the rule of law standards in the partner countries' application of the *acquis communautaire* notable in its previously analyzed Communication on "credible Enlargement perspective" for the Western Balkans.[33] Since the IPA II programming encompasses the period until 2020, it is, however, so far impossible to predict whether such shift will be reflected in the assistance programming.

Thus, CARDS has been the EU's only instrument of financial assistance to the Western Balkans that extensively referred to the rule of law standards in competition and public procurement legislation. Coupled with the delimitation between values and *acquis* conditionality, the institution-building focus of IPA I and IPA II led to relatively low attention to partner countries' implementation of the rule of law components in competition and public procurement domains, making the case of "deep" disciplines illustrative of the lacking coherence between the "regulation" and "action" dimensions of the EU activities.

Part 2. "Associated" Eastern Neighbourhood

1. AAs/DCFTAs in "soft" documents

As well as in the case of the Western Balkans, "soft" documents, underpinning the EU-"associated Neighbourhood" relations, are marked by differentiating connections

---

31 See, for instance: European Commission, Decision on a Multi-annual Indicative Planning Document (MIPD) 2007–2009 for the former Yugoslav Republic of Macedonia, C(2007) 1853 of 30 April, p. 20; European Commission, Decision on a Multi-annual Indicative Planning Document (MIPD) for Albania 2008–2010, C(2007)2245 of 31 May 2007, p. 17.

32 See, for instance, Commission Implementing Decision amending Commission Decision C(2014)5770 of 18 August 2014 adopting the Indicative Strategy Paper for Montenegro, C(2018)5027final of 3 August 2018, p. 2European Commission, Decision on a Multi-annual Indicative Planning Document (MIPD) for Albania 2008–2010, C(2007)2245 of 31 May 2007, pp. 2–4.

33 European Commission, Communication to the European Parliament, the Council, the European Economic and Social Committee and the Committee of the Regions: A Credible Enlargement Perspective for and Enhanced EU Engagement with the Western Balkans, COM(2018) 65 final of 6 February 2018, pp. 1–3.

154 *Internal coherence*

to the AAs/DCFTAs. While the 2004 Action Plans were marked by a strong linkage to the AAs/DCFTAs, such links were expectedly more detailed and less chaotic in the declarations of the EaP Summits, bringing together both associated and non-associated Neighbours (e.g. Georgia, Belarus).

In Part 2 of Chapter 5, we pointed to the in-depth nature of Internal Market–oriented dimension of reforms, preceding the negotiations of AAs/DCFTAs. In this vein, the 2014 EU-Ukraine Action Plan emphasized "the perspective of moving beyond cooperation to a significant degree of integration, including through a stake in the EU's Internal Market, and the possibility for Ukraine to participate progressively in key aspects of EU policies and programmes".[34] In less specific terms, the EU-Moldova Action Plan "will encourage and support Moldova's objective of further integration into European economic and social structures".[35] The Action Plans, thus, addressed two crucial "junctures" between the rule of law and trade liberalization, as well as economic development, more broadly: the improvement of business climate and the approximation of "deep disciplines"–related *acquis communautaire*.[36] Though far less elaborate, the Action Plans' points are consonant with the contents of the DCFTAs due to the partner countries' specific commitments in the domains of trade in services, establishment, "deep disciplines" and the approximation toward the WTO). Moreover, such commitments immediately referred to the rule of law standards, stipulated in the DCFTAs' chapters and previously addressed in Chapter 4. This statement can be, *inter alia*, exemplified by the referral to the EU-Georgia Action Plan's point on ensuring the enforcement of competition law "in particular . . . by enhancing the independence of the Free Trade and Competition Agency".[37] Thus point resonates quite evidently with Art. 204(2) of the EU-Georgia AA that requires the parties "to maintain an authority responsible and appropriately equipped for the effective enforcement of the competition laws".[38] Furthermore, the EU-Georgia Action Plan referred to specific rule of law principles in its part related to public procurement (i.e. transparency, non-discrimination, competition and the availability of judicial review), creating the foundation for the implementation of the AA's "Public Procurement" chapter.[39] The Action Plan also included the points related to the compliance with WTO rules, in general, and with regard to IP rights and phytosanitary rules, consonant with numerous AA provisions (e.g. Art.1[h] – "Objectives", Art.

---

34 European Union External Action Service, EU-Ukraine Action Plan 2004. [online] Available at: https://library.euneighbours.eu//content/eu-ukraine-action-plan-0 (hereinafter referred to as "EU-Ukraine Action Plan 2004"), p. 2.

35 European Union External Action Service, EU-Moldova Action Plan 2004. [online] Available at: https://eeas.europa.eu/sites/eeas/files/moldova_enp_ap_final_en.pdf (hereinafter referred to as "EU-Moldova Action Plan 2004"), p. 1.

36 EU-Ukraine Action Plan 2004; EU-Moldova Action Plan 2004; European Union External Action Service, EU-Georgia Action Plan 2004. [online] Available at: https://eeas.europa.eu/sites/eeas/files/georgia_enp_ap_final_en_0.pdf (hereinafter referred to as "EU-Georgia Action Plan 2004").

37 EU-Georgia Action Plan 2004, p. 29.

38 EU-Georgia Action Plan 2004, p. 29; EU-Georgia AA, Art.204(2).

39 EU-Georgia Action Plan 2004, p. 30; EU-Georgia AA, Art.141.

96[5] – "Mutual Recognition", Art.190 – "Enforcement of the general obligations in the field of IP rights").[40] These examples show that, despite being formally linked to framework Partnership and Cooperation Agreements (PCAs), the 2004 EU Action Plans for Ukraine, Moldova and Georgia were marked by in-detail market integration-oriented provisions and multiple connections toward the rule of law standards, included into the DCFTAs.

While the first decade of the EaP initiative's functioning has largely overlapped with the AAs/DCFTAs' negotiations, the 2008 Commission's Communication on the EaP distinguished the EU-Neighbours trade liberalization and the creation of the "Neighbourhood Economic Community" as pivotal aspects of the EU-Neighbours cooperation.[41] Declarations of the EaP Summits, adopted during the period 2009–2013, referred to economic cooperation without mentioning negotiations of the AAs/DCFTAs and the preparations for their implementation in partner countries. The move towards stronger attention to the AAs/DCFTAs, including their provisions at the crossroads between the rule of law and trade liberalization, can be only captured in the 2015 Riga Summit Declaration. Contrary to the previously adopted EaP Summit Declarations, the Riga Summit Declaration stressed the concepts of the rule of law and legal certainty as the prerequisites for successful economic integration and trade liberalization.[42] The 2017 revision of the EaP "20 Deliverables for 2020" also briefly referred to improving implementation of the DCFTAs through the strengthening of legal certainty and transparency dimensions of the rule of law.[43] Such insignificant degree of coherence between the EaP Summit Declarations and the DCFTAs can be explained by the fact that, as compared to the 2004 Action Plans, the EaP Summit Declarations are characterized by an aspirational nature, rather than a technical nature, and target "non-associated" Neighbours.

Ultimately, the two categories of ENP-related documents in question demonstrate differentiating degrees and instances of coherence with the rule of law standards contained in the DCFTAs. Despite having been adopted three years prior to the start of the AAs/DCFTAs negotiations, the 2004 Action Plans for Ukraine, Moldova and Georgia were found to contain several rule of law standards (e.g. in the domain of "deep disciplines") coherent with the ones embedded into the "deep disciplines" chapters of the DCFTAs. The analysis of the EaP Summit Declarations, however, demonstrated a lack of diplomatic support of the implementation of the DCFTAs-based rule of law standards. Similar to the "soft" documents, shaping the dynamics of the EU-Western Balkans relationships, the

40 EU-Georgia Action Plan 2004, pp. 25–26; EU-Georgia AA, Art.1(h); 96(5); 190.
41 European Commission to the European Parliament and the Council: Eastern Partnership, COM(2008) 823 final of 3 December 2008, p. 3.
42 European Council/Council of the EU, Joint Declaration of the Riga Eastern Partnership Summit of 21–22 May 2015. [online] Available at: www.consilium.europa.eu/en/meetings/international-summit/2015/05/21-22/.
43 European Commission/High Representative of the Union for Foreign Affairs and Security Policy, Joint Staff Working Document – Eastern Partnership – 20 Deliverables for 2020. Focusing on Key Priorities and Tangible Results, SWD (2017) 300 final of 9 June 2017.

156 *Internal coherence*

2004 ENP Action Plans and the EaP Summit Declarations tangentially refer to the "junctures" between the rule of law and economic development/trade liberalization not immediately captured by the DCFTAs.

2. *Rule of law standards in the AAs/DCFTAs and unilateral trade, financial and technical assistance instruments*

This part of the analysis will explore the key indications of (in)coherence between the rule of law requirements, contained in the DCFTAs, and conditionality structures and cooperation priorities, stipulated by the relevant unilateral trade, financial and technical assistance instruments (with a focus on those immediately supporting the observance of the DCFTAs). It will follow the research design used in the equivalent section dedicated to the coherence between the rule of law standards incorporated into the SAAs with Western Balkans, and the relevant unilateral trade, financial and technical assistance instruments. Thus, it will zoom in on the multidimensional conditionality, customs and trade facilitation, as well as "deep" disciplines.

Multidimensional conditionality

We show that, despite the centrality of the rule of law in the architecture of conditionality in the EU–associated Neighbours relations, the coherence of its functioning is impeded by several instances of incoherence.

As noted in Chapters 4–5, respectively, the rule of law constitutes an "essential element" of both the EU–associated Neighbours relations under the AAs and the EU-Ukraine relations with respect to EU's autonomous trade measures in favour of Ukraine.[44] Alongside this broad rule of law requirement (that, by analogy with the case of the Western Balkans, can be regarded as a component of "overarching conditionality"), the DCFTAs contain numerous Single Market *acquis*-related conditions, aimed to support the ambitious "integration without membership" finalité of the EU's relations with associated Neighbours.[45]

Compared with the SAAs conditionality structures, the DCFTAs-based Single Market *acquis* conditionality is marked by two crucial differences. First, the lack of a membership perspective for associated Eastern Neighbours under the AA determines the EU's need to introduce novel mechanisms aimed at ensuring Neighbours' compliance with their legislative approximation obligations. Therefore, the AAs combine values conditionality with the market access conditionality (Van der Loo, 2016, pp. 210–213). As exemplified by Art. 153–154 of the EU-Ukraine AA, market access conditionality allows for linking partner countries' progress in fulfilling legislative approximation obligations to the scope of access

---

44 See, for instance, EU-Ukraine AA, Art.2; Regulation (EU) No 374/2014 of the European Parliament and of the Council of 16 April 2014 on the reduction or elimination of customs duties on goods originating in Ukraine, OJ L 118 of 22 April 2014.

45 See, for instance, EU-Ukraine AA, Title IV, Chapters 6–8.

Internal coherence 157

to EU markets they obtain. Second, due to the "deep" nature of the DCFTAs, they regulate partner countries' legislative approximation obligations in more detail, compared to the SAAs. Nonetheless, neither the SAAs nor the DCFTAs create bridges between the overarching/values conditionality and the *acquis*/market access conditionality, thus not recognizing the Single Market-related standards as the ones falling within the scope of the rule of law concept.

As argued by Koeth (2014) in relation to the IPA II, the EU's application of unilateral assistance instruments aims to promote strategic local ownership-based reforms, rather than ensure target countries' compliance with specific condition-alities/benchmarks (pp. 14–15). Similarly, the ENPI and ENI demonstrate the trend toward converting the focus on fulfilling conditions, established by the EU, into the emphasis on local ownership, based on domestic political priorities and development strategies. For instance, the 2014 ENI Regulation substituted nega-tive conditionality, contained in the 2006 Regulation,[46] with the "incentive-based approach" which links the EU allocation of funds to the partner countries' "com-mitment to and progress in implementing mutually agreed political, economic and social reform objectives".[47] While linking the allocation of funds to part-ners' reform commitments, the Regulation does not explicitly connect it either to the progress in the domain of the rule of law or to implementation of the AAs/DCFTAs.[48] This does not, however, preclude the EU from the formal or informal attachment of respective conditions in terms of the political dialogue with partner countries.

Ultimately, considered from the standpoint of coherence between the "regula-tion" and "action" dimensions of the rule of law promotion through trade liberali-zation, the system of conditionality involves two crucial instances of incoherence. They are: (i) the lack of linkages between the values and market access condi-tionality and (ii) the absence of the formalized link between the observance of the DCFTAs-based rule of law standards and the allocation of funds under the ENI. The persistence of such instances of incoherence testifies to the fact that, inspired by the Enlargement policy design, the ENP context shares the issues of strict delimitation between values and *acquis* conditionality and resulting "politics-only" understanding of the rule of law.

Customs and trade facilitation

In contrast to the SAAs with the Western Balkans, the DCFTAs with Eastern Neighbours contain not only general provisions on administrative cooperation, but in-detail regulations as to cooperation in the domain of customs and trade

---

46 Regulation (EC) No 1638/2006 of the European Parliament and of the Council of 24 October 2006 laying down general provisions establishing a European Neighbourhood and Partnership Instru-ment, OJ L 310 of 9 November 2016.
47 Regulation (EU) No 232/2014 of the European Parliament and the European Council of 11 March 2014, establishing a European Neighbourhood Instrument, OJ L 77/27 of 15 March 2014, Art.4(1).
48 *Ibid.*

158 *Internal coherence*

facilitation. As demonstrated in Chapter 4, the DCFTAs' "Customs and Trade Facilitation" chapters uphold an array of the rule of law standards, such as **legality** (comprehensiveness of legislation), **legal certainty** (stability of the legal framework, predictability of the provisions and procedures, proportionality, the uniform application of laws and regulations), access to **judicial review** and **transparency**. Nonetheless, extensively contributing to the capacity-building of the relevant authorities in partner countries, relevant "unilateral instruments only implicitly addressed the previously mentioned rule of law standards.

Hence, Art. 2 of the Regulation No 374/2014 on the EU's unilateral trade measures in favour of Ukraine obliges it to comply with the "methods of administrative cooperation", stipulated in Art.121–122 of the Regulation (EEC) 2454/93.[49] As noted in Chapter 5, such methods immediately relate to the **legality** (substance of customs rules and procedures), **legal certainty** and **transparency** (the design of customs procedures) dimensions of the rule of law. Next, both the 2006 Regulation on the ENPI and the 2014 ENI Regulation provide for financing measures related to customs cooperation and trade facilitation.[50] For instance, according to the Regulation (EC) No 1638/2006 on the ENPI, the objectives of Community assistance include, amongst others, encouraging investment and global trade, as well as promoting the **transparency** of administrative cooperation.[51] In this vein, the Community assistance can be used, *inter alia*, "to finance technical assistance and targeted administrative measures".[52] Having consolidated previously existing cooperation objectives, the Regulation 232/2014 emphasized achieving partner countries' progressive integration into the Union Internal Market and enhanced sectoral cooperation, including through deep and comprehensive free trade areas.[53] This allowed for immediate support of the implementation of the DCFTAs' "Customs and Trade Facilitation" chapters.[54] Furthermore, the EU has continuously supported the capacity-building of the associated Neighbours' customs authorities through their participation in Twinning and TAIEX technical assistance projects, and ensuring the operation of the EU Border Assistance

---

49 Regulation (EU) No 374/2014 of the European Parliament and of the Council of 16 April 2014 on the reduction or elimination of customs duties on goods originating in Ukraine, OJ L 118 of 22 April 2014; Commission Regulation (EEC) No 2454/93 of 2 July 1993 laying down the provisions for the implementation of Council Regulation (EEC) No 2913/92 establishing the Community Customs Code, OJ L 253 of 11 October 1993.

50 Regulation (EC) No 1638/2006 of the European Parliament and of the Council of 24 October 2006 laying down general provisions establishing a European Neighbourhood and Partnership Instrument, OJ L 310 of 9 November 2016, Art.2; Regulation (EU) No 232/2014 of the European Parliament and the European Council of 11 March 2014, establishing a European Neighbourhood Instrument, OJ L 77/27 of 15 March 2014, Art.2.

51 Regulation (EC) No 1638/2006 of the European Parliament and of the Council of 24 October 2006 laying down general provisions establishing a European Neighbourhood and Partnership Instrument, OJ L 310 of 9 November 2016, Art.2(2)(n).

52 *Ibid.*, Art.15(2)(a).

53 Regulation (EU) No 232/2014 of the European Parliament and the European Council of 11 March 2014, establishing a European Neighbourhood Instrument, OJ L 77/27 of 15 March 2014, Art.2(2)(b).

54 *Ibid.*

Mission to Moldova and Ukraine (EUBAM).[55] Though it does not position itself as a rule of law promotion mission, the EUBAM's encompasses several rule of law aspects of customs cooperation and trade facilitation, such as customs authorities' compliance with the EU Customs Code, good governance and the transparency of administrative cooperation.[56]

To conclude, although the "Customs and Trade Facilitation" chapters of the DCFTAs contain multiple and tightly intertwined rule of law standards, they remain formally disentangled from the rule of law promotion under both the AA and related non-contractual instruments. Though not immediately referring to the rule of law concept, the examined unilateral assistance instruments aim to promote an array of the rule of law standards such as legality, legal certainty and transparency.

"Deep disciplines": competition and public procurement

Similar to the Western Balkans case, the DCFTAs' provisions on public procurement and competition are pierced with a number of the rule of law standards, such as **legality**, **legal certainty** (e.g. ensuring more stable and predictable legislative frameworks, meeting economic operators' legitimate expectation), **transparency**, **equality** and **non-discrimination**, and the **availability of judicial review**. Due to the envisaged degree of the integration of associated Neighbours into the Single Market, the DCFTAs combined a number of pathways to promote these standards, such as the imposition of basic standards, the combination of legislative approximation and market access conditionality, as well as the recourse to the parties' international obligations. Besides, the implementation of these standards was extensively supported in terms of the EU's novel sectoral approach to reform's support, predominantly applied in Ukraine (Wolczuk and Žeruolis, 2018, pp. 11–12).

As demonstrated in Chapter 5, prior to the AAs/DCFTAs conclusion, the programming of the EU's assistance to associated Neighbours tended to emphasize the political cooperation-related dimension of the rule of law (e.g. reforms of the judiciary and public administration), and selectively tackle regulatory reforms.[57]

---

55 See, for instance, European Commission (2007). TAIEX and Twinning Activity Report. [pdf] European Commission. Available at: https://ec.europa.eu/neighbourhood-enlargement/sites/near/files/taiex-and-twinning-2017-highlights_en.pdf, p. 3. See also EU Border Assistance Mission to Moldova and Ukraine (n.d.). Mandate of 2019. [online] EUBAM. Available at: http://eubam.org/who-we-are/.

56 EU Border Assistance Mission to Moldova and Ukraine (n.d.). Mandate of 2019. [online] Available at: http://eubam.org/who-we-are/.

57 See, for instance, European Commission DG "External Relations" (2007). Ukraine: National Indicative Programme 2007–2010 [online] Available at: https://library.euneighbours.eu/content/ukraine-national-indicative-programme-2007-2010; European Commission DG "External Relations" (2007). Moldova: National Indicative Programme 2007–2010. [online] Available at: https://library.euneighbours.eu/content/moldova-national-indicative-programme-2007-2010; European Commission DG "External Relations" (2007). Georgia: National Indicative Programme 2007–2010. [online]

160 *Internal coherence*

This statement can be substantiated by an insight into the Annual Action Programmes (AAPs), introduced under the auspices of the ENPI over the period 2007–2014 that predominantly channelled the EU's support of regulatory reforms through TAIEX and Twinning.[58]

The entry into force of the AAs/DCFTAs marked the EU's transfer to a sectoral approach in supporting the implementation of the "deep" disciplines. This statement can be exemplified by the EU's support for public procurement reforms in the associated Neighbourhood. Over the period 2013–2017, the EU has been supporting the implementation of public procurement reform in Ukraine through its project "Harmonization of Public Procurement System of Ukraine with EU Standards".[59] The analysis of the Project's description reveals its linkages to several aspects of the rule of law, such as **legality** (appropriateness and comprehensiveness of legal framework, institutions' compliance with the legislative framework), **legal certainty** (uniform application of public procurement legislation) and **transparency** and **accountability** of institutions.[60] In Moldova, the EU supports ongoing public procurement reform through co-financing the project jointly implemented by several NGOs and the European Bank for Reconstruction and Development (EBRD).[61] Similar to the Ukrainian case, the respective project promotes **legality**, **legal certainty**, **transparency** and **accountability** dimensions of the rule of law in the public procurement domain.[62] While the EU has not financed an overarching public procurement–related project in Georgia, it has been continuously supporting institution-building and capacity development measures under Georgia's Roadmap and Action Plan for the Implementation of Public Procurement Chapter of the EU-Georgia AA.[63]

Overall, the consolidation of the EU's sectoral approach to supporting reforms in the "associated" Neighbourhood can be viewed as a crucial step towards strengthening the coherence of the EU's assistance and the "joining-up" of EU

Available at: https://publications.europa.eu/en/publication-detail/-/publication/14729e8f-6edb-448c-b1c3-a05a60c30c7e/language-en.

58 See, for instance, European Commission DG "External Relations" (2011). Ukraine: National Indicative Programme 2011–2013. [pdf] European Commission. Available at: http://eeas.europa.eu/archives/docs/enp/pdf/pdf/country/2011_enpi_nip_ukraine_en.pdf, pp-10–11; European Commission DG "External Relations" (2011). Moldova: National Indicative Programme 2011–2013. [pdf] European Commission. Available at: https://ec.europa.eu/europeaid/sites/devco/files/nip-moldova-2011-2013_en.pdf, pp. 13–15.

59 Crown Agents (n.d.). Harmonization of Public Procurement System of Ukraine with EU Standards [online]. Available at: http://eupublicprocurement.org.ua/?lang=EN.

60 *Ibid.*

61 Western NIS Enterprise Fund (2017). Western NIS Enterprise Fund supports public procurement reform in Moldova. [online]. Available at: http://wnisef.org/medias/western-nis-enterprise-fund-supports-public-procurement-reform-moldova/.

62 *Ibid.*

63 State Procurement Agency of Georgia (2013). Roadmap and Action Plan for the Implementation of the Public-Procurement Chapter of the EU-Georgia Association Agreement. [online] Available at: www.dcfta.gov.ge/public/filemanager/implimentation/Roadmap%20and%20Action%20Plan%20in%20Public%20Procurement.pdf.

Internal coherence 161

instruments for the achievement of specific goals (Wolczuk and Žeruolis, 2018, pp. 11–12). Since both the "regulation" and "action" pertaining to "deep" disciplines embrace numerous aspects of the rule of law, the rule of law concept can be potentially utilized as a framework to assess the joined-up utilization of the EU's contractual and unilateral assistance instruments.

Part 3. Development EU-CARIFORUM EPA

1. CARIFORUM EPA and "soft" documents

As demonstrated in Chapter 5, "soft" documents framing the EU-CARIFORUM relations tend to strongly disentangle between the objectives concerning economic cooperation, on the one hand, and domestic reforms, on the other hand. Nonetheless, the Agenda 2030, adopted in 2015, and the 2016 Joint Communication "A Renewed Partnership with the Countries of Africa, the Caribbean and the Pacific" gave a strong impetus to the strengthening of the rule of law–trade liberalization nexus in EU-CARIFORUM relations.

To start, the 2008 and 2010 EU-LAC Summit Declarations, adopted in Lima and Madrid, respectively, predominantly linked economic development to the intra-region integration, rather than the internal reforms (such as the promotion of the rule of law) and EU-LAC region-to-region trade liberalization. Both Declarations, however, reaffirmed the parties' commitment to "shared objectives, commitments and joint positions" (without immediately referring to the rule of law).[64] Having welcomed the finalization of the EU-CARIFORUM EPA negotiations, the Declarations did not suggest specific actions to accompany the implementation of the EU-CARIFORUM EPA (or the EU FTAs with Central Africa and Andean Community, also mentioned in the Lima Declaration).[65] They also did not refer to the cooperation domains lying at the crossroads between the rule of law and economic development, distinguished by the 2005 European Commission's framework document "The European Union, Latin America and the Caribbean: A Strategic Partnership", such as "creating a climate favourable to trade and investment".[66]

In turn, the 2012Council Conclusions on the Joint Caribbean-EU Partnership Strategy emphasized the importance of the Cotonou Agreement, EU-CARIFORUM EPA and bi-regional political dialogue as the framework of EU-CARIFORUM relations.[67] The Strategy also reaffirmed both the parties' commitment to

---

64 *Ibid.*

65 *Ibid.*

66 European Commission (2005). the European Union, Latin America and the Caribbean: A Strategic Partnership. [pdf] European Commission. Available at: http://eeas.europa.eu/archives/docs/la/docs/guadal_04_en.pdf.

67 Council of the European Union, Council Conclusions on the Joint Caribbean-EU Partnership Strategy, 3199th Foreign Affairs Council meeting of 19 November 2012. Council of the European Union. [pdf] Available at: https://eeas.europa.eu/sites/eeas/files/partnership_strategy.pdf.

162 *Internal coherence*

democracy, human rights and the rule of law, without, however, linking the process of these values' advancement to the implementation of the EU-CARIFORUM EPA.[68] Instead, it suggested supporting the EPA's implementation via "strengthening regional integration and cooperation processes in the Caribbean region" and different forms of development assistance.

In line with the Agenda 2030, the 2016 Commission's and High Representative's Joint Communication "A Renewed Partnership with the Countries of Africa, the Caribbean and the Pacific" introduced "promoting peaceful and democratic societies, good governance, the rule of law and human rights for all" as a priority for the EU-CARIFORUM relations.[69] Notably, the 2016 Communication "instrumentalized" the rule of law as "a fundamental value, a necessary basis for sustainable development, a key component in preventing conflict, and a foundation for successful cooperation in other areas of interests for the EU" and stressed the EU commitment to promoting "effective and independent justice for citizens and business".[70] The Communication also reaffirmed the pivotal role of the EU-CARIFORUM EPA in the region-to-region relations, underlining their WTO compatibility and calling for "addressing all trade and trade-related areas in a holistic manner".[71] According to the Commission, exercising such a holistic approach to trade would require strengthening the parties' dialogue and cooperation related to trade in services, elimination of non-tariff barriers to trade, regulatory harmonization, investment, IP rights, competition policy and labour rights.[72] Although the 2016 Communication both underlined the importance of the rule of law for sustainable development and called for reinforcing the EU-CARIFORUM dialogue on trade and its liberalization, it did not immediately highlight the "junctures" between the implementation of the EPA and the rule of law promotion. A number of such "junctures" was, instead, distinguished in the CARIFORUM-specific part of the Communication (e.g. the promotion of good economic governance via "sound public finance management, transparency and accountability" including *inter alia* "strengthening the fight against corruption, money laundering, and illicit financial flows and tax havens").[73]

Ultimately, the "soft" documents, as previously considered, represent a crucial dynamic framework for the implementation of the EPA, as well as the region-to-region dialogue and cooperation on trade-related issues. Although the documents under study contain in-detail provisions regarding many cooperation areas (e.g. intra-regional integration, environmental protection and sustainability issues), the documents under study barely provide for "action" in support of the

---

68 *Ibid.*, p. 1.
69 European Commission, Communication to the European Parliament and the Council: A Renewed Partnership with the Countries of Africa, the Caribbean and the Pacific, JOIN(2016) 52final of 22 November 2016.
70 *Ibid.*, pp. 8–9.
71 *Ibid.*, p. 11.
72 *Ibid.*
73 *Ibid.*, pp. 18–20.

Internal coherence 163

rule of law standards contained in the EU-CARIFORUM EPA. Instead, they view the rule of law as a part of the political cooperation agenda and tangentially refer to it as a prerequisite for sustainable development.

2. *Rule of law standards in the EU-CARIFORUM EPA and the European Development Funds (EDFs)*

Marked by the "deepest" scope among the EU's EPAs with ACP countries, the EU-CARIFORUM EPA contains an array of standards pertaining to different disciplines.[74] Underlining the importance of technical assistance and capacity-building in facilitating the attainment of the Agreement's competition-related objectives, Art. 130 of the EU-CAIFORUM EPA can be viewed as a foundation for the interplay between the "regulation" and "action" dimensions of the rule of law promotion through trade liberalization.

The analysis of funding priorities under the 9th–11th EDFs demonstrates mixed results as regards their coherence with the rule of law standards, contained in the EU-CARIFORUM EPA. Among the three considered EDFs, the programming under the 9th EDF has been least concerned with the problématique of both political development and trade liberalization with the EU.[75] Instead, the 9th EDF primarily focused on supporting the intra-region cooperation and integration as well as the attainment of the MDGs (e.g. poverty eradication, achieving universal primary education and combating HIV/AIDS, malaria and other diseases).[76]

As opposed to the 9th EDF, the 10th EDF is marked by stronger coherence with the EU-CARIFORUM EPA, ensured through the financing of the multifaceted region-wide support programme to the implementation of the EPA.[77] Pursuant to the "Regional Economic Integration and Cooperation" component of the 10th EDF, this programme was directed *inter alia* to the implementation of the EU-CARIFORUM EPA's provisions on technical cooperation and removing technical barriers to trade, reforming legislative and regulatory frameworks for the services sector and raising the institutional and implementation capacity of the CARIFORUM countries.[78] Importantly, this regional programme did

---

74 For more details, see Chapter 4, Part 3.

75 For more details, see Chapter 5, Part 3.

76 See, for instance, Delegation of the European Commission in Barbados and the Eastern Caribbean (2007). Joint Action Report: Cooperation between the European Union and Grenada. [online] Available at: https://ec.europa.eu/europeaid/sites/devco/files/joint-annual-report-07-cooperation-eu-grenada-2008_en.pdf; Joint Evaluation Union (DevCO and EEAS) (2012). Country-Level Evaluation. Final Report [pdf] European Commission. Available at: https://ec.europa.eu/euro peaid/sites/devco/files/evaluation-cooperation-ec-jamaica-1314-main-report-201209_en.pdf, pp. 15–28.

77 European Commission (2007). CARIFORUM – Regional Strategy Paper and Regional Indicative Programme under the 10th EDF 2008–2013. [pdf] European Commission. Available at: https://eulacfoundation.org/en/system/files/EUROPEAN%20COMMUNITY%20_%20CARIB BEAN%20REGION%20%20REGIONAL%20STRATEGY%20PAPER.pdf, p. 37.

78 *Ibid.*

164 *Internal coherence*

not specifically target the legislative and regulatory changes stemming from the implementation of "deep disciplines" under the EU-CARIFORUM EPA.[79] Neither did it refer to the role of law concept. The NIPs, developed under the 10th EDF, are characterized by a considerable variation in objectives, ranging from those that concentrate on development *stricto sensu* (e.g. poverty reduction, road infrastructure) to the rule of law–oriented ones (e.g. the improvement of access to justice and human rights).[80] Neither of the NIPs under the 10th EDF, however, provided for support of the implementation of the EU-CARIFORUM EPA at the national level.[81]

Finally, similar to the 10th EDF, the regional dimension of the 11th EDF encompassed support of the implementation of the EU-CARIFORUM EPA without linking it to rule of law promotion.[82] Similar to the NIPs under the 10th EDF, the ones under the 11th EDF are characterized by significant variation and the pursuit of the rule of law-related objectives without the connection to the implementation of the EU-CARIFORUM EPA.[83]

Hence, the case of the EU-CARIFORUM EPA is marked by the mixed account of coherence between the "action" and "regulation" dimensions of the rule of law promotion through trade liberalization. Both the 11th and 12th EDFs envisaged funding for programmes supporting the implementation of numerous EPA chapters at the regional level, thus promoting the rule of law standards, encompassed by these chapters of the EPA (e.g. transparency of public procurement, the relationship between international and domestic law pertaining to administrative cooperation). Nevertheless, neither these regional programmes, nor the NIPs, encompassed the "junctures" between the implementation of the EPA and the rule of law promotion.

---

79 *Ibid.*
80 See, for instance, European Commission, Government of Jamaica (2007). Country Strategy Paper and National Indicative Programme for Jamaica for the period 2008–2013 [pdf] European Commission. Available at: https://ec.europa.eu/europeaid/sites/devco/files/csp-nip-jamaica-2008-2013_en.pdf, pp. 27–37; European Commission (2007). Government of Trinidad and Tobago – Country Strategy Paper and National Indicative Programme for Trinidad and Tobago 2008–2013. [pdf] European Commission. Available at: https://ec.europa.eu/europeaid/sites/devco/files/csp-nip-trinidad-tobago-2008-2013_en.pdf, pp. 23–31.
81 *Ibid.*
82 See, for instance, European Commission (2015). CARIFORUM, Caribbean Regional Indicative Programme under the 11th European Development Fund 2014–2020. European Commission. [pdf] Available at: https://ec.europa.eu/europeaid/sites/devco/files/caribbean-regional-indicative-programme_en.pdf, p. 31.
83 See, for instance, European Commission, the Government of Jamaica (2014). 11th EU Development Fund (EDF) National Indicative Programme (2014–2020) for cooperation between the European Union and Jamaica. [pdf] Available at: https://ec.europa.eu/europeaid/sites/devco/files/nip-edf11-jamaica-2014-2020_en.pdf, pp. 13–15; European Commission, the Government of the Republic of Trinidad and Tobago (2014). 11thEU Development Fund (EDF) National Indicative Programme (2014–2020) for cooperation between the European Union and the Republic of Trinidad and Tobago. [online] Available at: https://ec.europa.eu/europeaid/sites/devco/files/nip-edf11-trinidad-tobago-2014-2020_en.pdf, pp. 7–9.

Conclusion

This chapter aimed to explore the coherence of the "regulation" and "action" dimensions of the EU rule of law promotion through trade liberalization in the Enlargement, Neighbourhood and Development contexts. In all cases under study, "soft" (diplomatic) documents have constituted a crucial policy framework for implementation of the RTAs and the EU's role in this process. It is, however, noteworthy that across all policy contexts, "soft" documents have predominantly linked the rule of law to the political aspect of the EU cooperation with third countries.

The scope of the EU's "action" and volumes of assistance across contexts have significantly differed, depending on the objectives behind each particular policy and integration aspirations. The envisaged degree of integration of partner countries into the Single Market was found to be a crucial factor, impacting both the scope of the partner countries' rule of law obligations, included into the RTAs, and the scope of unilateral financial and technical assistance, utilized by the EU to support their implementation. This statement can be additionally supported by the differentiating "depth" and elaborateness of the partner countries' rule of law obligations within the same agreements (e.g. elaborate public procurement clauses in the EU-CARIFORUM EPA).

Although in many cases, the EU's "action" has fit the scope of relevant "regulation", the analysis allows for distinguishing several conceptual incoherencies between the EU "regulation" and "action" in partner countries.

Among them, one can first of all mention a number of conceptual issues and divides, such as:

- The "politics-only" understanding of the rule of law.
- A strict demarcation line between the domains of political and economic cooperation (yet not fully excluding the cross-cutting areas, such as the improvement of economic governance and the environment for doing business).
- And subsequently, a dividing line between the values and *acquis* conditionality.

Second, as a result of these dividing lines, numerous rule of law standards contained in the RTAs remain non-reflected in the EU "action", as well as disconnected from each other in the EU benchmarking and progress assessment activities. In other words, there is no methodology that would allow the EU to assess the impact of "deep" trade liberalization on the rule of law situation in third states, in general, and within the disciplines of particular RTAs, in particular. This statement is also true for cross-cutting cooperation areas, included into numerous EU "action" documents (e.g. economic governance, ensuring the ease of doing business). Third, the divides between the political and economic cooperation, and between the values and *acquis* conditionality, create lacunas and disconnects within the multidimensional conditionality systems the EU employs in all the explored policy contexts. Such disconnects encompass, for instance, the lack of

166   *Internal coherence*

interplay between political conditionality (rule of law as a fundamental value), Single Market *acquis* conditionality (rule of law standards, embedded into respective *acquis*) and market access conditionality. Due to the combination of these factors, the rule of law promotion through RTAs remains *de facto* disconnected from EU efforts to promote the rule of law as a fundamental value.

References

Anastasakis, O. and Bechev, D. (2003). *EU conditionality in South-East Europe: Bringing commitment to the process, South-Eastern European studies programme (University of Oxford)*. Working Paper, 2003. St Antony's College University of Oxford. [pdf] Available at: www.sant.ox.ac.uk/sites/default/files/euconditionality.pdf.

Börzel, T.A. and Van Hüllen, V. (2014). One voice, one message, but conflicting goals: Cohesiveness and consistency in the European neighbourhood policy. *Journal of European Public Policy*, 2, pp. 1033–1049.

Duke, S. (1999). *Consistency as an issue in EU external relations*. EIPA Working Paper 99/W/06. [online] Available at: http://aei.pitt.edu/542/1/99w06.pdf.

Ghazaryan, N. (2014). *The European neighbourhood policy and the democratic values of the EU: A legal analysis*. Oxford: Hart Publishing.

Gross, E. and Rotta, A. (2011). *The EEAS and the Western Balkans*. IAI Working Papers 2011/11. Istituto Affari Internazionali. [pdf] Available at: www.iai.it/sites/default/files/iaiwp1115.pdf.

Hofmann, H.C.H. (2008). Mapping the European administrative space. *West European Politics*, 31, pp. 662–676.

Juncos, A.E. (2017). The European Union and the Western Balkans. Enlargement as a security strategy. In: S. Economides and J. Sperling, eds., *EU security strategies. Extending the EU system of security governance*. London: Routledge, pp. 39–57.

Karadjoski, M., Memeti, M. and Dimeski, B. (2019). *Principles of openness and transparency as an immanent part of the European administrative space (EAP)*.[online] Available at: http://eprints.uklo.edu.mk/5144/.

Kochenov, D. (2009). The EU rule of law: Cutting paths through confusion. *Erasmus Law Review*, 2, pp. 5–24.

Koeth, W. (2014). *The new instrument for pre-accession assistance (IPA II): Less accession, more assistance*. Working Paper 2014/W/01. [online] Available at: www.eipa.eu/wp-content/uploads/2017/11/20160318134447_WorkingPaper_2014_W_01.pdf.

Magen, A. (2016). Overcoming the diversity-consistency dilemmas in the EU's rule of law external action. *AsiaEurope Journal*, 14, pp. 25–41.

Mendelski, M. (2015). The EU's pathological power: The failure of external rule of law promotion in South Eastern Europe. *Southeastern Europe*, 39, pp. 318–346.

Noutcheva, G. (2006). *EU conditionality and Balkan compliance: Does sovereignty matter?* PhD. Graduate School of Public and International Affairs at the University of Pittsburg. University of Pittsburg. [pdf] Available at: http://d-scholarship.pitt.edu/7279/1/DISSERTATIONGerganaNoutchevaApril2006.pdf.

Olsen, J. (2011). Towards a European administrative space? *Journal of European Public Policy*, 10, pp. 506–531.

Pech, L. (2016). The EU as a global rule of law promoter: The consistency and effectiveness challenges. *Asia Europe Journal*, 14, pp. 7–24.

Studiare Sviluppo. (2008/2009). *Technical assistance to tax and customs administrations in the Western Balkans.* [online] Available at: www.studiaresviluppo.it/politiche-doga nali/technical-assistance-to-tax-and-customs-administrations-tacta-in-the-western-bal kans-2008–2009/.

Van der Loo, G. (2016). *The EU-Ukraine association agreement and deep and comprehensive free trade area: A new legal instrument of EU integration without membership.* Leiden: Brill.

Wetzel, A. and Orbie, J. (2012). *The EU's promotion of external democracy. In: Search of the plot.* CEPS Policy Brief 2012/281. [online] Available at: www.ceps.eu/ceps-publications/eus-promotion-external-democracy-search-plot/.

Wolczuk, K. and Žeruolis, D. (2018). *Rebuilding Ukraine: An assessment of EU assistance.* Chatham House Research Paper 2018/08. The Royal Institute of International Affairs. [online] Available at: www.chathamhouse.org/publication/rebuilding-ukraine-assessing-eu-assistance-ukraine.

7 Coherence between the rule of law promotion through RTAs and EU broader rule of law promotion activities (external coherence)

The case of justice sector reforms

As mentioned earlier, our research on the coherence of the EU's rule of law promotion through trade liberalization comprises two parts. The first part, presented in Chapter 6, dealt with the interplay between the "regulation" and "action" dimensions of the rule of law promotion through RTAs (i.e. "internal coherence"). Building on this, this chapter will zoom in on the relationship between the rule of law promotion through RTAs (as a single field) and broader EU rule of law promotion activities (i.e. "external coherence").

The boundary between these two aspects of coherence may seem fuzzy. In this vein, the key criterion we used for delimitation has been the connection to trade in EU "soft" documents and unilateral assistance instruments. Chapter 6 predominantly focused on diplomatic and assistance instruments, immediately linked to RTA implementation or at least the cooperation areas, lying at the crossroads between economic development and the rule of law promotion (e.g. economic governance, ensuring the ease of doing business, etc.). Notably, the "connection to trade" criterion may be seen problematic, when applied to the "essential element" conditionality. However, since "essential element" clauses were initially designed to make use of trade relations as an instrument to safeguard values, we chose to consider them under the auspices of "internal coherence".

Simultaneously, as we demonstrated in Chapter 5, the "rule of law menu" (Carothers, 2010, p. 6), offered by the EU to third countries, goes far beyond the economic or trade-related dimensions of the concept, with reform of the judiciary and law enforcement agencies lying at the heart of the EU's action across all policy contexts in question. In the Balkans, rule of law promotion has been part of the broader region-building and stabilization agenda, encompassing, *inter alia*, fights against corruption and organized crime, institution-building and public administration reform. Nonetheless, according to the Commission's 2018 Communication "A Credible Enlargement Perspective for and Enhanced EU Engagement with the Western Balkans", "state capture, including links with organized crime and corruption at all levels of government, as well as strong entanglement of public and private interests" continue to challenge the region.[1] The Communication

---

1 European Commission, Communication to the European Parliament, the Council, the European Economic and Social Committee and the Committee of the Regions: A Credible Enlargement

External coherence 169

thus distinguished creating "visibly empowered and independent judiciary and accountable governments and administrations" as the essentials of the Balkans' successful accession process. Following the outbreak of crises in Ukraine, Syria and Libya, the 2015 ENP Review connected the rule of law agenda to ensuring security and stabilization in both the Eastern and Southern Neighbourhoods.[2] Similar to the Western Balkans case, "an independent, transparent and impartial justice system free from political interference" is regarded as a cornerstone of EU-Neighbourhood relations.[3] Finally, in line with the Agenda 2030, the 2016 Joint Communication on the Renewed Partnership with the ACP Countries linked the rule of law to the concept of human security and ensuring universal access to effective and independent justice.[4]

Against this background, this part of the analysis uses the case of the justice sector reform as a lens to investigate the coherence between the EU rule of law promotion through RTAs and its broader rule of law promotion activities in the Enlargement, Neighbourhood and Development policy contexts. This chapter defines the EU's support of "justice sector reforms" as encompassing the activities directed at ensuring the efficiency and independence of both partner countries' judiciaries and law enforcement agencies, broadly defined (e.g. Ministries for Internal Affairs, Offices of Public Prosecutors, police).[5]

This chapter conceptualizes the EU's support for the justice sector reform as a "juncture" between the EU's rule of law promotion through RTAs and broader EU rule of law promotion activities. The multidimensional nature of the EU's external rule of law promotion activities allows for revealing numerous "junctures" of the rule of law promotion through trade liberalization and the rule of law promotion, more broadly, such as stabilization, institution-building and the fight against corruption and organized crime. We chose to focus particularly on the justice sector reform for several reasons. First, this objective is shared across all the policy contexts under study, and hence is reflected in numerous diplomatic and legal documents. Second, despite the EU's multifaceted and systemic efforts, ensuring judicial independence and efficiency remains a challenge in all the studied contexts (e.g. Bojicic-Dzelilovic, Kostovicova and Randazzo, 2018; Batora

---

Perspective for and Enhanced EU Engagement with the Western Balkans, COM (2018)65 final of 6 February 2018.

2 European Commission, Joint Communication to the European Parliament, the Council, the European Economic and Social Committee and the Committee of the Region: Review of the European Neighbourhood Policy, JOIN 2015 (50), final of 18 November 2015, pp. 3–4.

3 *Ibid.*, pp. 5–6.

4 European Commission, Communication to the European Parliament and the Council: A Renewed Partnership with the Countries of Africa, the Caribbean and the Pacific, JOIN(2016) 52final of 22 November 2016, p. 19.

5 See, for instance, European Commission, Commission Implementing Decision on the Special Measure III 2016 on Support to Rule of Law Reforms in Ukraine (PRAVO) to be financed from the general budget of the European Union, C(2016)8266 final; European Commission, Instrument for Pre-Accession Assistance (IPA II) 2014–2020. Bosnia and Herzegovina. EU4Justice in Bosnia and Herzegovina. [pdf] Available at: https://ec.europa.eu/neighbourhood-enlargement/sites/near/files/ipa_2018_41501_ad5_bih_eu4justice_in_bosnia_and_herzegovina_phase_2_.pdf.

170   *External coherence*

and Rieker, 2018). Third, the focus on justice sector reforms allows us zooming in on the political aspects, rather than the economic aspects, of the rule of law.

Ultimately, Chapter 7 will supplement our understanding of the EU's rule of law promotion through trade liberalization with an insight into the political rule of law agenda in the Enlargement, Neighbourhood and Development contexts.

Part I. Enlargement (Western Balkans)

1. Strategies and key focus points

As mentioned previously, the justice sector reform has been an essential of the EU-Western Balkans policy dialogue since the early stages of the SAP. However, following the strict delimitation between the values and *acquis* conditionality, discussed previously, the justice sector reform has been instantly regarded as a part of the political cooperation agenda, rather than a prerequisite for implementing trade-related parts of the SAAs.

Already the 2006 Commission's Communication "The Western Balkans on the Road to the EU: Consolidating Stability and Raising Prosperity" referred to "the establishment of functioning institutions and judiciary" and "building up institutional capacities in the judiciaries" as the essentials for implementing the 2003 Thessaloniki Agenda, constitutive of EU-Western Balkans relations.[6] Similarly, the 2014 Berlin Conference on the Western Balkans reaffirmed their commitment to increase legal certainty and to "uphold and reinforce their judiciary".[7] Moreover, the judicial reform was recognized as a centrepiece of the rule of law promotion by the Final Declaration of the Chair of the 2016 Paris Western Balkans Summit.[8] Justice sector reforms were not, however, mentioned in the 2015 Vienna Declaration or the 2017 Trieste Declaration, with both documents mainly linking the rule of law to economic governance and the anti-corruption problématique. Acknowledging the incomplete nature of transformation in the Western Balkans, the 2018 Commission's Communication on a "credible European perspective" for the region called for more results-oriented justice sector and anti-corruption reforms.[9]

---

6 European Commission, Communication: The Western Balkans on the Road to the EU: Consolidating Stability and Raising prosperity, COM(2006) 27 final of 27 January 2006.

7 Final Declaration of the Chair on the Berlin Conference on the Western Balkans of 28 August 2014. [online] Available at: https://archiv.bundesregierung.de/archiv-de/meta/startseite/final-declaration-by-the-chair-of-the-conference-on-the-western-balkans-754634

8 Final Declaration of the Chair of the Paris Western Balkans Summit of 4 July 2016. [pdf] European Commission. Available at: https://ec.europa.eu/neighbourhood-enlargement/sites/near/files/pdf/policy-highlights/regional-cooperation/20160713-01.final-declaration-by-the-chair-of-the-paris-western-balkans-summit.pdf.

9 European Commission, Communication to the European Parliament, the Council, the European Economic and Social Committee and the Committee of the Regions: A Credible Enlargement Perspective for and Enhanced EU Engagement with the Western Balkans, COM (2018)65 final of 6 February 2018, p. 3.

External coherence 171

Discussing the framework for justice sector reforms in the Balkans, it is crucial to mention to mention their connection to a very particular, region-specific issue, i.e. overcoming the legacy of the Yugoslav Wars and solving remaining bilateral disputes in the region.[10] As compared to the situation existing at the moment, when the 2003 Thessaloniki Agenda was adopted, Western Balkan countries surely achieved considerable progress in this domain.[11] However, as noted by the European Commission, such progress is not enough to ensure the fully-fledged region's integration into the EU cooperation structures in the field of Justice and Home Affairs.[12] In other words, the Commission warned the Balkans against the "importing of disputes" and the instability this may entail amid the accession process and the Western Balkans' ambition to join the EU.[13] Thus, analyzing justice sector reforms in the Balkans requires taking into account the context of stabilization, the solution of persisting bilateral disputes (e.g. the long-lasting Serbia-Kosovo dispute over North Kosovo and Serbia's recognition of the Republic of Kosovo as a state) and the observance of post-Yugoslav Wars peace agreements.

Ultimately, although the justice sector reform lies at the heart of EU-Balkans relations, the respective problématique is barely linked to the implementation of the SAAs in general, and their trade-related chapters in particular. This, once again, demonstrates the endurance of the borderline between the political and economic criteria in terms of the values conditionality, as well as the values and *acquis* conditionality. In this vein, distinguishing synergies between the EU's justice sector support, exercised through SAAs, and its broader activities in this regard requires an insight into the relevant framework norms and the substance of the EU's justice sector support in the region.

2. Framework norms and substance of the EU's support of justice sector reforms in the Balkans

This section of the analysis aims to highlight key legal norms, constituting the framework of EU-Western Balkans relations, and major substantial themes, encompassed by the EU's support for justice sector reforms.

To start, it shall be mentioned that each of the SAAs between the EU and Western Balkan countries contains a title, dedicated to "Justice, Freedom and Security". Calling for "the reinforcement of institutions at all levels", the "Justice, Freedom and Security" titles contain partner countries' commitments to strengthening the independence of the judiciary, its efficiency and the improvement of the functioning of police and other law enforcement agencies.[14] In this way, the SAAs implicitly point to the need for the interplay between the judicial and public administration reforms and their financial and technical support.

10 *Ibid.*
11 *Ibid.*
12 *Ibid.*, p. 7.
13 *Ibid.*
14 *Ibid.*

172   *External coherence*

Specific targets and instruments of the EU's support for the implementation of justice sector reforms in the Balkans are reflected in the programming of the EU's assistance to the region, relevant region and country reports, and the EULEX documents.

Immediately following the formulations, contained in the SAAs, already the 2002–2006CARDS Regional Strategy primarily targeted the effectiveness dimension of the justice sector reform, expecting to achieve the functionality and interconnectedness of the Interpol networks in the region, create cross-regional functional networks of the judiciary and the opportunity of conducting cross-border crime-oriented joint investigations and prosecutions.[15] At the national level, the CSPs referred both to judicial independence and effectiveness. For instance, the 2002–2006 CSP for FYROM distinguished the promotion of an "independent and efficient judiciary" and support of the restructuring of the court system as the major objective of JHA projects to be implemented in the country.[16] Similarly, the 2002–2006 CSP for Bosnia and Herzegovina provided for "technical assistance, training and legal advice to the State Entities, Cantons and Municipalities and the courts" as the key means to reinforce judicial independence and improve effectiveness and efficiency of the judiciary.[17] Besides, the national dimension of the CARDS emphasized an array of specific **standards concerning the operation of the judiciary**, such as due process, the reduction of delays in the proceedings, an account of appropriate anti-corruption measures and the increase in the efficiency of court administration, the reduction of the number of non-implement court rulings and stronger cooperation between the courts and law enforcement agencies.[18] Notably, similar to the case of diplomatic documents, neither of the expectations or standards mentioned under the CSPs/MIPDs immediately engaged with the implementation of SAAs as a whole or their trade-related parts. This, once again, demonstrates the extent to which the design of the EU's assistance to Western

---

15 *Ibid.*, p. 41.

16 European Commission Directorate Western Balkans (2002). CARDS Assistance Programme Former Yugoslav Republic of Macedonia 2002–2006. [pdf] European Commission. Available at: https://ec.europa.eu/neighbourhood-enlargement/sites/near/files/pdf/financial_assistance/cards/publications/fyrom_strategy_paper_en.pdf, pp. 27–28.

17 European Commission Directorate Western Balkans (2004). CARDS Assistance Programme, Bosnia and Herzegovina 2005–2006. [pdf] European Commission. Available at: https://ec.europa.eu/neighbourhood-enlargement/sites/near/files/pdf/bosnia_and_herzegovina/mip_2005_2006_bih_en.pdf, p. 24.

18 European Commission Directorate Western Balkans (2002). CARDS Assistance Programme Former Yugoslav Republic of Macedonia 2002–2006. [pdf] Available at: https://ec.europa.eu/neighbourhood-enlargement/sites/near/files/pdf/financial_assistance/cards/publications/fyrom_strategy_paper_en.pdf, pp. 27–28; European Commission Directorate Western Balkans (2004). CARDS Assistance Programme, Bosnia and Herzegovina 2005–2006. [pdf] European Commission. Available at: https://ec.europa.eu/neighbourhood-enlargement/sites/near/files/pdf/bosnia_and_herzegovina/mip_2005_2006_bih_en.pdf, p. 24; European Commission, Directorate Western Balkans (2001). CARDS Assistance Programme Albania 2002–2006. [pdf] European Commission. Available at: https://ec.europa.eu/neighbourhood-enlargement/sites/near/files/pdf/financial_assistance/cards/publications/albania_strategy_paper_en.pdf.

External coherence 173

Balkans mirrored the structure of the Copenhagen criteria, preventing the cross-fertilization between the different aid domains.

Produced following the expiry of the CARDS assistance instrument, the 2006 Commission country reports on the Western Balkans testify to the limitedness of partner countries' progress in the justice sector reforms domain.[19] In all three cases under study, the Commission did not take a selective standard-by-standard approach to assessment, but addressed the situation in partner countries as a whole. As a result, judicial dependence on other branches of power (including the lack of constitutional protection and accountability of judges), as well as insufficient impartiality and transparency of the judiciary, remained key concerns in the countries in question.[20] At the same time, scholars criticized the CARDS-era EU's justice sector support for the Union's reluctance "to concert its declarations with its intentions and unprepared and unable to implement its pronounced will" (Fakiolas and Tzifakis, 2008, p. 377), limited ability to set concrete deadlines for far-reaching reforms (Trauner, 2009, p. 65) and inconsistent progress assessment (Anastasakis, 2008).

Not surprisingly, justice sector reform remained high on the agenda under the IPA I assistance scheme.[21] Marked by a stronger focus on ensuring Candidate countries' abilities to fulfil the accession criteria (as compared to the CARDS), the national-level programming under the IPA I focused on two dimensions of the JHA reforms: capacities and structures.[22] In comparison with the CARDS, the CSPs/MIPDs under the IPA I focus on more specific tasks, involving particular institutions (e.g. the establishment of the Judiciary Training Institute in North Macedonia, or constructing the Justice Palace in Tirana).[23] Furthermore, in line with the IPA I focus on "transition assistance and institution-building", the IPA I programming demonstrated tight interconnections between the justice sector and public administration reforms (e.g. cross-cutting action to counter corruption and

---

19 Commission of the European Communities, Commission Staff Working Document – The Former Yugoslav Republic of Macedonia 2007 Progress Report, SEC(2007) 1432 of 6 November 2007, pp. 6–12; Commission of the European Communities, Commission Staff Working Document – Albania 2007 Report, SEC(2007) 1429 of 6 November 2007, pp. 6–10; Commission of the European Communities, Commission Staff Working Document – Bosnia and Herzegovina 2007 Report, SEC(2007) 1430 of 6 November 2007, pp. 7–15.

20 European Commission, Commission Staff Working Document – The former Yugoslav Republic of Macedonia 2006 Progress Report, SEC(2006)1387 final of 8 November 2016; European Commission, Commission Staff Working Document – Albania 2006 Progress Report, SEC(2006) 1383 final of 8 November 2016; European Commission, Commission Staff Working Document – Bosnia and Herzegovina 2006 Progress Report, SEC(2006)1384 final of 6 November 2016.

21 Regulation (EC) 1085/2006 of the European Council of 17 July 2006 establishing an Instrument for Pre-Accession Assistance (IPA), OJ L 210/82 of 31 July 2006.

22 See, for instance, European Commission, Decision on a Multi-annual Indicative Planning Document (MIPD) 2007–2009 for the former Yugoslav Republic of Macedonia, C(2007) 1853 of 30 April 2007, p. 9; European Commission, Implementing Decision on adopting a National Programme for Albania under the IPA Transition Assistance and Institution-Building Component for the Year 2012, C(2012)8208 final of 9 November 2012, pp. 14–16.

23 *Ibid.*

174 *External coherence*

organized crime).[24] As well as the CARDS, the IPA I programming did not, however, take recourse to either the SAAs in general, or with regard to trade liberalization in particular.[25] In progress terms, the IPA I reports have taken the CARDS-like approach: though acknowledging some progress being made, the Commission pointed to numerous shortcomings in the domains of **judicial independence, impartiality** and **transparency**.[26] A surge in attention towards the fluctuations in target countries' compliance with the EU's conditionality (most commonly explained by the mismatch between the interests of the EU and partner countries) was characteristic for scholarly contributions, produced during IPA I times (e.g. Anastasakis, 2008; Bieber, 2011).

As well as the IPA I and the CARDS, the IPA II country programming mirrored the accession criteria, introducing rather limited connections between the different groups of criteria. Pointing to the incomplete nature of justice sector reforms across the region, respective CSPs re-introduced the emphasis on judicial independence (e.g. in 2014–2017, the IPA II served as a foundation for a massive effort to re-evaluate judges and prosecutors in Albania as a requirement for opening the accession negotiations with the EU). Apart from the judicial independenceproblématique, the EU's support of justice sector reforms in the Balkans has focused on the following issue areas:

* The infrastructure of the judiciary, education and training system for judges and law enforcement professionals (Albania and FYROM).
* The functioning of administrative justice (FYROM).
* Strengthening efficiency of the judiciary and ensuring full implementation of free legal aid (Bosnia and Herzegovina).
* Addressing the persisting challenges of transitional justice (Bosnia and Herzegovina).

As noted previously, despite the EU's extensive focus on the judicial reform and the reforms of law enforcement agencies in the CARDS, IPA I and IPA II, the justice sector reform remains a crucial priority amid the post-2018 intensification of the accession talks.

Ultimately, we found that the substance of the EU's support of justice sector reforms in the Balkans has encompassed, *inter alia*, judicial independence, quality and efficiency; due process; infrastructure for the judiciary and law enforcement

---

24 *Ibid.*

25 *Ibid.*

26 Commission of the European Communities, Commission Staff Working Document – The former Yugoslav Republic of Macedonia 2013 Progress Report, SWD(2013) 413 final of 16 October 2013, pp. 10–11; Commission of the European Communities, Commission Staff Working Document – Albania 2013Progress Report, SWD(2013) 414 final of 16 October 2013, p. 9; Commission of the European Communities, Commission Staff Working Document – Bosnia and Herzegovina 2013 Progress Report, SWD(2013) 415 final of 16 October 2013, p. 19.

External coherence   175

agencies; and raising the capacity of the judicial and law enforcement bodies. Based on this investigation, the following part of the analysis will collate them with the norms on judicial review, as provided for in the SAAs.

3. Justice sector reform in the Western Balkans and the rule of law standards in the SAAs

Simultaneous analysis of the "regulation" dimension of the rule of law promotion through SAAs and the substance of the EU support of justice sector reforms in the Western Balkans allows for distinguishing a number of implicit yet crucial "junctures" or synergies.

First of all, an independent and efficient justice sector represents an essential prerequisite for fulfilling an individual's right to judicial review, provided for in "deep" disciplines chapters of the SAAs and international law acts they rely on (e.g. WTO law). Put it differently, the previously mentioned enduring issues pertaining to judiciaries and law enforcement in the Western Balkans (e.g. judiciaries' dependence on other branches of power; high backlog of cases) constitute the obstacles to the fulfillment of judicial review requirements stipulated in the SAAs with regard to trade-related issues. These statements can be exemplified by Art. XVIII of the GPA that obliges the parties *to* "provide a timely, effective, non-discriminatory administrative or judicial review procedure" that may be used to challenge the breach of an Agreement or a party's measure implementing the Agreement. Moreover, the SAAs require the parties to comply with the Directive 89/665/EEC of 21 December 1989 on the coordination of the laws, regulations and administrative provisions relating to the application of review procedures to the award of public supply and public works contracts.[27] The analysis of this Directive, presented in Chapter IV, demonstrated that it creates multifaceted obligations for the Member States as to ensuring the possibility of the contracting authorities' decisions' review as rapidly as possible, and effective enforcement of decisions by bodies responsible for the review procedure.[28] Analogously to the programming under the CARDS and IPA instruments, the Directive underlines the connection between the independence and impartiality of the judiciary and public administration bodies and even explicitly extends such requirements to administrations.[29] As opposed to the case of public procurement, the SAAs' competition provisions do not specify partner countries' obligations as to judicial review, only applying the independence and impartiality requirement to authorities, responsible for enforcing competition law.[30] By analogy with the public procurement provisions,

---

27 See, for instance, EU-Albania SAA, Art.74; EU-Kosovo SAA, Art.79.

28 Directive 89/665/EEC of the European Council of 21 December 1989 on the coordination of the laws, regulations and administrative provisions relating to the application of review procedures to the award of public supply and public works contracts, OJ L 395 of 30 December 1989, pp. 33–35.

29 *Ibid.*

30 See, for instance, EU-Albania SAA, Art.71(3); EU-Kosovo SAA, Art.75(3).

176 *External coherence*

it can be, however, assumed that independent and efficient judiciary is required to ensure the administrations' effective enforcement of competition law, approximated with the provisions of the SAAs.

Second, the independence and efficiency of the judiciary and law enforcement are immediately linked to the fulfillment of the legal certainty and transparency principles, traced across the whole spectrum of considered instruments and disciplines under the SAAs. This statement can be substantiated as follows. To start, the very idea of the European Administrative Space (EAS), foundational for administrative and customs cooperation among the EU, its Member States and third countries, necessitates mechanisms to enforce a broad array of its components, including **legal certainty** and the **openness and transparency of administration** (Torma, 2011). Moreover, the transparency principle is specifically underlined by the SAAs' norms on customs and technical cooperation between the EU and the Western Balkans. The legal certainty and transparency principles are emphasized in the international agreements in the administrative and customs cooperation domains (e.g. the TBT). This allows arguing that the independence and efficiency of the domestic judicial system may also promote the implementation of international treaties in trade-related domains (alongside other means, such as political dialogue with the EU's and technical assistance).

Third, discussing the interplay between the "regulation" dimension of the SAAs and the EU's support of justice sector in the Balkans, one can also take the dissenting perspective and ask how the SAAs rule of law standards can benefit the justice sector reforms in partner countries. Answering this question, it is foremost important to point to the legally binding nature of the Single Market *acquis* conditionality, enshrined in the SAAs and containing the rule of law requirements. In contrast to the conditions, attached to the EU's unilateral funding instruments, the SAAs' norms are marked by lesser flexibility (even though, some trade-offs may be made in terms of compliance assessment) (Zhelyazkova et al., 2018). Hence, they constitute a crucial component of the contractual framework of the EU's rule of law promotion in the Western Balkans. Given the stable nature of such requirements and their connection to precise sectors/disciplines under the SAAs, they can be utilized by the EU as benchmarks to assess the performance of the justice sector in partner countries, *inter alia*, through getting an insight into stakeholders' perceptions. Creating bridges between the political (JHA-related) conditions attached to the EU's unilateral justice sector reform support and the judicial review requirement would create a more nuanced picture of the performance of judiciaries and law enforcement agencies with regard to specific sectors/disciplines. Additionally, such as an approach would be beneficial for facilitating stakeholders' engagement in the SAAs' implementation and departing from a single-dimensional understanding of the rule of law as a component of a political criterion for membership, rather than a value and a prerequisite for sustainable development.

Finally, the discussion of the synergies between the SAAs' judicial review standards and the EU's support for justice sector reforms in the region would not be complete without insight into the connections to public administration reforms. On the one hand, the capacity, openness, transparency and accountability of administrations constitute the inalienable principles of the EAS (Torma, 2011), and subsequently, the administrative and technical cooperation between the EU and partner countries, as provided by the SAAs. The Agreements also emphasize the institutional dimension of enforcing domestic norms, approximated to *acquis communautaire*, in numerous domains, such as public procurement, competition and IP rights protection. On the other hand, already the IPA I programming was marked by the presence of the cross-cutting "institution-building" component. It encompassed the capacity-building of both the judiciaries and public administrations in the region, as well as the anti-corruption and anti–organized crime initiatives (functioning across the institution-building and transition assistance components of the IPA I).[31] Similarly, largely capacity development-oriented programming under the IPA II emphasized the nexus between the public administration and judicial reforms (arguing that the capabilities of both administrations and the judiciary are decisive for the quality application and enforcement of the legislation).[32] This makes it relevant for Commission to create stronger links between the capacity-building packages of the administrations, judiciary and law enforcement agencies of SAAs countries, especially with regard to applying and enforcing the SAAs' rule of law standards.

In a nutshell, we find that, although the SAAs standards concerning judicial review and the EU's unilateral justice sector support of the Western Balkans lack formalized connections, there is a number of crucial synergies to be taken into account. The institutions' capacity to enforce the SAAs' rule of law norms can be conceptualized and further instrumentalized as a "unifying axis" for assessing the EU's institution-building activities in the Balkans and their relevance for implementing the SAAs.

Part 2. "Associated" Eastern Neighbourhood

1. Strategic documents

The launch of the ENP provoked an intense discussion in scholarship as to whether the EU would be capable of effectively promoting Neighbours' compliance with its rules amid the lack of a membership perspective (e.g. Magen, 2006; Schimmelfennig and Scholtz, 2008). Nonetheless, the design of the rule of law reforms, promoted by the EU in the region, is highly similar to the Enlargement-related

---

31 Regulation718/2007 of the European Communities of 12 June 2007 implementing Council Regulation (EC) No 1085/2006 establishing an instrument for pre-accession assistance (IPA), OJ L 170/1 of 26 June 2007.

32 Commission Implementing Decision amending Commission Decision C(2014)5770 of 18 August 2014 adopting the Indicative Strategy Paper for Albania for the period 2014–2020, C(2018)5027 final of 3 August 2018, p. 4; Commission Implementing Decision amending Commission Decision C(2014)8561 of 19 August 2014 adopting the Indicative Strategy Paper for the former Yugoslav Republic of Macedonia, C(2018) 524 final of 3 August, p. 1.

178   *External coherence*

ones. Similar to the Western Balkans' case, the EU's strategic documents framing its relations with the Eastern Neighbourhood do not conceptualize justice sector reforms as a means to facilitate the AAs' implementation or refer to cross-cutting themes, such as the independence and efficiency of judicial review in public procurement and competition domains.

As well as the early "soft" documents on the EU-Western Balkans relations, already the 2004 Commission's ENP Strategy Paper stressed the reform of the judiciary, as well as the enhancement of police and judicial cooperation as priorities to be addressed in terms of the 2004 Action Plans.[33] In the 2004 Action Plans for Ukraine, Moldova and Georgia, the EU took a three-dimensional approach to the judicial and law enforcement agencies in the Eastern Neighbourhood, encompassing:

- The reform of substantive and procedural legislation related to the operation of the judiciary and law enforcement agencies.
- Institutional independence- and efficiency-oriented reforms of the judiciary and law enforcement agencies.
- Building the capacity of judges, prosecutors and officials, working in the judiciary, administration, police and the penitentiary system.[34]

Such a multi-aspect approach to the justice sector, stipulated already in early policy frameworks, makes the ENP "soft" framework different from the early stage of the Enlargement context, whereby justice sector reform was addressed in far more general terms.[35] Despite their relatively detailed norms, the foundational ENP policy documents did not put the justice sector reform into the context of the association and FTA negotiations can be considered quite surprising, since the 2004 Action Plans explicitly provide for "convergence" with the key principles in respective *acquis communautaire*, including "access to legal recourse".[36] Most probably, the absence of such connections is rooted in the structure of the Copenhagen criteria that are believed to have considerably influenced the ENP's design (Kochenov, 2008).

"Conflict, rising extremism and terrorism, human rights violations and other challenges to international law" in both the Eastern and Southern Neighbourhoods created the demand for reforming the ENP.[37] In contrast to the largely reform-

---

33 Commission of the European Communities, Commission Communication, European Neighbourhood Policy – Strategy Paper, COM(2004) 373 final of 12 May 2004, p. 21.

34 See, for instance, EU-Ukraine Action Plan 2004. [online] Available at: https://library.euneighbours.eu//content/eu-ukraine-action-plan-0, pp. 5–6; EU-Moldova Action Plan 2004. [pdf] Available at: https://eeas.europa.eu/sites/eeas/files/moldova_enp_ap_final_en.pdf, pp. 7–8; EU-Georgia Action Plan 2004. [pdf] Available at: https://eeas.europa.eu/sites/eeas/files/georgia_enp_ap_final_en_0.pdf, pp. 6–7.

35 *Ibid.*

36 See, for instance, EU-Ukraine Action Plan 2004, p. 27.

37 European Commission, Joint Communication to the European Parliament, the Council, the European Economic and Social Committee and the Committee of the Region: Review of the European Neighbourhood Policy, JOIN 2015 (50), final of 18 November 2015, p. 2.

External coherence   179

oriented 2004 ENP Strategy Paper, the recurrent theme of the 2015 ENP Review has been the stabilization of the Neighbourhood.[38] Against this background, the Review stipulated that

> an independent, transparent and impartial judicial system free from political interference which guarantees equal access to justice, protection of human rights, gender equality and non-discrimination, and full application of the law will continue to be a goal for the EU with its partners.[39]

Simultaneously, the stabilization orientation of the ENP Review supplemented this broadly formulated objective with new emphases, such as the improvement of the legal framework for the EU-Neighbours judicial cooperation in criminal cases and the promotion of the intra-region judicial cooperation in criminal matters. Analogous to the 2004 ENP Strategy Paper, the 2015 ENP Review did not explicitly link the EU's support of justice sector reforms to the implementation of the AAs with Eastern Neighbours (as well as the AAs' negotiations with Morocco and Tunisia), preferring the vague formulation "full application of the law".[40]

In a nutshell, analogous to the case of the Western Balkans, "soft" documents pertaining to EU-Eastern Neighbourhood relations did not connect justice sector reforms to implementation of the AAs. They also did highlight relevant crosscutting themes, such as independent judicial review n public procurement and competition domains. Following the pattern, used in the previous section, we will proceed with analyzing framework norms on the EU's support of justice sector reforms in the "associated" Neighbourhood and mapping the substance of such support.

2. Framework norms and substance of the EU's support of justice sector reforms in the "associated" Eastern Neighbourhood

Representing the framework for Neighbours' Union "integration without membership", the AAs combine "essential elements" clauses with partner countries' obligations related to dialogue and cooperation regarding domestic reforms.[41] In contrast to the EU-Georgia and EU-Ukraine AAs that only refer to the umbrella rule of law concept, the EU-Moldova AA contains the parties' obligation to cooperate in the domains of judicial independence and administrative capacity, as well as the impartiality and effectiveness of law enforcement bodies.[42] Furthermore, the AAs' "Justice, Freedom and Security" chapters contain varying formulations of the parties' attachment to the justice sector reform. For instance, the EU-Ukraine AA provides for "the reinforcement of institutions at all levels in

---

38 *Ibid.*, p. 3.
39 *Ibid.*, p. 5.
40 *Ibid.*
41 See, for instance, EU-Ukraine AA, Art. 2, Art.6.
42 EU-Moldova AA, Art.4.

180   *External coherence*

the areas of administration in general and law enforcement and administration of justice in particular". The principle of **judicial independence** is also stressed in the "Justice, Freedom and Security" chapters of the EU-Georgia and EU-Moldova AAs, alongside the access to justice, the right to a fair trial and the impartiality and effectiveness of the law enforcement bodies.[43] Similar to the SAAs' JHA chapters, the AAs' "Justice, Freedom and Security" chapters imply some extent of coherence between the justice sector and public administration reforms, addressing both within the umbrella institution-building objective.[44]

Similar to the Western Balkans case, these provisions on justice sector reform tend to be disconnected from the judicial review requirements contained in the DCFTAs (highlighted in Chapter 4). However, as we show in what follows, the ENP programming and Single Support Frameworks (at least rhetorically) link justice sector reforms to a broader array of issues and contexts, as compared to the SAAs (e.g. countering corruption; security, stability and resilience, public administration reform; and the protection of economic operators' rights and interests).

Following the implementation of the 2004 ENP Action Plans, the justice sector reform has been distinguished as a priority for the EU-Eastern Neighbourhood cooperation under the 2007–2010 and 2011–2013 NIPs.[45] Our analysis shows that the specific reform objectives under the NIPs continued reflecting the previously mentioned three-dimensional approach to justice sector reforms that embraces the independence of the judiciary, its efficiency and capacity-building for judges, court administrative staff and law enforcement agency personnel.[46] Furthermore, as opposed to the CARDS and IPA programming for the Western Balkans, the 2007–2010 NIPs for Ukraine, Moldova and Georgia distinguished the reform of both substantive and procedural criminal and civil legislation as part to the programming for justice sector support.[47] Besides, the 2007–2010 NIPs for Ukraine, Moldova and Georgia stressed the importance of simplifying judicial and law enforcement procedures to protect the interests of economic operators. Assessing the implementation of the 2007–2010 NIPs, the Commission pointed to the overall "limited progress" achieved, while praising country-specific successes.[48] Neither of the country reports, however, touched upon the simplification

---

43 EU-Georgia AA, Art.13; EU-Moldova AA, Art.12.

44 *Ibid.*

45 See, European Commission DG "External Relations" (2007). Georgia: National Indicative Programme 2007–2010. [online] Available at: https://publications.europa.eu/en/publication-detail/-/publication/14729e8f-6edb-448c-b1c3-a05a60c30c7e/language-en, pp. 7–8; European Commission DG "External Relations" (2011). Moldova: National Indicative Programme 2011–2013. [online] Available at: https://ec.europa.eu/europeaid/sites/devco/files/nip-moldova-2011-2013_en.pdf, pp. 13–15.

46 *Ibid.*

47 *Ibid.*

48 European Commission/High Representative of the Union for Foreign Affairs and Security Policy, Joint Communication to the European Parliament and the Council, Commission Joint Staff Working Paper – Implementation of the European Neighbourhood Policy in 2010, Country Report on: Ukraine, SEC(2011) 646 of 25 May 2011, p. 5; European Commission, European External Action Service, Eastern Neighbours Partnership (ENP): Country Progress Report 2011 – Moldova, 2011,

External coherence 181

of judicial and law enforcement procedures in the context of economic operators' activities.

Against this background, the priority "Justice, Freedom and Security" experienced considerable changes in the 2011–2013 NIPs for "associated" Eastern Neighbours.[49] In particular, the 2011–2013 NIPs supplemented the programming of justice sector reform support with emphases on "respect for human rights by prosecution, law enforcement agencies, and penitentiary staff in accordance with international standards and best practices" and the implementation of anti-corruption policies (e.g. the functioning of the Authorized Agent for Anti-Corruption Policy in Ukraine).[50] The nexus between the implementation of anti-corruption policies and the justice sector reforms in partner countries was reinforced in the 2014–2015 Association Agendas, concluded by the EU with the Neighbours.[51] Besides, the Association Agendas emphasized the principles of independence, impartiality and integrity of the judiciary, as well as the efficiency in the administration of justice.[52] In contrast to both the 2007–2010 and 2011–2013 NIPs, neither of these programmatic documents pointed to the interests of economic operators or the connections between the justice sector and public administration reforms.

Following the AAs' conclusion, the justice sector reform continued to be a top priority for EU support of Eastern Neighbours after the conclusion of the AAs.[53] Additionally, this statement can be supported by the referral to Single Support Frameworks (SSFs) for the EU's support of Eastern Neighbours, adopted in terms of 2017–2020 ENI programming.[54] In contrast to the Association Agendas, all the

---

pp. 1–2; European Commission, European External Action Service, Eastern Neighbours Partnership (ENP): Country Progress Report 2011 – Georgia, 2011, pp. 2–3.

49 See, for instance, European Commission DG "External Relations" (2011). Ukraine: National Indicative Programme 2011–2013. [pdf] European Commission. Available at: http://eeas.europa.eu/archives/docs/enp/pdf/pdf/country/2011_enpi_nip_ukraine_en.pdf, pp. 10–11; European Commission DG "External Relations" (2011). Moldova: National Indicative Programme 2011–2013. [pdf] Available at: https://ec.europa.eu/europeaid/sites/devco/files/nip-moldova-2011-2013_en.pdf.

50 European Commission DG "External Relations", Ukraine: National Indicative Programme 2011–2013. [pdf] Available at: http://eeas.europa.eu/archives/docs/enp/pdf/pdf/country/2011_enpi_nip_ukraine_en.pdf, pp. 10–11.

51 See, for instance, EU-Ukraine Association Council (2015) EU-Ukraine Association Agenda to prepare and facilitate the implementation of the Association Agreement. [pdf] EU-Ukraine Association Council. Available at: http://eeas.europa.eu/archives/docs/ukraine/docs/st06978_15_en.pdf, pp. 3–4; EU-Georgia Association Council (2014). EU-Georgia Association Agenda. [online] Available at: https://eeas.europa.eu/sites/eeas/files/associationagenda_2014_en.pdf; EU-Moldova Association Council (2014). EU-Moldova Association Agenda. [pdf] EU-Moldova Association Council. Available at: http://eeas.europa.eu/archives/docs/moldova/pdf/eu-moldova-association-agenda-26_06_en.pdf, pp. 3–4.

52 *Ibid.*

53 Regulation (EU) 232/2014 of the European Parliament and of the Council of 11 March 2014 establishing a European Neighbourhood Instrument, OJ L 77/27 of 15 March 2014.

54 See, for instance, European Commission (2016). Programming of the European Neighbourhood Instrument (ENI) 2017–2020. Single Support Framework for EU Support to Moldova (2017–2020). [pdf] European Commission. Available at: https://ec.europa.eu/neighbourhood-enlargement/sites/near/files/single_support_framework_2017-2020.pdf; European Commission (2016).

182 *External coherence*

SSFs stressed the connection between the justice sector and public administration reforms, as well as the justice sector reform and the support of economic development under the umbrella "Strengthening institutions and good governance" priority.[55] Analogous to the Western Balkans case, the 2018 and 2019 Association Reports for Ukraine, Moldova and Georgia acknowledged the incomplete nature of justice sector reforms in all three countries, predominantly due to the persistence of corruption, including few convictions in high-level corruption cases.[56] Despite the SSFs' focus on the connection between the functioning justice sector and the protection of business' interests, neither the 2018 nor the 2019 Association Implementation Reports tried to assess its functioning.

Ultimately, as well as in the Balkans, the justice sector reform has been the continuous priority in the EU-"associated" Eastern Neighbourhood relations. Compared to the assistance programming under the SAAs, the ENP programming and SSFs (at least rhetorically) link justice sector reforms to a broader array of issues and contexts, such as countering corruption; promoting security, stability and resilience; and institution-building, public administration reform and good governance; as well as the protection of economic operators' rights and interests. Based on this, we will distinguish the key "junctures" between the AAs' norms on judicial review and the EU's support of justice sector reforms in the region.

3. EU justice sector assistance to "associated" Neighbours and the DCFTAs' rule of law standards

As demonstrated in Chapter 4, the DCFTAs with "associated" Eastern Neighbours are marked by the most comprehensive and in-detail rule of law standards, compared to the SAAs and the EU's EPAs with ACP countries. Our analysis will explore four key "junctures" between the DCFTAs' standards related to judicial review and the EU's justice sector support of the region.

First, in contrast to other considered agreements, the DCFTAs' "Transparency" chapters immediately oblige the parties "to establish or maintain judicial, arbitral or administrative tribunals or procedures for the purpose of the prompt review and,

---

Programming of the European Neighbourhood Instrument (ENI) 2017–2020. Single Support Framework for EU Support to Georgia (2017–2020). [pdf] European Commission. Available at: https://eeas.europa.eu/sites/eeas/files/georgia_2017-2020_ssf_final.pdf.

55 *Ibid.*

56 European Commission/High Representative of the Union for Foreign Affairs and Security Policy, Joint Communication to the European Parliament and the Council, Commission Joint Staff Working Paper – Association Implementation Report on Ukraine, SWD(2018) 462 final of 7 November 2018, pp. 7–8; European Commission/High Representative of the Union for Foreign Affairs and Security Policy, Joint Communication to the European Parliament and the Council, Commission Joint Staff Working Paper – Association Implementation Report on Moldova, SWD(2018) 94 final of 3 April 2018, p. 6; European Commission/High Representative of the Union for Foreign Affairs and Security Policy, Joint Communication to the European Parliament and the Council, Commission Joint Staff Working Paper – Association Implementation Report on Georgia, SWD(2019) 16 final of 30 January 2019, pp. 6–7.

External coherence   183

where warranted, the correction of administrative action" within the issue areas covered by the DCFTAs. In this vein, it can be argued that the EU's continuous and systemic support for justice sector reforms helps partner countries to comply with this broadly formulated requirement. However, the framework nature of this norm and the absence of definite criteria to assess its fulfillment made scholars doubt the feasibility of its operationalization amid the AAs' implementation (Van der Loo, 2016, p. 288). This concern is especially relevant, given the previously established disconnection between the EU's support of justice sector reform and the objectives pertaining to the AAs' implementation. In practice, fulfilling the parties' broadly formulated obligations as to judicial review and appeal in the domains, covered by the DCFTAs, would require specialized justice sector support. This suggestion can be, *inter alia*, illustrated by the "Property Rights and Ease of Business" focus point of the "PRAVO-Justice" project (aimed to support the justice sector reform in Ukraine based on Special Measure III on Support to Rule of Law in Ukraine).[57] By analogy, targeting EU justice sector support of specific disciplines under the DCFTA would provide better chances for partner countries to fulfil their obligations as to judicial review and appeal in the trade-related domain.

Second, alongside the framework judicial review and appeal obligation, the DCFTAs also contain numerous discipline-specific obligations related to the individual right to review and authorities' independence and impartiality. For instance, similar to the SAAs, the AAs require partner countries to transpose the Council Directive 89/665/EC on the coordination of the laws, regulations and administrative provisions relating to the application of review procedures to the award of public supply and public works contracts.[58] The partner countries' obligations to maintain or institute bodies or procedures responsible for the review of administrative action are also contained *inter alia* in "Establishment, trade in services and electronic commerce" and "Trade-related energy" chapters of the DCFTAs.[59] Therefore, the EU's unilateral support for justice sector (and partly also the public administration) reforms is conducive to the "associated" Neighbours' fulfillment of such discipline-specific obligations. Potentially, their fulfillment could be reinforced by a stronger nexus between the EU's support for public administration and the justice sector in the Neighbourhood.

Third, as shown in Chapter 4, the DCFTAs' provisions on administrative cooperation and customs and trade facilitation are of more detailed nature than the ones stipulated by the SAAs. As it can be exemplified by Chapter 3 of the EU-Ukraine AA "Technical Barriers to Trade", the approximation of technical regulations, standards and conformity assessment obliges Ukraine to provide an effective and transparent administrative system (Art. 56[2][iii]) and conduct administrative and

---

57 European Commission, Commission Implementing Decision on the Special Measure III 2016 on Support to Rule of Law Reforms in Ukraine (PRAVO) to be financed from the general budget of the European Union, C(2016)8266 final.

58 See, for instance, EU-Moldova AA, Art.272(1), Annex XXIX-B.

59 See, for instance, EU-Moldova AA, Art.220(2), Art.353(3).

184 *External coherence*

institutional reforms necessary to implement the AA and the envisaged Agreement on Conformity Assessment and Acceptance of Industrial Products (ACAA) (Art.56[2][ii]).[60] In turn, creating an effective and transparent administrative system and ensuring its sustainability requires building its capacity, as well as providing for the avenues to review administrative decisions concerning technical regulations, standards and conformity assessment. Hence, the EU's institution-building efforts in partner countries (including both the capacity-building of public administrations and support of the justice sector) are conducive to facilitating trade, administration and customs between the EU and "associated" Neighbours.

Fourth, compared to the SAAs, the EU's DCFTAs with "associated" Neighbours contain an even broader array of the rule of law standards, such as legal certainty, transparency, equality and non-discrimination. The implementation of these standards, in turn, requires independent and efficient judiciary and law enforcement agencies. Alongside the parties' umbrella obligation to "establish or maintain courts or the other independent tribunals"[61], the implementation of these standards is supported by the application of the EU unilateral assistance instruments. However, amid the lack of connections between the EU's justice sector support programming and the DCFTAs' implementation, there are no monitoring or benchmarking systems to tackle the effects the EU justice sector support on the implementation of the rule of law standards in the DCFTAs.

This brings us back to the problématique of targeting EU justice sector support of partner countries to the needs of framework agreements' implementation. Previously in this chapter, we showed that the EU's justice sector assistance to the Western Balkans has so far never been adapted to implementation of the trade-related parts of the SAAs. Similar refers to the programming under the ENPI and ENI funding instruments. In the "associated" Neighbourhood case, the foundation for substantively specialized assistance to the judiciary and law enforcement agencies was laid down within the "PRAVO-Justice" project conducted in Ukraine.[62] As mentioned previously, one of the priorities under the "PRAVO-Justice" project deals with the improvement of property rights protection and the ease of doing business.[63] Such a focus only indirectly concerns the implementation of the DCFTAs' standards. However, it bears the potential to improve the coherence between the EU's rule of law promotion through DCFTAs and its justice sector support for at least two reasons. First, the "Property Rights Protection and Ease of Business" priority exemplifies the cross-cutting focus of assistance. It is, *inter alia*, of particular relevance for the implementation of Agenda 2030, which views justice as a prerequisite for sustainable development. Second, the

---

60 EU-Ukraine AA, Art.56(2).

61 *Ibid.*, Art.360(1).

62 European Commission, Commission Implementing Decision on the Special Measure III 2016 on Support to Rule of Law Reforms in Ukraine (PRAVO) to be financed from the general budget of the European Union, C(2016)8266 final.

63 For the substance of the respective project focus, please visit the website of the project "PRAVO-JUSTICE" www.pravojustice.eu.

External coherence 185

planning, benchmarking and monitoring experience gathered in terms of this priority's implementation can be used to create specialized instruments of justice sector support linked to particular disciplines under the DCFTAs and possibly other EU RTAs with third countries.

In a nutshell, there are many crucial synergies between the rule of law standards, included into the DCFTAs, and the EU's justice sector support. First, the EU's support of an independent and efficient justice sector facilitates the partner countries' implementation of their umbrella obligations to ensure access to judicial review and appeal in matters related to the DCFTAs. Second, such support facilitates the fulfillment of "associated" Neighbours' DCFTAs' discipline-specific obligations related to judicial review and appeal. Third, functional and sustainable judiciary and law enforcement agencies are essential to ensure the partner countries' fulfillment of their obligations regarding technical and administrative cooperation with the EU. Last but not least, the DCFTAs' rule of law standards concerning judicial review and appeal can be used as benchmarks to make the EU's justice sector support of third countries better targeted and more specialized.

Part 3. Development (EU-CARIFORUM EPA)

For natural reasons, the EU-ACP relations lack integration objectives, and the EU's assistance to the region has been traditionally oriented on the fulfillment of primary development needs (e.g. access to clean water, healthcare and education). Therefore, this case allows for only a highly limited insight in the coherence between the rule of law standards in the EU-CARIFORUM EPA and the EU justice sector support of CARIFORUM countries.

1. Strategies and key focus points

As shown in Chapter 5, the vast majority of the EU-LAC unilateral and bilateral diplomatic documents adopted prior to 2012 contained general references to the rule of law and commitments to the rule of law, rather than references to specific reforms, such as reform of the judiciary.

Hence, the 2012 Joint Caribbean-EU Partnership Strategy was the first EU diplomatic document that pointed to the judicial reform and "strengthening cooperation and capacity building in areas such as policing, judicial processes" as the goals of the EU- CARIFORUM "joint partnership".[64] This Strategy did not, however, link support of this action to the protection of business community's interests and the implementation of the EU-CARIFORUM EPA.[65] It has been only the 2016 Commission's and High Representative's Joint Communication "A Renewed Partnership with the Countries of Africa, the Caribbean and the Pacific" that provided for "a clear commitment" to be made "to promote effective and independent

64 Council of the European Union, Council Conclusions on the Joint Caribbean-EU Partnership Strategy, 3199th Foreign Affairs Council meeting of 19 November 2012, p. 11.
65 *Ibid.*

186   *External coherence*

justice for citizens and business".[66]"Conducive business environment" was also emphasized with respect to countering corruption and organized crime – an issue area strongly related to promoting judicial independence and effectiveness.[67] According to the Communication, the EU and CARIFORUM countries shall also cooperate to ensure "access to effective and independent justice".[68] The Communication does not link this objective to any economic matters or the implementation of the EU-CARIFORUM EPA, more specifically. Instead, it conceptualizes "access to effective and independent justice" as a political cooperation objective, alongside the consolidation of democracy, the rule of law and human security.

Ultimately, similar to the cases of the Western Balkans and the "associated" Eastern Neighbourhood, neither of the considered "soft" documents created the bridge between the promotion of independent and efficient judiciary, on the one hand, and the implementation of the EU-CARIFORUM EPA, on the other hand. In the former cases, the absence of such a link could be substantiated by the impact of the accession criteria's structure. In the CARIFORUM case, it can be explained by: (i) the recent nature of the emphasis on access to justice in the development policy context and (ii) the EU's predominant focus on the intra-region integration in terms of its support of the implementation of the EU-CARIFORUM EPA (as explained in the relevant parts of Chapters 5–6).

2. *Limited rule of law standards in the EU-CARIFORUM EPA and EU development funds*

Based on the findings of the relevant parts of Chapters 4–5, we argue that, as compared to the cases of the Western Balkans and the "associated" Neighbourhood, the CARIFORUM case is marked by limited rule of law standards. Subsequently, the EU-CARIFORUM EPA and the EDFs offer much less room for synergies between the EPA's norms on judicial review and justice sector support programming.

In contrast to the DCFTAs, the EU-CARIFORUM EPA does contain the CARIFORUM countries' umbrella obligation to ensure judicial review and appeal. Instead, the Agreement introduces discipline-specific obligations as to judicial review, such as the obligation to "provide transparent, timely, impartial and effective procedures enabling suppliers to challenge domestic measures implementing this Chapter in the context of procurements in which they have, or have had, a legitimate commercial interest" ("Public Procurement" chapter).[69] Theoretically, the CARIFORUM countries can use administrative procedures to comply with this requirement. In practice, however, the right to review is closely intertwined with the right to appeal, the observance of which presupposes at least some extent of judicial independence and effectiveness.

---

66 European Commission, Communication to the European Parliament and the Council: A Renewed Partnership with the Countries of Africa, the Caribbean and the Pacific, JOIN(2016) 52 final of 22 November 2016, pp. 8–9.

67 *Ibid.*, p. 8.

68 *Ibid.*

69 EU-CARIFORUM EPA, Art. 179(1).

External coherence 187

In Chapter 5, we found that over the period from 2000 (the launch of the 9th EDF) until the time of writing, there have been no EU-funded projects directed towards the support of the justice system of CARIFORUM countries at the regional level. Over the same period, the NIPs for Jamaica under the 10th and 11th EDFs have been the sole indicative programmatic documents emphasizing the justice sector reform as a focal priority.[70] The NIP for Jamaica under the 10th EDF linked the reform to security, human rights protection and ensuring access to justice for all.[71] In the same vein, the NIP for Jamaica 2014–2020 introduced two specific objectives of the EU support of justice sector reform in Jamaica: "increased access to gender-responsive, accountable and effective justice services, especially for the vulnerable" and "improved treatment of children in the responsibility of the criminal justice system".[72] The formulations of these objectives testify to the EU's support's orientation on the interests of citizens, rather than the ones of EU and CARIFORUM businesses. Nonetheless, measures aimed at promoting judicial accountability and effectiveness are most likely conducive to Jamaica's fulfillment of its discipline-specific obligations as to judicial review and appeal. Similar argument is applicable to the NIP for Trinidad and Tobago under the 10th EDF that stipulated the justice sector reform as a non-focal cooperation area. At the same time, as discussed in Chapter 5, the EU's unilateral support for the implementation of the EU-CARIFORUM EPA primarily took the form of discipline-specific technical assistance (e.g. with respect to the introduction of the EU food standards) and the support of intra-regional integration, rather than strengthening businesses' judicial protection.

Hence, compared to the Western Balkans and "associated" Neighbours, the CARIFORUM case demonstrates the lowest actual coherence between the rule of law obligations, contained in the RTA and EU support of justice sector reforms.

Conclusion

This chapter examined the coherence between the EU's rule of law promotion through trade liberalization and the EU's broader efforts to promote the rule of law. The case of justice sector reform was chosen for the analysis, since this reform represents an essential part of the EU's external rule of law promotion

---

70 European Commission, Government of Jamaica (2007). Country Strategy Paper and National Indicative Programme for Jamaica for the period 2008–2013. [pdf] European Commission. Available at: https://ec.europa.eu/europeaid/sites/devco/files/csp-nip-jamaica-2008-2013_en.pdf, pp. 22–24; European Commission, the Government of Jamaica (2014). 11th EDF National Indicative Programme (2014–2020) for cooperation between the European Union and Jamaica. [pdf] European Commission. Available under: https://eeas.europa.eu/sites/eeas/files/nip_jamaica_signed.pdf, pp. 13–15.

71 European Commission, Government of Jamaica (2007). Country Strategy Paper and National Indicative Programme for Jamaica for the period 2008–2013. [pdf] European Commission. Available at: https://ec.europa.eu/europeaid/sites/devco/files/csp-nip-jamaica-2008-2013_en.pdf, pp. 23–24.

72 European Commission, the Government of Jamaica (2014). 11th EDF National Indicative Programme (2014–2020) for cooperation between the European Union and Jamaica. [pdf] European Commission. Available at: https://eeas.europa.eu/sites/eeas/files/nip_jamaica_signed.pdf, pp. 13–15.

188   *External coherence*

"menu", and was funded by the EU across all the policy contexts under study. In all three cases, we found that diplomatic documents and the assistance programming barely linked the EU's unilateral support of justice sector reforms to the interests of business or referred to it as a means to facilitate partner countries' obligations under the RTAs related to rule of law. Similarly to the case of the interplay between the overarching and Single Market *acquis* conditionality, the lack of "bridges" between the RTAs-based rule of law standards and the EU's support of justice sector reforms can be attributed to the structure of the Copenhagen criteria. This explanation is relevant for the Enlargement context and the ENP. In the development policy context, most feasible explanations include: (i) the limited reach of the rule of law standards in the EU-CARIFORUM EPA and (ii) the orientation of the EU's assistance with traditional development objectives (e.g. access to water, healthcare, education) and the support of intra-regional integration.

Notwithstanding this, we distinguished several "junctures" between the EU's rule of law promotion through trade liberalization and its broader rule of law promotion activities. These "junctures" are most relevant for the Enlargement and Neighbourhood contexts. Amid the development of the EU-CARIFORUM relations and the implementation of a new Africa-Europe Alliance for Sustainable Investment and Jobs,[73] they can be also reinforced in the Development policy context:

- **Juncture 1:** The EU's efforts to promote independence, efficiency and capacity of the judiciary and law enforcement agencies may facilitate the fulfillment of partner countries' umbrella and discipline-specific obligations as to judicial review and appeal.
- **Juncture 2:** The EU's unilateral support of the justice sector is conducive to the fulfillment of numerous other rule of law standards contained in the RTAs and secured via judicial review and appeal.
- **Juncture 3:** Justice sector reform can be understood as an essential prerequisite for the triangular relationship between the RTAs' rule of law norms, related partner countries' institution-building obligations (e.g. in public procurement and competition domains) and individuals' and legal entities' guaranteed right to review and appeal.
- **Juncture 4:** The rule of law standards contained in the RTAs can be used as benchmarks to promote and assess stronger specialization of the EU's justice sector support. In turn, stronger specialization of justice sector reform is expected to strengthen the EU's engagement with partner countries' businesses communities and facilitate the implementation of countries' discipline-specific rule of law obligations.

---

73 European Commission (2018). State of the Union Address: Strengthening the EU's Partnership with Africa. A new Africa-Europe Alliance for Sustainable Investment and Jobs of 12 September 2018. [pdf] European Commission. Available at: https://ec.europa.eu/commission/sites/beta-political/files/soteu2018-factsheet-africa-europe_en.pdf.

External coherence   189

It is suggested that these "junctures" are taken into account in terms of the programming of the EU's support of implementation of the RTAs and justice sector reforms in partner countries. Additional insights can be gained from the analysis of coherence between the EU rule of law promotion through RTAs and its rule of law activities, not considered in this chapter (e.g. public administration reforms and support of the creation and maintenance of anti-corruption institutions).

References

Anastasakis, O. (2008). The EU political conditionality in the Western Balkans: Towards a more pragmatic approach. *Southeast European and Black Sea Studies*, 8, pp. 365–377.

Batora, J. and Rieker, P. (2018). EU-supported reforms in the EU neighbourhood as organized anarchies: The case of post-Euromaidan Ukraine. *Journal of European Integration*, 40, pp. 461–478.

Bieber, F. (2011). Building impossible states? State-building strategies and EU membership in the Western Balkans. *Europe-Asia Studies*, 63(2011), pp. 1783–1802.

Bojicic-Dzelilovic, V., Kostovicova, D. and Randazzo, E. (2018). EU in the Western Balkans: Hybrid development, Hybrid security and Hybrid justice. In: M. Kaldor, I. Rangelov, and S. Selchow, eds., *EU global strategy and human security: Rethinking approaches to conflict*. Abingdon-on-Thames: Routledge, pp. 45–63.

Carothers, T. (2010). *Promoting the rule of law abroad: In search of knowledge*. Washington, DC: Brookings Intuition Press.

Fakiolas, E.T. and Tzifakis, N. (2008). Transformation or accession? Reflecting on the EU's strategy towards the Western Balkans. *European Foreign Affairs Review*, 13, pp. 377–398.

Kochenov, D. (2008). The ENP conditionality: Pre-accession mistakes repeated. In: L. Delcour and E. Tulmets, eds., *Pioneer Europe? Testing EU foreign policy in the neighbourhood*. Baden-Baden: Nomos, pp. 105–120.

Magen, A. (2005/2006). The shadow of enlargement: Can the European neighbourhood policy achieve compliance? *Columbia Journal of European Law*, 12, pp. 383–390.

Schimmelfenni, F. and Scholtz, H. (2008). EU democracy promotion in the European neighbourhood. Political conditionality. Economic development and transnational exchange. *European Union Politics*, 9, pp. 187–215.

Torma, A. (2011). The European administrative space. *European Integration Studies*, 9, pp. 149–161.

Trauner, F. (2009). Deconstructing the EU's routes of influence in justice and home affairs in the Western Balkans. *Journal of European Integration*, 31, pp. 65–82.

Van der Loo, G. (2016). *The EU-Ukraine association agreement and deep and comprehensive free trade area: A new legal instrument of EU integration without membership*. Leiden: Brill.

Zhelyazkova, A., Damjanovski, I., Nechev, Z. and Schimmelfennig, F. (2018). European Union conditionality in the Western Balkans: External incentives and Europeanisation. In: J. Džankić, S. Keil, and M. Kmezić, eds., *The Europeanization of the Western Balkans*. Berlin: Springer, pp. 15–37.

8 The EU-Ukraine DCFTA as an instrument of promoting the rule of law

Conflict, unique approaches to assistance and unexpected spillovers

This chapter aims to apply the conceptualization of the EU value-promoting RTAs to the case of Ukraine with a focus on the rule of law effects of the DCFTA. The case of the EU-Ukraine DCFTA is of special relevance for investigating RTAs' impact on the rule of law in a partner country due to three groups of reasons:

1   Those related to the scope and the peculiarities of the DCFTA.
2   Those stemming from the features of the European Neighbourhood Policy (ENP).
3   The sensitive context of the crisis in and around Ukraine[1] and the multifaceted nature of the EU's response thereto.

First, the EU-Ukraine DCFTA is marked by the highest number and most detailed nature of the rule of law standards by comparison among the value-promoting RTAs under study. Moreover, it promotes the rule of law standards through an array of novel means, such as the combination of market access conditionality and legislative approximation clauses, and the definition of partner countries' institutions' elaborate cooperation obligations. Additionally, as demonstrated in Chapter 5, the EU has been exercising an unprecedentedly ambitious unilateral multi-aspect support for the implementation of the EU-Ukraine AA/DCFTA.

Second, the relevance of the EU-Ukraine DCFTA's rule of law dimension stems from the ENP captured in a limbo between expectations and constraints. Initially, the ENP was introduced "to share the benefits of the EU's 2004 enlargement with neighbouring countries in strengthening security, stability and well-being for all concerned".[2] Following the 2003 ENP Strategy Paper, this objective was to be realized through "bring[ing] them [partner countries] closer to the EU" in a number of key areas, such as dialogue and reforms, trade and partner countries' gradual integration into the Internal Market and Justice and Home Affairs.[3] Thus, the

---

1   Given the sensitivity and politicization of the ongoing conflict in Ukraine, and multiplicity of narratives about it (ranging from "Russia-Ukraine war" [e.g. Kuzio, 2018] to "separatist war" [e.g. Katchanovski, 2017]), this part of the book will use the term "crisis in and around Ukraine" introduced by the OSCE, Crisis in and Around Ukraine, n.d. Available at: www.osce.org/ukrainecrisis.
2   European Commission, Communication - European Neighbourhood Policy – Strategy Paper, COM (2004)0373*final of 12 May 2004, p. 3.
3   *Ibid.*, p. 9.

very conceptual design of the ENP implied a difficult task for the EU: to promote domestic reforms in third states under the lack of a membership perspective and the policy's conscious disentanglement from the EU Enlargement process (Kelly, 2006). The ENP's design gave rise to intense scholarly doubts about whether the EU can achieve third states' compliance with its values and norms under the "integration without membership" framework (Magen, 2005/2006). It has also been debated whether the EU should eventually offer a membership perspective to best-performing Neighbours (e.g. Emmanoulidis, 2008; Sasse, 2008). In this vein, the key driver of uncertainty for the EU deals with Russia's ambition to sustain its leverage in the former Soviet space and the unpredictability of its reaction to the strengthening of the EU's influence in the region (e.g. Cadier, 2019). Hence, both the elaborateness of the rule of law standards under the DCFTA and intensity of the EU's assistance to Neighbours can be regarded as a peculiar attempt to compensate for lacking incentives.

Third, our choice of the case study deals with the ongoing crisis in and around Ukraine, and the critical role the support of the EU-Ukraine AA/DCFTA implementation has played in the EU's response to it. The ongoing conflict in Ukraine is a unique and complex challenge for the EU due to a number of mutually intertwined factors. Foremost, a protracted conflict, involving an illegal annexation of a part of a state close to the EU's border, represents an immediate security threat for the Union. Furthermore, Russia's outspoken violation of numerous international law norms in terms of its annexation of the Crimean peninsula has constituted a crucial challenge to the foundational principles of international law, such as states' sovereignty and inviolability of their borders the EU seeks to promote worldwide (Kemp and Lyubashenko, 2018). Moreover, since both the ENP's founding documents and the ENP Review emphasized peace, security and stability as essential objectives to be achieved in terms of the policy, any massive conflict in the Neighbourhood is perceived as a test for the EU's actorness in diplomatic, conflict resolution and peace-building terms, both at home and abroad (Cross and Karolewski, 2017). This statement is of special relevance for the conflict with a strong geopolitical dimension, whose origins are to a great extent rooted in the complexities of EU-Russia relations in the "contested" Neighbourhood (Haukkala, 2015). The foreign policy and security response of the EU and its Member States to the Ukraine crisis was structured along three key axes, namely: sanctions and diplomatic pressure *vis-à-vis* Russia, dialogue and selective engagement with Russia, and intensification of the EU-Ukraine engagement (Russel, 2018). The signing and implementation of the EU-Ukraine AA/DCFTA, and the EU's support of related reform processes in Ukraine, has played a pivotal role in the EU's crisis response (Van der Loo, 2016, pp. 1–4; Wolczuk and Žeruolis, 2018). This, in turn, opens up an exciting space for the interplay between the foreign policy, security and stability, development, state-building and integration aspects within the ENP, and its reflection in EU policy and legal documents (Rabinovych, 2019).

Our analysis of the EU-Ukraine DCFTA as a rule of law promotion instrument will be structured as follows. First, this chapter will briefly summarize our previous findings as to the scope of the rule of law standards, incorporated into the EU-Ukraine DCFTA. Next, it will highlight the peculiarities of the EU's sectoral

192   *The EU-Ukraine DCFTA*

approach to support of reforms in Ukraine. Based on this, we will explore the internal and external coherence of the EU's rule of law promotion through the DCFTA in Ukraine. Finally, this chapter will consider intermediary results/progress pertaining to the EU promotion of the rule of law through the DCFTA in two domains (public procurement and the deregulation reform).

Part 1. The "regulation" dimension of the EU rule of law promotion through the EU-Ukraine DCFTA

1. Substantive rule of law standards

As shown in Chapter 4, the EU-Ukraine AA/DCFTA embraces numerous mutually intertwined rule of law standards. Most expansive rule of law standards that relate to the whole scope of the trade-related part of the EU-Ukraine AA are contained in the DCFTA's "Transparency" chapter that stipulates rules and procedures pertaining to the **legal certainty, transparency, equality** and **non-discrimination**, and **judicial review** dimensions of the rule of law.[4] As opposed to the EU-Western Balkans SAAs, the "deep" disciplines chapters under the EU-Ukraine AA contain not only legislative approximation requirements, but also basic standards, embracing the rule of law requirements (**legality, legal certainty, transparency, equality and non-discrimination**). These requirements are closely intertwined and pursue the overarching aim of creating a favourable regulatory environment for cross-border business.[5] Furthermore, the "deep" disciplines and administrative cooperation, customs cooperation and trade facilitation chapters of the EU-Ukraine DCFTA also touch upon the **relationship between international and domestic law** by emphasizing Ukraine's obligations under the WTO and WCO law.[6]

Thus, based on the analysis presented in Chapter 4, it can be argued that the analyzed chapters of the EU-Ukraine AA embrace the whole spectrum of legal standards, incorporated into the working conceptualization of the rule of law (Chapter 1).

2. The mechanisms of promoting the rule of law standards in the EU-Ukraine AA

As compared to the SAAs and the EU-CARIFORUM EPA, an important feature of the EU-Ukraine DCFTA has been the diversity and elaborateness of legal instruments the parties can use to secure the implementation of the rule of law standards. These instruments can be conditionally subdivided into two groups: (i) those immediately provided for in the DCFTA and (ii) those located in the general part of the EU-Ukraine AA.

---

4 EU-Ukraine AA, Chapter 12.
5 See, for instance, EU-Ukraine AA, Art.254, Art.148.
6 See, for instance, EU-Ukraine AA, Art.54, Art.76.

The former group encompasses, *inter alia*, the imposition of basic standards related to specific aspects of the rule of law and the combination of legislative approximation and market access conditionality, as well as the recourses to international standards and the parties' obligations under international law. As compared to the SAAs with the Western Balkans and the EU-CARIFORUM EPA, the EU-Ukraine AA contains more elaborate clauses on administrative and customs cooperation that tend to target **legal certainty** and **transparency** standards. In some cases, the cooperation provisions *per se* can serve as an instrument of safeguarding the rule of law (e.g. Art. 267[3][b] of the EU-Ukraine AA that obliges the European Commission and Ukrainian authorities to conduct a joint review of Ukrainian regions' eligibility for state aid).

Among the key relevant instruments beyond the trade-related realm one can mention the multi-actor institutional framework of the AA's implementation, the gradual and dynamic nature of legislative approximation, enhanced monitoring clauses, and the Dispute Settlement Mechanism (DSM) (Rabinovych, 2017). According to Art. 460(1) of the AA, annual summit meetings at the highest political level are organized to provide the parties with "overall guidance" and the "opportunity to discuss any bilateral or multilateral issues of mutual importance". In turn, the specific function of supervising and monitoring the implementation of the AA, including its trade-related part, is conferred on the Association Council.[7] Importantly, established at the ministerial level, the Association Council has the powers to adopt legally binding decisions.[8] The Association Council is assisted by the Association Committee, responsible for appointing a specific body to address trade-related issues (the Trade Committee).[9] Besides, the AA provides for establishing the fora for interparliamentary and civil society cooperation.[10] Thus, ensuring the AA's implementation and providing for various fora for the parties' dialogue and cooperation, the institutional framework of the EU-Ukraine AA contributes to the promotion of the rule of law standards, as previously discussed.

An in-depth understanding of the scope and nature of Ukraine's obligations under the AA requires drawing the borderline between the concepts of "standard", "soft" and "gradual" approximation (Petrov, 2014). Contained in Art. 474 of the EU-Ukraine AA, the "gradual approximation" clause stipulates Ukraine's obligation to "carry out gradual approximation of its legislation to EU law as referred to in Annexes I–XLIV to this Agreement".[11] Compared to the framework "gradual" approximation clause, the "standard" approximation clauses, attached to different chapters of the EU-Ukraine AA, are far "deeper". First, alongside defining the relevant *acquis*, "standard" approximation clauses may also contain a partner country's obligations regarding the conduct of specific administrative and institutional

---

7 *Ibid.*, Art.461.
8 *Ibid.*
9 *Ibid.*, Art.464.
10 *Ibid.*, Art.467, Art.469.
11 *Ibid.*, Art.474.

194 The EU-Ukraine DCFTA

reforms (that may imply strengthening particular rule of law standards)[12] Second, the in-depth nature of market integration, envisaged by some of the DCFTA's disciplines (e.g. trade in services and establishment) also requires "taking due account of any modifications of the EU acquis occurring in the meantime".[13] Directed to ensuring the continuing legal uniformity between Ukrainian legislation and the *acquis communautaire*, the "dynamic approximation" requirement appears to be immediately linked to meeting a number of intertwined **legal certainty** and **legality** standards (e.g. consistency of the legal system). Third, some of the "standard" approximation clauses promote **legal uniformity** and **legal certainty** by obliging Ukraine "to take due account of the corresponding case law of the European Court of Justice".[14]

Next, Ukraine's compliance with the rule of law requirements in connection to legislative approximation is supported by enhanced monitoring clauses, largely inspired by the logic of pre-accession conditionality.[15] The key objectives of such monitoring include the continuity and systemic nature of legislative approximation, and uniform application of the *acquis communautaire*. A vital novelty in this respect has been the EU's right to deploy on-the-spot missions, aimed at proving whether the approximation process is of genuine nature, and goes beyond the formal adaptation of the *acquis*.[16] In turn, a market opening does not automatically follow a positive outcome of the monitoring, and is subject to the approval of the Association Council.[17]

On top of that, the EU-Ukraine AA provides for three issue-specific dispute settlement frameworks. First, disputes pertaining to the non-trade-related parts of the AA are settled by a binding decision of the Association Council following the period of consultations.[18] Second, Art. 300(6) of the EU-Ukraine AA defines the procedure for settlement of disputes arising from trade and sustainable development-related issues. Third, a quasi-judicial Dispute DSM is employed to resolve the disputes stemming from the DCFTA.[19] Under the DSM, the parties are first expected to attempt to solve the dispute through consultations. In case they fail to do so, either party can establish the arbitration panel to proceed with the settlement of a dispute, and another party is legally prevented from blocking the initiation of arbitration proceedings by way of refusing to appoint its arbitrator.[20] The rulings of the arbitration panel are of bingeing nature for the parties, and they are obliged to "take any measure necessary to comply in good faith with it".[21]

Ultimately, the EU-Ukraine DCFTA is marked by the sophisticated combination of the DCFTA-based and general instruments, directed to supporting the

---

12 *Ibid.*, Art.56.
13 *Ibid.*, Art.153.
14 *Ibid.*, Art.153(2).
15 *Ibid.*, Art.475.
16 *Ibid.*
17 *Ibid.*, Art.475(5).
18 *Ibid.*, Art. 477.
19 *Ibid.*, Art. 477, Art. 305.
20 EU-Ukraine AA, Art.294.
21 EU-Ukraine AA, Art.311.

The EU-Ukraine DCFTA 195

implementation of the rule of law standards, as previously addressed. Together with the substantive rule of law standards, incorporated into the DCFTA, such instruments constitute the core of the "regulation" dimension of the EU's promotion of the rule of law through the EU-Ukraine AA.

Part 2. EU's sectoral approach to reform support

Over the period from 2014–2020, the programming of the EU's financial and technical assistance to Ukraine has included two types of assistance. First, the EU assisted Ukraine via grants channelled through bilateral allocation instruments such as the ENI, Neighbourhood Investment Facility and Instrument contributing to Stability and Peace (IcSP) (European Court of Auditors, 2016, p. 13). Second, to address the challenges stemming from the crisis in and around Ukraine, the EU launched annual "Special Measures" financed from the general budget of the EU. While the "Special Measures" were intended to help Ukraine solve urgent state-building tasks (e.g. anti-corruption measures, reform of the justice sector, decentralization and electoral reform),[22] the focus of the ENI programming has been on supporting the AA/DCFTA's implementation.

As argued by Wolczuk and Žeruolis (2018), one of the key means by which the EU has managed the complexity of simultaneous integration and state-building has been the introduction of the sectoral (or sector-focused) support of reforms. Institutionally, the implementation of such an approach was made possible through the creation of the Support Group for Ukraine (SGUA) that aimed to act as a "catalyst, facilitator and supporter of reforms" (European Commission, 2016, p. 1). The SGUA's major task has been the coordination of efforts on assisting Ukraine across the European Commission's directorates-general (DGs) and the EEAS (*Ibid.*). In structural terms, the SGUA is divided into seven sector teams (e.g. Agriculture and Sanitary/Phytosanitary Matters, Economic and Fiscal Reforms, and Justice and Home Affairs, including anti-corruption), and its members bring along expertise and experiences from respective sectors (European Commission, n.d.). In combination, the coordination, liaison and sector reform support activities helped the SGUA become a vital depository of "local knowledge" about Ukraine and EU-supported reforms, along with the EU Delegation (Wolczuk and Žeruolis, 2018, p. 13).

In the EU Studies scholarship, there has long been a claim that the EU tends to transfer from financing small-scale projects to sector-specific reforms support (e.g. Börzel and Böttger, 2012, pp. 163–173). Having brought together case studies from both Eastern and Southern Neighbourhoods, Börzel and Böttger (2012) found such a transfer to be determined by the EU's ambition to overcome the ENP's initial flaws, such as the lack of leverage due to the absent membership perspective. In the case of post-Euromaidan Ukraine, the consolidated nature of the sectoral support approach has fitted the complexity of crisis settings and allowed the EU to meet Ukraine's specific needs in terms of the integration and

---

22 These measures will be discussed in more detail in Part 4 of this chapter.

196   *The EU-Ukraine DCFTA*

state-building assistance axes. Additionally, the added value of the sectoral reform support has been constituted by its comprehensiveness (i.e. the chance to bring together support of strategies and the formulation and implementation of policies, as well as capacity-building) and systemic order (proper sequencing and step-by-step implementation).

The EU's support for the implementation of the EU-Ukraine DCFTA has been exercised via two major strategies: (i) extensive support for capacity-building of ministries and (ii) the deployment of multiple on-site technical assistance projects led by EU professionals. The former approach can be exemplified by reference to the EU co-sponsoring so-called "reform support teams" (RSTs) at key Ukrainian ministries, together with the EBRD under the auspices of the EBRD-managed Ukraine Multi-Donor Account (MDA).[23] Comprised of non-civil servants, such teams were expected to "provide assistance in filling the capacity gaps in the design and implementation of policy reform strategies and programmes, while strengthening links and partnerships between the Ministry's priorities and relevant donor support".[24] Despite the RSTs' regular reporting obligation, there has, however, been no publicly available information on their specific role and accomplishments with regard to reform support. This makes it difficult to assess an extent to which the RSTs helped the EU and EBRD address capacity and coordination challenges pertaining to the sectoral reform support. Given the uniqueness of the RSTs as an implementing instrument of the EU's external action, an insight into their effectiveness and impact would be of great relevance for further research.

Alongside the co-financing of the RSTs, the EU's support of the capacity-building of Ukrainian ministries has been exercised through umbrella and discipline-specific support programmes. The former can be exemplified by the programmes "Association4U" (translation of *acquis communautaire*, deployment of experts and trainings for civil servants) and (ii) the "Advisory Fund for EU Association of Ukraine" (education programmes and trainings for civil servants).[25]

Beyond these rather recent umbrella initiatives, the EU has been supporting reforms to be implemented under the DCFTA even prior to its shift to sector-specific assistance. For instance, since 2005, the EU Border Assistance Mission to Moldova and Ukraine (EUBAM) has, *inter alia*, engaged with the "smooth implementation of border and customs related aspects of the DCFTA".[26] The Mission has also sought to contribute to the development of EU-Ukraine and EU-Moldova

---

23 For information about the RSTs and the EU's support of them, please visit the website of Foundation for Support of Reforms in Ukraine: https://fsr.org.ua/en/page/reform-support-teams.

24 For the complete overview of the tasks to be performed by the MEDT's RST, see recruitment announcements at the website: https://eeas.europa.eu/delegations/ukraine/58616/node/58616_zh-hans.

25 For information about the Association4U project, please visit: www.association4u.com.ua/index.php/en/; For information about the Advisory Fund for EU Association of Ukraine, please visit: www.giz.de/en/worldwide/64066.html?fbclid=IwAR3gvjMmh_JRB6Kc0y5qLlXPMuoz6rAuuVWdl-2WApvUbgvKWRcc-I3wTrg.

26 For the overview of the EUBAM's mandate, please visit: http://eubam.org/who-we-are/.

cross-border cooperation, including customs rules and procedures, as emphasized by the EU's DCFTAs with both countries.[27] Smaller-scale customs support projects, mostly oriented on capacity-building, have been continuously funded by the EU in terms of the ENPI/ENI Cross-Border Cooperation (CBC) component (e.g. the 2007–2013 project "Development of IT Infrastructure of Customs and Border Guards Service at Ukrainian-Polish border").[28] Simultaneously, a large part of Ukraine's "homework" regarding the harmonization of its customs procedures with EU standards remains outside the scope of the EU's assistance, and its implementation is found to lack coherence (Butin, 2019). This, in turn, has long prevented Ukraine from getting its economic operators recognized by the EU and joining the EU New Common Transit System (NCTS), which eventually started operating in Ukraine in a test mode since late 2019) (*Ibid.*). Similar issues have been impeding the adoption of Ukraine's legislation on conformity assessment and, in turn, Ukraine's progress towards the Agreement on Conformity Assessment and Acceptance of Industrial Products (ACAA) (Uriadovyi Portal, 2019). The reforms of technical regulation and conformity assessment in Ukraine were supported under the 2009–2015 sector budget support programme "Promoting mutual trade by removing technical barriers to trade between Ukraine and the European Union".[29] These examples illustrate two crucial challenges of the sectoral support idea, i.e.: (i) the pivotal role of the domestic legal framework in reforms' implementation and (ii) donors' limited engagement with domestic parliaments (Wolczuk and Žeruolis, 2018).

The cases of "deep disciplines" look less problematic. The EU supported the reforms of public procurement, as well as competition and state aid in Ukraine, through "chapter-specific" projects, namely:

- "Harmonization of Public Procurement System of Ukraine with EU standards" (2013–2017).
- "Support to the Antimonopoly Committee of Ukraine in conducting market studies and enforcement of competition rules according to best international standards" (2016–2019).
- "Support to the Establishment of the State Aid Control System in Ukraine" (2017).[30]

---

27 *Ibid.*
28 For more details about this project, please visit the official website of the European Union: 2007–2013 Poland-Belarus-Ukraine ENPI CBC (n.d.). Project "Development of IT Infrastructure of Ukrainian Customs and Border Guards Services at Ukrainian – Polish Border". [online] Available at: www.keep.eu/project/15893/development-of-it-infrastructure-of-ukrainian-customs-and-border-guards-services-at-ukrainian-%25E2%2580%2593-polish-border.
29 European Commission (n.d.) International Cooperation and Development "Sector Budget Support – Promoting Mutual Trade by Removing Technical Barriers to Trade between Ukraine and the European Union" [online] Available at: https://ec.europa.eu/europeaid/projects/sector-budget-support-promoting-mutual-trade-removing-technical-barriers-trade-between_en.
30 For information about the project "Harmonization of Public Procurement System of Ukraine with EU standards", please visit: http://eupublicprocurement.org.ua/category/progress?lang=en.

198   *The EU-Ukraine DCFTA*

Each of these projects targeted a particular state body (MEDT, the Antimonopoly Committee), aiming to promote its capacity and engaged in its activities related to the implementation of AA standards in respective fields.[31] As will be shown in what follows, these projects played an important role in ensuring Ukraine's progress at to "deep disciplines"–related reforms.

Ultimately, the EU's support of the implementation of the EU-Ukraine AA has been marked by numerous features, such as the co-existence and synergies with ambitious state-building measures, the application of sectoral assistance strategy and a considerable focus on strengthening the executive via the RSTs. The key challenges associated with the EU's sectoral approach to support of reforms encompass (but are not limited to) building and sustaining the capacity of executive bodies in a partner country, ensuring proper coordination between domestic actors and donors, and dependence on domestic strategies and legislative frameworks. Keeping these insights in mind, we will continue with exploring the coherence between the rule of law standards under the DCFTA and the "action" the EU has undertaken to support their implementation.

Part 3. Internal coherence

In Chapter 4, we established that the EU DCFTAs with Eastern Neighbours encompass a broad array of the rule of law standards, ranging from substantive **legality** and **legal certainty** requirements to partner countries' far-reaching obligations regarding the **right to judicial review** and **due process**. Bringing together the analysis of the rule of law standards, embraced by the EU-Ukraine AA[32] and an insight into the design of the EU assistance to Ukraine, we can make several statements regarding the internal coherence of the EU's rule of law promotion through the EU-Ukraine DCFTA.

First, it can be argued that the application of the sectoral approach to reform support *per se* implies a considerable degree of coherence between the DCFTA's norms and the EU's "action" in Ukraine. Such a degree of coherence is construed by the combination of two factors:

- Each of the researched DCFTA disciplines/cooperation areas (i.e. administrative and customs cooperation, competition, public procurement) was found capable of promoting the rule of law.

For information about the project "Support to the Antimonopoly Committee of Ukraine in conducting market studies and enforcement of competition rules according to best international standards", please visit: https://eeas.europa.eu/delegations/ukraine_tk/27857/Support%20to%20the%20Antimonopoly%20Committee%20of%20Ukraine%20in%20conducting%20market%20studies%20and%20enforcement%20of%20competition%20rules%20according%20to%20the%20best%20international%20standards.

For information about the project "Support to the Establishment of the State Aid Control System in Ukraine", please visit: www.aets-consultants.com/en/news,147.

31 *Ibid.*
32 See Chapter 4 and Part 2 of this chapter.

The EU-Ukraine DCFTA   199

- EU assistance aims at supporting the implementation of norms, encompassed by respective chapters.

This would mean by default that the previously considered projects contribute to the legality and legal certainty dimensions of the rule of law in those areas, as well as the rule of law standards, covered therein. This statement can be exemplified by recourse to the project "Harmonization of Public Procurement System of Ukraine with EU Standards", aimed at supporting the harmonization of Ukraine's public procurement legislation with the norms of the AA and the *acquis communautaire*. Simultaneously, as we established in Chapter 4, the "Public Procurement" chapter under the EU-Ukraine DCFTA stipulate an array of mutually intertwined rule of law standards such as legality, legal certainty, transparency and the right to judicial review as basic standards. Besides, numerous rule of law standards are contained in the EU's public procurement Directives (i.e. Directive 2014/24/EU, Directive 2014/23/EU, Directive 89/665/EC)[33] to be transposed into Ukraine's domestic legislation in accordance with the EU-Ukraine AA. Thus, by assisting Ukrainian authorities to implement basic standards, contained in Chapter 8 of the AA, and transpose the previously mentioned Directives into the legislation of Ukraine, the respective project has by default contributed to promotion of the rule of law.

Second, some of the EU sector-focused technical assistance projects specified particular rule of law standards they seek to promote, alongside their general support of the implementation of the relevant DCFTA chapters. For instance, one of the specific objectives under the previously mentioned project "Harmonization of Public Procurement System of Ukraine with EU Standards" dealt with the promotion of transparent public procurement. Simultaneously, pursuant to the EU Public Procurement Strategy and the European Parliament's and Council's Directives 2014/24/EU and 2014/23/EU, the transparency principle is essential for the effective functioning of public procurement and the liberalization of the EU's public procurement market with the ones in third countries.[34] Similarly, the previously mentioned project and the project "Support to the Establishment of the State Aid Control System in Ukraine" aimed at promoting the transparency

33 Directive 2014/24/EU of the European Parliament and of the Council of 26 February 2014 on public procurement and repealing Directive 2004/18/EC, OJ L 94 of 28 March 2014, p. 65–242; Directive 2014/23/EU of the European Parliament and of the Council of 26 February 2014 on the award of concession contracts, OJ L 9 of 28 March 2014; Council Directive 89/665/EEC on the coordination of the laws, regulations and administrative provisions relating to the application of review procedures to the award of public supply and public works contracts, OJ L 395 of 21 December 1989.

34 European Commission (n.d.). Public Procurement Strategy, Internal Market, Industry, Entrepreneurship and SMEs [online]. Available at: https://ec.europa.eu/growth/single-market/public-procurement/strategy_en; Directive 2014/24/EU of the European Parliament and of the Council of 26 February 2014 on public procurement and repealing Directive 2004/18/EC, OJ L 94 of 28 March 2014, p. 65–242; Directive 2014/23/EU of the European Parliament and of the Council of 26 February 2014 on the award of concession contracts, OJ L 94 of 28 March 2014.

200 *The EU-Ukraine DCFTA*

of newly established state aid system of Ukraine, in line with Art. 263 of the EU-Ukraine AA, governing the transparency dimension of launching the state aid system in Ukraine.[35] Thus, the recourse to the specific rule of law standards in defined domains represents a crucial axis of coherence between the EU's rule of law promotion through the DCFTAs and its sector-focused assistance to Ukraine.

Third, it may be argued that the EU's extensive efforts to strengthen the capacity of Ukrainian ministries and agencies responsible for the implementation of the DCFTA's standards is also generally coherent with the "regulation" dimension of the rule of law promotion through the DCFTA. Such efforts embrace the capacity-building dimension of the previously mentioned technical assistance projects, AA-wide general assistance programmes (e.g. the "Association4U") and the creation of the RSTs at the ministries. In this vein, it is, however, important to remember that the EU's support of the capacity-building of a partner country's executive does not necessarily result in the strengthening of its performance on fundamental values (Wetzel, 2015). On the contrary, the sole focus on technical capacity may result in unjustified bureaucratization, hampering democratization and the strengthening of the rule of law (*Ibid.*). In the case of Ukraine, such negative externalities may be prevented thanks to the multiplicity of connections between the EU's assistance to the capacity-building of Ukrainian ministries and agencies and other forms of support, such as the engagement of EU experts into reform support and funding civil society organizations as watchdogs of reforms.

Alongside this, an insight into the interplay between the "regulation" and "action" dimensions would not be complete without mentioning that both the DCFTA and the relevant unilateral documents typically do not use the rule of law concept in the context of trade liberalization. Nor they refer to specific rule of law standards. As discussed in Chapter 6, this phenomenon can be explained by several reasons:

- The EU's conceptualization of the rule of law in the solely political cooperation terms.
- A strict borderline between political and economic criteria, as well as the EU's overarching (or "common values") conditionality and Single Market *acquis* conditionality.
- Lacking explication of the logic behind cross-cutting components (e.g. support of the creation of favourable business environment).

As mentioned earlier, these factors lead to the selective reflection of the rule of law standards contained in the DCFTA in the legal and policy frameworks of the EU's support of the DCFTA's implementation. In turn, such selectiveness causes the lack of benchmarking or measurement strategies and instruments that would allow the EU and Ukrainian leadership to comprehensively assess the state of the

---

35 Crown Agents (n.d.). Harmonization of Public Procurement System of Ukraine with EU Standards. [online] Available at: http://eupublicprocurement.org.ua/?lang=EN. For information about the project "Support to the Establishment of the State Aid Control System in Ukraine", please visit: www.aets-consultants.com/en/news,147.

rule of law in the domains covered by the DCFTA and distinguish possible spillovers and synergies brought about by these standards.

Ultimately, the very idea behind the sector-focused approach towards the implementation of the EU-Ukraine DCFTA implies the coherence between DCFTA norms and the focus points of unilateral instruments directed towards its implementation. This statement is substantiated by the fact that the EU conducted separate technical assistance projects for nearly each of the DCFTA chapters considered for the purposes of this study. Some of these projects targeted specific rule of law standards, such as transparency. However, analogously to previously researched RTAs, the DCFTA and related unilateral support instruments do not apply the rule of law concept to create bridges between the "regulation" and "action" dimensions of EU performance or elaborate on the new strategies to assess partner countries' progress. In such a way, the existing coherence between the rule of law dimension of the DCFTA and relevant support programmes is shaped by the logic of market integration and a sector-focused approach to reform support, rather than the EU's intentional application of the DCFTA as a rule of law promotion instrument.

Part 4. External coherence

Mirroring the structure of analysis presented in Chapter 7, we will now proceed with the analysis of the coherence between the EU's rule of law promotion through the DCFTA and its broader rule of law promotion activities, zooming in on the case of the EU's justice sector support. As noted in Chapter 7, justice sector support has traditionally played a crucial role in the EU's assistance to Eastern Neighbours.

1. The peculiarities of EU justice sector reform support under conflict settings in Ukraine

As noted in Chapter 7, the EU has been exercising support for justice sector reforms in the Neighbourhood since the launch of the ENP and the approval of the 2004 Action Plans. We show that, being deeply concerned by the (lack of) resilience in the Neighbourhood and the challenging nature of the justice sector as a reform field, the EU has applied unprecedentedly comprehensive efforts to supporting the judiciary and law enforcement agencies in Ukraine amid the conflict.

To start, it shall be mentioned that already the 2004 EU-Ukraine Action Plan distinguished "further judicial and legal reform, so as to ensure the independence of the judiciary and strengthen its administrative capacity" as a key priority for the EU-Ukraine joint action.[36] This priority envisaged the following key points:

- The completion and implementation of court system reform, aimed at ensuring the independence, impartiality and efficiency of the judiciary.

---

36 EU-Ukraine Action Plan 2004. [online]. Available at: https://library.euneighbours.eu//content/eu-ukraine-action-plan-0.

202 *The EU-Ukraine DCFTA*

- The implementation of the EU-Ukraine Action Plan on JHA.
- The improvement of the training of judges, prosecutors and officials working in police, prisons and judicial administration.

Despite the EU's continuous support for the implementation of these objectives in accordance with the 2004 Action Plan and, later on, under the auspices of the ENPI, the 2011 and 2012 ENP country progress reports on Ukraine pointed to the persistence of an array of the rule of law issues in the country.[37] In particular, the Reports pointed to the persisting legacy of "politically-motivated selective justice" and convictions, the lack of judicial independence, corruption, conflict of interest and organized crime.[38] Moreover, since 2010, "the Commission has been more outspoken" about the rule of law-related risks, stemming from the oligarchic system in Ukraine, i.e. the dysfunctional nature of public administration, top-down corruption and the politicization of the judiciary.[39] Alongside the politics-related issues, the 2011 Report pointed to the need to "tackle specific obstacles to business and investment" and "address the trade and trade-related reforms with the intention facilitate the implementation of the future DCFTA".[40] The 2012 Report also touched upon the economic dimension of the rule of law by calling for "reversing the backsliding which occurred in 2012 on public procurement and budget transparency" and strengthening the transparency and accountability standards in the area of public finance management.[41] Hence, even prior to the outbreak of the crisis in and around Ukraine, the Commission repeatedly expressed its dissatisfaction with both the path of the judicial and law enforcement agencies' reform in Ukraine and the operation of the rule of law standards in the external economic relations/trade domain.

Amid the crisis in and around Ukraine, the geopolitical and security challenges became more explicit in the EU's cooperation with Ukraine and the ENP, more generally, as a consequence of Russia's reaction to the Euromaidan Revolution and the regime change in Ukraine in February 2020 (Haukkala, 2015; Browning, 2018). On the geopolitical level, the crisis demonstrated that the Eastern dimension of the ENP (especially, the EaP) is perceived from outside as a geopolitical interests–driven initiative (Browning, 2018). The strengthening of the EU's awareness about such a perception has, *inter alia*, given momentum to the EU's resilience-building efforts in the "associated" Neighbourhood, with a particular

---

37 EEAS (2012). ENP Country Progress Report 2011 – Ukraine. [pdf] EEAS. Available at: http:// eeas.europa.eu/archives/delegations/ukraine/documents/press_releases/memo_ukraine_clean.pdf; EEAS (2013) ENP Country Progress Report 2012 – Ukraine. [pdf] EEAS. Available at: https:// library.euneighbours.eu/content/ukraine-enp-progress-report-2012.

38 *Ibid.*

39 European Court of Auditors (2016). Special Report – EU Assistance to Ukraine. [pdf] European Court of Auditors. Available at: www.eca.europa.eu/Lists/ECADocuments/SR16_32/SR_UKRAINE_EN.pdf, p. 14.

40 EEAS (2012). ENP Country Progress Report 2011 – Ukraine. [pdf] EEAS. Available at: http://eeas.europa.eu/archives/delegations/ukraine/documents/press_releases/memo_ukraine_clean.pdf, p. 2.

41 EEAS (2013) ENP Country Progress Report 2012 – Ukraine. [pdf] Available at: https://library.euneighbours.eu/content/ukraine-enp-progress-report-2012, p. 4.

The EU-Ukraine DCFTA 203

emphasis on the justice sector and the rule of law (Johansson-Nogués, 2018). The EU's dissatisfaction with the path of the rule of law reforms in Ukraine, coupled with the instability and security implications of the crisis, has shaped the novel approach the EU has applied to the support of the judicial and law enforcement agencies' reform in post-Euromaidan Ukraine, encompassing:

- The strengthening of the security-rule of law nexus via the deployment of the EU Advisory Mission to Ukraine (EUAM) and granting support to a number of external security and rule of law projects in Ukraine (e.g. the UNDP project "Rule of Law and Community Justice for Conflict-Affected Areas in Ukraine").[42]
- The support of the justice sector and law enforcement agencies' reform in terms of the Special Measure III 2016 on Support to the Rule of Law Reforms in Ukraine (PRAVO).[43]

As provided for at the official website of the EUAM Ukraine, its key objective is "to assist the Ukrainian authorities towards a sustainable reform of the civilian sector through strategic advice and practical support for specific reform measures based on EU standards and international principles of good governance and human rights".[44] Pursuant to the EUAM, the concept of the "civilian sector" comprises a broad range of security and law enforcement agencies, such as the National Police, the Security Service of Ukraine and the General Prosecutor's Office, as well as local courts and anti-corruption bodies.[45] The EUAM's focus action areas are pierced by a number of rule of law components. First, the Mission's actions, directed at improving the delineation of competences between the Ukrainian civilian sector authorities, contribute to the institutional dimension of legality, as well as the principles of transparency and accountability. The latter principles are also addressed via the so-called community policing, aimed at "building trust within communities through direct interaction and dialogue".[46] Third, the "Public Order" pillar of the EUAM's activities is illustrative of the rule of law–human rights nexus, as it emphasizes the rule of law dimension of the right to peaceful assembly. Besides, under the "Human Resources" focus area, the Mission supplements its focus area–centred technical support of reforms through capacity-building activities.[47]

---

42 For information about the EUAM, please visit the website: www.euam-ukraine.eu/.
 For information about the UNDP project "Rule of Law and Community Justice for Conflict-Affected Areas in Ukraine", please visit the website: www.ua.undp.org/content/ukraine/en/home/projects/rule-of-law-for-stabilization-in-Ukraine.html.
43 European Commission Action Document for Support to Rule of Law Reforms in Ukraine (PRAVO), COM (2016) 8266 final of 12 December 2016.
44 EUAM Ukraine (n.d.) Our Priorities. [online] Available at: www.euam-ukraine.eu/our-mission/our-priorities/.
45 EUAM (n.d.). The Civilian Security Sector, What is The Civilian Security Sector? [online] Available at: www.euam-ukraine.eu/our-mission/the-civilian-security-sector/.
46 *Ibid.*
47 *Ibid.*

204 *The EU-Ukraine DCFTA*

In turn, the EU's support of the justice sector reform in Ukraine, channelled through the Special Measure III 2016 on Support to the Rule of Law Reforms in Ukraine (PRAVO), provides for two key action areas: (i) funding for the police reform (complementary to the EUAM) and (ii) reform of the judiciary and justice sector, more broadly. The latter has encompassed, *inter alia*, improved access to justice and the enforcement of judicial decisions, as well as the enhanced quality of state registers' functioning and the execution of sanctions.[48] In its 2016 Implementing Decision as to this previously mentioned Special Measure, the Commission pointed to a number of the rule of law standards to be pursued in terms of the on-site project "PRAVO-JUSTICE. European Justice for Ukraine".[49] For instance, the project addresses the legality dimension of the rule of law by assisting the government of Ukraine to reconsider the legal framework on the judiciary, the Office of Public Prosecutor and the enforcement of judicial decisions.[50] The transparency dimension of the concept is reflected in the project's experts' participation in the merit-based recruitment of judges and the administrative staff, working in courts.[51] Similar to the EUAM, the "PRAVO-JUSTICE" project envisions multi-aspect capacity-building activities targeting judges, the staffs of judicial and law enforcement bodies, and the Ministry of Justice of Ukraine, responsible for holding the previously mentioned public registers.[52]

In a nutshell, the EU's in-depth concern with the resilience of its Neighbours, coupled with its previously unsuccessful efforts to promote justice sector reform in Ukraine, has determined the comprehensiveness of the EU's support of reform of the judiciary and law enforcement agencies in Ukraine. The key substantial features of this support can be summarized as follows. First, the substance of the EUAM's activities testifies to the EU's focus on the resilience of Ukraine's civilian security sector and the securitization of the rule of law concept in terms of the EU's response to the crisis in and around Ukraine. Second, the design of the support under the EUAM and "PRAVO-JUSTICE" project mirrors the EU's sectoral approach to reform support, combining strategic advice, technical assistance and the support of capacity-building. Besides, both initiatives emphasize the law enforcement aspect of the reforms in question. Bearing these insights in mind, we will continue with exploring the coherence between the EU's support of the justice reform and the rule of law standards provided for in the DCFTA.

2. *External coherence*

The simultaneous analysis of the rule of law standards under the DCFTA and the substance of the EU's support of the justice sector reform in Ukraine allows for

---

48 *Ibid.*
49 For information about the project "PRAVO-JUSTICE", please visit the website: www.pravojus tice.eu/.
50 *Ibid.*
51 *Ibid.*
52 *Ibid.*

The EU-Ukraine DCFTA 205

distinguishing several "junctures", testifying to the coherence between the EU's promotion of the rule of law through trade liberalization and its support of justice sector reforms in Ukraine.

Foremost, amid the continuing annexation of Crimea and violence in Eastern Ukraine, security and stability constitute essential prerequisites for creating the environment, conducive to the implementation of the EU-Ukraine AA. This statement can be substantiated by the recourse to the World Bank's Worldwide Governance Indicators that point to the "Stability and Lack of Violence" as one of the key characteristics pertaining to successful economic governance within a state (Kaufmann, Kraay and Mastruzzi, 2010, p. 1). Moreover, peace, security and justice are referred to as the essentials of sustainable development under the UN Agenda 2030 and the New European Consensus on Development.[53] It can thus be argued that the EU's efforts to strengthen the rule of law–security nexus via the EUAM and the 2016 Special Measure are in coherence with the EU-Ukraine joint trade liberalization and facilitation endeavour.

Second, as mentioned in Chapter 7, the EU's justice sector assistance supports Ukraine's implementation of a number of general and discipline-specific obligations under the DCFTA in part concerning the judicial review. Ukraine's broadest obligation in this regard is contained in Art. 286 of the EU-Ukraine AA, under which each party to the Agreement "shall establish or maintain courts or other independent tribunals . . . for the purpose of the prompt review or, where warranted, correction of administrative action in areas covered by this Agreement". Ukraine's discipline-specific obligations concerning judicial review can be, *inter alia*, exemplified by the provisions of the Council Directive 89/665/EC on the coordination of the laws, regulations and administrative provisions relating to the application of review procedures to the award of public supply and public works contracts (public procurement).[54] Since the fulfillment of obligations under the previously mentioned Directive requires the functioning of independent and impartial judicial bodies, the EU's justice sector support is beyond the doubt supportive of Ukraine's fulfillment of its discipline-specific obligations under the DCFTA.

Third, Art. 286(3) of the EU-Ukraine AA obliges the parties to ensure the implementation of judicial decisions concerning the DCFTA by the office or authority, "competent with respect to the administrative action at issue". Similarly, discipline-specific obligations related to the right to judicial review and appeal may also encompass the law enforcement aspect (e.g. Art.2[7] of the Council Directive 89/665/EC, obliging the Member States to ensure effective enforcement of decisions by the bodies responsible for the judicial review).[55] According to the 2009–2018 country progress reports on Ukraine, the effective enforcement

---

53 United Nations General Assembly Resolution: Transforming our World: the 2030 Agenda for Sustainable Development, A/RES/70/01 of 21 October 2015; New European Consensus on Development.
54 Council Directive 89/665/EEC of 21 December 1989 on the coordination of the laws, regulations and administrative provisions relating to the application of review procedures to the award of public supply and public works contracts, OJ L 395 of 30 December 1989.
55 *Ibid.*, Art. 2(7).

206   *The EU-Ukraine DCFTA*

of judicial decisions constitutes the key challenge to the rule of law in Ukraine.[56] That is why the EU's post-Euromaidan focus on reforming Ukraine's law enforcement agencies and promoting their resilience goes in line with the parties' ambition to ensure functional nature of one's right to judicial review under the DCFTA.

Fourth, in contrast to the numerous previously researched EU initiatives in the justice sector domain, the "PRAVO-JUSTICE" project immediately tackles the rule of law–economic development nexus by introducing the priority "Property Rights Protection and Ease of Business".[57] Under this priority, the project has supported creation of the private enforcement service, improvement of the notary service, and adoption of the new Bankruptcy Code and relevant procedures.[58] In contrast to other technical assistance projects, discussed previously with respect to "Internal Coherence", the PRAVO-JUSTICE" project does not link its priorities to specific DCFTA-based norms/obligations.[59] This means that, analogously to an array of previously considered cases, the Ukrainian case is marked by the lack of a formalized connection between the partner countries' DCFTA-based obligations regarding the right to review and the design of the EU's reform support.

In sum, since the DCFTA obliges Ukraine to ensure one's right to judicial review in the domains covered by the Agreement, the EU's external assistance to Ukraine's justice sector reform creates a supportive environment for the implementation of such obligations. Moreover, given the complexities of the ongoing crisis, the EU's justice sector assistance has acquired a state-building character and is essential for ensuring security and stability as basic prerequisites for sustainable development. Despite the lack of the formalized connections between the DCFTA rules and the EU's justice sector assistance to Ukraine, it can be argued in favour of using the relevant DCFTA's obligations as benchmarks to assess the relevance and effectiveness of the EU's justice sector assistance.

Part 5. Reforms and their results/progress

This section of the analysis will shed light on the results/progress of major reforms concerning the DCFTA's chapters in question as of March 2019, paying particular attention to their rule of law dimension. In particular, the analysis will focus on the domains of public procurement and deregulation. Our choice of focus reform areas represents a combination of the domain, wherein Ukraine has very specific obligations in line with the DCFTA (public procurement), and the broader reform

---

56 See, for instance, EEAS (2015). ENP Country Progress Report 2014 – Ukraine "Implementation of the European Neighbourhood Policy in 2014". [online] Available at: https://library.euneighbours.eu/content/enp-country-progress-report-2014-%E2%80%93-ukraine, pp. 2–3; European Commission/High Representative of the Union for Foreign Affairs and Security Policy, Joint Communication to the European Parliament and the Council, Commission Joint Staff Working Paper – Association Implementation Report on Ukraine, SWD(2018) 462 final of 7 November 2018, p. 8.
57 For an insight into the scope of the "Property Rights Protection and Ease of Business" priority under the "PRAVO-JUSTICE" project, please visit the website: www.pravojustice.eu/.
58 *Ibid.*
59 *Ibid.*

area pertaining to the Agreement but marked with lesser precision of the obligations (deregulation).

Notably, the major domestic law framework for Ukraine's implementation of its AA/DCFTA obligations is constituted by the Cabinet of Ministers Resolution "On the implementation of the Association Agreement between Ukraine, on the one side, and the European Union, the Euratom and their Member States, on the other side" of 25 October 2017. The Resolution presented Ukraine's obligations as to the AA/DCFTA implementation in the form of 7,500 actions, broken down by 2,000 tasks.[60] The key institution responsible for the inter-agency coordination of these tasks' implementation is the Government Office for Coordination of European and Euro-Atlantic Integration.[61] According to the Office's 2018 and 2019 Reports, Ukraine managed to fulfil 52% and 37% of all tasks planned for those respective years (the lack of progress in 2019 can be attributed to the bureaucratic challenges due to the election of the new President Volodymyr Zelenskyy).[62] As shown at the government's information website "Pulse of the Agreement", Ukraine fulfilled the vast majority of its obligations in the domains of public procurement (countering technical barriers to trade) (82%), public procurement (80%) and deregulation and business (79%), as well as the area of freedom, justice and security (83%).[63] The worst performance was noted in the domains of IP rights (22%); transport, transport infrastructure and postal services (25%); and the financial sector (30%). As shown earlier, a considerable role in hampering the implementation of Ukraine's commitments under the AA belongs to the Verkhovna Rada, or Parliament, with the performance rate of 12% in 2019 (i.e. meaning the fulfillment of 12% of all the tasks planned for the year).[64]

Bearing these figures and insights in mind, the chapter will proceed with analysis of Ukraine's progress in the aforementioned reform domains.

1. Public procurement

Chapter 8 of the EU-Ukraine AA envisages the comprehensive gradual mutual opening of the parties' public procurement markets. As demonstrated in Chapter 4,

---

60 *Ibid.*

61 *Ibid.*

62 Government Office for European and Euro-Atlantic Integration of Ukraine, Vice Prime-Minister's Office for European and Euro-Atlantic Integration of Ukraine (2019). Report on Implementation of the Association Agreement between Ukraine and the European Union 2018. [pdf] EU-UA. Available at: https://eu-ua.org/sites/default/files/inline/files/association-agreement-implementation-report-2018-english.pdf, pp. 2–4; Government Office for European and Euro-Atlantic Integration of Ukraine, Vice Prime-Minister's Office for European and Euro-Atlantic Integration of Ukraine (2020). Report on Implementation of the Association Agreement between Ukraine and the European Union 2019. [pdf] EU-UA. Available at: https://eu-ua.org/sites/default/files/inline/files/ar_aa_implementation-2019-4_eng.pdf, pp. 6–9.

63 Euro-Integration Portal (n.d.) Pulse of the Agreement. [online] Available at: https://pulse.eu-ua.org/

64 Government Office for European and Euro-Atlantic Integration of Ukraine, Vice Prime-Minister's Office for European and Euro-Atlantic Integration of Ukraine (2020). Report on Implementation of the Association Agreement between Ukraine and the European Union 2019. [pdf] EU-UA. Available at: https://eu-ua.org/sites/default/files/inline/files/ar_aa_implementation-2019-4_eng.pdf, p. 9.

208 *The EU-Ukraine DCFTA*

for "associated" Neighbours, the implementation of such openings is concerned equates to an in-depth rule of law-oriented reform of the public procurement system.

Prior to the AA's conclusion, there were at least three attempts to create a transparent public procurement system, and each of them failed due to the persistent legacy of neopatrimonialism (Stewart, 2013). As noted by Stewart (2013), each of prior framework laws, attempting to reform the public procurement system in Ukraine, was initially regarded as a success that was, however, soon "wiped off" by amendments, adopted in the interest of particular oligarchic groups (pp. 201–202). So far, the case of 2016 Law of Ukraine "On Public Procurement" (hereinafter referred as "2016 Law") seems to be different, for two reasons. First, the provisions of the 2016 Law are of more general nature and, as compared to the former framework laws, contain fewer exceptions to the application of the general DCFTA-compliant public procurement procedure.[65] Second, the 2016 reform is marked by the launch of two electronic public procurement systems (e-platforms), "Prozorro" and "Dozorro", aimed at ensuring the observance of the legality, legal certainty and transparency aspects of the rule of law in the public procurement domain.

Before elaborating on these systems, we would like to briefly address the substance of the rule of law-oriented novelties, introduced by the 2016 Law "On Public Procurement". Foremost, as opposed to the 2014 Law "On State Procurement", adopted as a transitory step towards the public procurement reform, the 2016 Law stipulated the obligatory application of the innovative electronic tendering (e-tendering) system "Prozorro" to all public contracts.[66] Simultaneously, the 2016 Law increased the minimum purchase cost for mandatory tendering from 100,000 to 200,000 UAH for goods and services from 1–1.5 million UAH for works, requiring an obligatory report on conducted procurement to be provided to the Anti-Monopoly Committee of Ukraine (AMCU) in case of a procurement, whose value is between 50,000 and 200,000 UAH.[67] The 2016 Law also is marked by a number of transparency-oriented changes pertaining to both state institutions in the public procurement domain and tenderers. For instance, it specifically pointed to state institutions and bodies authorized to intervene in procurement procedures, limiting their number.[68] Another crucial transparency-oriented novelty of the Law has been the requirement of verification of the final beneficiary of participating companies.[69] Besides, in case of a tender, whose value equals to or exceeds 20 million UAH, an entity can only be eligible for participation if it presents an anti-corruption programme and appoints a representative responsible for countering corruption.[70]

---

65 Verkhovna Rada of Ukraine (2016). Zakon Ukrainy "Pro Publichni Zakupivli" (Law of Ukraine "On Public Procurement") No 922-VIII of 25 December 2015. [online] Available at: https://zakon.rada.gov.ua/laws/show/922-19#Text.
66 *Ibid.*, Art.2.
67 *Ibid.*, Art.2, Art.7.
68 *Ibid.*, Art.7–8.
69 *Ibid.*, Art.1(29), Art.22(2).
70 *Ibid.*, Art.17(10).

Importantly, the public procurement reform would not be complete without the reform of the Anti-Monopoly Committee of Ukraine as the key regulatory institution in the domains of public procurement and competition. As noted by the OECD in its 2016 Review of Competition Law and Policy, both the leadership and staff of the AMCU demonstrated an in-depth commitment to implementing the DCFTA-driven reforms both amid the political and economic turmoil of 2014–2015 and later (OECD, 2016). In particular, the AMCU played a central role in implementing "Prozorro" as the unified e-tendering platform (OECD, 2016, p. 58). In partnership with several international organizations and mechanisms (Transparency International Ukraine, USAID and the EBRD's Ukraine's Stabilization and Sustainable Growth MDA), the AMCU supported the launch of the e-platform "Dozorro".[71] It serves as an e-platform for the community of tenderers and NGOs to share concerns about suspicious procurements and experiences of protecting economic operators' interests with regard to public procurement procedures.[72] The key issue that would, however, prevent us from calling "Dozorro" an ultimate success is that it does not follow the practices of appeal against the AMCU's decisions in courts. Notably, particularly the appeal against AMCU's decisions constitutes the most vulnerable point of the reform at issue, with only 0.13% of cases won by economic operators. The reasons behind such a situation include courts' application of the concept of discretionary authorities of state bodies[73] and jurisdictional discontents between administrative and business courts, authorized to consider different aspects of cases pertaining to public procurement (Vinnichuk and Holovn'ov, 2018). Hence, following the opinions of multiple foreign donors and experts, the protection of economic operators interests remain the key challenge to be addressed in the public procurement domain (e.g. Rudenko, 2020).

Hence, it can be concluded that, extensively supported by the EU and other donors, Ukraine managed to make progress with regard to the **legality**, **legal certainty** and **transparency** dimensions of the rule of law in the public procurement domain. Nonetheless, the newly created system of regulating public contracts remains vulnerable to neo-patrimonial challenges that become especially dangerous amid the statistically low probability for economic operators to protect their interests in courts.

2. Deregulation and business development

In contrast with the public procurement case, the DCFTA does not contain in-detail provisions as to conducting the deregulation reform. Nonetheless, its rationale immediately stems from the establishment of "conditions for enhanced economic and trade relations leading towards Ukraine's gradual integration in the

---

71 For information about "Dozorro", please visit the website: https://dozorro.org/.

72 *Ibid.*

73 This means a court can only acknowledge the unlawfulness of AMCU's decisions without substituting its decisions with the ones it makes on its own.

210 *The EU-Ukraine DCFTA*

EU Internal Market . . . and support Ukrainian efforts to complete the transition into a functioning market economy".[74] Furthermore, the conduct of deregulation reform is consonant with a number of the DCFTA's chapter-specific objectives, such as the maintenance of "an effective and predictable regulatory environment for economic operators" or ensuring free and undistorted competition.[75] As provided for by the Office of Reforms at the Cabinet of Ministers of Ukraine, the reform of deregulation and business development was designed to pursue three intertwined objectives, namely:

- The reduction of regulatory pressure on SMEs and costs pertaining to administering business.
- The creation of an environment favourable to domestic and foreign investments.
- Promoting healthy market competition.[76]

Accordingly, the deregulation reform has comprised three strands of efforts, i.e.: (i) strategizing the improvement of business environment for economic operators; (ii) the application of a "regulatory guillotine", providing for the full review of applicable standards and the radical elimination of standards "non-alignable" to EU rules and (iii) concentrated efforts to improve Ukraine's positions in World Bank's "Doing Business" rating (with the umbrella objective of reaching the Top30 by 2020).[77] In this vein, the reform has been strongly connected to at least three crucial domains under the DCFTA:

- The promotion of international trade (via the definition and abolition of ineffective, unlawful and corrupt regulations, limits and quotas, as well as the harmonization of Ukraine's technical and food security standards with the EU ones).
- Strengthening of the customs cooperation.
- Fair competition.

Moreover, these strands of efforts may contribute to the improvement of multiple aspects of the rule of law. This statement can be, *inter alia*, exemplified by the "Doing Business" rating that encompasses states' adherence to the **legality**, **legal certainty** and **transparency** principles with respect to the key "doing business" issues, such as the launch of a new business, obtaining permits for land use and construction, registering property rights, protecting minority investors and engagement in cross-border trade.[78] Besides, the "Doing Business" rating encompasses the "enforcement of contracts" indicator that combines the measurement

---

74 EU-Ukraine AA, Art. 1.
75 *Ibid.*, Art. 282.
76 Office of Reforms at the Cabinet of Ministers of Ukraine (n.d.). Business Climate Improvement. [online] Available at: https://rdo.in.ua/en/direction/business-climate-improvement.
77 *Ibid.*
78 For an insight into the methodology of Doing Business rating, please visit the website: www.doingbusiness.org/en/methodology.

of time and costs necessary to resolve a commercial dispute in a local fist-instance court, and the index of judicial processes' quality.[79]

Prior to the start of the deregulation reform, Ukraine held the 137th position in the Doing Business rating.[80] During 2013– 2019, it managed to improve by 66 places, having reached 71st and becoming one of the regional leaders.[81] Pursuant to the 2013 Doing Business rating, Ukraine demonstrated the poorest performance with respect to getting construction permits (183rd) and access to electricity (166th), as well as taxation (165th) and dealing with bankruptcy (157th).[82] Ukraine's best results were achieved on access to loans (23rd) and the registration of enterprises (50th).[83] By comparison, the 2019 Report demonstrated an impressive improvement with respect to the acquisition of construction permits (30th), taxation (54th) and the protection of minority shareholders (from 117th to 72nd).[84] Nonetheless, a number of positions remained unchanged or even worsened (e.g. enforcement of contracts) (57th in 2019), dealing with bankruptcy (145th in 2019) and registration of new enterprises (63rd in 2019).[85] According to governmental experts, the key legislative novelties that allowed Ukraine to achieve a considerable improvement of its position in the Doing Business Rating since 2013 concern: (i) the multi-sector "rolling review" of regulatory acts in terms of the "regulatory guillotine" initiative; (ii) the de-bureaucratization of the procedure for getting construction permits; (iii) corporate law reform regarding transparency and protection of minority shareholders (e.g. requirements regarding the disclosure of beneficial ownership) and (iv) the ongoing efforts related to the harmonization of technical and food security standards with the ones of the EU.[86] Importantly, these legislative changes were accompanied by the implementation of numerous capacity-building programmes for SMEs led by national and foreign donors, ranging from the almost €200 million worth "EU4Business" programme to the "She Exports" project of the Ukraine Office of Export Promotion, directed towards the capacity-building of women exporters.[87]

Simultaneously, despite Ukraine's continuous improvement of its positions in the Doing Business rating, a number of critical points should be mentioned. First, there is much skepticism as regards the Doing Business rating's objectivity,

---

79 *Ibid.*
80 The World Bank (n.d.). Doing Business, Measuring Business Regulations, Ease of Doing Business in Ukraine. [online] Available at: www.doingbusiness.org/en/data/exploreeconomies/ukraine.
81 *Ibid.*
82 *Ibid.*
83 *Ibid.*
84 *Ibid.*
85 *Ibid.*
86 Ministry for Development Trade and Agriculture (2019). Ogliad dosiahnen reform derehuliatsii gospodars'koyi diyalnosti za 2018 rik [Overview of the Achievements of the Deregulation Reform for Year 2018]. [online] Available at: https://issuu.com/mineconomdev/docs/_____ _____2018_____._2.
87 For information about the activities of the EU4Business programme in Ukraine, please visit the website: www.eu4business.eu/ukraine. For information about "She Exports" programme, please visit the website: https://epo.org.ua/en/.

212 *The EU-Ukraine DCFTA*

mainly because the Rating considers the legislative and regulatory framework for doing business, rather than the actual dynamics of a country's attracting investments (The World Bank, n.d.). Moreover, the Rating does not take into account the impact which the ongoing crisis in and around Ukraine may have on decisions as regards making investments in Ukraine. The Rating's non-comprehensive nature can be also substantiated by the fact that it barely considers the lawfulness and effectiveness of activities performed by law enforcement agencies exercising states' supervision and control over businesses, as well as the enforcement of judicial decisions in commercial cases. Simultaneously, relations between the state, law enforcement agencies and businesses remain strained in Ukraine, with businesses being frequently subjected to searches and seizures of property in both commercial and criminal cases (e.g. Vox Ukraine, 2018). Given the post-Soviet legacy of neo-patrimonial complex interlinkages between businesses and state bodies (Malygina, 2012; Kyselova, 2015), such searches and seizures may be intentionally applied as a means of acquiring an illegal advantage over competitors (Vox Ukraine, 2018). Although many businesses manage to successfully counter seizures through appeal, the trend is capable of significantly lowering the trust of businesses and investors in legality, legal certainty and transparency as achievements of deregulation reform.

In sum, linked to many aspects of the DCFTA's implementation, Ukraine's ongoing deregulation reform managed to significantly reduce the number of formal obstacles to running a business or investing in Ukraine. These achievements related to legality, legal certainty and transparency have been reflected in the rapid improvement of Ukraine's positions in the World Bank's Doing Business rating. At the same time, the difficulties pertaining to the enforcement of judicial decisions by respective bodies and the persistence of non-formal practices of pressure on business have conditioned the businesses' insufficient trust into the reform's achievements –thus, similarly to the public procurement case, in particular the non-formal practices, rather than deficiencies in formal regulations.

Conclusion

The final part of this study aimed at conducting an in-detail analysis of the EU-Ukraine DCFTA as an instrument of the EU's rule of law promotion in Ukraine.

We found the DCFTA to be marked by comprehensiveness and the complex interplay of the rule of law standards (e.g. legality, legal certainty, transparency), especially in chapters related to "deep disciplines", as well as customs cooperation and trade facilitation. They also contain numerous instruments aimed to ensure the observance of these standards, such as the imposition of basic standards, the referral to the parties' obligations under international law and the combination of legislative approximation obligations and market access conditionality. Besides, the EU-Ukraine AA also encompasses an array of more general mechanisms supportive of the implementation of the rule of law standards, such as the AA's multilevel institutional framework, the gradual and dynamic nature of the AA-driven legislative approximation and enhanced monitoring clauses.

One of the key peculiarities of the EU's assistance to Ukraine amid the crisis has been the combination of assistance immediately related to the implementation of the EU-Ukraine AA and state-building measures, encompassing, *inter alia*, the support of the civilian security and justice sectors. In this vein, the EU's sectoral approach to reform support inevitably implies a considerable degree of coherence between the "regulation" and "action" dimensions of the rule of law promotion through the DCFTA by: (i) focusing on the domestic transposition and implementation of the DCFTA-based rule of law standards and (ii) building the capacity of civil servants and experts engaged in implementation of reforms.

With regard to external coherence, it was established that the EU's support of the rule of law in Ukraine through civilian security and justice sector reforms has contributed to the environment supportive of the implementation of the rule of law standards, as contained in the DCFTA. The key "junctures" of such coherence include:

- The civil sector reform's contribution to security and stability as the critical prerequisites of sustainable development.
- Support of the implementation of the DCFTA's general and discipline-specific obligations on the right to judicial review.
- The introduction of the "Property Rights' Protection and Ease of Business" focus area in terms of PARVO-JUSTICE project.

There is, however, no formalized coordination between the EU's support of the DCFTA's implementation and its support of justice sector reform. In our view, more attention shall be dedicated to such coordination, since particularly ensuring the right to judicial review remains the key challenge in the context of both the public procurement and deregulation reforms.

In both the public procurement and deregulation domains, Ukraine managed to introduce an array of crucial strategies and framework laws in line with the *acquis communautaire*. Moreover, these reform fields were marked by crucial innovations, leading to the strengthened observance of the legality, legal certainty, transparency, equality and non-discrimination standards. The persistence of neo-patrimonial non-formal practices and the emergence of new ones can be regarded as a crucial challenge on the way to ensuring the sufficient judicial protection of investors' rights and promoting the economic rule of law in Ukraine more broadly.

Despite the remaining neo-patrimonial challenges in the explored reform domains, the "depth" of envisaged market integration, as well as the sector-focused nature and intensity of EU's support of the DCFTA's implementation and state-building in Ukraine, makes the Ukrainian case illustrative of the entire idea of instrumentalizing RTAs for rule of law promotion purposes, as suggested by this analysis.

References

Börzel, Tanja A. and Böttger, K. (2012). Conclusion: The power to transform lies in the detail. In: B. Börzel, eds., *Policy change in the EU's immediate neighbourhood: A sectoral approach*. Baden-Baden: Brill, pp. 163–173.

214 *The EU-Ukraine DCFTA*

Browning, C.S. (2018). Geostrategies, geopolitics and ontological security in the Eastern neighbourhood: The European Union and the "new cold war". *Political Geography*, 62, pp. 106–115.

Butin, A. (2019). *Streamlining EU-Ukraine customs procedures*. Civic Synergy. [pdf] Available at: www.civic-synergy.org.ua/wp-content/uploads/2018/04/STREAMLINING-EU-UKRAINE-CUSTOMS-PROCEDURES_en_2019.pdf.

Cadier, D. (2019). The Geopoliticisation of the EU's Eastern partnership. *Geopolitics*, 24(1), pp. 71–99.

Cross, M.K. and Karolewski, I.P. (2017). What type of power has the EU exercised in the Ukraine – Russia crisis? A framework of analysis. *Journal of Common Market Studies*, 55(1), pp. 3–19.

Emmanouilidis, J. (2008). *Alternatives between full membership and non-membership. Fata morgana or silver bullet?* Paper for the Bertelsmann Stiftung Conference "The EU and its Neighbours: In Search for New Forms of Partnership". [pdf] Available at: www.emmanouilidis.eu/download/Emmanouilidis_Fata-Morgana-or-Silver-Bullet.pdf.

European Commission. (n.d). *Support group for Ukraine*. [online] Available at: https://ec.europa.eu/neighbourhood-enlargement/neighbourhood/countries/ukraine/sgua_en.

European Commission. (2016). *Support group for Ukraine. Activity report. The first 18 months*. [pdf] Available at: https://ec.europa.eu/neighbourhood-enlargement/sites/near/files/neighbourhood/pdf/key-documents/ukraine/20161028-report-sgua.pdf.

European Court of Auditors. (2016). *Special report No. 32 – EU assistance to Ukraine*. [pdf] Available at: https://www.eca.europa.eu/Lists/ECADocuments/SR16_32/SR_UKRAINE_EN.pdf.

Haukkala, H. (2015). From cooperative to contested Europe? The conflict in Ukraine as a culmination of a long-term crisis in EU – Russia relations. *Journal of Contemporary European Studies*, 23(1), pp. 25–40.

Johansson-Nogués, E. (2018). The EU's ontological(In)security: Stabilizing the ENP area . . . and the EU's self? *Cooperation and Conflict*, 53, pp. 528–544.

Katchanovski, I. (2017). The separatist war in Donbas: A violent break-up of Ukraine? In: P. Nicolai, ed., *Ukraine in crisis*. London: Routledge, pp. 53–70.

Kaufmann, K., Kraay, A. and Mastruzzi, M. (2010). *The worldwide governance indicators (WGI). Methdology and analytical issues*. The World Bank Policy Research Working Paper 5430. [online] Available at: https://papers.ssrn.com/sol3/papers.cfm?abstract_id=1682130.

Kelly, J. (2006). New wine in old wineskins: Promoting political reforms through the new European neighbourhood policy. *Journal of Common Market Studies*, 44, pp. 29–55.

Kemp, G. and Lyubashenko, I. (2018). The conflict in Ukrainian Donbas: International, regional and comparative perspectives on the jus post bellum options. In: S. Sayapin and E. Tsybulenko, eds., *The use of force against Ukraine and international law*. Berlin: Springer, pp. 329–355.

Kuzio, T. (2018). National minorities in Putin's Russia. Diversity and assimilation. *Europe-Asia Studies*, 70, pp. 1167–1169.

Kyselova, T. (2015). The role of state in Ukrainian business: Violent bedspread and profitable partner. *Kyiv-Mohyla Law and Politics Journal*, 1, pp. 83–112.

Magen, A. (2005/2006). The shadow of enlargement: Can the European neighbourhood policy achieve compliance. *Columbia Journal of European Law*, 12, pp. 383–390.

OECD. (2016). *OECD reviews of competition law and policy*. Ukraine 2016. [pdf] Available at: http://www.oecd.org/daf/competition/UKRAINE-OECD-Reviews-of-Competition-Law-and-Policy_WEBENG.pdf.

Malygina, K. (2012). Ukraine as a neo-patrimonial state: Understanding political change in Ukraine in 2005–2010. *Journal for Labour and Social Affairs in Eastern Europe*, 13(1), pp. 7–27.

Petrov, R. (2014). *Zblyzhennia Zakonodavstva v Uhodi pro Asotsiatsiiu Mizh Ukrainoiui Y ES [Approximation of laws in the EU-Ukraine association agreement]*. [online] Available at: http://ekmair.ukma.edu.ua/handle/123456789/3266.

Rabinovych, M. (2017). The rule of law promotion through trade in the "associated" Eastern neighbourhood. *Polish Yearbook of International Law*, 37, pp. 71–100.

Rabinovych, M. (2019). EU's development policy vis-à-vis Ukraine after the Euromaidan: Securitisation, state-building and integration. *East European Politics*, 35(3), pp. 332–350.

Rudenko, T. (2020). *Chomu Rishennya AMKU ne Zavzhdy Spravedlyvi [Why are the decisions of the antimonopoly committee not always fair?]* Dozorro.org. [online] Available at: https://dozorro.org/blog/chomu-rishennya-amku-ne-zavzhdi-spravedlivi.

Russel, M. (2018). *The EU's Russia policy. Five guiding principles, European parliament research service briefing*. European Parliament. [pdf] Available at: www.europarl.europa.eu/RegData/etudes/BRIE/2018/614698/EPRS_BRI(2018)614698_EN.pdf.

Sasse, G. (2008). The European neighbourhood policy: Conditionality revisited for the EU's Eastern neighbours. *Europe-Asia Studies*, 60(2), pp. 295–316.

Stewart, S. (2013). Public procurement reform in Ukraine: The implications of neopatrimonialism for external actors. *Demokratizatsiya*, 21(2), pp. 194–214.

Uriadovyi Portal. (2019). *Klimpush-Cincadze: "Industrial 'Visa Liberalization' with the EU possible in 2020"*. [online] Available at: www.kmu.gov.ua/ua/news/promislovij-bezviz-z-yes-mozhlivij-u-2020-roci-ivanna-klimpush-cincadze.

Van der Loo, G. (2016). *The EU-Ukraine association agreement and deep and comprehensive free trade area: A new legal instrument of EU integration without membership*. Leiden: Brill.

Vox Ukraine. (2018). *Anatomiya Pressinga*. Chto analiz boleye 2000 sudebnykh resheniy govorit o biznes-klimate v Ukraine [The anatomy of oppression: What does the analysis of more than 2000 court decisions say about business climate in Ukraine?] [online] Available at: https://voxukraine.org/ru/anatomiya-pressinga-chto-analiz-bolee-2000-sudebnyh-reshenij-govorit-o-biznes-klimate-v-ukraine/.

Vinnichuk, Y. and Holovn'ov, S. (2018). *Yak Obmanuty Systemu Derzhzakupivel na ProZorro [How to deceive the public procurement system on Prozorro?]* Business Tsensor. [online] Available at: https://biz.censor.net.ua/resonance/3086528/yak_obmanuti_sistemu_derjzakupvel_na_prozorro.

Wetzel, A. (2015). The substance of the EU democracy promotion: Introduction and conceptual framework. In: A. Wetzel and J. Orbie, eds., *The substance of EU democracy promotion: Concepts and cases*. Berlin: Springer, pp. 1–23.

Wolczuk, K. and Žeruolis, D. (2018). *Rebuilding Ukraine: An assessment of EU assistance*. Chatham House Research Paper 2018/08. Chatham House. [online] Available at: www.chathamhouse.org/publication/rebuilding-ukraine-assessing-eu-assistance-ukraine.

The World Bank. (n.d.). *Doing business, measuring business regulations, methodology*. [online]. Available at: www.doingbusiness.org/en/methodology.

Outlook and recommendations

The very idea behind this study has been to find out whether and, if yes, to which extent and how EU RTAs are and can potentially be instrumentalized for the purposes of promoting the rule of law in third states. This research question emerged from our curiosity to find out whether the ever-increasing "depth" of EU RTAs with third countries may grant the EU an opportunity to strengthen its ability to project its norms beyond its borders under the widely discussed intertwined crises of the liberal agenda globally and within the EU.

Already at the start of our theoretical enquiry, we encountered a crucial gap in existing knowledge on the interconnections between the rule of law (or law, in broader terms) and trade liberalization (or regional economic integration, in broader terms). Since the early post-war era, law and development scholars and practitioners have been generating multiple explanations of the role law plays in facilitating economic development and integration. However, despite the proliferation of bilateral and plurilateral trade regimes and their ever-expanding scope, **virtually no research has dealt with the trade liberalization's implications for the dynamics of the rule of law in partner countries.** Furthermore, although the EU's policies *vis-à-vis* third countries and regions typically combine political and economic development agendas, not much has been written on the policy and legal aspects of the interplay between them. Against this background and based on insights from the literature on law and development, EU external rule transfer, and normative and market power Europe, we introduced the concept of "EU value-promoting RTAs" to capture the set of circumstances, under which the EU is capable of promoting its values via the RTAs. It was established that, driven by the combination of EU normative and market powers, the Union's ability to instrumentalize each particular RTA for the purposes of value-promotion is shaped by the unique combination of factors, determining the EU bargaining power in each particular case, such as a counterpart's economic characteristics and its role at global and regional markets, its political regime, dependency on development aid and the vision of future relations with the EU, as well as respective strategic interests of the Union. Thus, the EU was found to have its best chances for instrumentalizing its RTAs for value-promotion purposes in terms of its relations with young (and frequently also "flawed") democracies, dependent on the EU in terms of imports/exports and development aid that may have European aspirations.

Based on the examples of the EU SAAs with the Western Balkans, AAs with Neighbours and EU EPAs with ACP countries, we found that **EU value-promoting RTAs entail a broad spectrum of the rule of law components, such as legality, legal certainty, the right to review and appeal, equality and non-discrimination, transparency and public accountability, and the relationship between domestic and international law.** While these norms in some cases are marked with a very narrow chapter-specific scope, others can create partner countries' obligations pertaining to the legal system as a whole. The RTAs promote respective standards through a number of legal instruments, such as the **setting of substantive standards, legislative approximation obligations and market access conditionality, obligations related to exchange of information, and cooperation and referrals to the partner country's obligations under international law.**

At the same time, the analysis of coherence between the rule of standards contained in value-promoting RTAs and the scope of EU diplomatic and unilateral assistance instruments used to support their implementation showed mixed results. While each sector in question manifested particular instances of coherence, we found that **both the rule of law concept as a whole and its components have been seldom depicted in the programming of the EU's unilateral assistance**, including "expected results" and "progress indicators" sections. It was also established that the EU's broader efforts to promote the rule of law in the Western Balkans, "associated" Eastern Neighbourhood and CARIFORUM countries are to a high extent consonant with/supportive of the implementation of the partner countries' rule of law obligations (e.g. with regard to the protection of businesses' interests and due process). However, similar to the case of "internal coherence", **virtually no instruments were introduced by the EU to synergize the application of the rule of law clauses in the RTAs and EU efforts to strengthen partner countries' justice sectors**. Thus, largely due to the EU's tendency to relate the rule of law solely to the domain of political cooperation with third countries and strict borderlines, and as it draws between values and *acquis* conditionality, and political and economic cooperation, **the RTAs' rule of law promotion potential is overlooked. The same applies to the synergies between the RTA norms and the EU's diplomatic and unilateral assistance instruments.** These findings were confirmed by our in-depth insight into the case of the EU rule of law promotion through the DCFTA with Ukraine and its application of sectoral approach to reform support. The case of Ukraine also helped us illustrate complex nexuses between security/stability, the rule of law promotion and trade liberalization support in the policy and legal design of the EU response to the crisis in and around Ukraine, and the importance of addressing persisting legacies of neo-patrimonialism while implementing the EU-Ukraine DCFTA.

Against this background, a number of recommendations can be suggested to relevant EU institutions. Foremost, according to our research, presented in Chapter 4, EU value-promoting RTAs contain numerous rule of law standards, whose implementation is secured by multiple legal mechanisms, ranging from the imposition of basic standards to complex information exchange and cooperation

218 *Outlook and recommendations*

structures. However, as demonstrated in Chapters 6–7, the implementation of these standards tends to be reinforced by the application of EU unilateral support instruments only on a case-by-case basis. Subsequently, on a most general level, we **suggest exploring the added value of instrumentalizing existing and future trade liberalization/market integration arrangements for the purposes of promoting values, in general, and the rule of law standards, in particular.** As exemplified by the case of Ukraine, presented in Chapter 8, such instrumentalization can be of special value in the context of limited opportunities for advancing political cooperation and/or strong contestation of EU values. Additionally, this recommendation can be supported by the referral to the theory of "democracy promotion by functional cooperation" that illustrates the pathways for functional cooperation-related rules to advance different aspects of democracy (e.g. public accountability) outside the traditional democracy promotion agenda. Hence, the instrumentalization of RTAs for the purposes of value-promotion deserves the special attention of EU institutions amid the global and intra-EU trend to the contestation of liberal values and the rise of geopolitical competition in the Neighbourhood and ACP countries.

Second, a crucial step towards strategizing the application of RTAs as instruments of promoting values, in general, and the rule of law, in particular, is concerned with **removing key conceptual obstacles on the way to the internally and externally coherent rule of law promotion through trade liberalization.** We revealed at least three such obstacles. First of all, **the EU frames the rule of law as a concept pertaining solely to political cooperation** and primarily links it to reforming the judiciary and law enforcement agencies, countering corruption and organized crime and institutional development, broadly defined. Hence, the instrumentalization of the EU RTAs for the rule of law promotion purposes would require supplementing the existing understanding of the rule of law with an economic dimension and introducing a stronger emphasis on business interests with regard to conventional components of the EU-driven rule of law reforms (e.g. functioning of the judiciary). Besides, the notion of an economic dimension of the rule of law may be applied to develop benchmarks and indicators to assess the performance of respective assistance projects and partner countries' progress. Next, there is a crucial **gap between "common values" and *acquis* conditionality,** due to which the rule of law effects, produced by sectoral *acquis,* tend not to be considered with regard to the programming of the EU unilateral external rule of law promotion instruments. The need for bridging this gap can be substantiated by our in-depth analysis of multiple implicit synergies between the EU promotion of the rule of law through trade liberalization and its unilaterally granted support of justice sector reforms, presented in Chapter 7. Additionally, the "politics-only" understanding of the rule of law and the strong borderline between "common values" and *acquis* conditionality leads to the **lack of the EU action at crossroads between economic and political cooperation** (e.g. the creation of an environment conducive to running business and attracting FDI or the protection of investors' interests). Thus, the key takeaway from our research is that increasing the potential of "deep" RTAs to serve as rule of law promotion frameworks

Outlook and recommendations 219

requires tackling an array of conceptual barriers that may, in turn, lead to the need for institutional changes.

Third, the suggested emphasis on addressing the gaps between "common values" and *acquis* conditionality, and political and economic cooperation, is consonant with the global ambition to make use of the synergies between the SDGs and increase the role of trade as a cross-cutting component for development, provided for in the Agenda 2030. Having committed itself to be a "frontrunner in implementing the 2030 Agenda and the SDGs"[1], the EU distinguished the CCP – as well as its Enlargement, Neighbourhood and Development policies – as key to support implementation of the SDGs externally. Thus, **bridging the previously mentioned conceptual gaps may be embedded into the EU's ongoing efforts to streamline its external policies in accordance with the Agenda 2030.** Similar refers to increasing the role of trade liberalization in promoting the rule of law, recognized by the Agenda 2030 as both a development objective and a crucial prerequisite for sustainable development.

Fourth, apart from emphasizing the interlinkages between the goals, Agenda 2030 puts significant value on coherence between different policies pertaining to development (based on the concept of Policy Coherence for Sustainable Development or PCSD). Notwithstanding conceptual gaps that may exist between the PCSD and the EU concept of Policy Coherence for Development, the PCD is generally consonant with the Agenda 2030 ambition to promote the interlinkages between the goals and coherence between different policies concerning development. However, as discussed in Chapter 6, the EU PCD concept has never been explicitly linked to the Union's value-promotion efforts. Given the many connections between trade liberalization/market integration, development and the rule of law revealed in terms of this study, we would like to argue in favour of **including fundamental values into the scope of the analysis under the PCD, and potentially also the PCSD framework** (if adopted by the EU following the example of Agenda 2030). The incorporation of fundamental values into the scope of the PCD would allow relevant EU institutions strengthen their role in the EU external action-wide understanding of development and ensure the coherence of the EU efforts, directed to the implementation of Agenda 2030.

Fifth, to support the instrumentalization of the RTAs for the value-promoting purposes, in general, and the rule of law promotion, in particular, it is suggested to **create the methodology for assessing the value-promoting potential of existing RTAs and those being negotiated.** Such a methodology shall be based on assessing the negotiating positions and interests of the EU and its counterparts in trade negotiations. As demonstrated in Chapter 3, the factors to be taken into account in terms of such assessment with respect to the counterpart's bargaining power shall relate to its economic resources and capabilities, imports/exports orientation, the state and prospects of its integration into a global market, dependency on

---

1 European Commission, Communication to the Council, the European Parliament, the European Economic and Social Committee and the Committee of the Regions: Next Steps for a Sustainable European Future, COM(2016) 739 final of 22 November 2016.

220 *Outlook and recommendations*

development aid, its political regime and its views on future of relations with the EU. Moreover, such an assessment shall take into account the strategic interests of the EU and its counterpart (e.g. in the domains of sustaining security/stability, countering illegal migration and organized crime). The assessment of the value-promotion potential of an RTA is envisaged as a foundation for strategizing the application of a particular RTA for value-promotion purposes.

Sixth, based on our insights into the "regulation" and "action" of the EU rule of law promotion through RTAs, **we would like to suggest two algorithms for respective strategy-making: for RTAs being negotiated, and for existing RTAs.**

The algorithm of **strategizing the application of RTAs currently being negotiated**, for the purposes of promoting the rule of law, shall include the following indicative steps:

1 Distinguishing the components of the rule of law to be included into each RTA's chapter.
2 Deciding which of the respective standards are strictly "discipline-specific" and which ones can be designed the way to generate spillovers to other areas not immediately encompassed by an RTA (as in case of partner countries' broadly formulated obligations with regard to the judiciary, contained in "Transparency" chapters of EU DCFTAs with "associated" Eastern Neighbours).
3 Deciding on the legal mechanisms that can best match respective substantive standards, given the context of a particular third state and its relationships with the EU.
4 Planning the synergies between the rule of law dimension of RTAs, programming of the instruments immediately aimed to promote the implementation of partner countries' obligations under an RTA ("internal coherence") and broader EU efforts to promote the rule of law in a given country or region ("external coherence").

In turn, characterized with a significantly more limited scope of possibilities as compared to the case of RTAs currently negotiated, the **respective algorithm for existing RTAs** shall include the following steps:

1 Mapping the rule of law promotion dimension of an existing RTA.
2 Assessing partner countries' performance with regard to the rule of law obligations contained in an RTA, and distinguishing key deficiencies therein.
3 Where possible, introducing changes to the programming of unilaterally granted assistance to address the above deficiencies and capture the synergies between the rule of law dimension of RTAs and unilateral assistance instruments.

It is suggested that, where possible, such broadly formulated algorithms can be applied to put in practice our previously formulated recommendations regarding the RTAs' instrumentalization for the value-promotion purposes.

Outlook and recommendations 221

Seventh, our analysis of the coherence between the EU rule of law promotion through trade liberalization and the EU support for justice sector reforms in third states, presented in Chapter 7, revealed that EU unilateral support of justice sector reforms in the Western Balkans, the "associated" Eastern Neighbourhood and CARIFORUM countries was seldom tailored to the protection of business interests. In this vein, the "PRAVO-JUSTICE" project, launched by the EU in Ukraine in 2016, has been the only EU project analyzed in terms of this book that specifically tackled the protection of business interests. Given the importance of high-quality judicial protection for facilitating cross-border trade and investment, **we recommend responsible EU institutions to take into account the problématique of business interests while designing the programming of justice sector reforms in third countries** and, if necessary, target the protection of business interests through specific programme components.

Eighth, while international trade is widely recognized as a cross-cutting instrument of promoting sustainable development, **we suggest relevant EU institutions aim at forming and sustaining ever stronger multi-stakeholder partnerships for the promotion of the rule of law in the context of trade liberalization/market integration.** Such partnerships are expected to engage EU institutions, parliaments of Member States and partner countries, international organizations, sectoral bodies, business representatives and civil society, and may also be formed as part of the "Global Partnership for Sustainable Development" envisaged by Agenda 2030. Their launch can be viewed as a promising starting point for the global effort to create a stronger rule of law–oriented multilateral, bilateral and plurilateral trade liberalization.

Ultimately, our study revealed that the ever-increasing "depth" of the EU RTAs with third countries can be viewed as a valuable opportunity for the EU to both strengthen its ability to project its norms beyond its borders under the widely discussed crisis of international liberal order and become a frontrunner of the movement towards a stronger normative agenda of global trade.

Index

access to justice 137, 179, 180, 186
accountability 16, 19–20, 22, 25, 50, 62,
    64, 70, 84, 101, 109–111, 120–121,
    130–131, 139–141, 147, 150, 160, 162,
    173, 177, 187, 203, 217–218
acquis communautaire 50, 89, 91, 95,
    97–98, 115, 140, 149, 153, 178, 194,
    196, 199, 213
African, Caribbean and Pacific (ACP)
    countries 1, 5, 28, 30–35, 54, 56, 61,
    68, 71, 93, 95, 100, 132–134, 138, 140,
    163, 169, 182, 217–218
Agenda 2030 2, 61, 70, 140, 161, 162, 169,
    184, 205, 219, 221
aid: development aid 29, 56, 61, **63**, 216;
    foreign aid 54–55, 64
Albania 31, 31n6, 56–57, 71, 71n11,
    81n42, 88, 88n77, 89, 113n21,
    114, 114n28, 114n29, 116–117,
    117nn38–40, 118, 118n41, 119, 119n47,
    119n48, 119n50, 120, 120n52, 151,
    151n26, 152, 152n29, 153n31, 153n32,
    172n18, 173n19, 173n20, 173n22, 174,
    174n26, 175n27, 175n30, 177n32
"associated": Neighbourhood 121, 140,
    179, 184, 186, 202; Neighbours 73, 81,
    84, 86, 97, 122, 133, 182–185, 187, 208
autonomous trade measures 111–112,
    126–127, 127n82, 133, 147, 149–150,
    152, 156

basic standards 92, 94–95, 97–98, 100–101,
    150, 159, 192–193, 199, 212, 217
business environment 75, 77, 123, 126,
    129, 147, 186, 200, 210

Common Commercial Policy (CCP) 37,
    41–42, 43
competition 2, 5, 8, 32, 36, 48, 50, 62, 63,
    68, 88, 90, 92, 95–97, 99–104, 109,
111, 115–116, 123–124, 129–130,
    130n105, 140, 150, 152–154, 159,
    162–163, 175–179, 188, 197–198,
    209–210, 214, 218
conditionality: *acquis* conditionality
    110–111, 113, 117, 120, 148–150, 153,
    156–158, 165–166, 170–171, 188, 200,
    218–219; market access conditionality
    63, 73, 86, 91, 92, 100, 101, 102, 156,
    157, 159, 166, 190, 193, 212, 217;
    values conditionality 69, 72, 149,
    156–157, 171
cooperation: administrative cooperation
    68, 80–84, 102, 111, 126, 147,
    150–151, 157–159, 185, 192; customs
    cooperation 80–82, 86, 102, 158–159,
    176, 192, 198, 210, 212
Cotonou Agreement 1, 32, 61, **63**, 70, 132, 161

Deep and Comprehensive Free Trade
    Agreement (DCFTA) 6–8, 59,
    61–62, **63**, 64, 68, 73–86, 91–93, 95,
    97–102, 122, 125, 128, 130–132, 140,
    153–160, 180, 182–186, 190–210,
    212–213, 217, 220
democracy 2, 12, 14, 17, 17n9, 18–20,
    24–27, 31, 47, 50, 52, 55–56, 58–59,
    61, 63–64, 66–67, 71, 74, 79, 84, 104,
    111–114, 119, 125, 129, 133, 138, 141,
    142, 146, 162, 167, 186, 189, 215, 218
democracy promotion through functional
    cooperation 50
dependency 44–46, **63**, 216, 219
deregulation 62, 192, 20–27, 209–211,
    211n86, 212–213

economic development 18, 33, 44–46, 57,
    59, 64, 66, 93, 109–111, 123–124, 126,
    128–134, 137, 139, 141, 149, 154, 156,
    161, 168, 189, 206, 216

Index

economic integration 44–45, 56, 111, 124, 130, 136–137, 155, 163, 216

Economic Partnership Agreement 5, 42, 61, 104–105, 142; *see also* EPA

enlargement 4, 8, 14, 23n20, 24, 24n30, 30, 52, 56–57, 57nn7–8, 58, 58n14, **63**–66, 72, 80, 88, 107, 110nn9–10, 120, 122, 140–143, 145–148, 153, 153n33, 157, 165–166, 168, 168n1, 169–170, 170n9, 177–178, 188–191, 214, 219

EPA 5, 33, 36, 61, 62n27, 62n30, **63**, 68, 70, 70n10, 71–72, 93, 93n102, 94–95, 100, 100n139, 101, 102, 133, 137–140, 161–165, 182, 185–186, 186n69, 187–188, 192–193, 217

equality 2, 15–17, 24–25, 27, 62, 75, 77, 79, 89–92, 94, 100, 102–103, 126, 128, 152, 159, 179, 184, 192, 213, 217

"essential element" clause 5, 8, 33, 69–74, 101, 111–112, 127, 034, 149, 168

EU external economic policy 4, 8, 28, 40, 43

European Development Fund (EDF) 60, 106, 134, 135n126, 136, 138, 138nn144–145, 139n146, 163, 164n82

Everything But Arms (EBA) 1, 5

foreign policy objective 26, 38, 51–52, 66, 136, 146

Former Yugoslav Republic of Macedonia 113n21, 117n38, 117n40, 118n43, 151n26, 152n29, 153n31, 172n18, 172n23

Generalized Scheme of Preferences 9, 30; *see also* GSP

Georgia 33, 33n10, 55–56, 59, 73, 75, 75n20, 76, 76n26, 77, 77n26, 77n29–31, 77n33, 78nn35–37, 78n39, 82n51, 83n52, 83n54, 83nn57–60, 83n62, 85nn65–66, 86n68, 86n69, 91n89, 97, 97nn119–120, 100, 122–123, 126, 128, 128n88, 130n102, 130n104, 131, 131n106, 140, 154, 154nn36–39, 155, 155n40, 159n57, 160, 178–180, 181n48, 181n51, 182, 182n54, 182n56

GPA (Agreement on Government Procurement) 87–89, 93, 95, 102, 147, 175

GSP 1, 5, 36

human rights 2, 3, 10, 12, 14–17, 19–20, 21n15, 25, 27, 31, 33, 37, 38, 41–42, 47, 51–52, 54–55, 57–58, 69, 69n3, 70–74, 103–106, 106n2, 111–112, 123, 125, 129, 133, 162, 164, 178, 181, 187, 203

impartiality 13, 24–25, 77–79, 83, 85, 89, 92, 95, 97, 99–100, 102, 115, 119–121, 123, 147–148, 173–175, 179–181, 183, 201

information exchange 100, 115, 151, 217

intellectual property rights 32, 62n31, 114, 114n26; *see also* IP rights

IP rights 2, 62, 72, 77, 83, 114–115, 140, 150, 154–155, 162, 177, 207

Jamaica 8, 135, 135n129, 136, 136n132, 137, 139, 139n147, 164n80, 187

judicial independence 13, 24–25, 78–90, 95, 121, 123, 147, 169, 172, 174, 179–180, 186, 202

judicial review 23, 89–92, 96–97, 102, 112, 115, 149, 152, 154, 158–159, 175–176, 178–180, 182–183, 185–188, 192, 198–199, 205–206, 213

Kosovo 57, 58n11, 62, 62n27, 62nn29–30, 65, 71–72, 80–81, 81n42, 44, 88, **107**, 116, 120–121, 142, 171, 171n27, 171n30

Law and Development Movement 44, 45

legal certainty 21, 22, 25–26, 62, 75–76, 79, 83, 85–86, 88–81, 93–100, 102, 110, 112, 14–15, 117–118, 121, 123, 125–126, 128, 148, 150–155, 158–160, 170, 176, 192–193, 198–199, 208, 210, 212–213, 217

legality 18, 20–21, 23, 25, 62, 79, 81–83, 85, 88, 96–102, 111, 114–115, 118, 120–121, 123, 127, 142, 150, 152, 158–160, 192, 194, 198–199, 203–204, 208–210, 212–213, 217

legislative approximation 88, 89, 91–92, 95, 97, 100, 102, 116, 120, 125, 128–129, 147, 150, 152, 156–157, 190, 192–194, 212, 217

Lisbon Treaty 13, 18, 28, 37–40, 145

market power Europe 3, 9, 65; *see also* MPE

modernization theory 44, 45

Moldova 33, 55–56, 59, 64, 73, 75nn20–21, 76, 76n26, 77, 77nn29–33,

224   *Index*

78, 78nn35–39, 82n46, 82n51,
   83, 83n52, 83n54, 84nn57–62,
   85nn65–66, 86nn68–69, 91n89, 93, 97,
   97nn119–120, 100, 122–123, 123n61,
   123n62, 126, 128, 128nn90–91, 130,
   130n105, 131, 140, 154–155, 159,
   159nn56–57, 160, 160n58, 160n61,
   178, 178n34, 179–180, 181n49,
   181n51, 181n54, 182, 182n56,
   182nn58–59, 196
monitoring 31, 35–36, 68, 121, 184–185,
   193–194, 212
Montenegro 57, 71n11, 89, 119n48,
   146n10, 151n26, 153n32
MPE 3, 50, 55, 64

new institutional economics 46, 47
non-discrimination 24–25, 62, 75, 77,
   83–85, 87–94, 97, 100, 102, 126, 128,
   139, 152, 154, 159, 179, 184, 192, 213
non-trade policy objective 2
normative power Europe 7, 49, 65–66;
   see also NPE
North Macedonia 58, 116, 120
NPE 50, 52–53, 63, 64

policy coherence for development 2, 4,
   4n9, 9, 60, 219
public procurement 2, 5, 8, 53, 59, 62–**63**,
   68, 86–87, 87n72, 87n73, 87n76, 88,
   89n82, 89–90, 90n82, 90n88, 91–94,
   97–98, 100, 102–103, 105, 109–111,
   115–116, 118, 124, 129, 129n105, 140,
   147–148, 152–154, 159–160, 160n159,
   164–165, 175, 177, 179, 186, 192, 197,
   197n30, 198–199, 199n33, 199n64,
   200n35, 205–208, 208n65, 209,
   212–213, 215

regional trade agreements 1, 2; *see also*
   RTAs
relationship between international and
   domestic law 79, 82, 97, 164
right to judicial review 90–92, 96, 102,
   175, 198, 205–206, 213
RTAs 1–8, 34–36, 39, 44, 49–56, 59–64,
   68–70, 73–74, 80–81, 86–88, 95–96,
   101–103, 106, 107, 140–141, 144, 146,
   165–166, 169, 185, 187–190, 201, 213,
   216–221
Rule of Law Checklist 17n9, 20–22, 24

SAA 5, 58n11, 62, 62n27, 62n29, 62n30,
   63, 68, 71, 71n11, 72, 72n13, 73, 80–81,

81n40, 81n42, 82n44, 88, 88n77, 89,
   91, 92–94, 96, 96nn113–115, 97,
   97nn117–118, 98, 101, 107, 109, 111,
   113–114, 116, 120–121, 140, 147–149,
   149n19, 150, 152, 156–157, 170–172,
   174–175, 175n27, 175n30, 176–177,
   180, 182–184, 192–193, 217
Serbia 56–57, 96nn113–115, 121, 146n10,
   149n19
Stabilization and Association Agreements
   5, 71; *see also* SAA
sustainable development 2–3, 9, 32,
   36–37, 41, 60–61, 64, 70–71, 73, 87,
   104, 130n105, 134, 140, 162–163, 184,
   205, 213, 219, 221
Sustainable Development Goals (SDGs)
   60–61, 219

technical assistance 7, 29, 35, 86, 97,
   101–102, **107**, 107, 108–109, 113, 115,
   121–122, 127, 132–134, 146, 149–152,
   156, 163, 165, 167, 172, 176, 187,
   195–196, 199, 201, 204, 206
technical cooperation 5, 64, 163, 176–177
trade and sustainable development chapter
   15; *see also* TSD
trade facilitation 32, 34–35, 35n14, 36, 80,
   82–86, 102, 105, 151, 156–159, 183, 212
trade liberalization 1, 4–6, 8–9, 28, 31,
   34, 38, 40–41, 44, 46, 48–49, 54–56,
   58–59, 62, 64, 70, 73, 75, 96, 101,
   106, 108, 111–114, 117, 119, 125–126,
   131–134, 136, 140–141, 144, 149, 155,
   161, 163–165, 168–170, 187–188, 200,
   205, 216, 218–219, 221
trade power Europe 50, 52
transparency 5, 8, 19–23, 25, 50, 62,
   64, 68, 70, 74–87, 89–94, 96–102,
   109–115, 117, 119–123, 125–128, 131,
   134, 139–140, 148–152, 158–160,
   162, 164, 173–174, 176–177, 182, 184,
   192–193, 199, 200–203, 208–213, 217
Trinidad and Tobago 135, 135n129,
   136n131, 137, 137n141, 139, 139n149,
   164n80, 164n83, 187
TSD 3–4, 36, 41, 52

Ukraine 6–7, 10, 33, 33n10, 55–56, 59,
   59n19, 62, 62nn25–26, 62nn28–30, 73,
   73n14, 75, 75nn20–22, 76, 76nn25–26,
   77, 77nn29–33, 78, 78nn34–39, 80–81,
   81n40, 81n42, 82nn44–45, 82n51,
   83n52, 83nn54–56, 84nn57–60, 84n62,
   85nn55–56, 86nn68–69, 91nn89–91,

92, 92n97, 97, 98, 98n121, 99, 99n137, 100, 104–105, 122–123, 123n62, 126, 126n78, 127, 127n82, 128, 128n87, 128n90, 130, 130n100, 130n105, 131n105, 132, 132n109, 132n111, 140, 154, 154n34, 154n36, 155, 156nn44–45, 158, 158n49, 159, 159nn55–57, 160, 160nn58–59, 167, 169, 169n5, 178, 178nn34–36, 179, 179n41, 180, 180n48, 181, 181nn49–51, 182, 182n56, 183, 183n57, 184, 184n60, 184n62, 189, 190, 190n1, 191, 192, 192nn4–6, 193, 194, 194nn20–21, 195, 196n23, 196n25, 197, 197nn28–30, 198, 199, 200, 200n35, 201, 201n36, 202, 202n37, 202n39, 202nn40–41, 203, 203nn42–44, 204, 205, 206, 206n56, 207, 207nn62–64, 208, 208n65, 209–210, 210n74, 210n76, 211, 211n80, 211n87, 212–215, 217–218, 221

value-promotion 1, 20, 49–53, 55–56, 60, 74, 106, 135, 216, 218–219, 220

Washington Consensus 45–48, 61–62, 64, 66, 72, 79, 104
Western Balkans 6, 58, **63**, 6–8, 71–73, 88, 92, 95–98, 104, 107–108, 108n4, 109, 109n6, 110, 110nn8–10, 111, 113, 113nn22–23, 114n28, 115n31, 116, 116n34, 116n36, 119–121, 123, 141–143, 145–147, 147nn13–14, 148, 148n18, 149–150, 150n21, 151, 151n23, 152nn28–29, 153, 153n33, 155–157, 159, 166–169, 169n1, 170, 170nn6–9, 171, 172nn16–18, 173, 175–179, 180, 182, 184, 186–187, 189, 192–193, 217, 221
world-systems theory 45–46
World Trade Organization 1, 32n7, 85n63, 114n26; *see also* WTO
WTO 1, 28, 31–35, 35n14, 36n21, 41n41, 42, 47, 48n2, 61n2, 62nn31–32, 64–65, 76–78, 80–85, 87–89, 93, 97, 97n118, 100–103, 105, 112, 114, 123, 132, 134, 141, 147, 154, 162, 175, 192

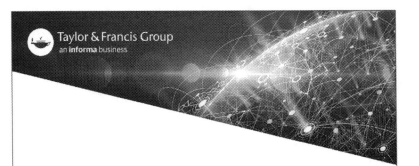

Printed in the United States
By Bookmasters